SCHIZOPHRENIA:
AN INTEGRATED APPROACH TO RESEARCH AND TREATMENT

M J Birchwood
S E Hallett
M C Preston

LONGMAN
London and New York

Longman Group UK Limited,
Longman House, Burnt Mill, Harlow,
Essex CM20 2JE, England
and Associated Companies throughout the world.

Published in the United States of America
by Longman Inc., New York

© Longman Group UK Limited 1988

First published 1988

British Library Cataloguing in Publication Data
Birchwood, M. J.
  Schizophrenia: an integrated approach to
  research and treatment.
  1. Schizophrenia
  I. Title II. Hallett, S. E. III. Preston,
  M. C.
  616.89′82 RC514

ISBN 0-582-29607-2

Library of Congress Cataloging in Publication Data
Birchwood, M. J.
  Schizophrenia: an integrated approach to
research and treatment.

  Bibliography: p.
  Includes index.
  1. Schizophrenia. I. Hallett, S. E. II. Preston,
M. C. III. Title. [DNLM: 1. Schizophrenia.
WM 203 B617s]
RC514.B54 1987   616.89′82   87-3014
ISBN 0-582-29607-2

Set in Linotron 202 10/11 pt Times
Produced by Longman Group (FE) Limited
Printed in Hong Kong

CONTENTS

PREFACE

The original intention was that this book would form part of the Longman Applied Psychology Series. My editorial preface to the series refers to 'authoritative short books' directed at both students and professionals, yet 'well within the grasp of the interested general reader'. But as the writing of *Schizophrenia* progressed it became clear that the authors were producing a 'state-of-the-art' book which should indeed be published by Longman but separately from the series.

The result is a major contribution to scholarship. It collates, expends and above all integrates a vast quantity of theory and research into the description, explanation and treatment of the most destructive mental illness of all, one which affects about one per cent of the population world-wide, knowing no national or social boundaries.

Birchwood, Hallett and Preston have given due weight to a range of both biological and environmental factors in causation and to their interactions. Their section on treatment is similarly comprehensive, and includes both physical and psychosocial approaches. The final part sets out an integrated model of causation and draws out the implications of the model for what is modestly, but properly termed amelioration. The model also has major consequences for future research programmes spanning the range from bio-social causation to preventative work with 'at risk' individuals.

Schizophrenia has been written by three clinical psychologists who have full time appointments at a typical British mental hospital. It is, to say the least, a major achievement to have combined their day-to-day practical work with the conception and execution of this impressive book.

Philip Feldman

ACKNOWLEDGEMENTS

We would like to acknowledge our professional colleagues at All Saints Hospital who have encouraged our interest and work in schizophrenia over the years. We would also like to thank the many schizophrenic patients and their families who have given up their time to take part in our research programmes.

In the preparation of this book the authors would particularly like to thank Professor Feldman for his guidance as editor and our wives Frankie, Ellen and Marian for their tolerance during the many hours spent writing. Finally we would thank Janet Morris for the unenviable job of typing the manuscript.

The writing of this book has been a collaborative effort. Ordering of authorship is, for convenience, alphabetical.

Part one

THE PROBLEM AND CONCEPT OF SCHIZOPHRENIA

Chapter one

THE PROBLEM OF SCHIZOPHRENIA

The concept of schizophrenia is now almost a hundred years old. Its lifetime has been marked by intense controversy about its nature, definition, social function and indeed its very existence.

Prominent among the disbelievers is Thomas Szasz who has over the years argued powerfully for the abandonment of the concept. He views schizophrenia as the 'sacred symbol' of a mistaken application of the techniques of medicine to those society needs to consider disturbed or deviant in conduct. Szasz writes (1979: 89, 204):

> (Schizophrenia is) fatally flawed by a single logical error: namely all of the contributions to it treat 'schizophrenia' as if it were the shorthand description of a *disease*, when in fact it is the shorthand *prescription of a disposition*; in other words, they use the term schizophrenia as if it were a *proposition* asserting something about psychotics when in fact it is a *justification legitimising* something that *psychiatrists* do to them.

> . . . schizophrenia will remain the central problem of psychiatry so long as society supports the sorts of interventions that are defined as therapeutic for it and are imposed on persons diagnosed as schizophrenic; it will cease to be a problem when society withdraws its support from these interventions and the institutions that now promote and profit from them.

At the other end of the spectrum there are those who argue that schizophrenia sits properly alongside medical diagnoses such as Diabetes Mellitus and that its 'cure' will be biological in nature:

> . . . I do have a personal idea of what schizophrenia is that structures how I approach diagnostic evaluation, treatment and research in schizophrenia. In my view schizophrenia should be seen as a phenotype, a group of disorders of the central nervous system of diverse etiology which produce a range of clinical signs and symptoms that include various combinations of delusions, hallucinations, thought

3

disorder, affective disturbances . . . the majority of schizophrenic patients do have persisting psychotic symptoms as well as severe deficits in intellectual and affective capacities and work and social relationships . . . (Meltzer 1982: 433).

What then are we to make of the concept of schizophrenia? Is schizophrenia a valid, meaningful concept or is it simply a figment of the psychiatrist's imagination? In this book we shall attempt to address these issues particularly from the standpoint of the therapeutic and explanatory utility of the concept. Such an outlook rests of course on the assumption that those who fall within the concept **want** and are in **need** of help. Indeed, in the ebb and flow of debate about 'schizophrenia', the problem it represents to the individual, his family and to society in general is sometimes forgotten. We shall begin therefore by attempting to 'anchor' the concept in human terms before proceeding to consider some of the evidence.

THE INDIVIDUAL WITH SCHIZOPHRENIA

There can be little doubt that the group of people labelled 'schizophrenic' do undergo a major change in their mental and social functioning. For some these changes are transient but in the majority of cases the changes are episodic or permanent. It has been estimated for example that less than a third can expect to return to an 'average' level of functioning (Keith *et al*. 1976). The changes that are observed seem to build up with time and present a complicated picture to describe. The British social psychiatrist John Wing argues that a distinction should be drawn between the impairments which are *intrinsic* to the disorder (largely psychological in nature) and those which are secondary and result from the impinging of the primary impairments on the social environment. Such secondary impairments are of a kind which any disadvantaged or disabled group might expect to experience and as such could be largely prevented. The most common of these impairments are shown in Table 1. Let us start by considering the intrinsic impairments.

Prominent among these are hallucinations and delusions. Hallucinations are perceptions often in the auditory modality and occur in the absence of identifiable external stimulation. Frequently termed 'voices', they often 'speak' in the third person and may offer comments on the person's action or thoughts, make accusatory suggestions or instruct the individual in some way. Sometimes the voices can be amusing. In most instances the individual will believe that the 'voices' are alien but real, must be taken seriously and sometimes obeyed. The best illustrations of these experiences are

TABLE 1   Some common problems associated with schizophrenia

Intrinsic impairments
Persisting symptoms (hallucinations, delusions, thought
   disorders)
Tendency to withdrawal, apathy, emotional blunting ('negative'
   symptoms)
Cognitive impairments: attention and problem-solving
Vulnerability to further schizophrenic episodes

Secondary impairments

Social
Unemployment, downward social drift
Social adversity: housing, finance etc
Institutionalisation
Diminished social network
Family discord or rejection
Social prejudice to mental illness

Psychological
Loss of confidence and achievement motivation
Social and community survival skills impaired or fall into disuse
Dependent or semi-dependent on family or institutions
Distress due to poor coping with persisting symptoms (e.g. auditory
   hallucinations)

---

provided by the individuals themselves.

This person was a doctor working in a busy hospital who suddenly without reason started to hear voices and believe his thoughts were being controlled:

> . . . I saw the cross, and then God spoke to me. With this certainty
> my thoughts then took control. They were religious thoughts . . . and
> I began to hear an intermittent voice. Just prior to my acute
> admission I announced to my aged father, who was in bed, that Satan
> in the form of the Loch Ness Monster was going to land on the lawn
> and do for us if we both remained together in the house. By this
> time, I heard the voice pretty constantly . . . the voice continued for
> four months. One day I was sitting listening to it when it suddenly
> said . . . 'This is the final transmission: Over and out'. I have never
> heard it since . . . Again . . . my thoughts took control; it was a
> period of wildly erotic sensations, lack of sleep, being out walking at
> any time from 1 a.m. onwards, marked tiredness, and frequent ideas
> of reference. Messages were being transmitted by car registration
> numbers and many written sentences had messages hidden in them in
> code . . .

At the age of twenty-two this person was working in a bank. His parents noticed a gradual change in his behaviour resulting in his becoming more withdrawn:

> . . . I sat down at home and my mother says I just started talking a load of utter rubbish . . . I was examined very thoroughly but the doctors could not find anything wrong physically and put it all down to 'nerves' . . . I complained of hearing voices telling me to do different things, which I felt compelled to do . . . I felt everyone was against me even the nurses and doctors . . . I did not clean my teeth, wash myself or comb my hair for the first two months . . . I just existed till I felt better when I gradually started to look after myself again. I used to sit all by myself and would hardly say anything to anyone . . .

Delusions represent beliefs which are not shared by the individual's cultural peer group. In schizophrenia these are mainly of three general kinds. In the first the individual may believe (and feel) that his behaviour is being influenced or controlled by some external force (delusions of influence or control). In the second the person may believe that he is being watched, followed or persecuted in some way (delusions of persecution). Third, the individual may lose his sense of identity or purpose and may believe he has powers or abilities out of the ordinary (delusions of identity). The following description vividly portrays the experience of delusional identity and the acute distress which accompanies the lonely feeling of a delusion of persecution. This twenty-three year old man worked as a store-keeper in a departmental store:

> . . . in my flat I began to get delusions. I was a storekeeper at the time. I wrote out 'Supreme New Plan', a system of life which I had worked out for myself . . . I wrote out notebooks full of plans. I kept thinking the Mafia were after me, and the FBI were protecting me, ready to send me away to be trained. I kept thinking my parents were Jews. I would ask my landlady, in my loneliness, if I could watch their television and I would cry all the way through the programmes. Finally, I tried to get away to my Aunt Mary's: all I had with me was a suitcase with a bible in it. The police picked me up, and I made a false confession of murder so that they would incarcerate me and protect me from the Mafia . . . my doctor said I needed a rest. Sometime, next day, a medical superintendent and my mother came to certify me at the flat. A social worker, took me to the hospital. I didn't resist; I thought it was all part of the plan . . .

Hallucinations, delusions and other thought disorders are often termed the 'positive' symptoms. Another set of 'negative' symptoms are usually also associated with the concept of schizophrenia. As the name suggests these represent a loss to the individual's functions in particular those of emotion and motivation. Characteristically, the individual may withdraw from social contact and find him (or her) self overcome by a sense of apathy, listlessness and a difficulty in sustaining attention. A feeling of emotional blunting is sometimes experienced: the individual may find himself emotionless, unable to laugh or cry, or in some cases the full range of emotions are expressed but the individual may do so inappropriately.

This young man describes experiences of negative symptoms following a sudden episode of schizophrenia characterised by florid positive symptoms:

> . . . I used to like football – really like it, on the telly, you know.
> I'd sit up late and watch it, if it was on. But now, it's as if I don't
> care – I go to bed at 7.30 sometimes – well, most nights. I sleep
> OK, but I wake up in a sweat. And him (pointing to infant son, aged
> 5), well of course, I still love him, but I don't feel it here, inside.
> Even a drink, you know, I go sometimes for a drink with my brother.
> It's as if I can't get drunk any more, well . . . it used to give me a
> lift. Not now, though. I don't seem to get hungry, either. I eat OK,
> but I can't get, well, really hungry . . . every day is the same. It all
> seems pointless somehow. I don't care about the weather, you know,
> like if it's a nice day, I don't care, it doesn't matter to me. I went to
> the hairdresser today, and he told me a joke – and before I would
> have laughed – but I didn't. It wasn't that it wasn't funny, I just,
> well – it wasn't funny enough . . . There's not much difference
> between being awake or sleeping. Do other people get this? As long
> as it doesn't go on forever.

Perhaps the great cost to the person affected by these experiences are their social and psychological consequences. It may after all be argued that there are many in society whose behaviour is statistically abnormal yet who do not bring themselves, or are not brought by others, to public attention. It is when such behaviour leads to a serious deterioration in the quality of life or results in danger to the well-being of the individual or others that the person concerned, his family and society in general feels a need to respond. Unemployment, social drift, social adversity, loss of confidence, drive and even loss of the skills of independent living are among the most serious of these social and psychological effects (Table 1). Once again this is best illustrated by some actual case examples:

> Colin worked as a general labourer in a Birmingham factory making
> garden tools. At 19 years of age he was living with his mother and
> sister in a council flat in a deprived area of the city. He had always
> been a quiet person with few friends. His interests were
> predominantly solitary (fishing, gardening) although he occasionally
> spent evenings out with his brother. One summer, after visiting a
> fortune teller at a local fair, Colin felt convinced that she had cast a
> spell upon him and that she exerted almost total control over his
> behaviour and thoughts. Colin became increasingly withdrawn and
> started to absent himself from work. He became suspicious of people,
> including his relatives as he thought they were agents of the fortune
> teller. His mother reported that he spent much of the day in his

bedroom talking and laughing to himself. It was discovered that Colin was hearing voices which he thought was an attempt by the fortune teller to drive him insane. The voices sometimes commented on his thoughts or behaviour ('He's going to sleep' [laughter]); sometimes they criticized him ('The way you act makes me sick'; 'You're daft I am') and sometimes they were bizarre or humorous ('He's not well liked but he's well liked', 'Monster crabs claws for you old boy'). Colin refused to watch TV as he felt he heard thinly disguised references to him and to his sanity. Colin's family had no previous acquaintance with such behaviour and at the time were resistant to identify it as mental illness, preferring to view it as a 'phase' he was going through. Their perceptions changed suddenly when they realised that he had not eaten for three days and they called their family doctor who immediately admitted him to the local psychiatric hospital.

Following two months at the hospital Colin was much improved but he nonetheless continued to hear voices. He was unable to keep his job as the voices were too intrusive and distressing. At home, Colin withdrew further and his family were finding difficulty motivating him.

Two years later Colin rarely laughs and seems to find it hard to understand what is said to him. He has given up the idea of working again and spends 3 days a week in a day centre. He spends much of the time alone in his room.

Barry was described by his parents as having been a lively, popular boy at school having numerous friends and enjoying outdoor activities. They felt, however, that in spite of his apparent confidence that he was sensitive to criticism and felt inferior to his brother and sister who were doing well in their careers. On leaving school at 16 Barry was unable to find work and he became somewhat despondent, and was felt by his parents to have become lazy and disinterested in work. During the course of the following year Barry became very quarrelsome with his parents and on one occasion hit out at his mother. He left the home for a short time and it was discovered that he had indulged in drug and alcohol abuse. He was spending many nights out and returning drunk. His relationship with his parents worsened still further. His excesses continued for over 12 months and were brought to a head when he was picked up by the police who discovered him shouting and swearing at cars passing in the road. The police physician arranged for him to be admitted to a psychiatric hospital as he continued to be aggressive and threatening after the effects of the alcohol wore off. Barry refused to answer questions and his behaviour was observed to become increasingly aggressive and bizarre. It was subsequently discovered that he thought that the occupants of passing cars were shouting abusive comments to him. He claimed that his parents had attempted to poison him. Barry improved with medication. His aggressive and rebellious demeanour was unchanged however and at home he became increasingly lethargic. Barry's condition worsened on a number of occasions and prompted his readmission to hospital. His behaviour continued to worsen to the extent that his parents refused to accept him home until his behaviour improved. Barry has become continually hallucinated in spite of high dosages of medication. He now lives in sheltered accommodation, takes poor care of himself and shows little interest in people.

These anecdotal observations are underlined by the numerous studies which have followed up schizophrenic patients discharged from hospital (see Ch. 12). One such study was that conducted by Eve Johnstone and her colleagues (Johnstone *et al.* 1984). They attempted to recontact a cohort of 120 schizophrenic patients discharged from hospital over a period of five to nine years. They found that only 18 per cent had recovered to the extent that they had *no* significant symptoms and were functioning satisfactorily. Personal care (hygiene, appearance, diet) was impaired in 38 per cent and again 38 per cent were functioning poorly in their social role (e.g. work, home etc).

These findings might surprise those who would point to the advances in the pharmacological treatment of schizophrenia over the last thirty years. The phenothiazine group of drugs have indeed been shown in carefully controlled investigations to reduce or eliminate 'psychotic' symptoms and to halve the rate of relapse (e.g. Hogarty *et al.* 1974). There is also evidence (see Ch. 12) that the outlook for schizophrenia has improved since the advent of these drugs. These developments notwithstanding, the proportion of cases that continue to deteriorate into a chronic disorder[1] remains unchanged and the rate of relapse on medication approaches nearly 50 per cent over two years (see again Ch. 12). In conjunction with the problems of persisting impairments and social disadvantage documented earlier, these facts taken together must strongly temper the optimism with which the introduction of these drugs was heralded. Clearly those individuals who fall within the classification of schizophrenia can, as a whole, anticipate a poor quality of life.

SCHIZOPHRENIA AND THE FAMILY

A large proportion of those diagnosed with schizophrenia reside in the home environment. In the majority of cases this is the parental home, which is especially so for males. This arises because the disorder tends to start quite early in life (18 to 35 years), often before the individual has left home to marry or live independently (Cooper 1978). Thus the immediate family are frequently the ones on whom the major burden of support will fall. This burden has increased over the years with the trend towards non-custodial, community management. As we have already noted the discharge from hospital is rarely accompanied by a remission of symptoms and sometime quite profound changes to the personality can occur. These behavioural changes have been documented in some systematic studies of schizophrenics living with their families. Among the first of these was Creer and Wing's (1973) study of 80 schizophrenics living at home. They found that some three-quarters were observed by relatives to be socially withdrawn, lacking conversation, slow in their actions and to be generally underactive. This preponderance of 'negative' symptoms observed by relatives was later confirmed by Birchwood (1983) and Gibbons *et al.* (1984). Related to this Creer and Wing noted that schizophrenics' social role within and outside the home was regarded by 71 per cent of relatives as 'unsatisfactory', that is, making little contribution in terms of money, household chores or general companionship. These observations may be summarised simply in terms of the families' growing feeling that their schizophrenic relative has become insidiously dependent on them. Many families, however, do not find their relative so quiescent. Birchwood (op. cit.) finds that 36 per cent of relatives interviewed reported their relative expressing delusional or hallucinatory ideas; a further 30 per cent noted incidents of aggression directed toward them, of restless, overactive behaviour and bizarre, unpredictable or offensive behaviour (see Table 2).

TABLE 2 Behaviours observed by relatives of acute* schizophrenic patients living at home

	Per cent observing
Withdrawal	51
Staying in bed	
Emotional detachment	
Avoiding social contact	
Psychotic symptoms	36
Expressing passivity ideas	
Persecutory delusions	
Hallucinatory behaviour	
Behavioural excesses	31
Aggression to relatives	
Restlessness	
Provoking family discord	
Impaired social performance	51
Self-care	
Domestic tasks	
Independence skills	

* Mean age = 26 yrs mean admission = 1.7 mean illness duration = 2.2 yrs (*N* = 53)

Much of this behavioural disturbance can be attributed to the symptoms we described in the previous section. Thus Birchwood (1983) reports a significant correlation of r = 0.70 between measures of behavioural disturbance and psychotic symptoms, a result also found by Gibbons *et al.* (1984).

It may be readily appreciated that these changes in behaviour and personality can prove profoundly distressing for close family members. On the one hand there is the difficult emotional adjustment in coming to terms with a disintegration of personality in a family member. On the other, the behavioural problems can prove extremely taxing to cope with and in time frequently lead to ambivalence in the relationship, and sometimes outright rejection. This distress can be translated into severe stress symptoms. Birchwood (1983) using a standardised stress scale, the Symptom Rating Test, found that 38 per cent of his sample of families scored in a 'pathological' range in terms of depression, anxiety, somatic symptoms and self-image. Similarly Gibbons *et al.* (1984) find a high level of emotional distress in 32 per cent of their sample using the General Health Questionnaire.

Studies clearly point to the persisting behavioural disturbance and its consequences as being the major source of this distress. Birchwood (1983) and Gibbons *et al.* (1984) both find a substantial relationship between the level of disturbance and distress reported by families. However, it is often not so much the disturbance *per se* which is distressing rather the family's problems in *coping* with the behaviour. The following extract from an interview illustrates the conflict which is aroused in relatives when such disturbance impinges directly on them. The interviewee is the mother of a young person discussing her reactions to her son's accusations that she is trying to poison him:

> . . . he was always a quiet thoughtful sort of lad . . . we were very close . . . much more than with (father) . . . he didn't have many friends at school you know . . . we were devastated when the doctor told us what he'd got – I can't believe it even now . . . nearly two years on . . . the worst of it is the hate in his eyes, sometimes I don't know how he thinks we could do something like that . . . I do know he's been ill but sometimes I get angry inside, I mean, how would you react if your son said that to you? . . . it's difficult to know what to say to him, if you say you're not (poisoning him) that's what he expects . . . I tried once to tell him it was his illness but he just laughed . . . (Birchwood 1983).

In this instance as in many others the family's difficulty in coming to terms with these changes can lead to guilt and compensatory over-involvement but in some families their positive feelings can be eroded and replaced by criticism, antipathy and frank rejection. These feelings may be exacerbated by other severe consequences for the family: in particular, stigma, embarrassment, financial hardship and a significant level of tension which can erupt into arguments and recrimination. The resources available to families to support them in their task is meagre indeed both in the UK and USA (Pringle and Pyke-Lees 1982; Willis 1982), and self-help groups have sprung up to campaign for their needs to be recognised by the mental-health services (e.g. the National Schizophrenia Fellowship in the UK). Probably for many families, beyond their immediate problems and needs, is a major worry of how the individual will manage as parents approach old age, particularly in view of the paucity of community resources for the mentally disordered (Creer and Wing 1973).

THE SOCIAL PROBLEM OF SCHIZOPHRENIA

Whether or not one accepts the concept of schizophrenia and its 'treatment' the fact remains that there exist many individuals whose behaviour and phenomenology would fall within this classification. In fact the percentage of the population that could be so classified is surprisingly high. Before considering these figures it is important to distinguish between three statistics which describe the frequency of a characteristic within a population. *Morbidity* or *lifetime* risk estimates the percentage of the population developing the characteristic in the course of a lifetime. *Incidence* estimates the rate of *inception* of the characteristic (e.g. number of new cases per 1,000 population). *Prevalence* estimates the total number of individuals with this characteristic at a given point in time. If the characteristic (e.g. a disease) has a short duration then incidence will equal prevalence. Over the past fifty years many epidemiological studies have been conducted in the USA, Europe and the Far East. However, a major barrier to the establishment of a definitive figure is that there are no universally accepted criteria for the classification of schizophrenia and some countries such as the USA have in the past adopted broad criteria.

The majority of studies find a lifetime expectancy falling somewhat short of 1 per cent. Helgosan (1964) in Iceland studied a group of 5,000 people aged between 15 and 49 years (the maximum risk period) using birth registers and identified the numbers in contact with the psychiatric services. He found 0.73 per cent of this group received a diagnosis of schizophrenia. A similar study by Fremming (1951) on Bornholm Island established a lifetime risk of 0.90 per cent. In the United States the lifetime risk has been established somewhat higher at between 1 per cent and 2 per cent (Yolles and Kramer 1969), due in part to more 'liberal' diagnostic practices at that time. With the exception of the United States the published findings show a surprisingly high measure of agreement between different countries. The prevalence rates are similarly consistent with most showing between 2 and 4 cases per 1,000 (i.e. 0.2% to 0.4%) of the population (Jablensky and Sartorious 1975). Incidence rates are much lower but tend to be more variable: thus in Salford, England, Edelstein *et al.* (1968) find 0.3 new cases per 1,000 population; Hofner and Reiman (1970) in Mannheim, Germany find 0.53 new cases per 1,000 and Babigan (1975) finds 0.72 new cases per 1,000 in New York State.

These data suggest two things. First by extrapolation there will be at least 100,000 schizophrenics in the UK and approaching half a million in the USA. It may be readily appreciated that the scale of provision required to meet this need will be considerable in organizational and financial terms. It has been calculated for example that the overall economic cost to the US was approximately $10 billion in 1975 or 2 per cent of the gross national product (Gunderson and Mosher 1975). A similar figure was arrived at in Australia where the costs per case of schizophrenia was six times that for heart disease in spite of the latter being afforded priority for public funding. Second, since prevalence is greater than incidence, this suggests that many receiving a diagnosis of schizophrenia will continue to be in contact with the psychiatric services, reflecting in part the chronic nature of the problem in some individuals. This is underlined when we look at the numbers of individuals resident in our psychiatric hospitals. In the UK (population approximately 55 million) there were 152,000 people resident in psychiatric hospitals in 1954. However, by 1971 this had dropped to 111,000 and by 1980 to 56,000 (Nodder 1980). A large proportion of these will be diagnosed with schizophrenia.

The reduction in the hospital population suggested by these figures arose due to community placement policies in the 1960s following the introduction of new drug treatments. This community policy did not, however, eliminate the problem. It soon became apparent that those individuals discharged into the community were in many cases experiencing a quality of life no better than they were when institutionalised (Lamb and Goertzel 1971). Studies conducted in the 1970s have also drawn attention to a 'new' population of 'long-stay' patients who through repeated readmissions and failure to survive in the community, are gradually filtering back into hospital (Mann and Cree 1976). These observations have of course more to do with the shortfall in the level of social provision that is made for these individuals rather than schizophrenia itself, but are mentioned here to illustrate that simply 'releasing' people called schizophrenic from hospital does not necessarily eliminate their or society's problem.

CONCLUSION

We started this chapter with a quote from Thomas Szasz who seems to suggest that schizophrenia (and thereby the people described by the term) is only a problem because society and its institutions need, and choose, to respond to it as a problem. Take away the societal response and we no longer have a problem (except perhaps in terms of reduced profits for drug companies and unemployment among psychiatrists). We hope to have convinced the reader that whether he accepts or rejects the concept, and whatever stance he ultimately takes on the epistemiology of schizophrenia, that he accepts the testimony of 'schizophrenics' and their families of the tragic impact it can have on the individual's mental, emotional and social life.

NOTES

1. 'Chronic' schizophrenia is a term used to describe the evolution of a long-term unremitting or undulating disorder usually characterised by a preponderance of 'negative' symptoms sometimes known as the 'deficit syndrome'. Acute schizophrenia describes a fairly sudden onset of predominantly 'positive' symptoms.

Chapter two

THE CONCEPT, DEFINITION AND VALIDITY OF SCHIZOPHRENIA

HISTORICAL PERSPECTIVE

Our present concept of schizophrenia owes a great deal to the insights of Emil Kraeplin, a German physician who in the late nineteenth century suggested that what was then regarded simply as 'insanity', comprised two distinct disorders. The first, *manic-depression*, included characteristics such as euphoria, grandiose ideas and 'pressure' of speech which he regarded as bearing a favourable prognosis. *Dementia Praecox*, on the other hand, was distinguished by symptoms such as hallucinations, delusions and emotional dysfunction (e.g. inappropriate or blunted emotions) and Kraeplin speculated that this usually followed a deteriorating course.

Kraeplin's suggestion was fundamentally a practical one born of a need to understand and help those people afflicted with these profoundly debilitating problems. As a scientist his instincts were to define and classify his subject matter in order to facilitate understanding and treatment. This was perhaps quite a reasonable step in view of the advances afforded by classification in other sciences, such as for example the role played by the periodic table in chemistry. Kraeplin maintained his emphasis on description and classification in his subsequent writings, and although he suggested *Dementia Praecox* as a unifying concept, he later proposed subtypes, which in fact forms the basis of subtyping today. He proposed a *catatonic* group in which motor retardation was prominent, a *paranoid* group in which delusions were salient and a *hebephrenic* group characterised by emotional incongruity. However, Kraeplin's ideas were essentially hypothetical. He rigidly maintained an atheoretical position believing that his work was a tentative step towards the application of scientific principles to 'insanity'.

Eugen Bleuler (1857–1939) took up Kraeplin's concept and was

15

largely responsible for the application of Freudian theory to these disorders. He claimed that the common denominator linking the various types of *Dementia Praecox* was a 'breaking of associative threads' which in normals would link together thoughts, emotions and behaviour into a coherent whole facilitating rational, purposive behaviour. This disorganisation, he argued, arose as a result of powerful intrapsychic conflicts which were symbolised by the peculiar content of hallucinations and delusions. Bleuler coined the term schizophrenia to capture the meaning underlying his theory (derived from the Greek 'skhizo' [split] and 'phren' [mind]).

Freudian theory is very much concerned with people as individuals rather than as members of diagnostic classes. Adolf Meyer, a prominent figure in American psychiatry in the first half of the century, was particularly influenced by Bleuler's thinking. He tended to regard schizophrenia as a description not of behaviour and experiences, but of certain intrapsychic processes. For this reason the concept of schizophrenia became attached to non-observable, theoretical descriptors with the inevitable consequence that the concept was much more widely applied than was originally anticipated by Kraeplin. Thus according to Kuriansky *et al.* (1974) up to 80 per cent of patients in psychiatric hospitals in the USA were diagnosed 'schizophrenic' and in effect schizophrenia merely became shortened for 'insanity' (Cooper *et al.* 1972). Thus from being a hypothetical concept, schizophrenia was imbued with a sense of certainty, of a spurious foundation in a secure knowledge base. As schizophrenia has become more remote from Kraeplin's hypothesis and reified in the minds of psychiatrists and the community at large, so the problems have accumulated for the concept.

As previously indicated, the term has been carelessly over-applied and diagnosis based on ill-defined, 'clinical', judgements of psychiatrists. It came as somewhat of a shock to the psychiatric community when it was discovered that substantial disagreement existed between psychiatrists in their diagnosis of schizophrenia when diagnostic practices in Europe and the USA were compared (Cooper *et al.* 1972). In contrast, general medical diagnostic concepts are much sharper but also directly determine treatment; critics of psychiatric medicine such as Thomas Szasz (1979) have pointed to the lamentable state of affairs in which the application of certain drug treatments bears a poor relationship to the characteristics of their recipients. Furthermore, drug treatments were often applied in an empirical way sometimes with the aim of inferring the diagnosis from the clinical effects of these treatments (Kendall 1975).

A second and related issue concerns the over-zealous application of a medical framework. In general medicine, the diagnosis embodies all (medical) treatment implications and it was assumed that a diagnosis of schizophrenia would also; thus the personal and social circumstances of people diagnosed schizophrenic were thought to be no more relevant to treatment than, say, those of an individual with influenza. In view of the psychological nature of the abnormalities, this is a speculative assumption and one which has stifled the acceptance and development of non-medical, psycho-social, interventions. The medical framework itself also implies a *unitary* disorder, which Kraeplin did not intend, and research has tended to be applied to the syndrome itself rather than individual symptoms (e.g. hallucinations) when in fact the hypothetical nature of the concept (or indeed the logic of scientific enquiry) would not prefer either approach.

The concept of schizophrenia has become so cemented within the psychiatric (and lay) vocabulary that the label has become attached to the individual as well as his 'disease': the stigma of 'mental illness' has given the concept a pejorative meaning to the social detriment of those so labelled (Brown *et al.* 1966). The acceptance of Kraeplin's hypothesis of inevitable deterioration may have also had harmful consequences in that large custodial hospitals were built on this premise and public money did not find its way into alternative forms of social management. The negative effects of institutions are well documented (Wing and Brown 1970) and have perhaps served to fulfil Kraeplin's expectations.

Observations such as these fuelled a vociferous anti-schizophrenia lobby in the 1960s which challenged the validity of Kraeplin's concept and the very nature of medicine in this context.

It must be recognised, however, that these criticisms are concerned with the abuse of the *application* of the concept rather than the utility of the concept itself. In our view, those who argue for the rejection of the concept confuse the issue of its scientific utility in terms of improving understanding and treatment, with its *application* in contemporary psychiatric practice. Any evaluation of the concept must be concerned with the former rather than the latter. Schizophrenia has undoubtedly become uncritically assimilated into the medical framework which has had many harmful consequences and has stifled its scientific development.

Debate about the concept of schizophrenia has revolved around two issues. The first concerns the *disjunctive* nature of the definition of the concept; that is, it is defined on the basis of one or more of a set of characteristics, thus there are no necessary and sufficient conditions for class inclusion. The effect of this type of definition is that two individuals with 'schizophrenia' may have no symptoms in common.

Disjunctive definitions are not unusual and in fact few definitions are based on necessary *and* sufficient conditions (a 'monothetic' definition). In zoology for example, classifications of mammals, birds, reptiles, etc are 'polythetic', that is, they are defined by the presence of some or most of a set of features, none of which are essential (Kendall 1975). Zoological classifications are valid as they seem to bear some evolutionary significance.

The second issue relates to the existence of schizophrenia. The question is often asked, 'where is the schizophrenia that exists beyond the presence of these unusual experiences?' Many argue (e.g. Szasz 1979) that schizophrenia has no existence other than in the minds of psychiatrists and that persons with these experiences should first and foremost be regarded as individuals and not members of a class (the 'idiopathic' approach). Again this is an assumption equally as unfounded as the medical doctrine that a diagnosis of schizophrenia will ultimately be sufficient to determine all treatment implications.

In our view, schizophrenia is best viewed as a hypothetical, heuristic concept whose validity should stand or fall by the strength of the aetiological and therapeutic implications it embodies. Thus therapeutic and aetiological research into schizophrenia should ultimately lead to the clarification, subdivision or even rejection of the concept. Psychological concepts such as 'anxiety' and 'short-term memory', and in fact many medical diagnoses such as migraine are hypothetical in nature and their validity can only be judged on the basis of their scientific utility and not upon epistemiological issues. This position is not logically incompatible with the 'idiopathic' approach or an approach based on an analysis of individual symptoms (e.g. hallucinations). At this early stage in our understanding, all approaches should be encouraged without the premature rejection of either. At the conclusion of this book we shall suggest how both the 'idiopathic' and 'diagnostic' approaches can be blended to rationally determine the nature of treatment.

VALIDITY ISSUES

The reliability with which different assessors can identify and agree on instances of schizophrenia will determine the upper limit of its validity – the clear definition of its subject matter is the very basis on which science depends.

Spitzer and Fleiss (1974) evaluated the reliability of diagnosing schizophrenia using data from a number of studies and found that the coefficient of agreement between assessors ('kappa') averaged only 0.6. Beck *et al.* (1962) found that 32 per cent of the disagreement arose as a result of poor and inconsistent measurement of symptomatology and 63 per cent due to unclear and differing criteria. In view of the former, a number of standardised rating schedules have been developed, the most widely used being Wing's Present State Examination (PSE), which provides a structured interview protocol and a rating system based on carefully defined criteria. A high level of agreement between raters can be achieved (Wing *et al.* 1974). The PSE is now widely used in psychiatric research and has largely solved the problem of unreliable measurement (although the retest reliability of the PSE is not as high as inter-rater reliability due to variations in patients' self reports over time [Brockington and Meltzer 1982]).

The major factor limiting the reliable identification of schizophrenia is the lack of consensus on the precise definition of the concept. This was vividly demonstrated in the UK/US diagnostic project (Cooper *et al.* 1972) in which video-taped interviews with psychiatric patients were submitted to psychiatrists in London and New York for their diagnostic judgements. It was found that British psychiatrists used a much more restricted definition and that the US definition included many who would have been classified in Britain as manic, depressed, personality disorder or even neurotic. (This particular study was in fact responsible for the tightening of US diagnostic practice which is now more similar to the European approach.)

The diagnostic systems employed by US and UK psychiatrists were clinical in nature; that is, they were based on the unspecified judgements of psychiatrists. As the specific result of this study, a number of objectively defined ('operational') criteria have been proposed to capture the meaning of the concept.

Ten of the most prominent criteria have been examined in terms of their concordance with one another and inter-rater reliability by Brockington *et al.* (1978). These workers found that 55 per cent of their sample of hospital admissions met at least one definition and 25 per cent at least four. There was a moderate degree of overlap between the ten definitions particularly among those placing emphasis on the 'positive' symptoms such as hallucinations or delusions. Two definitions placed greater emphasis on 'negative' symptoms (blunted affect, loss of volition, social withdrawal) and tended to be very restrictive in their application; however those emphasising positive symptoms tended to identify a similar proportion of patients as schizophrenic (about 30 per cent).

Common to the majority of these operational definitions were the following symptoms: auditory hallucinations; believing that thoughts are inserted, withdrawn or 'broadcast' from the mind; feeling that one's behaviour is under 'alien' control; persecutory delusions and the *absence* of depressive symptoms. The definitions mainly varied in the number of such symptoms, or their precise form which they must take, to qualify for schizophrenia.

The study by Brockington *et al.* highlights a number of important characteristics about the schizophrenia concept. First, once the symptoms have been reliably assessed and operational criteria employed, inter-rater reliability can be high, particularly where positive symptoms are emphasised. Second, there seems to be a core group of patients, described above, who are common to all definitions (about 30 per cent) but beyond this core group there is considerable diagnostic uncertainty. Third, the definition of schizophrenia essentially remains an arbitrary affair particularly in terms of the 'limits' of its application: there is as yet no means of preferring one definition over another except perhaps on the limited grounds of inter-rater reliability, which is why diagnoses based principally on positive symptoms are so current (e.g. Schneider's 'First Rank' Symptoms 1959).

There can be few instances in science where there is so much uncertainty regarding the definition of its subject matter. However, we have seen that once clear criteria are laid down, this considerably enhances its reliability of identification and that these operational definitions show a significant degree of overlap particularly where the positive symptoms are prominent in the definition. This state of affairs is perhaps the best that can be achieved until such time as further studies validating the concept clarify its definition – either by establishing a definitive definition, sub-dividing the concept or even possibly rejecting the concept altogether.

CORE PHENOMENOLOGY

The operational definitions appear to have in common a core group of phenomenological symptoms which would lead to a diagnosis of schizophrenia under a majority of these definitions. These symptoms broadly correspond to Kurt Schneider's 'First Rank' Symptom (1959), a definition which enjoys considerable favour in Europe and features strongly in the computer classification based on the PSE ('CATEGO'). As 'first-rank' symptoms only partly capture the concept embodied in many definitions, it is regarded by some as restrictive. However for research purposes, a homogeneous group is preferable to avoid the problems of 'liberal' diagnosis discussed earlier. The first-rank symptoms include the following:

AUDITORY HALLUCINATIONS

1. Voice (or voices) commenting on the individual's thoughts or actions. The voice(s) speak *about* the subject and therefore refer to him in the third person.
2. Voices conversing to each other *about* the individual (again in the third person).

DELUSIONS OF INFLUENCE

1. Delusion of Control: the subject *feels* that his will is replaced by that of some other force or agency. He may experience impulses to do or say something which was not of his own volition. This is a basic experience and may be elaborated in delusional terms (e.g. the individual is the victim of demonic possession).
2. Somatic Passivity: an external force is believed to have penetrated the mind or body from outside (e.g. X-rays, spirits or radio implanted into the subject's brain).

THOUGHT DISORDERS

1. Thought Insertion: the subject experiences thoughts which are *not his own*, intruding into his consciousness.
2. Thought Broadcast: the individual believes his thoughts to be shared with others often over long distances.
3. Audible Thoughts: the individual experiences his thoughts spoken out loud in his mind.
4. Thought Withdrawal: the individual experiences an abrupt cessation of all thoughts not due to activity or distractibility and believes that his thoughts have been removed from his mind by an alien force.

CONCLUSION

The studies described here have illustrated that there is to some degree a consensus among academic psychiatrists in the reliable definition of Kraeplin's concept. Consensus does not of course provide a scientific basis to support the validity of any concept, particularly one so controversial as schizophrenia.

How should one undertake to establish the validity of a concept such as this? Essentially this would involve establishing any lawful relationship into which the concept enters. Thus one might anticipate some of the following characteristics: (a) the concept might show a phenomenology and/or demography distinct and not continuous with other categories, and to have a similar form across cultures, (b) a distinct, possibly homogeneous aetiology and (c) those falling within the concept could be expected to demonstrate a different prognosis and prove responsive to different kinds of treatment compared to other psychiatric groups. On this basis then, it is clear that the validity of the concept is inextricably bound up with its *therapeutic and explanatory utility*.

This book is in a sense an analysis of these various aspects of validity as applied to the concept of schizophrenia. Our aim will be to examine validity at various levels of analysis (e.g. biochemical, familial, cultural) and in the concluding chapter to synthesise this information in terms of whether the concept has or will prove a useful one to those charged with the responsibility of effecting beneficial changes to these individuals.

Chapter three

SCHIZOPHRENIA IN CROSS-CULTURAL PERSPECTIVE

When Kraeplin first distinguished the syndrome of schizophrenia he recognised that if the concept was to have any validity, then it must be observable in countries other than his own. Kraeplin himself reported cases of *Dementia Praecox* in remote areas of the Far East since which time many anthropological investigations of schizophrenia have been undertaken. Such studies have been mainly concerned with validity, but they may also assist in shedding some light on the role of the environment in the genesis, recognition and form of the disorder.

THE CULTURAL RELATIVITY OF SCHIZOPHRENIA

Anthropologists, using a methodology which includes an analysis of language, have examined a number of disparate and remote cultures as a means to discover whether they, like us, have concepts of 'sanity' and 'insanity' and what behaviour patterns underlie these terms. Typical of this approach is the study by Murphy (1976) of the *Yorubas* tribes of tropical Nigeria and the *Eskimos* of North-western Alaska. She found that these very different cultures distinguish between norm-violating behaviours considered 'bad conduct' from those considered to represent a disorder of the mind, spirit or soul. Among the Eskimos the sickness label *nuthkavihak* included such phenomena as talking to oneself, screaming at someone who does not exist, believing that one's child or husband was murdered by witchcraft, believing oneself to be an animal, threatening people and believing that food is poisoned. Similarly, the *Yorubas* have a similar term *were* characterised by such behaviour as laughing when there's nothing to laugh at, defecating in public, picking up sticks for no purpose, refusing to eat certain foods, hitting someone with no reason and believing one emits a pungent odour. Implicit in the meaning of both terms is the idea of a loss of volitional control over behaviour. In both cases, people described by this term were felt to require healing rather than reprimand, a finding also reported by Waxler (1979) in Sri Lanka. The similarity between these putative diagnostic criteria and those for 'schizophrenia' is striking. The anthropological studies have suggested then that abnormalities of behaviour and thought, similar to schizophrenia, are found in most cultures and are sufficiently salient to have attached to them a label, the consequence of which is a desire to heal rather than punish (Leff 1982).

The comparability of such 'diagnoses' across cultures is an issue which has been explored with considerable sophistication by the International Pilot Study of Schizophrenia (WHO 1979). Using standardised assessment methods, it was found that the pattern of symptoms shown by 'psychotic' patients in nine centres throughout the world, east and west, were remarkably similar and under a given definition a large proportion of patients in each country fell within the rubric of schizophrenia, showing impressive consistency in the profile of symptoms presented. Intensive *psychiatric* study of individual races and cultures – such as the Igbo race in Nigeria (Ihezue and Kumaraswamy 1984) – generally point to a similar conclusion.

Similarly, comparisons of incidence and morbidity risk across several countries throughout the world is more notable for its consistency than variability, particularly where similar definitions are used (Jablensky and Sartorius 1976). However, a low prevalence among some non-industrialised countries has been observed (e.g. in Papua New Guinea [Torrey *et al.* 1974]).

It would seem, therefore, that most countries experience and recognise individuals with behavioural and phenomenological aberrations very similar in form to our concept of schizophrenia and most regard such persons as 'treatment-worthy'. This evidence argues against a substantial influence of culture on the *presentation* of schizophrenia. However, this general conclusion requires some qualification.

First, it is necessary to distinguish between the *form* and *content* of schizophrenic symptoms. The forms of a symptom are those characteristics which define into which *class* the symptom falls. For example, the feeling that alien forces are influencing or controlling the mind may be described as the form of a delusion; where this is elaborated, for example, in terms of the presence of a radio receiver having been implanted in the brain, controlling the individual's thoughts and actions, this would be described as the content of the delusion.

It may be readily appreciated from the latter example that the content of hallucinations and delusions are determined by the cultural milieu in which the patient lives: the Yorubas may choose an explanation in terms of witchcraft whereas modern western culture might lean towards high technology. The *form* of the symptoms therefore corresponds to 'primary' psychotic experiences such as hallucinations, perceptual distortions, delusions of control etc and the content to the *expression* or the *delusional elaboration* of the primary experience. The content of many delusions may therefore be seen as an attempt by the individual to develop some degree of psychological consistency between the constructions of reality afforded by their culture and the apparent reality of their phenomenological experience which are seemingly culturally independent.

A second qualification concerns the degree to which the definition of a delusion or hallucination is culturally relative. It was suggested previously that the 'symptoms' of schizophrenia are universally recognised and acted upon, yet it is clearly the case that the accepted beliefs of some cultures (e.g. that witchcraft causes physical illness or the existence of God) would be regarded as delusional (and perhaps even suggestive of schizophrenia) in others. This means that the delusional status of an individual's beliefs and experiences must be judged in terms of their being inconsistent with (a) the available evidence and (b) the prevailing beliefs of the social or cultural group. Psychiatrists, when assessing persons of a different culture to their own must therefore be fully cognisant of the beliefs of that culture in order not to mislabel such beliefs as delusional. With this in mind, many have argued that if psychiatrists could feasibly make such errors then is it not possible that what they diagnose as 'schizophrenia' in their own culture may simply represent *sub*cultural beliefs? Indeed the reasoning appears correct: if one accepts that 'delusions' can only be defined in cultural context, then schizophrenic delusions would not seem to be *qualitatively* different from other beliefs or experiences. Therefore the notion of the universality of schizophrenia should be brought into question. The issue then is whether *subcultural* beliefs and experiences do in fact differ qualitatively from 'schizophrenic' delusions. There are many reasons to support such a distinction.

As previously discussed, 'schizophrenic' delusions tend to occur in the context of a syndrome of perceptual, behavioural and cognitive abnormalities – not in isolation – and when they do so, their form shows strong similarities across cultures (cf. WHO, 1973, 1979). Second, subcultural beliefs are acquired socially or vicariously and have a degree of permanence about them. Schizophrenic delusions, on the other hand, are usually acquired suddenly without social or vicarious experience (Stone and Eldred 1959) and frequently disappear and re-appear in an episodic fashion (WHO 1979). A final point concerns the degree of acceptance abnormal beliefs find within a society – the greater their acceptance the more 'schizophrenics' are likely to be camouflaged within society. There are a number of countries, particularly the underdeveloped nations, where there exists a greater acceptance and tolerance towards the mentally disordered (Murphy 1978; Waxler 1979) yet, as noted above, this is apparently no obstacle to the recognition and 'treatment' of such persons.

CONCLUSION

The limits of the influence of culture on the presentation of schizophrenia appears predominantly to lie in the effect it has on the content of delusions and hallucinations. Many cultures express beliefs which, from an egocentric point of view, might be regarded as delusions. There are some cultures which positively value the experience of hallucinations (Leff 1982) and within cultures there are those who adhere to 'bizarre' or 'unusual' views yet who find acceptance. In spite of this *prima facie* evidence for the cultural relativity in the definition and acceptance of 'abnormal' beliefs, the quality of a *delusion* indicative of schizophrenia is universally recognised, has a fairly constant form and prevalence, and is widely regarded as treatment-worthy.

Part two
BIOLOGICAL FACTORS

Chapter four

GENETICS

Is schizophrenia inherited? If so, how is it transmitted? Is there a single underlying process to the vast range of clinical phenomena observed? Do specific genetic and environmental factors play a role in the production of different subtypes within the spectrum of the schizophrenic disorders? Our present knowledge permits us to answer only some of the issues raised by these questions but does indicate the way in which others may be clarified.

In this first section we will review evidence from family, twin and adoption studies which suggests that the predisposition to schizophrenia is genetically transmitted. Although the exact mode of transmission has not been determined, in the next section we will attempt to evaluate the extent to which the available data are compatible with established mathematical models of genetic transmission. It should, however, be stated at the outset that few contemporary researchers would advance an hypothesis of the aetiology of schizophrenia which relies solely on the contribution of genetic (or indeed environmental) variables. It is clear that the complex clinical phenomenon of schizophrenia is not in itself inherited. Rather, as is the case for many complex behaviours and characteristics, the development of schizophrenia probably represents a complex interaction between genetically transmitted capacities and environmental influences.

THE EVIDENCE

POPULATION AND FAMILY STUDIES

Early investigators attempted to address the question of a genetic predisposition to schizophrenia by determining the rates of schizophrenia in the biological relatives of schizophrenics and comparing

29

these with rates in the general population. One conclusion they arrived at was that schizophrenia was a disorder which clustered in families. Collating the data from a large number of independent population studies yields a median lifetime or morbidity risk[1] for the general population of approximately 0.85 per cent (Neale and Oltmanns 1980).

Variations in morbidity risk were most apparent across studies, ranging from 0.35 ± 0.35 (Panse 1936) to 2.85 ± 0.31 (Book 1953), however such variations largely reflected differences in sampling techniques and diagnostic criteria, and the range of the 'risk period' used by the investigators. Compared, however, to this median rate of 0.85 per cent the risk in all classes of relatives of schizophrenics (ascertained by tracing the biological relatives of registered schizophrenic index cases) is substantially elevated. Furthermore, the risk for schizophrenia among relatives of a schizophrenic individual increases as a function of familial relatedness to that individual (e.g. 2.4% for first cousins, 3% for nephews or nieces and 12.8% for the children of a schizophrenic [Gottesman and Shields 1982]). The trend is a consistent one across investigations despite some degree of disparity in absolute percentage rates again reflecting differential diagnostic and sampling procedures.

Gottesman and Shields (1972) interpret this trend as being compatible with a genetic hypothesis – the variation reflecting the degree of gene overlap with a schizophrenic – and cite as additional evidence the fact that incidence rates in the general population are largely comparable across many countries despite wide variation in obstetric and child-rearing practices and cultural ecologies.

Nevertheless, the data from family investigations in themselves can provide no definitive support for a genetic predisposition as it has quite appropriately been pointed out that the increasing morbidity risk may equally reflect greater environmental similarities.

Finally, certain opponents of the genetic viewpoint might raise as evidence against a genetic hypothesis the fact that the morbidity risk in parents of schizophrenics is somewhat lower than for children of schizophrenics despite the fact that as first-degree relatives they both average 50 per cent gene overlap with the schizophrenic individual. Gottesman and Shields (1982) however suggest that the reduced rates in parents indicate that marriage may select against psychopathology, that is 'the process of marriage and reproduction leads to a positive "selection" for mental health compared to those who remain unmarried' (Gottesman and Shields 1982: 4).

TWIN INVESTIGATIONS

The possibility of investigating and comparing identical and fraternal twin pairs, one of whom had been diagnosed as schizo-phrenic in adulthood, offered an important opportunity with which to partition the respective weights of genetic and environmental factors. Monozygotic (MZ), or identical twins develop from a single fertilized ovum, sharing 100 per cent of their genetic material and representing a unique sub-population in respect of embryonic devel-opment. Dizygotic (DZ), or fraternal, twins, develop simul-taneously from two separate fertilizations and are no more genetically alike than ordinary siblings. Monozygotic and dizygotic twin pairs therefore differ in terms of the percentage of genes each individual shares with their co-twin whilst it may be assumed that in both MZ and DZ pairs each twin shares a similar environment with its co-twin. If then, given that this latter assumption is valid, genetic variables are important contributors to the liability for schizo-phrenia, we might expect when one of the twin pair has been diagnosed as schizophrenic, that rates of schizophrenia in the co-twins should be appreciably higher in MZ than in DZ pairs.

Before considering the results and their implications, it is first necessary to raise two methodological issues which have contributed to disparities in results between early and more recent investi-gations. In twin investigations rates of schizophrenia are expressed in terms of 'concordance', the proportion of twin pairs in which *both* co-twins are diagnosed as schizophrenic. This is ascertained in prac-tice by identifying a schizophrenic index case and then tracing his or her co-twin for evidence of diagnostic classification. Earlier investigations determined concordance by 'pairwise' analysis whereby one simply calculates the proportion of all twin pairs in which both are affected. This analysis did not take into consider-ation the fact that in any given twin pair either might have been independently registered as an index case and hence both traced for psychopathology. Whilst, therefore, the pairwise method would count this twin pair once only in determining concordance, the more recently employed 'probandwise' method would not discount such independently ascertained pairs, but would count them twice. The probandwise analysis therefore generates somewhat higher but arguably more realistic concordance rates.

A second issue to be considered when comparing studies concerns the determination of mono-versus di-zygosity. Early inves-tigations relied upon observation, by independent raters, of simi-larities in physical appearance to determine whether twin pairs were identical or fraternal. Such practices could result in misclassification and hence spurious inflation or deflation of concordance rates according to the nature of the misclassification. In addition to the above practice of rating, more recent investigations have employed both fingerprint and blood-typing to arrive at a more valid esti-mation of zygosity.

Having taken these issues into consideration, the results from contemporary investigations employing objective determination of zygosity yield concordance rates (corrected by the probandwise analysis) ranging from 9 per cent (Pollin *et al.* 1969) to 27 per cent (Fischer *et al.* 1969) in DZ twins and from 35 per cent (Tienari 1963, 1971) to 58 per cent (Gottesman and Shields 1972) for monozygotic pairs. Having pooled data from five recent investigations, Gottesman and Shields (1982) arrived at weighted averages of 46 per cent for MZ and 14 per cent for DZ pairs, values which we may take as representative and which strongly implicate genetic factors in the predisposition to schizophrenia. Further analysis of the twin data indicates that the incidence of schizophrenia in the offspring of discordant monozygotic twins is as high as for clinically concordant pairs – an important observation which we will return to when considering models of genetic transmission. Furthermore, female MZ twins and male MZ twins are equally concordant, and opposite sex DZ pairs are as concordant as same sex DZ pairs, a finding which suggests that gender may not be relevant in the investigation of schizophrenia and genetics but perhaps only relevant in respect of the onset of schizophrenic illness, where there are obvious sex differences (see Ch. 1).

Finally, the fact that concordance for schizophrenia in monozygotic twins is always substantially less than 100 per cent indicates that a specific genetic predisposition to schizophrenia is not a sufficient causal explanation and provides the most impressive evidence that environmental variables are also significant contributors.

It is, perhaps, necessary at this stage to be aware that the term 'environmental' serves to cover a vast range of influences which might contribute to the aetiology, precipitation, and exacerbation (as well as amelioration) of schizophrenia; this comprises potential somatic influences such as intrauterine experiences, obstetric and birth complications and the effects of other independently transmitted characteristics; as well as intrafamilial, interpersonal and sociocultural factors.

Specifically, concerning the implications of the data from MZ twin concordance rates, it must be acknowledged that whilst MZ twins develop from genetically identical embryos, their *effective* genotypes may differ at any stage from the point of fertilization as a function of uncontrolled intrauterine experiences (Gottesman and Shields 1982). The identification of specific environmental factors as stressors investigated by comparison of clinically discordant MZ twin pairs has, however, proven a difficult task primarily because of the small sample sizes involved and the retrospective nature of these studies.

There appears to be little consistent evidence that lowered birthweight or other perinatal difficulties play a specific role (McNeil and Kaij 1978), and differences in birth weight are unable to differentiate reliably between the schizophrenic and the non-schizophrenic co-twin. Boklage (1977) has, however, argued that in virtually every case of discordance in monozygotic twin pairs there is evidence of asymmetric cerebral hemisphere specialisation. Using handedness as his index of cerebral lateralisation, Boklage demonstrated that 95 per cent of concordant MZ twins were both right handed whilst 80 per cent of discordant MZ twins were either both left handed or opposite (one left the other right) handed. This finding has since been independently replicated by Luchins *et al.* (1979).

Whilst there are certain reservations with accepting a one-to-one relationship between handedness and the lateralisation of function to a single hemisphere, cerebral lateralisation, itself to some degree under independent genetic control, might constitute a somatic factor which could exert a modifying influence on the expression of schizophrenia.

Notwithstanding the importance of the twin data, there are several methodological problems with these studies. Methods of determining zygosity and concordance as well as small sample size, retrospective identification and misdiagnosis must all be taken into consideration. Furthermore, Jackson (1960) has questioned the assumption that the MZ/DZ comparison holds environmental components constant, arguing that identical twins are less likely to be separated from each other and more likely to be treated and dressed alike. Whilst this may be the case, environmental variation within twins is likely to be limited. Whether they could account for a threefold increase in risk from fraternal to identical twins is perhaps questionable. Additionally, Kendler (1983) has argued that assortive mating, the twin-transfusion syndrome,[2] and factors in the social environment which are likely to increase differences in personality in MZ twins, may act to produce a 'Reverse Bias', that is, to decrease differences in concordance between MZ and DZ twins.

Finally, in highlighting specific environmental factors one must be careful in not generalising from such potentially 'twin-specific' variables to our understanding of the singleton schizophrenic. Such factors may represent *relative* differences between twin co-pairs and may have no absolute validity in non-twin individuals.

ADOPTION STUDIES

The results of the adoption strategies have served two useful functions. First, they strengthened the genetic hypothesis by demonstrating that children of schizophrenics, adopted away, still become schizophrenic in adulthood at an increased rate. Secondly, they were able to rule out certain environmental factors considered previously to be important. Two specific approaches have been employed in the adoption strategy. The 'prospective' approach concerns the identification and follow-up into adulthood of children of schizophrenics who were adopted away shortly after their birth into unaffected families. Reported rates of schizophrenia in such studies represent the proportion of children diagnosed as schizophrenic in adulthood. The second approach entails the identification of registered schizophrenics who were adopted away shortly after birth, and the subsequent tracing of their biological and adopting relatives for independent evidence of diagnosed psychopathology.

Employing the first approach, Heston (1966) compared the raw prevalence (number of identified cases) of schizophrenia in his adopted away high-risk children and a group of children of normal parentage similarly adopted away but for reasons other than psychopathology. Whereas no cases of schizophrenia were diagnosed in the normal controls, 10.6 per cent of the adopted high-risk children had received a diagnosis of schizophrenia. This percentage is very close to the weighted average of 10 per cent in high-risk children reared by their biological parents. A similar investigation by Rosenthal *et al.* (1968, 1975) yielded a percentage rate of 'hard spectrum' schizophrenia (see later) of 18.8 per cent in the adopted away high-risk children compared to 10.1 per cent in the adopted controls. Kety *et al.* (1978) in a more recent investigation employing the second approach identified seventy-four adult schizophrenics who were adopted, and a normal control adopted sample, tracing both biological and adopting families. They report prevalence rates of schizophrenia of 6.2 per cent for biological and 4.4 per cent for the adopting parents of the control group versus 12.1 per cent for biological parents and 1.6 per cent for adopting parents of the schizophrenic probands. These investigations provide evidence compatible with a genetic hypothesis and suggest that gross adverse intrafamilial influence such as schizophrenogenic environments do not appear to account for the familial clustering of schizophrenic cases. The investigations of both Kety *et al.* and Rosenthal *et al.* are of additional interest because they throw further light on the question concerning the possible role of pregnancy and birth complications.

In Kety *et al.*'s study, included in the data was an analysis of the biological half-siblings of the schizophrenic proband (i.e. brothers or sisters sharing one parent with the schizophrenic); 22.2 per cent of the paternal half-siblings were diagnosed as definite or uncertain schizophrenics compared to 14.6 per cent for maternal half-siblings. The higher percentage in paternal half-siblings who do not share the same intrauterine environment is in the opposite direction to that predicted by the proposed contribution of perinatal difficulties.

Rosenthal's investigation of adopted children further weakens the argument that perinatal difficulties act as specific stresses. Whilst in Heston's (1966) study all schizophrenic parents were mothers, in Rosenthal's sample fully one-third were fathers. Furthermore, only five of the seventy-two mothers gave birth to the child after their first psychiatric hospitalisation, a fact, as Gottesmann and Shields point out, which weakens the role 'attributed to birth factors associated with psychosis or its treatment . . .' (1982: 125).

One further study deserves consideration. In the adoption strategy of Wender *et al.* (1971, 1974), a small sample of adoptees of normal parentage adopted into unaffected families in whom one parent was subsequently diagnosed as schizophrenic were identified. The incidence of 'hard' spectrum diagnosis in this 'cross-fostered' group emerged at 10.7 per cent comparable to the rate of 10.1 per cent in the normal control sample (biological and adopting parents unaffected) and numerically lower than, but not significantly different from the rate of 18.8 per cent in the 'high-risk' sample of children adopted into normal families (all groups being matched for age and socio-economic status of the adopting parents).

Wender *et al.* (1974) subsequently purified their samples by eliminating all subjects coming from adopting families in whom any evidence of disturbance prior to adoption was available, and by excluding any children from the cross-fostered group if one of their biological parents has received a psychiatric diagnosis at interview. The rates emerging from the 'purification' were 10.7 per cent for normal adoptees, 4.8 per cent for the cross-fostered group and 19.7 per cent for the high-risk adoptees. These results were interpreted as suggesting that the influences of a grossly disruptive familial environment may be ineffective in producing schizophrenia in an individual not genetically predisposed. Further evidence against any simple formulation of the relationship of parental psychopathology, abnormal parenting and the production of pathology in their offspring can be drawn from Wender's analysis within the cross-fostered group, where the severity of psychopathology in children raised by schizophrenic mothers or schizophrenic fathers were comparable (Neale and Oltmanns 1980).

Whilst Wender *et al.*'s results are thought-provoking, the study does require to be independently replicated in view of certain methodological complications. Noting their use of broad diagnostic criteria (from process to borderline) and their relatively small sample of cross-fostered children (N = 29) a more crucial complication concerns the fact that within the cross-fostered group most of the parents were not overtly psychotic or hospitalised during the period of their adopted child's development (Neale and Oltmanns 1980). This time period would, of course, be considered one during which proposed intrafamilial disruptive influences due to parental psychopathology might be expected to play a vital role.

Consideration of the data from the adoption studies does, however, provide consistent evidence compatible with, perhaps even conclusively validating, the genetic hypothesis. The investigations are, of course, not without their methodological problems. Sampling techniques, sample size and diagnostic practice are all factors of some concern and ones which have been raised earlier. Additionally, Wender *et al.* (1971) and Horn *et al.* (1975) provide evidence which raises the question as to whether families who give their children for adoption are representative as 'normal' for the purposes of controls. Notwithstanding these issues, combining the data from the adoption, family and twin investigations leaves little doubt that genetic factors are necessary operatives in the aetiology of schizophrenia.

In concluding this review one further issue relating to diagnostic practice needs to be considered briefly. It may have been apparent that the adoption studies of Kety *et al.* (1978), Rosenthal *et al.* (1975) and Wender *et al.* (1974) report far higher incidence rates of schizophrenia in both experimental *and* normal control groups compared to the study of Heston (1966) and the family studies. These inflated rates reflect primarily the former authors' acceptance and usage of the concept of the schizophrenic 'spectrum' of disorders which encompasses psychopathology considered to be related to schizophrenia but less severe and merging into the normal range. The concept of the schizophrenic spectrum derives from the fact that schizophrenia as a clinical phenomenon does not exhibit clear cut boundaries and also from the observation that certain borderline conditions cluster in families of schizophrenics. This spectrum has been divided into 'hard' spectrum and 'soft' spectrum diagnoses. The hard spectrum comprises both *certain* diagnoses of acute, chronic, and latent schizophrenia and *uncertain* diagnoses – schizoid and cases uncertain due to lack of diagnostic information. Within the soft spectrum are included non-recurrent acute episodes and schizophrenic personalities such as undifferentiated, inadequate, or subparanoid, and schizoid personalities (Rosenthal 1975: 202). Evidence from Kety *et al.*'s (1975) adoption study suggests that hard spectrum diagnosis tend to cluster together among the biological relatives of schizophrenics, and may be considered as genetically related to schizophrenia (Kessler 1980). However, the position regarding the relationship between schizophrenia and soft spectrum diagnoses is less clear. In Heston's (1966) study approximately 19 per cent of the adopted children of schizophrenic mothers were diagnosed within the soft spectrum compared to only 4 per cent in the control group. Kety *et al.* (1975) on the other hand found that soft spectrum diagnoses were distributed equally among biological relatives of schizophrenics and non-schizophrenic adoptees. Furthermore, there is no evidence from twin studies (Shields *et al*. 1975) that soft and hard spectrum diagnoses are genetically continuous. Gottesman and Shields (1982) argue that the fact that the inclusion of soft spectrum diagnoses dramatically inflates the incidence rates in the normal population indicates the need for narrower criteria in genetic studies. Whilst further investigation is necessary to clarify this debate it would seem parsimonious to assume, for the moment, that whilst the hard spectrum may be considered a genetic variant of schizophrenia, the soft spectrum comprises abnormalities of personality seen in some relatives of schizophrenics with characteristics suggestive of schizophrenia but which is not genetically continuous with schizophrenia.

MODELS OF GENETIC TRANSMISSION

Despite the fact that a good deal is now known about the specific mechanisms of heredity and that geneticists have been successful in delineating the genetic patterns in certain human diseases, there are many characteristics about schizophrenia and its investigation which have made genetic studies concerned with this disorder extremely difficult.

Under any circumstances humans are difficult subjects for genetic analysis and fulfil few of the prime criteria for adequate investigation (Burns 1980). The life span is too long, the number of offspring too few, and for obvious reasons geneticists are unable to control matings and environmental conditions.

When considering certain human disorders and diseases a variety of factors have frustrated attempts at specifying their particular modes of genetic transmission. Indeed Smith has concluded that 'with sampling errors, ascertainment biases, mortality, variable onset age, heterogeneity and many other complicating factors, discrimination between different modes of inheritance is likely to be very difficult indeed' (1971: 303).

All of the problems outlined by Smith are inherent in schizophrenia. Nevertheless, in the face of these seemingly overwhelming obstacles the attention paid to genetic theorising in schizophrenia research is not without its justification in view of the potential rewards in understanding *how* genetic factors may affect the development of schizophrenic processes. At the very least the development of a working model may be of some heuristic value in focusing the attention of new research programmes. Ultimately a precise understanding of the mechanisms involved in the inheritance of schizophrenia will have important theoretical and practical value, not least to clinicians in the realm of genetic and post-natal counselling.

In view of the applied orientation of the present book the aim in this section is to provide an introduction to the field of genetic analysis and to acquaint the reader with current models of genetic transmission and their application to schizophrenia. For those wishing to come to grips with the mathematical complexities of genetic theories and schizophrenia, we refer the reader to Gottesman and Shields (1982) for a most comprehensive exposition.

Before considering specific attempts at estimating the compatibility between mathematical models of transmission and the incidence (or risk) rates of diagnosed schizophrenia obtained from the studies detailed earlier, it is necessary to familiarise ourselves with the basic issues in genetic analysis.

GENETICS: ISSUES AND MODELS

The basic blocks of heredity are chromosomes and genes. Chromosomes are rod-like nucleoprotein structures contained within the nucleus of each cell. Humans are endowed with forty-six such 'filaments' ordered as twenty-three pairs with one member of each pair being inherited from each parent. Genes are chains of deoxyribose nucleic acid (DNA) ordered in fixed sequences and specific positions (or loci) on the chromosomes. Genes provide the basic genetic code from which amino acids and subsequently proteins are built. All chromosome pairs (apart from the sex chromosomes) are structurally alike. Any pair of chromosomes will, therefore, under normal circumstances, have genes ordered in the same relative sequence along their length. Within a given gene pair both may be dominant, both recessive, or one dominant and the other recessive; dominant genes being expressed regardless of the status of its co-gene while recessive genes are only expressed if the co-gene is also recessive.

Few human characteristics (or phenotypes) are determined by the action of a single pair of genes (termed monogenic inheritance). Most may appear as a function of the interaction between genes at two or more chromosomal loci (polygenic inheritance). Genetic models of transmission, then, are models defining the manner in which genes interact to produce observable characteristics. Initially such models are mathematical hypotheses of gene action which are then tested against the observable prevalence rates of a particular characteristic, or trait, in general populations and genetically related subgroups.

The simplest pattern is that observed and quantified by Gregor

Mendel and referred to as Mendelian inheritance or single major locus transmission. This model seeks to define the action whereby a single pair of genes, operating in a dominant-recessive relationship, is responsible for the expression of an observable characteristic (when both genes are dominant or both recessive they are referred to as homozygous; when one is dominant and the other recessive they are termed heterozygous). This form of inheritance predicts that specific percentages of the offspring will manifest that characteristic (25%, 50%, 75% or 100%). These frequencies of expression assume a 1:1 relationship between the presence of specific genetic material (the genotype) and the manifestation of the characteristic. Through both observation of the phenotype in certain traits known to be transmitted by Mendelian modes, and with the advent of sophisticated microcellular techniques, it is now known that the expression of genetic material is, in many cases, influenced by environmental factors and by the operation of other genes acting as independent modifiers. These influences result in *incomplete penetrance* whereby a given genotype is not expressed at all in a certain proportion of cases; and *incomplete* expression whereby variations in the phenotype are apparent in the offspring. The consequence of incomplete penetrance and expression are, respectively, a deviation from strict Mendelian percentages and the observation of a spectrum of characteristics. Furthermore, a single major locus model may be modified to incorporate a threshold above which individuals are considered to exhibit the full phenotype and below which the incompletely expressed characteristics are ordered.

At the other end of the genetic continuum is the concept of polygenic inheritance. Polygenic theories hold that certain traits are determined by the action of a number of pairs of genes (two or more). Simply stated, this multiple gene action may be purely cumulative, in that a trait is only expressed in its full form when the required number of genes operate together (with incomplete expression when fewer genes are operative) or it may be interactive – the full expression resulting from the action of multiple gene pairs in a specific pattern and hence incomplete expression resulting from slightly different patterns. The polygenic model explicitly utilises a threshold concept and implicates a spectrum of expression. Furthermore some polygenic models incorporate the action of independent genetic modifiers and environmental factors which may either contribute towards the liability of expression or work in the opposite direction to inhibit expression. Such a model is referred to as 'multifactorial'.

Finally, a further concept utilised in genetic analysis is that of 'distinct heterogeneity'. This formulation is a descriptive one and suggests that a particular characteristic may be determined in several distinct and independent ways, some of which are primarily genetically transmitted and others environmentally determined. This concept is descriptive in as much as it does not propose to evaluate the exact mode of transmission of the genetically determined characteristics but it is of significance in terms of our understanding of schizophrenia and genetic transmission by bringing to our attention the possibility of different causal pathways to the same phenotype, and also to the need to eliminate mimics of the disorder from genetic research. For example, there are instances in which the ingestion of psychotropic drugs or traumatic brain pathology may produce symptoms indistinguishable from schizophrenia or diagnoses falling within the schizophrenic spectrum. Certainly, if we are to reach an understanding of the genetics of schizophrenia, such mimics of the disorder need to be ruled out from research samples.

Having introduced some of the basic issues in the field of genetic analysis we may now proceed to evaluate the success with which these accepted models of genetic transmission have been applied to the data on schizophrenia.

GENETIC MODELS AND SCHIZOPHRENIA

Early investigations attempted to fit the available data on schizophrenia to a simple single locus model where the gene for schizophrenia had been viewed as either dominant or recessive. The fact that approximately 90 per cent of all schizophrenics did not have a parent who was schizophrenic suggested that the 'schizophrenic gene' must be recessive. This, of course, implied that to express the trait an individual would have to be a homozygous recessive whilst heterozygous individuals would not overtly manifest schizophrenia but would act as 'carriers'. A simple recessive model does not, however, fit the available data on risk rates in families of schizophrenics. Furthermore, it could not account for the observation that the incidence of schizophrenia in the offspring of concordant MZ twins is as high as for discordant MZ twins. Nevertheless, Slater and Cowie (1971) have developed a modified recessive model incorporating reduced penetrance and expression which is compatible with the data. In spite of this compatibility two other issues remained unresolved. First, a recessive model would predict dramatic differences in the percentage of schizophrenic offspring as a function of whether one or both parents were schizophrenic. Thus if one parent were schizophrenic and the other normal the percentage of schizophrenia in the offspring would be 0 per cent; if both parents were schizophrenic the percentage would be 100 per cent. In fact, the observed discrepancy is in order of 30 per cent.

Second, the fall off in Mendelian ratios from first- to second-degree relatives is not consistent with the sharp reduction in the observed rates evident from family studies of schizophrenia.

Some attention has also been given to the possibility that schizophrenia was transmitted by a dominant but incompletely penetrant gene (it was, of course, essential that the gene be incompletely penetrant to account for the low rates of schizophrenia in the parents of schizophrenics). Again, several problems are immediately apparent with such a model. First, the morbidity risk for schizophrenia is far higher than other diseases with known dominance. Second, dominant 'disorder' traits tend to decrease in frequency in the general population because of their disadvantageous effects on the individual. Some dominant disorder traits *do* continue in the population because the heterozygous state appears to confer a compensatory advantage over normal individuals (a phenomenon known as balanced polymorphism). There is, however, no strong evidence that this phenomenon operates in schizophrenia. Finally, Neale and Oltmanns (1980) argue that, unlike other dominant traits, schizophrenia has not been shown to have a common underlying biological defect. Whilst this is a cogent remark, it is difficult to evaluate whether this merely reflects the present state of biological investigation.

Both recessive and dominant models can be manipulated to fit the empirical data on schizophrenia risk rates by employing the concepts of penetrance, expression, threshold, and gene frequency (the proportion of one of a pair or series of genes in the general population). The extent to which this is possible serves to highlight the fact that merely achieving compatibility between observed and expected rates does not in itself provide definitive confirmation that a particular pattern of inheritance is operative in schizophrenia. Rather it is essential to evaluate each model against other objective criteria gleaned from analysis of other diseases of known genetic transmission. Whilst the concepts of penetrance and expression reflect valid mechanisms of gene action we must be careful to use them to explain data rather than, as Rosenthal (1970) points out, to explain away data.

Currently, emphasis has moved away from monogenic models to the suggestion that the gene action in schizophrenia is polygenic. Polygenic inheritance, as we discussed earlier, refers to the interaction and combination of a number of genes to produce a particular characteristic. The attraction of a polygenic model lies in its ability to account for a dimension of severity in schizophrenia, where there is an observed correlation between severity in the proband and risk in the relatives, by assuming that the more severe eases of the disorder have more of the relevant genes and pass more of them on. Furthermore, a polygenic approach is entirely compatible with a spectrum disorder in schizophrenia and additionally, by its explicit use of a threshold, is compatible with a segregation of 'pure' or process schizophrenia lying beyond the threshold and the genetically related but milder 'hard spectrum' disorders located below the threshold and merging into the normal population in a quasi-continous manner. Finally, a polygenic model is able to accommodate several areas of concern raised as problems for the monogenic hypotheses. For example, the inability to detect a common biological component in schizophrenia is incompatible with a formulation where all schizophrenics are considered to possess the same abnormal gene at the same locus but not for a polygenic model where it would be assumed that not all schizophrenics would have exactly the same combination of genes in an identical pattern.

Two further and related issues concerned the high frequency of schizophrenia and its maintenance across generations despite a clear compensatory advantage. Both observations are compatible with a polygenic approach if it is assumed that the individual genes are, in themselves, *normal* but combined in an unfortunate or deleterious way in an individual to produce schizophrenia. If this assumption is correct the specific genes are assured of their continuity in the gene pool (this would not be the case if the individual genes were themselves pathological).

The strength of a polygenic approach lies in its heuristic value, its ability to address the above anomalies and to account for the comparability in the incidence in offspring of discordant and concordant MZ twins; the sharp fall in incidence rates from closest to remote relatives; and the low rates in parents of schizophrenics. Its appeal is further bolstered by the inability to identify an analogue of schizophrenia which is of known monogenic inheritance but which is as common as schizophrenia and with similar characteristics in the observed risk rates. There are, of course, specific weaknesses with a polygenic model. To a large extent the inability, so far, to achieve compatibility with the empirical data lies with our, as yet, meagre understanding of the mechanisms whereby polygene systems interact and in determining just how many gene pairs interact to produce schizophrenia (although it is likely that only a few genes contribute most variance). Notwithstanding these difficulties, Gottesman and Shield (1982) in their extensive review of the field provide sound arguments for its use as a heuristic model. Additionally, they argue for a multifactorial-polygenic model whereby one can best understand the inheritance of schizophrenia and the schizophrenic spectrum in terms of the combined action of both genetic and environmental factors. Incorporating a threshold in their model they argue for the operation of three specific groups of contributors:

1. A specific genetic predisposition to schizophrenia transmitted

polygenically. By 'specific' the above authors mean that whatever other effects certain individual genes may have on other traits, when combined in a particular way they contribute to the liability for schizophrenia as opposed to any other disorder.

2. General genetic contributors. Such contributors are independently transmitted characteristics which may either act as liabilities – by pushing an individual near to the critical threshold; or as assets innoculating against the manifestation of schizophrenic disorders.

3. General environmental contributors. These may again act also as contributors for liability or as assets.

Gottesman and Shields (1982) argue that the extent to which environmental contribution may be crucial is dependent upon the overall weighting of genetic liability. Hence an individual at 'very high' genetic risk would require only a modest detrimental environmental contribution to precipitate the manifestation of schizophrenia, and perhaps a marked enrichment of the environment to ensure innoculation against full manifestation. This model, therefore, explicitly incorporates the concept of distinct heterogeneity by implicating alternative causal pathways to schizophrenia as a function of differential input from the contributors outlined above.

Whilst at the present moment there appears to be both disadvantages and advantages with each of the models discussed, and there is as yet no conclusive evidence which would lead us to reject or accept any one, the most elegant and cohesive would seem to be the multifactorial hypothesis. We are, however, far from providing a definitive evaluation of models of genetic transmission. To a large extent this reflects our reliance on the heterogenous data base, since the mathematical models of transmission have been evaluated in terms of their compatibility with risk rates in various populations, and the difficulties associated with the use of different diagnostic practices. Ultimately, if we are to arrive at a definitive model of the inheritance of schizophrenia it is crucial that the schizophrenic phenotype be documented more reliably than appears possible on the basis of clinical phenomenology and diagnosis. With the advent of new technologies such as Computerised Axial Tomography and Positron Emission Tomography, and with further developments in the already rapidly expanding fields of neurochemistry, neurophysiology, neuropsychology, and high-risk research it seems likely that we will be able to identify important and relevant biological variables which may be associated with the development of schizophrenia. This may result in a more reliable identification of specific neurological phenotype markers of the schizophrenic genotype, and may also aid in the identification of crucial environmental contributors. In the following chapters we will review these areas of biological investigation.

NOTES

1. Morbidity risk calculates the probability that a person surviving through the risk period (approximately 15–45 years) will develop schizophrenia. This calculation has generally replaced other standardised indices of *prevalence* (the total number of cases now alive expressed at a rate per 1,000 of the general population) and *incidence* (the number of new cases in a specified time period expressed at a rate per 100,000 or 1 million of the general population). Unlike the latter two indices, morbidity risk takes into account deceased individuals and an estimate of those who will develop schizophrenia but who have not yet entered the risk period.

2. The Twin Transfusional Syndrome (Kendler 1983) refers to the substantial transfusion of blood which occurs from one twin to the other in gestation and results in large differences in weight and robustness of the twins at birth. This transfusion occurs in some 20 per cent of MZ twins (two-thirds of whom share the same chorionic membrane) but not in DZ twins (all of whom have separate chorions).

Chapter five
BIOCHEMISTRY

The oldest, most thoroughly explored, and probably most influential approach to the explanation of schizophrenia is that which ascribes a pathogenic role to abnormal brain biochemistry. Preliminary expressions of this approach can be traced back many years, Thudichum (1884) for example suggesting that 'insanity' might represent the effects on the brain of 'poisons fermented within the body', and Bleuler (1911) emphasising the potential importance of chemical disturbance in his classic treatise on *Dementia Praecox*.

Theories advanced in the first half of the century were, however, inevitably constrained by the availability of only modest techniques for biochemical assay and analysis, and by a limited understanding of intact neurophysiologic functioning and the chemical bases of normal behaviour. While relatively prominent, such early theories remained, therefore, unsupported by any strong confirmatory evidence, and are today considered of only historical interest. More substantive and potentially testable biochemical theories have, however, proved possible on the basis of advances in the technology of nervous system analysis and the accompanying emergence of a more sophisticated understanding of neural structure and function. Considerable impetus for the proposal of such hypotheses has more-over been provided by observations that certain pharmacological compounds can induce psychotic states analogous to naturally occurring schizophrenia, while others can alleviate some of the central features of the clinical condition. Bolstered by such inferential evidence, biochemical theories have therefore proliferated over the last thirty years, and are considered by many to offer the best prospects for discovering the key which unlocks the disorders' aetiopathologic secrets.

Of the several contemporary lines of biochemical enquiry, some, echoing Thudichum's (1884) speculations concerning 'fermented poisons', have continued to explore the possibility that schizophrenia arises through some metabolic abnormality which produces

45

an endogenous psychotogenic toxin. The extensive search for a unique 'toxic metabolite' has however proved singularly unrewarding, and recent attention has in the main shifted to examination of possible abnormalities of neurophysiologic function and, in particular, to investigation of putative dysfunction of the neurochemical messenger systems which mediate and regulate interneuronal communication. The foci of most current theories have therefore been the chemicals known as neurotransmitters, which are released from nerve cell endings, diffuse through the synaptic cleft, act upon specific receptor sites in adjacent neurons and thereby serve to carry impulses from nerve to nerve. The study of such neurochemical bridging systems has advanced rapidly as powerful new techniques such as immunoassay and immunohistochemical staining procedures, receptor-binding incubation and autoradiography and high performance liquid chromatography have permitted major developments in the identification, mapping and understanding of neurotransmitter substances. Thus, while relatively few neurotransmitters were until recently well described, the list of likely candidates now exceeds forty substances and includes a number of monoamines (acetylcholine, dopamine, noradrenaline, adrenaline, serotonin and histamine), several aminoacids (gammaaminobutyric acid, glycine, glutamic acid and aspartic acid), and more than thirty recently discovered neuropeptide transmitters (including such opioid peptides as beta-endorphin, met-enkephalin, leu-enkephalin, dynorphin and kyotorphin, as well as pituitary peptides, circulatory hormones, gut hormones, and hypothalamic releasing hormones). The precise biological significance of this wide, and perhaps incomplete, range of transmitter candidates is still unclear, their variety perhaps suggesting that chemical coding plays as important a role in interneuronal communication as does point-to-point impulse transfer (Iversen 1982). There is however broad agreement that intact transmitter function is critical to the integrity of those neuronal interactions which underlie and modulate normal human behaviour, and accordingly that transmitter dysfunction is likely to produce significant changes in experiential and behavioural functioning. Many researchers have, therefore, contended that schizophrenia almost certainly reflects in the last analysis a state of central nervous system neurotransmitter imbalance.

Attempts to identify and describe critical transmitter abnormalities have given rise to a now vast research enterprise, most of the monoamine, aminoacid and neuropeptide messengers being the subject of close scrutiny as potential pathogenic candidates. Numerous speculations have also been offered concerning the hypothetical causes of putative transmitter imbalance. Some have, for example, suggested that the primary pathology is confined to the brain, and involves some disturbance of synaptic transmission arising from abnormal transmitter storage or release, changes in receptor density or altered receptor sensitivity. Others have suggested that a transmitter imbalance may be secondary to a metabolic abnormality within the brain, which has as a consequence, for example, deficient manufacture or inactivation of a transmitter, or indeed the production of an endogenous toxin which compromises transmitter integrity. Others still have argued that the primary pathology may be extracerebral, or involve biochemical processes which are common to the brain and extracerebral systems, including for example changes in metabolic processes or pathways arising from some organ pathology, nutritional deficiency or infection. The data generated in pursuit of these lines of enquiry is by now both voluminous and complex. In view of the prominence, and widespread acceptance of the biochemical approach to schizophrenia, a fairly detailed critical evaluation of contemporary hypotheses is, however, appropriate.

THE DOPAMINE HYPOTHESIS

The predominant and undoubtedly most generative biochemical model of schizophrenia is that which suggests a critical role for the catecholamine neurotransmitter dopamine, and which specifically implicates relative or absolute dopaminergic hyperactivity due to increased production or release of the substance at nerve terminals, increased receptor sensitivity, or reduced activity of dopamine antagonists. As the subject of intense investigation over the last fifteen years, the hypothesis may now be appraised by reference to a substantial body of data emerging from several direct and indirect lines of enquiry.

DRUG-INDUCED ANALOGUES OF PSYCHOSIS

One of the most compelling sources of support for the hypothesis has been evidence that 'model' psychoses may be induced by pharmacological compounds which increase dopaminergic activity. In this respect particular attention has been focused on the effects and mechanisms of the stimulant drug amphetamine, which in large or repeated doses can induce a psychotic state closely resembling naturally occurring schizophrenia (Angrist *et al.* 1974; Young and Scoville 1938). Attempts to specify the drugs' *modus operandi*, and by inference the chemical mechanisms of schizophrenia itself, have in fact been constrained by amphetamines' widespread effects and its stimulation of both dopamine and noradrenaline transmitter systems. On the basis however of animal studies in which amphetamine induced behavioural stereotypes are reversed by the destruction of dopamine terminals and by drugs which prevent the formation of dopamine or which block dopamine receptors (see McKinney and Moran 1981), and in view of the studies in humans of the effects of dopamine receptor blocking agents and synthesis inhibitors, and of· dopamine metabolites following amphetamine administration (see Crow 1981a), most workers agree that amphetamines' psychotogenic properties are mediated by increased central dopamine turnover.

Additionally bolstered by evidence concerning the induction of paranoid psychoses by several other stimulant drugs thought to potentiate dopaminergic transmission, the dopamine hypothesis is widely considered to receive strong indirect support from the mechanism of amphetamines' effects. The generality of amphetamine psychosis as a model for all forms of the naturally occurring disorder, and the validity of the animal behavioural syndrome as an analogue of the human clinical state, must however be considered questionable. Moreover, as noted by Crow (1981a), the dopamine hypothesis is seriously challenged by evidence of drugs which induce psychosis with minimal dopamine release or which potentiate dopaminergic function without associated psychosis. Ephedrine is, for example, reported to produce a typical psychosis but is a weak releaser of dopamine, while even more problematic is the absence of psychotic symptoms following the administration of apomorphine and ET-495 which act directly on dopamine receptors.

PHARMACOLOGICAL EXACERBATION OF SCHIZOPHRENIC SYMPTOMATOLOGY

If correct, the dopamine hypothesis would predict that drugs which increase dopaminergic activity should exacerbate the existing psychotic symptomatology of schizophrenic patients. While tests of this prediction involve the ethically suspect strategy of administering drugs with the expectation of inducing clinical deterioration, a number of workers have nonetheless variously administered amphetamine, methylphenidate, L-Dopa, ET-495, apomorphine and bromocriptine to groups of both chronic and acute schizophrenic subjects. Results of the strategy have however been largely inconclusive, Van Kammen *et al.* (1982a), for example, emphasising the very marked heterogeneity in symptomatic response that may be observed following amphetamine administration with clinical populations. Reviewing the literature in the area published since 1937, Van Kammen *et al.* selected twelve publications containing sufficient information to permit a re-evaluation of published data, and noted that of 285 drug free patients listed in fact only 72 showed symptomatic exacerbation after amphetamine, 132 showed no change, and 81 actually showed definite clinical improvement. In their own placebo-paired, double-blind study, Van Kammen *et al.* similarly noted improvement in 13 of 45 of their schizophrenic subjects, and worsening in only 18. Surveying 24 studies in which a variety of dopamine agonists had been employed, Haracz (1982) has also noted the variability and inconsistency of results across studies and subject samples, and the presence of almost as many reports of clinical improvement as there are of symptomatic exacerbation. As Haracz observes, a sift of the data does perhaps suggest that dopamine agonist administration more commonly worsens symptoms in younger, more acutely ill subjects, and that it produces insignificant or beneficial effects primarily in respect of those negative symptoms of withdrawal, retardation and blunted affect typical of the disorders' chronic stage. Even these trends, which raise the possibility that acute and chronic schizophrenia involve different types of dysfunction, have not however been consistently replicated.

A similar picture has moreover emerged from studies of the administration of monoamine oxidase inhibitors, which through reducing the deactivation of dopamine by the enzyme monoamine oxidase, should in terms of the dopamine hypothesis worsen already present symptoms. While some studies have reported this to be the case, the reviews of Price and Hopkinson (1968) and Brenner and Shopsin (1980) have however again suggested the evidence to be generally inconclusive. Thus Brenner and Shopsin have noted that in fourteen studies involving large numbers of schizophrenic subjects, 71 per cent were unchanged, 26 per cent were improved, and only 3 per cent worsened following monoamine oxidase inhibitor administration. Together with the results of studies of dopamine agonist administration, such findings therefore appear to offer little support for a simple dopamine hypothesis.

DRUG-INDUCED AMELIORATION OF SCHIZOPHRENIC SYMPTOMATOLOGY

The contention that schizophrenia involves some type of neuro-chemical dysfunction has received considerable encouragement from observations of the apparently specific antipsychotic effects of the neuroleptic drugs. The prototypic neuroleptic, the phenothiazine derivative chlorpromazine, was in fact initially synthesised as an antihistamine, but proved so sedating that it was thought unlikely to have much clinical applicability. Investigating its potential in calming schizophrenic patients, Delay and Deniker (1952) however made the serendipitous discovery that it appeared to reduce core schizophrenic symptoms. Such observations were subsequently confirmed by several controlled trials, and the efficacy of chlorpromazine is now widely considered to be established (Davis 1965; Klein and Davis 1969). Several other apparently effective phenothiazine derivatives such as fluphenazine, trifluoperazine, and thioridazine have now also been introduced, as well as members of other chemical classes of neuroleptic including thioxanthenes (e.g. flupenthixol), and the butyrophenones (e.g. haloperidol, spiroperidol) and their phenylbutylpiperadine analogues (such as pimozide). The effects of these neuroleptics appear quite specific to schizophrenia, and that they are not simply due to sedation has been established by controlled comparisons with standard barbiturates such as phenobarbital, and with anxiolytics such as the benzodiazepine compounds valium and librium.

Considerable attention has therefore been focused on elucidating the *modus operandi* of the neuroleptic compounds in the hope that the biochemical dysfunction they ameliorate might therefore be revealed. Since neuroleptics are chemically very reactive, affecting for example DNA metabolism and protein synthesis, and virtually every transmitter system evaluated, such a task has not been easy. Following Carlsson and Lindqvists' (1963) early observation concerning the neuroleptic blockade of central dopaminergic transmission, several lines of evidence have however converged to suggest that neuroleptics exert their therapeutic effects by acting as antagonists at CNS dopamine receptors. It has been noted, for example, that neuroleptics can selectively inhibit the dopamine dependent behavioural effects of agonists such as amphetamine, and that the power of different classes of neuroleptic in this respect corresponds well with their relative clinical potencies in treating schizophrenia. Fairly direct evaluation of the effects of neuroleptics at dopamine receptors has moreover been facilitated by the development of *in vitro* techniques for investigating receptor mechanisms. Thus following the discovery that dopamine receptors in the brain are coupled to the enzyme adenylate cyclase, it has been shown that activation of the enzyme by dopamine can be antagonised by antipsychotic drugs and that the potencies of various phenothiazines on this test are similar to their potencies as antipsychotic agents (see Iversen 1978). The clinical potencies of various neuroleptics also appear to parallel their ability to inhibit electrically stimulated dopamine release from brain slices (Seeman and Lee 1975), their *in vitro* inhibition of dopamine receptor binding (Creese *et al.* 1976) and their ability to elicit changes in dopamine responsive plasma prolactin levels (Langer *et al.* 1977).

Several observations therefore suggest that neuroleptics act against schizophrenia by blocking receptor sites for dopamine in the brain, with the most likely site of their antipsychotic action being the nucleus accumbens or mesocortical areas of the brain (Crow 1981a; Snyder 1982). While such observations are often cited in support of a simple dopamine hypothesis, the extent to which dopamine overactivity provides necessary and sufficient conditions for schizophrenia is however seriously questioned by evidence concerning the time course of neuroleptic effects, and in particular by that suggesting the maximum therapeutic benefit to be in fact effected some considerable time after the achievement of dopamine receptor blockade. Crow (1981a) has suggested therefore that receptor blockade may be important for the antipsychotic effect primarily because it is a condition for some slower process to take place. The dopamine hypothesis is moreover challenged by equivocal data on the effects of alpha-methyl-p-tyrosine and alpha-methyldopa, which in reducing brain dopamine concentrations should in terms of the hypothesis produce a favourable clinical outcome. Reviewing relevant studies Haracz (1982) notes that neither drug alone seems to be of therapeutic benefit, and while some work suggests their potentiation of neuroleptic effects in a subgroup of chronic subjects, results are far from consistent. In the last analysis it must anyway be noted that observations concerning the action of neuroleptics do not establish dopaminergic systems as the locus of schizophrenia, the fundamental abnormality being perhaps several steps removed and only indirectly influenced by alterations in dopaminergic activity. In this respect it may be noted that the efficacy of anticholinergic drugs in Parkinson's Disease did not ultimately indicate an abnormality in brain cholinergic mechanisms, but imbalance between cholinergic and dopaminergic influences in the basal ganglia.

INVESTIGATION OF POST-MORTEM TISSUE

A rather more direct method of evaluating the dopamine hypothesis has involved examination of dopaminergic mechanisms and enzymatic processes in post-mortem brains. Results of this approach have to date however proved disappointingly unsupportive. Thus while a few studies have reported altered levels of dopamine and its metabolite homovanillic acid in specific brain regions, results of investigations covering the caudate, nucleus accumbens, putamen, cingulate gyrus, frontal lobe and septal region have been in the main essentially negative or inconclusive (Haracz 1982). In respect of the putatively important nucleus accumbens for example Haracz (op. cit.) cites fourteen studies of which only one reported increased dopamine levels. Post-mortem investigations of monoamine oxidase, an enzyme which degrades dopamine and whose activity some workers (e.g. Wyatt *et al.* 1979a) suggest might be decreased in schizophrenia, have proved similarly inconclusive. Thus studies covering a wide range of brain areas and using various monoamine substrates, have reported no difference in the enzyme between schizophrenics and controls (e.g. Reveley *et al* 1981). Mainly negative findings have also been reported in respect of the deactivating enzyme catechol-o-methyl transferase (e.g. Crow *et al.* 1979a).

A number of investigators have however recently explored the possibility of post-synaptic receptor pathology through studies of post-mortem tissue. Of those employing the butyrophenone binding technique, several (e.g. Owen *et al.* 1978; Reisine *et al.* 1980) have in fact reported increased numbers of dopamine receptors known as type D2, and Crow *et al.* (1982b) have argued a strong case for a link between type D2 supersensitivity and the schizophrenic syndrome involving positive symptoms and good neuroleptic response. Reynolds *et al.* (1981) however found no difference between schizophrenics and controls in post-mortem putamen binding, and data evaluation in this area is confounded by possible receptor increases as a function of prior neuroleptic medication. As noted by Snyder (1982), several lines of evidence suggest that a deprivation of neurotransmitters may result in receptor supersensitivity manifest by augmented numbers of receptor binding sites, the chronic blocking effected by neuroleptics producing a substantial increase in the number of D2 receptors. In this respect Mackay *et al.* (1980) report evidence of D2 receptor increase only in patients maintained on medication until the time of death. In contrast however others (e.g. Cross *et al.* 1981; Reisine *et al.* 1980) have reported elevated binding in members of their sample who were drug free before death, and Crow *et al.* (1982b) argue that receptor supersensitivity is not a drug effect. Given its potential importance, future research is clearly required to resolve the apparent conflict in available data.

INDICES OF DOPAMINE METABOLISM IN CEREBROSPINAL FLUID, BLOOD AND URINE

A further vehicle for evaluating the dopamine hypothesis has involved the estimation of central dopaminergic activity via CSF, blood and urine measurement of dopamine metabolites and related compounds. The strategy has however been sparsely employed, and its few results offer the hypothesis little substantive comfort. Studies of CSF metabolite concentrations have for example suggested that schizophrenics show essentially normal basal levels of homovanillic acid (e.g. Sedvall and Wode-Helgodt 1980; Gattaz *et al.* 1982), and generally unremarkable patterns of metabolite accumulations following the administration of probenecid, a compound which inhibits the transport of amine metabolites to the blood stream (e.g. Berger *et al.* 1980; Leckman *et al.* 1981). In opposition to the hypothesis a few studies have moreover reported a negative correlation between post-probenecid homovanillic acid levels and the presence and severity of Schneiderian first-rank symptoms (Bowers 1973; Post *et al.* 1975). The utility of CSF analyses must anyway remain questionable while measures may be confounded by local spinal cord monoamine metabolism, differences in metabolite transport and CSF hydrodynamics, and so on.

Similar reservations have been expressed concerning the utility of blood and urine measures in providing indices of central amine turnover, the confounds of local metabolism and environmental influences being marked and the extensive early literature in the area being inconclusive and characterised by an absence of reproducible findings. An exception to the current relative disinterest in such measures however has concerned the investigation of monoamine oxidase activity in blood platelets, Murphy and Wyatt's (1972) initial observation of reduced activity in chronic schizophrenics proving in fact to be probably the most widely reproduced finding of all biochemical investigations of the disorder (Wyatt *et al.* 1980; Meltzer *et al.* 1982). While encouraging the inference of reduced central monoamine oxidase activity and hence of reduced deactivation of dopamine, the relevance of the finding to schizophrenia and the dopamine hypothesis have however been questioned by the failure to detect consistent evidence of altered monoamine oxidase activity in post-mortem schizophrenic brains, by the failure of monoamine oxidase inhibitors to induce analogue psychoses, and by the observations of low platelet monoamine oxidase activity in several groups of normal subjects (Wyatt *et al.* 1980). Moreover, several recent studies have provided strong evidence to suggest that reduced monoamine oxidase activity in chronic schizophrenics is the effect of neuroleptic medication (see Meltzer *et al.* 1982).

NEUROENDOCRINE INDICES OF DOPAMINERGIC ACTIVITY

A final tactic used to evaluate the dopamine hypothesis has involved the measurement of pituitary hormones whose release is altered by the activity of dopamine in the hypothalamic-pituitary system. Essentially the approach is based on the assumption that any dopaminergic abnormality in schizophrenia would be present in the hypothalamus as well as elsewhere in the brain, and that its effects might therefore be detected in abnormal basal plasma levels of pituitary hormones or in hormone responses to dopamine agonists. In this respect particular attention has been paid to the, respectively, inhibitory and stimulatory influence of hypothalamic dopamine on prolactin and growth hormone, the hypothesis in its simplest form predicting that schizophrenics should show decreased serum concentrations of prolactin and elevated levels of growth hormone. Unfortunately, however, studies of basal prolactin and growth hormone levels have in the main failed to detect significant differences between schizophrenics and controls, Haracz (1982) in fact identifying positive results in only three of fifteen studies reviewed. Investigations of endocrine responses to indirect dopamine agonists such as amphetamine and L-dopa have similarly revealed few differences between schizophrenics and other groups, and have offered the hypothesis little substantive support (Haracz 1982). Certain exceptions to this negative trend may be discerned, Johnstone *et al.* (1977) reporting an inverse relationship between prolactin secretion and positive symptomatology, Kleinman *et al.* (1982) confirming this observation in schizophrenics with normal ventricular size, and a number of studies reporting exaggerated growth hormone responses to apomorphine in predominantly unmedicated subjects (e.g. Meltzer *et al.* 1980a; Rotrosen *et al.* 1979). While raising the possibility of dopamine receptor supersensitivity in some schizophrenics, the significance of the latter findings is however uncertain in view of negative findings concerning basal hormone levels, and the unconfirmed assumption that an abnormality in the hypothalamic-pituitary system would be indicative of dysfunction elsewhere. On the whole, therefore, results of the neuroendocrine approach cannot be considered strongly supportive of a generalised dopamine hypothesis.

EVALUATION OF THE DOPAMINE HYPOTHESIS

Results of the variously direct and indirect investigative strategies reviewed above clearly fail to provide the robust body of supportive evidence necessary for validation of the dopamine hypothesis in its original form. If it is to be maintained, the hypothesis would appear therefore to require substantial modification and refinement, and in particular reformulation in terms other than those implicating simple unilateral and generalised dopaminergic overactivity.

The possibilities of developing model variants that remain consistent with the pharmacological bases of the original thesis are in fact several, Haracz (1982) suggesting as potential hypotheses the involvement of dopamine malfunction which is confined to a discrete region of the brain, the existence of minor abnormalities in dopaminergic transmission which collectively occasion serious dysfunction, the presence of an abnormality in some other transmitter system which interacts with dopamine (again perhaps anatomically restricted to a particular brain area), or the existence of several 'schizophrenias' with dopamine dysfunction of primary relevance to only some. Of these, the last possibility is the subject of considerable current interest in view of the many studies which have reported inconclusive or contradictory evidence in terms of a simple dopamine hypothesis, but which have also noted biochemical differences between subgroups of schizophrenics selected initially as members of a single diagnostic class. Such subgroups have rarely been the major focus of investigation, and variable descriptors have been used across studies (e.g. acute versus chronic, positive versus negative symptoms, many versus few Schneiderian first rank symptoms, good versus poor prognosis, drug responsive versus unresponsive, normal versus enlarged ventricles, family history versus no family history, paranoid versus non-paranoid and so on). The observation of subject variability does however appear to support the possibility that dopamine dysfunction characterises at least some schizophrenics, and that the apparent confusion in the literature reflects in part the inclusion of effectively heterogenous experimental samples. Several workers have therefore suggested that more sustainable variants of the dopamine hypothesis may emerge as typologies within the overall schizophrenic population are discerned and validated. In this respect a preliminary typological framework has been advanced by Crow and his colleagues (Crow 1980; Crow *et al.* 1982b), in terms of which it is suggested that schizophrenia comprises at least two identifiable pathological syndromes. The first, Type I, is characterised by the presence of positive symptoms, is most typically seen in acute psychosis, tends to be associated with good response to neuroleptic medication, is associated with no evidence of intellectual impairment or structural brain damage, and has a relatively good (reversible) prognosis. The Type II syndrome is by contrast associated with negative symptoms such as affective flattening and poverty of speech, is characteristically associated with intellectual impairment, may involve cellular loss and structural changes in the brain, and may be irreversible. Such syndromes are conceived not as separate diseases, but as overlapping constellations of symptoms of which both might be present in a patient at one point of time. While the variability of this typology is itself the subject of continuing debate (see Luchins 1982; Nasrallah *et al.* 1982a), Crow *et al.* (1982b) have suggested that dopaminergic dysfunction, perhaps involving receptor supersensitivity, is centrally implicated in Type I schizophrenia but not Type II.

The possibility of a typological variation in dopaminergic disturbance may help resolve some of the conflicting data evident within the current literature, and would appear to offer a heuristically useful framework for guiding future research. Explorations within this framework are as yet however preliminary, and the extent to which even a modified dopamine hypothesis might be maintained is accordingly uncertain. In lieu of the outcome of such explorations, and in view of the disappointing results in terms of the original hypothesis, several workers have therefore directed their attention to the potential role of other neurotransmitter systems in schizophrenias' aetiopathology. Studies which have investigated the importance of the other neurotransmitters via their interaction with dopamine, and in their own right, are reviewed in the following sections.

THE PHENYLETHYLAMINE HYPOTHESIS

Since the demonstration of amphetamine psychosis remains suggestive of the operation of some sort of biochemical abnormality in schizophrenia, some workers have advanced the parsimonious possibility that the natural disorder is in fact the product of an endogenously manufactured amphetamine-like substance. The most likely candidate for such a substance is phenylethylamine (PEA), a monoamine whose structure differs from amphetamine only in respect of the latter's possession of an alpha-methyl group, whose pharmacological and behavioural effects parallel those of amphetamine, and whose effects are similarly blocked by antipsychotic compounds.

The possible involvement of PEA overactivity in schizophrenia, first suggested by Fischer *et al.* (1972), has been most thoroughly articulated in Sandler and Reynolds' (1976) hypothesis that PEA receptors exist in the brain, that both PEA and amphetamine exert their effects by direct action on such receptors, and that schizophrenia represents the effects of abnormally increased synthesis or decreased degradation of PEA, or PEA supersensitivity. More recently Wyatt *et al.* (1977; 1979b) have similarly suggested a potential role for elevated PEA arising from reduced central or peripheral monoamine oxidase activity, and hence reduced PEA deactivation. Unfortunately however there is as yet little evidence available in terms of which a direct or indirect role for PEA can be adequately evaluated. As noted in connection with the dopamine hypothesis, an elevation of central PEA arising from reduced central monoamine oxidase activity seems improbable in view of the failure to detect abnormal monoamine oxidase activity in post-mortem schizophrenic brains (e.g. Meltzer *et al.* 1980b), although in view of the ability of PEA to cross the blood brain barrier, elevated levels arising from reduced peripheral monoamine oxidase activity might however reach the brain and produce psychotic symptoms even in the absence of reduced central monoamine oxidase activity. Consistent with the latter possibility, and in general with a PEA hypothesis of schizophrenia, several studies have in fact reported elevated PEA levels in the urine of some, particularly paranoid, schizophrenic subjects (Jeste *et al.* 1981; Wyatt *et al.* 1980). The significance of the urine PEA results is however unclear in view of the failure of some studies to detect a significant level elevation, the uncertain status of evidence concerning peripheral monoamine oxidase activity in schizophrenia, and in particular the failure to observe behavioural improvements in schizophrenics following the reduction of PEA by pharmacological and dietary methods (Wyatt *et al.* 1979c). Further investigation is therefore clearly required if a potentially significant role for PEA is to be substantiated.

NORADRENALINE AND SCHIZOPHRENIA

Recent investigations of noradrenaline and schizophrenia have in the main examined the possibility of noradrenergic overactivity and of abnormal interactions between noradrenergic and other transmitter systems. In an early theory however, Stein and Wise (1971) proposed that the anhedonia characteristic of the schizophrenic deficit state reflects a metabolic abnormality which in fact produces a noradrenergic deficiency. The hypothesis represents a development of the authors' previous work, in which Wise and Stein (1969) suggested that the effects of reward are biochemically mediated by an ascending system of noradrenergic neurons. On the grounds that damage to this system produces deficiencies in goal directed behaviour similar to certain features of schizophrenia, Stein and Wise (1971) suggest therefore that the disorder may arise because the noradrenergic reward system is damaged by an endogenous toxin. The most likely candidate for such a toxin they suggest to be 6-hydroxydopamine, an aberrant metabolite of dopamine which can deplete brain noradrenaline and produce degeneration of noradrenergic neurones. Specifically Stein and Wise propose that a pathological gene produces a reduction in the activity of dopamine-beta hydroxylase (the enzyme which synthesises noradrenaline from dopamine) and that as a result a mixture of noradrenaline and dopamine is stored in noradrenergic terminals of the reward system. When stimulated by a nerve impulse it is suggested that both noradrenaline and dopamine are released into the synaptic cleft, the dopamine being converted into 6-hydroxydopamine and exerting toxic effects when taken up by the noradrenergic terminal.

In support of their hypothesis, Wise *et al.* (1974) subsequently reported significantly decreased dopamine-beta-hydroxylase activity in several regions of post-mortem schizophrenic brains. Later post-mortem studies by other groups have however failed to replicate these findings (e.g. Crow *et al.* 1979a), and studies of CSF (e.g. Lerner *et al.* 1974) and plasma (e.g. Castellani *et al.* 1982) dopamine-beta-hydroxylase activity have proved similarly negative from the point of view of Stein and Wises' thesis. The indirect support apparently offered by the neuroleptic blockade of 6-hydroxy-dopamine noradrenaline depletion has also been weakened by evidence that 6-hydroxydopamine may destroy any catecholamine system, and that chlorpromazine is unlikely to exert its therapeutic effect by blocking 6-hydroxydopamine uptake.

The general lack of support for the specific hypothesis of Stein and Wise does not in itself of course exclude the possible involvement of noradrenergic deficiency in schizophrenia. Reports that L-dopa in combination with neuroleptics may have therapeutic effects on some negative symptoms in chronic patients (Inanaga *et al.* 1975) may for example suggest that enhancement of noradrenaline release and receptor activation relative to dopaminergic activity is important in at least some cases. Some studies have moreover reported inverse relationships between symptom severity and CSF (Post *et al.* 1975) and urine (Joseph *et al.* 1976) noradrenaline metabolites. Differences between schizophrenic and controls in mean noradrenaline levels have not however been widely reported, and in general interest in the involvement of noradrenaline has passed to consideration of noradrenergic overactivity.

The contributory role of overactivity and impaired regulation of noradrenaline in schizophrenic psychosis has been suggested by several lines of indirect evidence. Thus, it has been observed that such features of psychosis as agitation, hyperactivity, anxiety, affective lability and sleeplessness are consistent with noradrenergic hyperfunction (Sternberg *et al.* 1982), while many of the drugs which produce model psychoses, exacerbate existing symptomatology, or afford therapeutic relief, affect central noradrenaline as well as dopamine and other neurotransmitter systems. Given the inconsistency of the results of studies in which amphetamine has been administered to schizophrenic patients, the possibility that noradrenaline plays an important modulatory role cannot, for example, be excluded (Van Kammen *et al.* 1982a). Similarly since neuroleptics such as clozapine are relatively weak dopamine blockers, their more potent effects as alpha-adrenergic antagonists may be therapeutically relevant (Snyder 1982). Some studies (e.g.

Hanssen *et al.* 1980) have moreover suggested that the beta-adrenergic receptor blocker propranolol may be an effective anti-psychotic for at least some schizophrenics.

More direct evidence of noradrenergic hyperfunction has however been provided by studies reporting elevated noradrenaline levels in the limbic forebrain of post-mortem schizophrenic brains (e.g. Bird *et al.* 1979), and by evidence of elevated CSF noradren-aline levels which decline after neuroleptic treatment in association with therapeutic improvement (e.g. Sternberg *et al.* 1981). Studies of CSF noradrenaline metabolite levels (e.g. Gattaz *et al.* 1982), plasma noradrenaline levels (e.g. Castellani *et al.* 1982) and urinary metabolite (e.g. Joseph *et al.* 1976) have been less conclusive, but abnormalities in adrenergic regulation have been suggested by the differential effects of the alpha$_2$ adrenergic agonist drug clonidine in schizophrenics compared to controls. Several lines of evidence suggest the existence of presynaptic alpha adrenergic receptors which inhibit noradrenaline release, stimulation of which by cloni-dine should therefore reduce noradrenaline turnover and lower plasma levels of noradrenaline metabolites. In a recent study, Stern-berg *et al.* (1982) have reported a significantly reduced level of plasma metabolite levels following clonidine in schizophrenics, which they suggest to be consistent with a functional subsensitivity of the inhibitory presynaptic alpha$_2$ adrenergic receptor, and which leads to increased noradrenaline turnover. The results of Matussek *et al.* (1980) on growth hormone response to clonidine however suggests post synaptic alpha$_2$ adrenergic receptors may be normal in schizophrenic patients, and it would appear that post-mortem binding studies are required to clarify the status of both pre- and post-synaptic central adrenergic receptors.

SEROTONIN AND SCHIZOPHRENIA

In comparison with other monamines, the possible role of serotonin has been the subject of relatively little investigation in biochemical studies of schizophrenia. That it might merit attention is of course suggested by observation of the powerful psychotomimetic proper-ties of the drug LSD, and by evidence that LSD inhibits the firing of serotonin neurons of the raphe nuclei and reduces serotonin turn-over via stimulation of pre- and post-synaptic serotonin receptors. Several authors, noting the general absence of delusions and reten-tion of insight, have however questioned the validity of acute LSD psychosis as an analogue of naturally occuring schizophrenia (see Crow 1981a), and suggest therefore that LSD effects provide at best very weak support for the involvement of serotonergic mechanisms in the clinical disorder. While many neuroleptics can act as serotonin antagonists, it also seems unlikely that that such effects are critical to their therapeutic potency. Moreover, the few studies of the effects of serotonin antagonists have been essentially inconsistent, Yorkston *et al.* (1974) reporting some benefit with 1-propranolol, but Holden *et al.* (1971) noting no therapeutic effects of the antiserotonergic drug cinanserin. While a serotonin over-activity hypothesis thus receives little consistent support, a serotonin deficiency hypothesis is equally questioned by the failure to detect consistent therapeutic improvement following administration of the serotonin precursors tryptophan and 5-hydroxytryptophan (e.g. Gillin *et al.* 1976). Studies of tritiated LSD binding to frontal cortex (e.g. Whitaker *et al.* 1981), of brain levels of tryptophan, serotonin or serotonin metabolites, of basal and post probenecid CSF metabolite levels (e.g. Gattaz *et al.* 1982; Post *et al.* 1975; Sedvall and Wode-Helgodt 1980), and of platelet and whole blood serotonin concentrations (e.g. Freedman *et al.* 1981; Joseph *et al.* 1977), have similarly produced an inconclusive pattern of mixed and inconsistent or negative results. The potential importance of subgrouping schizophrenics in some biological basis has however been again suggested by the observation of DeLisi *et al.* (1981) who report higher mean serotonin concentrations in patients with abnormal CT brain scans compared to schizophrenics with normal CT scans and controls.

METHYLATED AMINES AS ENDOGENOUS HALLUCINOGENS

One of the oldest and most durable biochemical theories of schizophrenia is that which suggests a causal role for methylated amine neurotransmitters which are endogenously manufactured and which possess psychotogenic properties. Now commonly known as the 'transmethylation hypothesis', the idea owes its origin to two main sets of observations. First, a number of experimental investigations in the 1940s and 1950s suggested that certain natural and synthetic substances such as mescaline, psilocybin, dimethyltryptamine (DMT) and LSD could produce striking experimental distortions similar to some of the features of naturally occurring psychosis. Second, in 1952 Osmond and Smythies noted the structural similarity between the transmitter noradrenaline and the hallucinogenic drug mescaline, since which time many 'psychedelics' have been shown to be methylated amines (i.e. they are derived from the same nuclei as brain amines but by a process of methylation rather than hydroxylation). On the basis of these observations, several workers suggested therefore that schizophrenia might be the result of a metabolic abnormality by which endogenous hallucinogens are produced from naturally occurring dopamine, noradrenaline or serotonin by an aberrant process of methylation.

One strategy used to test this hypothesis has involved examination of the effects of methyl-rich substances on schizophrenic patients, an exacerbation of symptoms being expected if additional methyl donors were compounding the effects of an already existing aberrant methylation process. Such a strategy did indeed provide the first apparently supportive evidence, Pollin *et al.* (1961) reporting a worsening of symptoms in four of nine patients given the methyl-rich amino acid methionine, and the finding being subsequently replicated in at least ten other studies (see Cohen *et al.* 1974). While bolstering the transmethylation hypothesis over several years, the significance of this finding is in fact far from clear. Thus Baldessarini *et al.* (1979) have reported that methionine administration has no effects on normal humans, that it does not increase blood concentrations of S-adenosylmethionine (the substance that actually donates the methyl group), and that in animals neither methionine or S-adenosylmethionine have any significant effect on the methylation of L-dopa, while they actually decrease the production of DMT. Further, Erdelyi *et al.* (1978) found no difference in S-adenosylmethionine activity in autopsied brain material between schizophrenics and controls. In sum, methionine does not appear to produce its psychotic worsening effects by increasing the production of methylated catechol or indoleamines.

The second strategy adopted to test the hypothesis has been to administer methyl acceptor substances which should, if the hypothesis is correct, lessen symptoms. While however Hoffer and Osmond (1964) reported that large doses of the methyl acceptor nicotinic acid (Vitamin B) were of therapeutic benefit, the finding has not been widely replicated (e.g. Gillin *et al.* 1978), and nicotinic acid does not appear anyway to lower the level of S-adenosylmethionine in the brain (Baldessarini *et al.* 1979).

The third research strategy has been to search for methylated amines or their metabolites in the body fluids of schizophrenics, great excitement being aroused when Friedhoff and Van Winkle (1962) reported that a urinary metabolite having properties analogous to the psychedelic amine DMPEA (a methylated derivative of dopamine) was found in schizophrenics but not controls, showing up on chromatographic testing as a 'pink spot'. Attempts to replicate the results have however produced a welter of contradictory positive and negative findings (see Wyatt *et al.* 1971), and several studies suggesting it to be an artefact of diet or medication. More refined methods of biochemical assay have moreover indicated that the 'pink spot' contains several compounds other than DMPEA, while observations that DMPEA can appear in the urine of 'normal' individuals and that its ingestion does not appear to produce psychosis-like effects have together tended to reduce interest in the area. In the absence of studies excluding nonspecific factors, the DMPEA hypothesis nonetheless survives for want of definite disconfirmation.

More recent studies have therefore concentrated on methylated indoleamines, such as DMT and bufotenin, although results have again as a whole proved rather inconclusive. In respect of bufotenin Wyatt *et al.*'s (1971) review noted both positive and negative findings and the frequent confounds of diet and medication, and despite some positive results in later studies (e.g. Cottrell *et al.* 1977), the evidence for bufotenin's hallucinogenic properties is not convincing (Turner and Merlis 1959). Positive (e.g. Narasimhachari *et al.* 1974) and negative (e.g. Angrist *et al.* 1976) findings have also been noted in relation to DMT, and some have suggested that anyway the presence of DMT is not specific to schizophrenia (e.g. Rodnight *et al.* 1976). Studies of enzyme function are also inconsistent, Wyatt *et al.* (1973) for example reporting that indolethylamine-N-methyltransferase (which catalyses the methylation of indoleamines) is higher in schizophrenics, but the result not been supported by others (e.g. Strahilevitz *et al.* 1975).

In sum, while the transmethylation hypothesis has not been conclusively refuted, a consistent pattern of supportive evidence cannot be marshalled in its favour in respect of either catechol or indoleamines. It moreover remains the case that the mental disturbance produced by psychedelic drugs differs in many respects from that of naturally occurring schizophrenia. Accordingly, while an explanation of methionine effects may yet provide useful clues to a chemical basis of schizophrenia, interest has in the main passed to other areas.

ACETYLCHOLINE AND SCHIZOPHRENIA

On the basis of largely indirect evidence, a number of workers (e.g. Davis and Janowsky 1975) have suggested the possible contributory role of acetylcholine deficiency in the expression of schizophrenic symptoms, particularly in view of its interactive relationship with the neurotransmitter dopamine.

One line of evidence used to support an acetylcholine hypothesis has concerned reports of psychosis, including visual and auditory

hallucinations and delusions of persecution, following the administration of anticholinergic drugs in normal volunteers and parkin-
sonian patients. Since the effects of cholinergic blockade appear to
be more pronounced in the elderly, and also include impairment of
the capacity to learn, Crow (1981a) has however noted that anticholinergic drugs may be considered to induce a typical exogenous
psychotic reaction or acute confusional state rather than a clear
analogue of schizophrenia. Moreover, no clear or consistent
evidence has emerged to suggest that anticholinergic drugs exacerbate existing schizophrenic symptomatology, Crow (1981a) again
noting that the widespread use of anticholinergics with neuroleptics
is presumably based on the clinical impression that concomitant
usage does not in fact reduce the latter's efficiency. In addition,
some neuroleptics with a strong anticholinergic activity (e.g.
thioridazine, clozapine) appear to be effective antipsychotic agents.

A further explored strategy has involved the administration of
drugs which increase cholinergic activity, and which the hypothesis
would predict should improve symptomatology. Some animal
studies have suggested that the effects of amphetamine can be
reduced by cholinomimetics such as oxotremorine and the cholin-
esterase inhibitor physostigmine (e.g. Davis *et al.* 1978), and in
humans the worsening of psychosis following methylphenidate has
been reversed by physostigmine (Davis and Janowsky 1975). Some
early reports also suggested that cholinomimetics could produce
brief periods of lucidity in withdrawn schizophrenics, while Rosenthal and Bigelow (1973) noted short-term beneficial effects of
physostigmine in conjunction with neuroleptics. Such effects were
however short lived, and Davis *et al.* (1980) have recently noted no
significant effects on symptoms following either physostigmine or
choline chloride (the precursor of acetylcholine). Moreover Davis
et al. (1979) found no evidence of altered acetylcholinesterase (a
metabolising enzyme) in schizophrenic CSF, while Domino *et al.*
(1973) reported no change at post mortem in the enzyme choline
acetyltransferase in most areas.

In sum, despite the interactions of acetylcholine and dopamine
and the possible deleterious effects of an alteration in their relative
balance, the hypothesis of acetylcholine deficiency remains at this
stage unestablished.

GABA AND SCHIZOPHRENIA

The aminoacid neurotransmitter gamma-aminobutyric acid (GABA)
is one of the most widely distributed substances in the brain, some

30 per cent of all synapses being GABAergic compared to less than 1 per cent of neurons using catecholamines in neurotransmission. Moreover GABA may inhibit all neuronal pathways in mammalian brain, and act in particular as an inhibitory feedback neurotransmitter in relation to dopamine. Given its inhibitory action Roberts (1972) therefore proposed a GABA-deficit hypothesis of schizophrenia, later revised to a GABA-imbalance hypothesis (Roberts 1976), while others have proposed a similar GABA-dopamine imbalance model as an extension to the original unitary dopamine hypothesis (e.g. Van Kammen 1977).

Unfortunately, as the role of GABA has been better characterised, it has become clear that its interactions with dopaminergic pathways are extremely complex. Thus recent evidence suggests that GABA does not in fact always inhibit dopamine function and may in certain cases actually activate dopamine neurons, that GABA may both increase and decrease dopamine turnover depending upon the brain region assayed and the duration of stimulation, and that its effects on dopamine mediated behaviour are subtle and vary depending upon anatomical location, dosage and duration of action (Garbutt and Van Kammen 1983). In view of these complexities, it is perhaps not surprising that clinical trials of GABA stimulation in schizophrenics have been essentially inconclusive, Garbutt and Van Kammen's (op. cit.) review noting an inconsistent pattern of positive, negative and neutral findings following the administration of GABA agonists such as baclofen, gamma hydroxybutycate, muscimol and SL-76-002, and drugs which inhibit the GABA degrading substance GABA-T such as dipropylacetic acid. Investigations of GABAergic function in schizophrenic patients via post-mortem measures of GABA levels, GABA receptor binding and levels of the synthesising enzyme glutamic acid decarboxylase, and of GABA levels in schizophrenic CSF, have been similarly inconsistent and inconclusive (see Garbutt and Van Kammen, op. cit.).

As yet therefore neither a GABA deficiency nor imbalance hypothesis has been substantiated, although in view of the evidence for dopamine-GABA interactions, the area continues to receive interested attention. Van Kammen *et al.* (1982b) have for example speculated that recently ill schizophrenics who respond to GABA stimulation with symptomatic worsening have low GABA levels secondary to dopamine supersensitivity, while chronically ill patients may be unresponsive. It seems likely, therefore, that the potential role of GABA will continue to be studied, and that it may become clearer as appropriate experimental advances are made and as specific and non-toxic GABAergic drugs are identified.

NEUROPEPTIDES AND SCHIZOPHRENIA

While the existence of peptide hormones in CNS neurons and nerve terminals and their status as transmitters or neuromodulators has been only recently recognised, the description of more than 30 neuropeptide candidates in recent years suggests that they in fact comprise the largest group of chemical messengers in the CNS. Considerable attention has therefore been paid to the possible role of such substances in schizophrenia's pathogenesis, and in particular to the involvement of opioid peptides or endorphins, which have pharmacological properties similar to those of morphine and other opiates, and which are of interest in view both of their particular anatomical location in brain areas thought to be important in the regulation of mood and affect (e.g. limbic structures), and evidence for their extensive interactions with other transmitters implicated in the disorder's aetiology. Thus, given the known mood altering capacities of opiates such as morphine, and evidence that beta-endorphin administration can produce catatonic-like behaviour in animals, several workers have suggested that schizophrenia may reflect the direct or interactive influence of excessive endogenous opioid activity.

Although investigations of the hypothesis are as yet preliminary, results available to date are nonetheless disappointingly inconclusive. Of several studies in which opiate antagonists such as naloxone have been administered on the grounds that endorphin blockade should produce therapeutic improvement, some have for example reported decreased symptomatology (e.g. Davis *et al.* 1979; Watson *et al.* 1978), but as many have found no clear evidence of significant clinical effects (e.g. Janowsky *et al.* 1977; Lipinski *et al.* 1978). Even were significant changes noted following naloxone, its effects other than opiate blockade (e.g. GABA receptor antagonism) render interpretation difficult. A simple endorphin hypothesis is also challenged by the failure of opiate agonists to induce a convincing analogue of schizophrenia, and as Berger (1981) notes by the several uncontrolled studies over the last century which have in fact reported clinical improvement following exogenous peptide administration.

More recently therapeutic benefits in schizophrenia have similarly been reported following the administration of beta-endorphin (e.g. Lehmann *et al.* 1979) and des-tyrosine-y-endorphin (e.g. Verhoeven *et al.* 1982), and some authors suggest such results if anything to support an endorphin deficiency hypothesis. Other studies however have failed to replicate such findings (e.g. Berger *et al.* 1980; Tamminga *et al.* 1981), while Gerner *et al.* (1980) reported worsening of symptoms following beta-endorphin administration more in line with the excess hypothesis. Studies of endorphin and opiate activity in body fluids have proved no more conclusive, normal and elevated CSF beta-endorphin levels being variously and inconsistently reported across studies of acute, chronic, mixed and unmedicated schizophrenics (e.g. Domschke *et al.* 1979; Emrich *et al.* 1979; Naber *et al.* 1981). Initial reports of the benefit of renal dialysis in schizophrenia (Wagemaker and Cade. 1977) attributed the removal of elevated leucine-5-beta-endorphin (Palmour *et al.* 1979) have also failed to receive support, Schulz *et al.* (1981) finding no therapeutic benefit of haemodialysis in a double blind trial, and the existence of elevated endorphins in dialysate or plasma not being confirmed (e.g. Emrich *et al.* 1979).

In considering opioid peptides and psychosis Watson *et al.* (1979) have noted the several difficulties which constrain both research and the evaluation of current findings, including the existence of several opiate peptide systems in the brain with possibly different receptor pools, and the still limited understanding of their interaction with other neuronal systems implicated in schizophrenia. Watson *et al.* also suggest that inconclusive naloxone results may reflect variable dose levels across studies, as well as the problem of measuring subjective symptom change following a substance whose duration of action is short. At this stage therefore further basic research is required to understand opioid systems and their direct and interactive functional roles, and to determine agents which specifically modify the several types of opiate receptors postulated. In lieu of such research, attempts to implicate endorphins in all or subpopulations of schizophrenics must remain speculative.

PROSTAGLANDINS AND SCHIZOPHRENIA

The ubiquitously distributed prostaglandins whose potent physiologic effects have been known for many years, play an important regulatory role in respect of various endocrine and metabolic processes, inflammatory and immunological reactions, and other bodily functions. Evidence has however now emerged for their existence and synthesis in the brain, and while not themselves considered neurotransmitters, it seems that CNS prostaglandins can both modulate neuronal responses to neurotransmitters and hormones, and influence the presynaptic release of catecholamines.

While their functional role in the CNS is still poorly understood, both excessive and deficient prostaglandin activity have already been implicated in schizophrenia's aetiopathology. In noting the role of prostoglandin in fever production, Feldberg (1976) for example has cited reports of symptomatic worsening in schizophrenics with fever as supportive of a prostaglandin excess hypothesis, and also suggests as supportive evidence the induction of catatonic-like behaviour in animals following prostaglandin administration, and elevated CSF prostaglandin in cataleptic states. Horrobin (1977) however has postulated a role for prostaglandin deficiency in schizophrenia, noting the involvement of prostaglandin in arthritis, inflammation, pain and vasodepression, and citing as supportive evidence therefore the apparent incompatibility of schizophrenia and arthritis, and the enhanced vasoconstrictor and reduced pain and inflammatory responses sometimes reported in schizophrenics. As further supportive evidence Horrobin also notes the possibility that the therapeutic action of neuroleptics may be mediated through prolactin stimulation which stimulates prostaglandin synthesis.

To date little substantive experimental evidence is available in terms of which either model can be evaluated. Neither prostaglandin induced catatonic-like behaviour, nor the toxic confusional state following prostaglandin antagonists, can be considered convincing analogues of schizophrenia. Moreover a prostaglandin excess model gains little support from the failure of paracetamol (a synthesis inhibitor) to exert therapeutic effects, while reports of the possible benefits of primrose oil (a prostaglandin precursor), zinc and penicillin (synthesis enhancers) can at most be considered very preliminary support of a deficiency model. Some support for a functional prostaglandin deficiency model has been afforded through platelet studies in schizophrenics which suggest both reduced prostaglandin synthesis and reduced responsivity to exogenous prostaglandins (see Rotrosen *et al.* 1980), although Pandey *et al.* (1977) reported exaggerated responses to prostaglandins in acute patients.

In reviewing the area Rotrosen *et al.* (1980) have suggested that functional prostaglandin activity could provide a basis for dopaminergic overactivity, that it may account for the blunted growth hormone responses seen in some schizophrenics, and that it could be compatible with the endorphin excess theories and those relating to symptoms to the consumption of cereal grain. In the light of the limited available evidence, and lack of evidence regarding prostaglandin function in the brains of schizophrenics, such possibilities remain as yet intriguing avenues for research.

IMMUNOLOGICAL AND VIRAL FACTORS IN SCHIZOPHRENIA

The possible involvement in schizophrenia of abnormal proteins, viral infections or disordered immunological regulation, has been the focus of intermittent interest over a period of several years. Apparent parallels between schizophrenia and certain autoimmune diseases, including identical twin variation, the 'juvenile grace gap' and characteristic episodes of remission and relapse, have for example suggested to some investigators that schizophrenia may itself be an autoimmune condition. Probably the best known of the immunological theories is that proposed by Heath (Heath and Krupp 1967), based on the reported discovery in schizophrenia of an abnormal blood protein (taraxein) which possesses psychotomimetic properties when injected into healthy volunteers. Subsequent work by Heath suggested taraxein to be present in a subfraction of the antibody gamma-G-immunoglobulin (IgG), and that at post mortem IgG could be found bound to cell nuclei in the septal area of schizophrenic brains. It was suggested therefore that schizophrenia is an autoimmune disease, in which taraxein containing antibodies are produced to combat antigens in the septal area of the brain and that they interfere with neural functioning. Attempts to replicate the reported psychotomimetic properties of taraxein have however been generally unsuccessful (e.g. Durell and Archer 1976). Studies of IgG at post mortem have also failed to reveal its presence (Logan and Deodhar 1970) or its presence specific to schizophrenia (Boehme *et al*. 1974).

More recently, Knight (1982) has proposed an autoimmune hypothesis which seeks also to account for some of the conflicting data collected in terms of the dopamine hypothesis. Knight suggests that acute positive symptoms are occasioned by auto-antibodies which interact with and stimulate dopamine receptors, or by antibodies which block presynaptic autoreceptors, while chronic negative symptoms represent an autoimmune encephalitis-like syndrome in which a viral infection triggers a destructive autoimmune response against certain dopaminergic pathways. The hypothesis however awaits evaluation.

The possible involvement of viral factors in schizophrenia's aetiology has however been suggested by several other investigators (see Bergsma and Goldstein 1978), particularly in view of the advances in characterising the role of slow viruses in CNS disease. It is now clear that slow viruses may cause subtle neurological dysfunction for months or years before hard signs of impairment become apparent, and that they may proceed without demonstrable biochemical or immunological abnormalities in the blood or CNS. Several investigators have noted similarities between such disorders and schizophrenia in terms of the insidious onset and episodic progression, as well as suggesting that the excess of winter births in schizophrenia may implicate a viral aetiology. In this respect Crow and colleagues (Crow *et al*. 1979b; Tyrrell *et al*. 1979) have recently reported a Virus Like Agent (VLA) in the CSF of some patients with schizophrenia like illness, although VLA was also present in other patients with chronic neurological disease.

In general terms the involvement in and role of abnormal proteins, viral agents or immunological disturbance in schizophrenia remain unclear. Differences between schizophrenia and controls in terms of blood proteins such as alpha-2-globulin (the Frohman Factor) and beta-lipoprotein, in terms of immunoglobin antibodies (Pulkkinen 1977) and in terms of lymphocytes, have been variously reported, and some studies have reported an association between HLA antigens and schizophrenia which might be a genetic marker for the disorder. In respect of each of these areas however findings have tended to be inconsistent across studies, and no clearly replicable results specific to schizophrenia have emerged. Such inconclusive findings do not exclude an important role for immunological or viral factors in schizophrenia's aetiology, particularly in view of the increasing understanding of the mechanisms of autoimmune conditions and slow viruses. At this stage however a suggested role must be considered rather speculative and one that must be subject to further experimental scrutiny.

CONCLUSION

The hypothesised involvement of neurochemical imbalance in schizophrenia's aetiopathology has clearly been the focus of a massive body of technologically sophisticated research. The findings of such research however have been frequently uncertain in terms of both fact and interpretation, and have not provided a consistent and replicable body of evidence implicating a critical dysfunction specific to the clinical condition. Given reports of the pharmacological induction and amelioration of psychotic symptoms, and the sheer volume of studies in which abnormalities have been variously detected, many investigators remain convinced that biochemical factors play some role in the disorder's emergence and course. The nature and mechanism of the critical chemical disturbance remains however disappointingly elusive.

The reasons for this continuing uncertainty are several and varied. In the first instance however, the formulation of testable biochemical hypotheses of schizophrenia has been constrained by the still relatively poor understanding of the neurochemical bases of normal behaviour. Recent years have of course witnessed major advances in basic knowledge, the development of powerful new techniques of biochemical assay permitting an increasingly precise identification and mapping of the brain's neurochemical systems.

Such advances however have been matched by a growing appreciation of the quite astonishing complexity of the chemical communication network, and of the major task investigators face in clarifying the functional roles and interrelationships of the messengers now identified. Many new transmitters have been described over the last few years, and it now seems that while some are responsible for fast, point-to-point signalling, others serve a more diffuse regulatory and modulatory role in respect of neuronal activity. It also now appears that many neurons secrete not a single neurotransmitter at their terminals, but contain more than one biologically active substance which reside in co-existence. As Iversen (1982) has noted, the biological significance of such multiple chemical signals is as yet unknown, though it seems likely that complex chemical coding, and not merely point-to-point connection plays an important role in CNS communication. Evidence has also emerged for the possibility of neurochemical laterality in the human brain, Glick (1983) for example reporting neurochemical asymmetries in several structures and transmitter systems in post-mortem human brain, as well as noting findings from animal studies of endogenous asymmetries in striatal dopamine content, of lateralisation of neurochemical reward mechanisms and of differential dose-related effects of certain drugs on the two hemispheres. Such observations may prove to be of particular importance given the possibilities noted elsewhere in this book of functional asymmetries in the expression of schizophrenia. Given the above it is perhaps not surprising that hypotheses of schizophrenia implicating simple unilateral transmitter excesses or deficiencies are likely to be gross oversimplifications of a vastly complex situation.

Research on the chemical bases of normal behaviour is of course itself constrained by the considerable methodological problems which limit access to those processes of primary interest in human subjects, and which confound data interpretation. Such problems however apply equally to the evaluation of hypotheses of schizophrenia, and have undoubtedly also contributed to their still uncertain status. A major obstacle to research is for example posed by the blood-brain barrier, whose presence precludes direct access to the living human brain and necessitates the employment of variously indirect investigative strategies for hypothesis testing. Unfortunately the foci of such strategies, including peripheral body fluids, deceased brains, the effects of pharmacological substances and animals, may provide relatively poor indices of what is happening in the brain of a living schizophrenic. Many workers for example consider the assessment of such body fluids as blood or urine to be a relatively weak investigative strategy, whose results may reflect primarily the influence of peripheral systems, while even CSF measures, rarely used because of the unpleasant nature of sample collection, are confounded by the uncertain contribution of peripheral versus cerebral sources to the substances detected. Similarly, while the analysis of brain tissue at post-mortem has permitted more direct access to those neuronal systems thought related to the disorder, the strategy is still several steps removed from the living brain, and may be confounded by changes in the sample as a consequence of the lapse of time or preservative technique used, or by differences in the cause of death, and so on. Attempts to infer biochemical defects in schizophrenia from the *modus operandi* of drugs which induce, exacerbate or ameliorate psychotic symptoms are also fraught with difficulties, the behavioural effects of such drugs being as previously noted frequently variable, their pharmacological properties being very general and involving several transmitter systems, and the status of drug-induced analogues of schizophrenia being in many respects questionable. Similarly, rigorous extrapolations cannot be made from animal studies, where the status of analogues of human schizophrenia must be considered even more suspect.

The difficulties with indirect measures however highlight a more general interpretational problem associated with the essentially correlational nature of much biochemical research. In many instances an abnormality of presumed causal and pathological significance is inferred on the basis of an observed relationship or correlation between some biochemical parameter and the diagnosis of schizophrenia. A correlation may however reflect not a simple directional or causal relationship, but the effect of some other unobserved factors. A detectable biochemical difference between schizophrenics and controls, even one representative of activity within the brain, may in principle therefore be secondary to the influence of for example hospitalization, diet, psychosocial treatment, stress, medication, or some other circumstance arising from illness and the diagnosis of schizophrenia. Unless such extraneous sources of variance are carefully controlled, an abnormality of apparently primary causal relevance may prove to be quite spurious. Secondary abnormalities arising from the stress of illness may for example be difficult to exclude, particularly given the very wide range of response in the normal population, while as noted previously the interpretation of bodily fluid and post-mortem studies have been particularly confounded by the possible effects of prolonged neuroleptic medication. Even were an abnormality detected independent of the effects of medication, its primary causal status would still however prove difficult to demonstrate. Given the complex interactions between neurotransmitter systems, an observed abnormality may in fact be an ephiphenomenon or consequence of a primary disturbance elsewhere (although its identification would at least be useful as a biological marker for the condition). A similar problem confounds the interpretation of drug studies, where the behavioural and clinical effects of even a compound affecting a single biochemical system may depend not, or not only, on the transmitter it first affects, but on others which interact with the first.

Such interpretational difficulties are unfortunately further compounded in the field of schizophrenia by the evident inconsistency between many of the research results available, an inconsistency in large part reflective of the variability across studies in methodology and in the care paid to experimental design. Procedures for biochemical analysis have been in the main sophisticated and carefully controlled, although it is probable that at least some conflicting results reflect the use across studies of analytic methods differentially sensitive to biochemicals present in low concentrations. A marked imbalance has however existed between the careful attention paid to the collection, preservation and assay of biological samples, and the inconsistency and variable quality of procedures for subject description and selection, control of confounding variables within samples, and objective measurement of behaviour change across time and condition. The sophistication of biochemical assay is largely irrelevant if the subject groups classed as schizophrenic are in fact heterogeneous in composition, or if subjects within and across studies are differentially exposed to environmental circumstances of potential biochemical significance.

The selection of homogeneous samples and data interpretation is a major problem in any area of biochemical research, given the considerable biochemical variation in the normal population, individual differences in for example responsivity to stress or metabolism, differences associated with age, sex, physique, and so on. If such factors have however been poorly considered in many studies of schizophrenia, of even greater concern is the uncertain homogeneity in clinical terms of the subject samples investigated. As noted elsewhere in this book, the diagnosis and discrimination of schizophrenia has been fraught with problems of validity and reliability, which even the development of more objective research nosologies has not fully resolved. Given only limited agreement about how to select and classify schizophrenia subjects, and the uncertain validity and reliability of those procedures used, there must be doubt that subjects seen by different investigators, or even within single studies, represent a totally homogeneous group. Such doubts exist even in respect of those studies employing the same classificatory system, but are particularly acute when comparing the results of studies which have used different diagnostic criteria. Further uncertainty is occasioned by the frequent mixing within samples, and differential representation across studies, of various loosely defined subgroups (e.g. chronic, acute, paranoid etc), as well as by the variable inclusion of subjects whose symptom patterns overlap with those of other conditions which may have their own biochemical correlates. There seems little doubt therefore that many apparently conflicting results reflect the inclusion of subjects heterogeneous in terms of symptomatology and aetiology.

Inconsistent results may also reflect in part the variability within and between subject samples in terms of exposure to other factors which might influence biochemical functioning. The most obvious example in this respect is again medication, some studies reporting on medicated subjects and others on those who are drug free, and most reporting on a mix of the two (and also often on medicated subjects who vary in terms of the type of medication, dosage, period on drugs etc). Variability of diet between subjects may also be an important factor, particularly in view of the suggestion that the gluten component of cereal grain may exacerbate the overt symptoms of schizophrenia (Dohan 1966). Support for this idea has been provided by the apparently high correlation between changes in wheat consumption during the war and hospital admissions for schizophrenia, by the increased incidence of celiac disease in schizophrenics and the prevalent psychotic symptoms in celiac patients, and by reports that gluten-free diets may be of therapeutic value (Dohan 1976). Ashkenazi *et al.* (1979) have reported a lymphocyte antigenic response to gluten in some schizophrenics that is similar to responses in celiac patients, and Klee *et al.* (1978) have noted that the polypeptides derived from gluten have endorphin and opioid antagonist properties. In the light of inconsistent results from other studies (see Storms *et al.* 1982), the importance of wheat gluten is, as many other factors in schizophrenia, highly controversial. The area does however highlight the possible confounds in other biochemical studies if even exposure to foodstuffs is not controlled between subjects. A further potentially important source of variance between subjects, particularly in studies involving the administration of drugs, concerns differences in the nature and level of their ongoing behavioural activity. Substantial evidence from the field of behavioural pharmacology suggests that the behavioural effects of drugs such as amphetamine depend not merely on their chemical properties, their dosage or the physiology of the recipient, but also critically on the nature of the subject's ongoing behaviour and the conditions of reinforcement under which it is maintained when the drug is administered (Blackman 1974). While simple universal predictions about the behavioural effects of drugs cannot therefore be made without reference to existing behavioural patterns and the conditions under which they occur, such factors have rarely been considered in clinical drug trials or studies of the effects of putative psychotomimetics. Such studies have moreover been frequently characterised by the use of measures of behaviour and behaviour change which are global, unreliable and extremely unsophisticated in their objectivity and sensitivity. Behavioural psychologists, particularly those working in the fields of operant conditioning, behavioural pharmacology and behaviour modification, have of course developed sophisticated methodologies for the objective assessment of behaviour. Procedures for carefully defining behaviour and for reliably measuring its occurrence are therefore readily available, as are many powerful experimental designs which are extremely sensitive to behavioural change (e.g. prolonged baseline designs, reversal designs, multiple baseline designs across subjects and conditions). Again however such methodologies have rarely been employed in biochemical or drug studies, the predominant use of global rating scales undoubtedly therefore contributing to the frequent difficulties in replication. Given such methodological problems and theoretical problems of interpretation, it is perhaps surprising neither that the field has been confused by inconsistent and inconclusive findings, nor that many theories have been found wanting and premature. Several early hypotheses, focusing on putative toxic substances or simple unilateral biological abnormalities, are now in fact considered of largely historical interest, and certain others survive more through want of definite disconfirmation that the availability of compelling support. However, even the dopamine hypothesis, for several years the dominant guide for biochemical enquiry, lacks a substantive body of direct support and owes much of its continuing appeal to indirect pharmacological observation. Given moreover apparent limitations in its theoretical power and in the range of diagnosed schizophrenics to which it may apply, even proponents of the hypothesis concede the need for modification and refinement if it is to be sustained as a major explanatory model. Similarly studies of other monoamines, amino acids, neuropeptides and so on, while giving rise to several intriguing speculations, have yet to provide solid evidence of their causal role in either their own right or through their balance and interaction with dopamine.

The status of biochemical hypotheses must at this stage therefore be considered uncertain and rather disappointing. They have in the main been unsupported by replicable evidence, they have not provided convincing accounts of for example symptomatology, phenomenology or social aspects of the disorder, and they have not been readily related to work in the field of genetics or that implicating the influence of social and other environmental factors. Perhaps even more importantly the biochemical approach has not provided a model in terms of which treatment can be logically deduced from pathology, and has not made a major impact on the development of pharmacological interventions. The discovery and rational administration of more specific, more effective and less toxic drug treatments is perhaps the single most important *raison d'être* for the biochemical research effort. Chemotherapeutic advances have however been based primarily on initial serendipitous discovery and subsequent empirical development within the field of clinical pharmacology, and have owed little to biochemical hypotheses of schizophrenia. Indeed, pharmacological research has guided rather than followed such hypotheses, and has provided the latter's clearest support. Moreover biochemical assay plays no significant part in routine clinical diagnosis, the selection of a treatment modality or the monitoring and evaluation of treatment response. Treatment is not therefore based upon an identified biochemical pathology.

The search for more effective, less toxic drug treatment remains an important justification for exploring the biochemistry of the disorder itself. If significant advances are to be made however, several issues would seem to merit attention. First, biochemical research focuses in the main not on dependent and independent variables which are both 'organic' in nature, but on relationships between chemical dependent variables and independent variables which are behavioural or diagnostic. Given the biological-behavioural interaction implicit in the field therefore it seems crucial that the imbalance in methodology between sophisticated chemical assay and unsophisticated subject selection, description and assessment be redressed. In this respect the development of improved operational definitions of schizophrenia, the consistent use of more objective behavioural assessment procedures and more powerful experimental designs, and the greater control of environmental factors that influence behaviour and biochemistry, would seem of particular importance. Secondly, while the initial search for a simple biological abnormality was not itself unreasonable, contemporary theories must now clearly address the complex nature of brain chemistry and physiology, and the massive and intricate interaction between neurotransmitter systems and other biological processes. Such theories must also address the possibility that a dysfunction may involve not only several transmitter systems, but that an imbalance may not be characterised in terms of a simple linear or sequential causal relationship. Thirdly it seems increasingly clear that schizophrenia is indeed a disorder of heterogeneous composition, in which variable but overlapping symptom patterns, and even essentially similar behavioural presentations, may be associated with critically different aetiopathologies. One of the most important developments in recent years has been the gradual distillation from the massive research literature of possible schizophrenic subgroups which have particular combinations of behavioural, physiological and biochemical characteristics. The attempt to determine reliable discriminatory markers, and in particular to describe a biochemical classification, seems of critical importance if research is to produce a replicable body of findings. Clearly a rational biochemical classification is also important if drugs are to be prescribed on a logical and individually tailored basis. Finally, it is now clear that a 'golden bullet' biochemical explanation of schizophrenia is likely neither in practice nor principle. Indeed it seems improbable that any single level of investigation, be it genetic, developmental, physiological, social, environmental or behavioural, will be able to account for the full range of the disorder's manifestations and correlates. This should come as no surprise, since any adequate account of normal or abnormal human behaviour and experience must acknowledge its functional dependence on a reciprocal interaction between biology, behaviour and the environment. The biochemical approach can hope to describe only one element of this complex interactive whole, and not stand as an autonomous level of explanation.

Chapter six

NEUROANATOMICAL INVESTIGATIONS

NEUROHISTOLOGICAL EXAMINATION

Over the last five to seven years there has been a resurgence of interest in neuropathological investigations of morphological changes in the brains of schizophrenic patients. This, in part, probably reflects the increased availability and refinement of advanced technological procedures such as computerised transaxial tomography. Interest in neuropathological changes in schizophrenia was, however, high well before the 1950s during which time histopathological investigations of post-mortem schizophrenic brains were carried out. The results of these studies were somewhat dichotomous in their findings (Stevens 1982a).

On the one hand it was considered that Nissl and Myelin staining techniques pointed to discrete and specific changes in the basal ganglia, basal forebrain and the cerebral cortex of schizophrenic brains. Other investigators, however, reported only diffuse alterations and were largely of the opinion that all the reported neuronal abnormalities most probably reflected the effects of long-term medication, surgical interventions and post-mortem changes. Certainly, given the absence of 'normal' control preparations in these studies, very little could be inferred from their observations regarding the significance of these morphological alterations to the schizophrenic condition.

Recent investigations by Stevens (1982a,b) employed highly sophisticated preparation and staining techniques and were able to include a non-psychiatric control group in the analyses. She reports observations of degenerative changes within the neurons and an increase of the supporting glial cells (termed fibrillary gliosis) within the central nervous system of the schizophrenic brains.

These morphological alterations were maximal in the 'subependymal regions and at the origin and terminus of major pathways between the amygdala and the basal forebrain and in the hypothalamus, globus pallidus, medial hypothalamus and midbrain' (Stevens 1982b). Furthermore, Stevens points out that the observed alterations were similar to those characteristically reported in infectious inflammatory diseases such as viral encephalitis and considered the changes in the schizophrenic brains to be consistent with a 'healed inflammatory' process.

Whilst the use of sophisticated histological examinations in schizophrenia are still in their preliminary stages it is of interest to mention that there are several factors in schizophrenia which may be consistent with the above view of viral aetiology. Thus the observation of seasonal variations in breakdown and social class clustering in schizophrenia (Torrey *et al.* 1977; Kohn 1973) are phenomena which are commonly associated with other known viral disorders. Similarly, the detection of a transferable virus-like agent in the cerebrospinal fluid of some schizophrenics (Crow *et al.* 1979b) adds further weight to this suggestion.

It is worthwhile noting that the possible discovery of a viral causation does not contradict the considerable evidence for genetic transmission in schizophrenia since viral genomes can become incorporated in the cell nucleus and hence transmitted with the genetic material of the host cell.

Finally, several studies have pointed to anatomical abnormalities in the callosums of schizophrenics. In the earliest of such studies Rosenthal and Bigelow (1972) reported significantly enlarged corpus callosum width in schizophrenic compared with normal brains. Bigelow *et al.* (1983) in a direct replication of the above study report that in their sample this enlargement was significant in the frontal but not occipital areas. Furthermore, Nasrallah *et al.* (1979) have suggested that these are associated with early onset hebephrenic but not late onset schizophrenia. Histological analysis of the corpus callosum (Nasrallah *et al.* 1982c) suggests that this enlargement may reflect an increase of gliosis of the corpus callosum rather than an increase in the number of fibres.

COMPUTERISED TOMOGRAPHIC STUDIES

The issue of whether morphological abnormalities could be detected in the 'living' brains of schizophrenics and whether these might be relevant to the schizophrenic process began in the early 1900s following the development of the technique of pneumoencephalography (PEG). This clinical technique involves the injection of air into the subarachnoid space of the lumber spinal region which then eventually finds its way into the fluid filled ventricles and the convexities of the brain, providing a contrast medium for X-ray examination. Early studies employing PEG were, to a large extent, characterised by poor methodological design and invariably an absence of adequate controls. Additionally, there was some evidence the PEG introduced an artifact in that the injection of air could, on occasions, enlarge the ventricular spaces (LeMay 1967) hence rendering any interpretation on the basis of ventricular size somewhat spurious. Finally, PEG is a difficult procedure involving some risk to the individual as a consequence of which many of the subjects included in both the schizophrenic and control groups were not randomly selected but had been referred for PEG because of suspected organicity or diagnostic uncertainty.

Nevertheless, several investigations which have attempted to control for these factors, notably those of Haug (1962) and Asano (1967), reported evidence of ventricular enlargement in their schizophrenic samples. Because, however, the technique of PEG appeared poorly suited for investigating psychotic patients, refinements of the technique did not occur and it was only with the advent of computerised transaxial tomography that interest in morphological alterations in schizophrenia was renewed.

Computerised tomography (hereafter CT) is now a widely used clinical diagnostic tool which involves virtually no risk to the subject. The technique employs an X-ray beam and an array of detectors revolved around the subject's head to calculate the density of tissue in a particular 'slice' of the brain. The density indices are then reconstructed by computer assisted analysis into a two-dimensional analogue picture of the brain in the plane swept by the X-rays.

The application of CT to the identification of morphological abnormalities in schizophrenia has been of considerable importance, not only because of the increased sensitivity of detecting abnormalities in the CNS structures (the resolution power being, in principle, possible to 0.3 mm) but, because it has provided information regarding abnormalities of hemispheric asymmetries in the cerebral cortex of some schizophrenics.

Generally speaking the findings from CT studies may be divided into those reporting changes in the ventricular cavities, and suggestive of cortical atrophy, and those specifically addressing the issue of cerebral hemispheric asymmetry.

VENTRICULAR SIZE

The ventricles are cavities within the brain filled with cerebrospinal fluid, forming a continuous channel between the four ventricles and the central canal of the upper end of the spinal cord. Enlargement or dilation of the ventricles, most notably as a result of local obstruction, may result in increased intracranial pressure and is associated with wasting or atrophy of the surrounding brain tissue. This is most noticable in hydrocephalus and more insidiously and discretely in the dementias.

The first reported investigation using CT with schizophrenic patients was that of Johnstone *et al.* (1976) in which they observed that in excess of 50 per cent of their schizophrenic sample there was evidence of significantly enlarged ventricles. Since that time a number of similar studies have been reported across which striking differences in the prevalence of ventricular enlargement in schizophrenics have been observed.

Golden *et al.* (1980b), for example, reported enlarged ventricles in approximately 60 per cent of their schizophrenic patients whilst Andreason *et al.* (1982c) observed enlargement in only 6 per cent. Furthermore, Jernigan *et al.* (1982) concluded that there were no significant differences in ventricular size between healthy volunteers and young schizophrenics. In a study by Weinberger *et al.* (1982) 24 per cent of their chronic schizophrenic sample exhibited ventricular enlargement as compared to 22 per cent in a group classified as first-episode schizophreniform psychosis.

Such disparities have lead, almost within the same year, to seemingly different conclusions. Thus Jernigan *et al.* (1982) concluded that 'the presence of ventricular enlargement in a large proportion of the schizophrenic population has not been established', whilst Weinberger and Wyatt (1983) concluded that 'CAT studies . . . . indicate evidence of brain atrophy in some patients with a diagnosis of chronic schizophrenia'. These conclusions are, in fact, not mutually exclusive when one considers the variation across studies in terms of sampling and measurement procedures. Indeed, in view of the possible implications of the observations of increased ventricular size in some schizophrenics, it is perhaps appropriate to discuss the studies in the context of several methodological issues.

Several factors, notably age, chronicity, control samples and measurement technique appear intimately associated with the differences observed in prevalence of ventricular enlargement in schizophrenics. Generally speaking, those studies reporting negative findings, that is, normal ventricle size in schizophrenics (e.g. Benes *et al.* 1982; Jernigan *et al.* 1982), recruited samples of schizophrenics which were both young and hospitalised for a period of less than five years. As an example, in Jernigan *et al.*'s (1982) study, fully one-third of the schizophrenics were outpatients and all subjects were unmedicated during the period preceding and including CT scanning. Jernigan *et al.* observed no significant differences in ventricular size in their schizophrenic sample compared to a normal control either in terms of a global measure of fluid volume or on a semi-automated analysis plotting a ratio between ventricular size and total brain weight (termed ventricular brain ratio or VBR). This study is of particular interest in as much as Jernigan *et al.*'s techniques were largely comparable to those of Weinberger *et al.* (1982) who had observed a prevalence of ventricular enlargement of some 24 per cent in their schizophrenic sample.

Whilst, therefore, there is probably very little difference in respect of the measurement procedures used between the two studies it is crucial to note that Weinberger *et al.*'s sample comprised older, chronic schizophrenics who had been recruited to a research ward as a function of poor response to conventional treatment.

Furthermore, Benes *et al.* (1982), employing five measures of ventricular size including VBR, observed a high correlation between each measurement but no significant abnormalities in the schizophrenic group. Again, noticably, the schizophrenic sample were both young and acute with a mean length of hospitalisation of only 1.1 years. Finally, whilst Gross *et al.* (1982) observed an overall prevalence of 28 per cent ventricular enlargement in their schizophrenic sample, an analysis of ventricular size and age demonstrated no significant differences between schizophrenics and normals except in the age group 50 and above. It would therefore appear to be the case that ventricular enlargement may be associated with older, chronic schizophrenics.

One further, but associated, factor which might account for some of the variance across studies concerns the nature of the subgroups diagnosis within the overall category of schizophrenia.

Thus in the study by Nasrallah *et al.* (1982a) significant enlargement of the ventricles was observed in a combined schizophrenic group. However, differentiating between 'paranoid', 'non-paranoid hebephrenic', and 'non-paranoid undifferentiated' schizophrenics indicated that those subjects with the largest ventricular abnormality (defined as VBR of greater than two standard deviations from the control group mean) were concentrated in the paranoid and non-paranoid hebephrenic groups but not in the undifferentiated sample, an important finding in its own right but one which additionally indicates the need to report more specifically the diagnostic characteristics of the groups recruited for assessment. On a similar issue Andreason *et al.* (1982b) reports that large VBR's appear to be associated with the presence of negative symptoms (apathy, withdrawal etc) whilst subjects with the smallest VBR's exhibited a greater prominence of positive symptoms such as delusions and auditory hallucinations.

The issue of appropriate control groups has been less stringently examined however it is apparent that in a number of studies the controls were recruited from neurological clinics in which the primary referral was for headaches and dizziness of suspected organic aetiology. In all cases only those subjects receiving a normal diagnosis, either by the CT scan itself or more commonly by independent neurological investigation, were included. Nevertheless, whilst it may be assumed that the majority of controls obtained in the manner are likely to be appropriate, Gur (personal communication) has pointed out that reasonable caution must be exercised with respect to their neurological status given that CT scans are usually only employed if there is independent evidence consistent with organicity (although this practice must vary geographically).

To highlight this point Andreason *et al.* (1982c) observed a significant difference in ventricular size between their sample of young, briefly hospitalised schizophrenics and the normal control group. Comparison of their controls with those of similar investigations, however, indicated that Andreason *et al.*'s controls had lower VBR's (hence smaller ventricles) than those of the other studies – an observation which suggests a spurious inflation within the schizophrenic sample compared to the controls. Similarly, one must be aware of the reverse phenomenon (abnormally large ventricles within the controls) which might lead one to conclude that no ventricular enlargement is apparent in the schizophrenic group.

Regarding measurement and analysis, Luchins (1982) has commented, after reviewing a number of CT studies, that slight differences in CT equipment image reproduction and measurement technique may have a profound effect on determining abnormalities for research comparisons. One example would be the level or slice at which the CT scan is obtained for analysis, and whether this corresponds to the maximal prominence of ventricular size, slight differences in which across subject, groups, and studies will inevitably influence objective comparisons. Furthermore, a two dimensional versus three dimensional analysis may contribute an artefact to the determination of relative abnormality. Thus, for example, Golden *et al.* (1980b) who observed a 60 per cent incidence of enlarged ventricles in their schizophrenic sample employed both a lateral and ventral measurement to arrive at a three-dimensional volume index, and this may well have accounted for their somewhat excessive incidence rates.

In spite of the apparent differences between CT investigations there is, we feel, enough evidence to conclude that abnormally increased ventricular size is demonstrable in some schizophrenics who fall into the chronic, elderly, long-stay group. Additionally, several investigations report an association between the presence of ventricular enlargement and functional deficits on standardised neuropsychological tests (see Luchins 1982). Thus in those schizophrenics characterised by increased ventricular size there is evidence of neuropsychological performance decrements consistent with intellectual deterioration and chronic organic brain syndrome, whilst normal scans are largely associated with normal (i.e. non-organic) neuropsychological profiles.

Several questions, however, remain partially unanswered and have been summarised by Nasrallah (1982): '. . . is ventricular size a meaningful biologic sign with diagnostic, clinical, therapeutic and prognostic significance? When does ventricular enlargement occur in schizophrenia and is it progressive or static?'

Certainly the fact that ventricular enlargement does not appear to be associated with young, acute populations of schizophrenics suggests that enlarged ventricles may be associated with chronicity, and given that the majority of schizophrenics have normal scans it seems unlikely that ventricular enlargement could be a pathognomic sign of schizophrenia. Furthermore, the observation of increased ventricular size in non-schizophrenic subjects, notably schizophreniform psychosis (Weinberger *et al.* 1982) and mania (Nasrallah *et al.* 1981b; Pearlson and Veroff 1981) adds further weight to the suggestion that enlargement of the ventricles may be a non-specific correlate of psychosis associated with age related organicity.

CEREBRAL ASYMMETRY

It is well known that functional asymmetries of the brain, notably in terms of language comprehension and speech production, are associated with and perhaps ultimately determined by neuro-anatomical asymmetries. Thus with respect to language the observed functional lateralisation of language predominantly to a single hemisphere (derived from investigations with normal and split-brain subjects) appears closely associated with anatomical differences in the temporal lobes (Springer and Deutsch 1981). Knowledge of such asymmetries of performance and anatomy has provoked extensive research into the conceptual and investigative area of cerebral laterality and schizophrenia.

As we will observe later, there is an abundance of evidence from neurophysiological and neuropsychological investigations which is clearly consistent with the hypothesis that in some groups of schizophrenics abnormalities of functional lateralisation are present. Given this vast body of evidence it is, perhaps, not surprising that neuroanatomical correlates of these functional abnormalities have been sought after. Specifically, CT studies of abnormal lateralisation in schizophrenia have derived from the observation that in normal, right-handed individuals the right frontal lobe is larger, laterally, than the left and the left occipital lobe larger than the right (Le May

1976; Le May and Kido 1978). CT studies with schizophrenic populations have raised the question as to whether some schizophrenics exhibit a reversal of this normal anatomical asymmetry. It should be pointed out, however, that whilst this is an important field of enquiry relatively few studies have addressed this issue to date.

In one such investigation by Luchins *et al.* (1982) the lateral surface of the left and right occipital lobes was measured in a group of schizophrenics and normal controls. Luchins and his colleagues omit measurement of the frontal lobes on the basis that frontal but not occipital asymmetry appears to be affected by the degree of brain pathology. As a group their seventy-nine schizophrenics contained a significant proportion of individuals who demonstrated occipital reversal (right greater than left), these reversals being negatively correlated with the presence of cortical atrophy and were associated with poor verbal relative to non-verbal IQ. Those schizophrenic subjects in whom normal asymmetry was evident were reported to have higher verbal than non-verbal IQ's.

Luchins *et al.* (1982) suggest that these 'reversals', which may be possible determinants of unusual or anomalous language specialisation, are more likely to constitute abnormalities of cerebral development, rather than being a consequence of left hemisphere cerebral insult. As evidence in support of this hypothesis they argued that if occipital reversal were a direct consequence of left hemisphere damage then the left lateral ventricles would be more frequently enlarged in their 'reversal' group as compared to the 'non-reversal' subjects – a finding which was not observed in their data. Luchins *et al.*'s results have since been independently confirmed by Lee *et al.* (1985).

Golden *et al.* (1980a, 1981) employed a somewhat different, and arguably more sensitive, measure of cerebral morphology which involved selecting three separate slices from the CT scan, the lowest of which corresponded to the greatest prominence of ventricular size. This and the next two, superior, slices were then compared for analysis of brain density using the primary density indices from the CT readout (it should be remembered that initial CT readouts are in the form of density indices which are then converted by an analogue computer programme to yield a reconstructed two dimensional visual film).

In their initial report (Golden *et al.* 1980a) brain density measures were obtained separately for the left and right cerebral hemispheres for each of the three slices. In all but the second level right hemisphere slices the schizophrenic group exhibited significantly less density than controls. Additionally, in both groups, left hemisphere density was greater than right hemisphere density, a finding which indicates normal asymmetry and one which appeared to add further weight to the suggestion of cortical atrophy in schizophrenic groups. In a later study, however, Golden *et al.* (1981) elaborated upon the assessment by dividing each hemisphere into four discrete dorsal sections (anterior to posterior) at each of the three slices, yielding a total of twenty-four separate density measures.

Overall, Golden *et al.* report that the schizophrenics exhibited a significantly lower overall mean density, most prominently in the anterior (frontal) left hemisphere sections. Golden and colleagues argued that the reduced density, and specifically the reduced left frontal density (perhaps indicative of discrete abnormalities in lateralisation), did not necessarily implicate enlarged ventricular size (which would, by definition, reduce cerebral density) as density measures were significantly lower in the second and third slices where the ventricles are particularly sparse – the third slice being the highest and furthest away from the ventricles. Finally, the absence of a positive correlation between increasing age and decreasing density provoked Golden *et al.* to speculate that reduced density is not an 'age-related' degenerative process but is, perhaps, more consistent with a developmental retardation in the growth of neuronal tissue. Bearing in mind Luchin's (1982) comment in terms of the effect of organic pathology on frontal prominence it is difficult to determine whether Golden's findings are consistent with a reversal of anatomical asymmetry *per se* or whether they might reflect upon overall neuronal density reduction as a function of some other specific pathology.

In contradistinction to the above findings Andreason *et al.* (1982a); Weinberger *et al.* (1982) and Nasrallah *et al.* (1982a) report no evidence of reversed asymmetry in their groups of chronic schizophrenics.

As with the determination of increased ventricular size, sampling styles and differences in patient composition may account for the disparities in the reported findings. Chronicity, in particular, appears to be an important factor for consideration. Those chronic schizophrenics in whom there is evidence of cortical atrophy are less likely to exhibit reversal of asymmetries (Luchins 1982).

One final, but important, consideration is that there appears to be little consensus on how CT asymmetries should be measured, what the normal distribution of asymmetries are, and what factors may be crucial in their determination and distribution in a particular population. As an example, the position regarding handedness (as one index of cerebral laterality) in non-psychiatric populations is still unclear given the consistency with which the relationship between handedness and functional asymmetry is reported in the literature. As Luchins (1982) states 'the relationship between handedness and these (CT) asymmetries has produced diametrically opposite findings'.

85

SUMMARY

In attempting to summarise the findings from CT investigations several tentative conclusions may be offered for future refutation. Evidence of cerebral atrophy and ventricular enlargement in some schizophrenics is available and appears to be associated with chronic, elderly schizophrenics who show no evidence of reversed cerebral asymmetry and who exhibit neuropsychological performance decrements consistent with diffuse organicity.

Specifically with respect to schizophrenia such individuals may form a particular subgroup associated with a predominance of negative symptoms and possibly consistent with the 'defect state', or Type 2, schizophrenia of Crow *et al.* (1982a). However, the further question of whether the abnormalities are in themselves specific to schizophrenia is unclear. In view of the increased prevalence of ventricular enlargement in non-schizophrenic populations such abnormalities may indeed rather reflect non-specific correlates of psychosis-factors possibly associated with chronicity, age, institutionalisation and medication. Additionally, since the majority of schizophrenics have normal scans (particularly the young, acute schizophrenics) the observed abnormalities cannot be considered pathognomic of schizophrenia.

With respect to cerebral asymmetry, the finding are relatively sparse, however evidence does suggest that reversed cerebral asymmetry is evident in a small group of schizophrenics in whom there is no evidence of cortical atrophy or ventricular enlargement. This group appears to comprise schizophrenics characterised by the presence of positive symptoms. As yet there are too few studies to forward any specific conclusions relating to the presence of reversed asymmetry and the demonstration of specific neuropsychological performance deficits indicative of functional abnormalities of lateralisation or cerebral hemispheric specialisation.

Finally, whilst there is some evidence that, unlike cortical atrophy and ventricular enlargement, reversed anatomical lateralisation may reflect developmental retardation of cerebral systems, further evidence is required to fully evaluate this claim.

Chapter seven

REGIONAL MEASURES

INTRODUCTION

In an attempt to understand the brain 'in action' various physiological and functional measures may be utilised. Unlike anatomical techniques, the more dynamic physiological indices have been able to address the issue of 'regional' activity within the brain and hence regional abnormalities in schizophrenia.

One of the most obvious regional divisions, apparent both physiologically and functionally, is that between the left and right cerebral cortices, the exploration of which has resulted in a major field of enquiry into gross asymmetries of brain activity and function. In the previous section we discussed the, as yet, preliminary findings suggestive of reversed asymmetry in some schizophrenic populations. This enquiry into 'lateral asymmetries' and anomalies of asymmetry will be taken further in this chapter.

REGIONAL CEREBRAL BLOOD FLOW

The term Regional Cerebral Blood Flow (rCBF) refers to the perfusion of blood through the extensive arterial system of the central nervous system. The CNS is one of the most metabolically active structures of the body and its oxygen and nutrient requirements are extensive, being possibly as high as one-fifth that of the entire body (Walsh 1978). The regional distribution of blood represents a dynamic system which may alter as a function of cerebral activity on specific tasks, and, more simply, even as a function of changes in head position.

Generally speaking, hyperactivity in the brain, such as a seizure, is associated with a parallel increase in blood flow whilst hypo-activity (e.g. slow wave sleep, or coma) is associated with reduced blood flow. More discretely, regional activity within the brain is accompanied by relatively higher blood flow within the active brain systems compared to those not activated. Risberg *et al.* (1975), for example, observed that when subjects were engaged on a verbal task rCBF was greater in the left, verbally dominant, hemisphere. The reverse asymmetry was observed during a spatial task. Additionally, Ingvar and Schwartz (1974) report that overt speech is associated with high precentral (frontal) flow in the left, or verbally dominant hemisphere.

Therefore it can be said that as a direct function of neuronal and metabolic activity in the brain, blood flow, oxygen consumption and glucose uptake alter and are closely correlated as indices of brain activity. The measure of regional blood flow may therefore be considered a reasonably reliable index of brain function and hence offers an important method of addressing the issue of altered brain function in schizophrenia.

The technique of rCBF involves the injection, and more recently the inhalation, of a diffusable radioisotope which is then monitored by high resolution scintillation detectors attached to the scalp surface.

Relying on the assumption that an injected isotope will be conveyed differentially (along with nutrients and oxygen) to regions of the brain as a function of cerebral activity, the technique of rCBF measures the initial perfusion and the later rate of clearance of the radioisotope in various brain regions when a subject is either at rest or engaged in a specific cognitive activity (the rate of clearance varying as a direct function of oxygen metabolism in the active brain region). Before considering those investigations which have utilised the rCBF technique with schizophrenic populations it is pertinent to discuss the various methods which are traditionally employed, as each specific technique has its own discrete limitations which need to be recognised when reviewing the findings.

One of the most commonly used, contemporary, methods involves the inhalation of a mixture of air and the radioisotope Xenon-133, a biochemically inert and freely diffusable gas. The more established method, however, involves introducing Xenon-133 by injection via the carotid arteries. It is important to note that intracarotid injection conveys the isotope predominantly to a single hemisphere which is ipsilateral to the injected arterial site (although there may be a slight leakage across the hemisphere systems).

Inhalation, however, results in the perfusion of isotope to both hemispheres at the same time, permitting the monitoring of both cerebral hemispheres and the identification of dynamic asymmetries whilst the subject is working on a task. Additionally, whilst Xenon-

133 is the radioisotope of choice, earlier investigators employed nitrous oxide. This earlier technique was based on the assumption that a quantity of a given substance taken up by an organ in a given time from arterial blood equals the amount of the substance carried to the organ minus the amount removed. Whilst this assumption is, within certain limits, valid, there were several limitations to the nitrous oxide method not least of which was that localised changes in blood flow and oxygen uptake are not directly identified since the nitrous oxide technique measures only overall blood flow and overall oxygen uptake or consumption. Furthermore, the nitrous oxide method is unable to identify blood flow or metabolic changes that occur in a relatively short period of time since the method requires blood sampling over a period of at least ten minutes.

Having discussed the essential technical issues we can now proceed to review regional cerebral blood flow investigations with schizophrenic populations.

REGIONAL CEREBRAL BLOOD FLOW STUDIES AND SCHIZOPHRENIA

One of the first rCBF studies, employing the nitrous oxide method, reported no abnormalities of regional blood flow in schizophrenics (Kety *et al.* 1948). Since that time, however, several investigations using the Xenon-133 technique have reported reasonably consistent findings. Ingvar and Franzen (1974), for example, noted from the computerised clearance curves of Xenon-133 following intracarotid injection that, whilst the mean overall left hemisphere blood flow did not differ significantly between schizophrenic and control samples, there were differences in regional distribution. Thus whilst the controls were characterised by high blood flow in the frontal and pre-central areas with a gradient towards lowest blood flow in posterior regions, the schizophrenic group exhibited a significant reduction in frontal blood flow with a significant increase in posterior areas, a reversal of the normal pattern. (These results refer to grey matter blood flow, correlated with neuronal activity, evident from the fast clearance curves of Xenon-133. Typically, normal subjects exhibit this 'hyperfrontality' in grey matter flow which is approximately equal for homologous areas of the left and right hemispheres).

The specific findings of this study, and their implications for understanding the relevance of such abnormalities for schizophrenia, were somewhat weakened by the demonstration of a significant correlation between mean blood flow and cognitive dysfunction, and also by the observation that this pattern of blood flow was most clearly demonstrated in the chronic patients (less so in the younger, acute schizophrenics). Nevertheless the observed reverse pattern of blood flow distribution with the overall mean hemisphere flow being normal is of particular interest since it raises the question of abnormal *distribution* of function.

The finding of 'hypofrontality' in schizophrenics following Xenon-133 injection appears a consistent one across comparable studies and has also been reported by Franzen and Ingvar (1975) in their samples of chronic schizophrenics. A similar investigation by Ariel *et al*. (1982) also included the recording of regional blood flow whilst subjects were engaged on a specific mental task. The resting blood flow in normal controls showed the typical pattern of hyperfrontality whilst the chronic schizophrenics and a small number of the younger schizophrenics exhibited the hypofrontal distribution (the majority of acute patients exhibiting the 'normal' pattern). On a cognitive activation task (a test of abstraction) the younger schizophrenics and controls exhibited an increase in frontal and post central blood flow (less dramatic for the schizophrenics) whilst the older schizophrenics showed none of these changes, a finding which Ariel *et al*. suggests may reflect a dysfunction in the arousal systems of older schizophrenics.

There are several methodological problems with Ariel *et al*.'s (1982) study which create difficulties in interpreting the results and comparing them to the normal 'inhalation' studies of Risberg *et al*. (1975). (It will be remembered that Risberg *et al*. had demonstrated asymmetries of hemispheric blood flow distribution in normals when engaged on verbal or non-verbal tasks.) First, Ariel *et al*.'s 'normal' controls were chronic alcoholics whose mean age was greater than the schizophrenic sample. Second the sample sizes were relatively small (N = 13). But perhaps the most important factor concerns the fact that Ariel's results are based upon intracarotoid injection and hence only a single hemisphere's activity would be monitored. In contrast, Risberg *et al*. 1975, were able to plot dynamic inter-hemispheric differences after inhalation of the radioisotope.

A series of investigations by Mathews provides an interesting contrast to the above studies in that they report the use of inhalation rCBF in schizophrenic samples. Their initial investigation, reported in Mathews *et al*. (1981), compared six chronic schizophrenics and six controls matched for age. Compared to the control subjects, the schizophrenics were characterised by significantly lower blood flow in the right and a non-significant reduction in left hemisphere flow. There was, however, no evidence of the 'hypofrontal' pattern observed in the previous studies although the authors point out, that in contrast to these other investigations, the schizophrenics were not 'productive', or symptomatic, at the time of testing.

Following from this relatively small investigation Mathews *et al.* (1982) compared neurologically normal individuals and age matched schizophrenics. As in the studies reported earlier, the normal subjects exhibited the typical resting pattern of hyperfrontality in grey matter blood flow in both the left and right hemispheres. The schizophrenic group however exhibited gross hemispheric differences with the normal hyperfrontal pattern (and anterior-posterior gradient) evident in the right hemisphere but with no significant differences between the anterior and posterior regions of the left hemisphere (i.e. a reduced superiority for anterior over posterior grey flow). No gross differences were observed between the left and right hemispheres of either schizophrenics or normals; however the schizophrenic group demonstrated lower overall blood flow.

Overall Mathews *et al.* (1982) concluded that the schizophrenics may differ from other psychiatric and neurological patients by showing a relatively greater left frontal blood flow reduction rather than a simple bilateral lowering in overall grey matter flow, a conclusion which is consistent with Golden *et al.*'s (1981) finding of reduced left frontal brain density in schizophrenic patients using CAT.

The results of Mathews *et al.*'s investigations are particularly interesting since all patients were drug free for one week prior to testing, thereby to some extent minimizing the possible effects of medication as an interacting variable. Furthermore, the authors monitored carbon dioxide and oxygen uptake levels during testing and report no significant difference between groups, an important observation since oxygen and particularly, carbon dioxide levels are perhaps the most important variables affecting changes in blood flow (Purves 1972). Whilst, therefore, it is possible that certain non-specific factors may have contributed to the observed results, Mathews *et al.* concluded that the most likely explanation of reduced blood flow in the schizophrenic groups was decreased neuronal activity.

In their most recent investigation, Mathews *et al.* (1982) report similar findings to their earlier investigations and additionally observed that the presence of hallucinatory behaviour in the schizophrenic group (as determined by the administration of the Brief Psychiatric Rating Scale on the day of testing) correlated inversely with regional blood flow in the left frontal, left temporal, right temporal-parietal, and right occipital lobes. Furthermore, they found no evidence of interhemispheric differences or imbalance in the schizophrenic (or normal) groups. They point out, however, that such differences, if they were present, may have been blurred by the contamination of radiation from one hemisphere to the other. In their last study carbon dioxide levels were in fact lower in the schizophrenic group and these differences cannot be ruled out as significant factors in the observed group differences.

More recently Kurachi *et al.* (1985) measured rCBF using the inhalation technique. The authors report that frontal blood flow was significantly lower, bilaterally, in the schizophrenic versus an age-related normal control group.

In addition those schizophrenics with a prominent history of auditory hallucinations showed a significantly increased blood flow in the left temporal region. Those without a history of hallucinations showed a comparable but smaller increase in right temporal blood flow.

They tentatively conclude that the negative symptoms of schizophrenia are related to bilateral hypofrontal activity whilst positive symptoms may reflect hyperfrontal activity, predominantly in the left hemisphere.

For a number of reasons, it is difficult to compare the investigations of Mathews *et al.* and Kurachi *et al.* with those that have employed the injection technique. First, as we have mentioned earlier, lack of consistency in findings between unilateral and simultaneous bilateral recordings may reflect not so much on the absolute validity of the results but rather on the necessity of determining a single hemisphere's activity at rest or on task relative to the activity of the contralateral hemisphere. Ultimately the inhalation technique would seem to be of greatest value both in terms of its ability to assess the whole cerebral system and hence in respect of comparing rCBF activity with other indices of cerebral organisation and lateralisation of function. Unfortunately, because of the possibility of interhemispheric contamination (or 'cross talk') and the relatively lower regional resolution, the inhalation technique may prove to be less reliable than the more intrusive injection procedures.

A second area of difficulty concerns the fact that the correction factors for oxygen and particularly carbon dioxide levels are derived from injection techniques and may not be entirely applicable to inhalation, hence possibly introducing an artefact into group results. This issue is a crucial one to clarify since, as we outlined earlier, carbon dioxide level is probably the single most important determinant of regional cerebral blood flow.

Finally, as a general issue of concern it is necessary when reviewing the data to be aware that regional blood flow itself may be affected by several non-specific factors such as circadian type rhythm and time of day, menstrual cycle and anxiety in addition to non-specific factors associated with psychopathology including age, chronicity, cognitive dysfunction and long term medication.

In summarising the findings it is impossible to arrive at any definitive conclusions in respect of the implications of regional blood flow studies in schizophrenia. The injection procedure, being an intrusive technique, carries some risk to the patient and may only have been used in subjects in whom diagnosis was uncertain or compounded by possible organic factors. The use of inhalation provides a more satisfactory procedure. However, too few studies have as yet been carried out with schizophrenic, other psychiatric, neurological and normal individuals to permit any but tentative conclusions. In spite of these apparent difficulties, perhaps the most consistent observation across many of the studies has been the demonstration of hypofrontality, or reduced left hemisphere anterior blood flow (relative to posterior flow) in, largely, chronic samples of schizophrenics. This finding is in accord with observations of reduced neuronal density in the same regions ascertained by Computerised Tomographic Scanning, and is possibly consistent with electrophysiological and neuropsychological abnormalities suggestive of left hemisphere frontal involvement (see Chs. 8 and 9).

Whether this pattern of reduced frontal blood flow represents an index of brain function central to schizophrenia or reflects a non-specific correlate of psychosis and chronicity is difficult to determine in the absence of further data. The observations, however, of hypofrontality in some acute schizophrenics and in productive or symptomatic schizophrenics but not in non-productive patients, in conjunction with significant correlations between the presence of specific schizophrenic symptomatology and abnormal distributions in regional flow, indicates that rCBF abnormalities may reflect alterations in brain organisation and activity which may relate more directly to the process of schizophrenia.

In the final analysis the value of rCBF may be in the ability to correlate regional flow changes with both specific cognitive activity and perhaps electrophysiological recording. The possibility of correlating rCBF with EEG recording also carries with it vast methodological difficulties in terms of the ability to assess both variables simultaneously and regionally and to plot parallel distributions accurately. With the advent of the inhalation technique certain methodological and ethical problems have been reduced, at the expense, however, of less reliability in resolution power. Nevertheless, the need for normal controls requires the utilisation of less intrusive techniques.

Because of this need for adequate controls and additionally the fact that cerebral metabolism, cognitive activation, and EEG are invariably responsive to environmental factors, a less invasive, faster, and regionally more discrete technique may be appropriate. One possible candidate to meet these criteria is the newly developed technique of Positron Emission Tomography.

POSITRON EMISSION TOMOGRAPHY

The technique of Positron Emission Tomography (PET) initially developed from an autoradiographic method in which local glucose consumption in animals was measured.

This quantitative assessment, developed by Sokoloff (1977) involves the administration of Deoxyglucose (2-(11C) Deoxylglucose) which is taken up by the brain in competition with glucose. Deoxyglucose (2DG) is then metabolised to Deoxylglucose-6-phosphate, the accumulation of which in neural tissue is proportional to glucose use. Positron Emission Tomography involves the injection of 2DG which is labelled with a fast-decay positron emitter (18F). The accumulation of the 2DG-18F complex in active neural tissue can then be detected by scanning and the data reconstituted by emission tomography into a two-dimensional energy picture. Whilst PET has a resolution power comparable to the Xenon-133 blood flow technique (0.1 mm) it has several distinct advantages which includes the ability to map the entire brain (cortical, subcortical and brainstem) and that glucose uptake is labelled prior to scanning so that closer control over the subject's state can be effected. Furthermore, glucose uptake is regionally very localised within the resting and active brain and thus PET can provide information which is more accurately related to regional tissue metabolism.

As yet only relatively few studies have been reported in the literature, the most notable being those of Buchsbaum and associates. Buchsbaum and Ingvar (1982), for example, report an investigation assessing local glucose metabolism by PET, after injection of 18F-2DG, in unmedicated schizophrenics and normal controls matched for age and sex. They report that in most normals there is a higher 2DG uptake in the frontal cortex relative to occipital (posterior) regions; however this pattern was reversed in the schizophrenics. These investigations are consistent with the pioneering PET findings of Farkas (1980) and also with the blood flow studies reported earlier.

Buchsbaum and Ingvar (1982) additionally report correlations between glucose uptake and specific schizophrenic symptomatology, an example of which was the observation of elevated glucose metabolism in the superior temporal auditory area of the left but not the right temporal cortex in one patient who reported auditory hallucinations during the scanning period.

In an earlier study Buchsbaum (1981) had reported similar peaks of glucose uptake in the left auditory (temporal) cortex and bilaterally over the occipital areas in four hallucinating schizophrenics. Two further preliminary findings are worthy of mention. Firstly Buchsbaum (1981) reported an investigation in which glucose uptake was monitored during somatosensory stimulation. Unlike the normal controls who exhibited high uptake in frontal regions as well as the sensory (postcentral) strip, the schizophrenic patients demonstrated increased uptake only in the sensory regions, a finding which prompted Buchsbaum to conclude that there may be a functional 'intrahemispheric' disconnection between these two cerebral regions in some schizophrenics. Finally, Sheppard (1981) reports several interesting observations of regional oxygen uptake employing the inhalation of O^{15} (acting as a positron emitter) and monitoring by PET. Consistent with previous findings the schizophrenics exhibited hypofrontality in respect of oxygen consumption. Additionally, whilst the normal controls (matched for age, sex, and handedness) exhibited a higher resting oxygen uptake in the left compared to the right hemisphere, these normal asymmetries were less obvious in the schizophrenics, i.e. schizophrenics demonstrated a more symmetrical distribution of oxygen metabolism.

Whilst it is too early to make any firm conclusions, it is encouraging that the initial findings from PET are in accord with those of cerebral blood flow, which are suggestive of altered hemisphere activity in some schizophrenics. The exact nature of the relationship between these two indices awaits further investigation in which both processes may be measured within the same subject. Furthermore, the observations of correlations between glucose (and perhaps oxygen) uptake and symptomatic behaviour during testing raises the exciting prospect of delineating the cerebral mechanisms and regional systems responsible for their action.

Chapter eight

ELECTROENCEPHALOGRAPHY

INTRODUCTION

The results of CT scanning, regional blood flow, and glucose uptake studies converge to suggest that some schizophrenics may be characterised by an alteration in cerebral organisation. Whilst alterations in both cerebral hemispheres are implicated, the majority of studies specifically point to a maximal dominant cerebral hemispheric abnormality to the extent that a reversal of the normal pattern of hemisphere activation is apparent in some schizophrenics whilst at rest or engaged on task.

These studies of regional cerebral activity form part of a large data base derived from investigations of the relationship between schizophrenia and altered brain function. As raised earlier, the most readily apparent division in respect of brain anatomy and function is that concerned with lateralisation – the observation of anatomical and functional asymmetries between the two cerebral hemispheres. The investigation of hemisphere asymmetries is not a new field of enquiry. It has long been known that within most sensory modalities there are orderly afferent projections to each cerebral hemisphere (the phenomenon of contralateral projection being most apparent in the visual and manual modalities) and that specific cognitive functions are to a large degree lateralised in the normal human brain. This is not to imply a simplistic division of function to readily localisable regions of both cerebral hemispheres; it is fully acknowledged that the determination of mental, cognitive and affective states must be one of complex interaction between lateralised systems. Nevertheless the vast body of literature investigating the functional consequences of discrete or gross brain damage does suggest that the phenomena of lateralisation and localisation have some validity.

Accepting the validity of this approach, whilst being cognisant of the dangers of oversimplification, it has been possible to infer from electrophysiological and neurophysiological data the relationship between schizophrenia and abnormal brain function.

Two specific hypotheses have been forwarded and since supported. The first derived from observations that a small group of individuals with dominant temporal lobe epilepsy presented with symptoms comparable to schizophrenia (Flor-Henry 1969; Slater and Beard 1963). This initial observation gave rise to many studies aimed at determining whether schizophrenics might exhibit electrophysiological and cognitive difficulties consistent with dominant temporal lobe dysfunction (this, of course, did not assume a common aetiology between schizophrenia and temporal lobe epilepsy). The results of these investigations have supported this hypothesis but additionally implicate dominant frontal and limbic systems.

A second, perhaps less impressive, body of data supports the hypothesis that schizophrenia may be characterised by a disturbance of communication between, and integration of, the two cerebral hemispheres.

Whilst these two hypotheses have been considered by some as mutually exclusive, the observations of impaired interhemispheric integration in schizophrenics may reflect a disturbance in reception, output or transmission. It is therefore, possible to argue either that disturbed integration may give rise to unilateral dysfunction or as Flor-Henry (1983) has suggested, that an overactivated or dysfunctional left hemisphere may give rise to a secondary disturbance of hemispheric relations since the corpus callosum acts as a strong 'coupling' system between the two hemispheres and is involved in the transmission of information between the two hemispheres and in the inhibition of one hemisphere's activity by the other.

In an attempt to expand upon and clarify the above discussion, two further major areas will be considered in some detail, namely EEG and neuropsychology (see Ch. 9). It is evident that within these two broad fields of enquiry much of the data base concerning lateralised dysfunction in schizophrenia has been generated.

This does not negate the contribution of other important areas of investigation such as psychophysiological recording (GSR, Heart Rate etc). Nevertheless it is apparent that debate still continues as to the precise interpretation of such measures as, for example, GSR. Thus it is still unclear as to whether lateralised galvanic responses are under ipsi, or contralateral control, an important point to clarify prior to determining the implications of such results.

Furthermore, unlike EEG investigations, psychophysiological methodologies have only relatively recently addressed the issue of lateralised impairment in schizophrenia, earlier investigations were either global in nature or employed to investigate more general theories such as attention, arousal etc.

Whilst, therefore, psychophysiological assessment has provided supportive evidence for the main thesis of altered cortical function in schizophrenia this field will not be discussed in this section. Rather the authors refer the reader to Spohn and Patterson (1980) for a detailed review.

ELECTROENCEPHALOGRAPHY

The use of electroencephalography (EEG) to study the electrical activity of the brain is widely acknowledged as a valuable clinical and research tool. Despite the fact that the existence of electrical potentials originating from the brain (and recordable from the scalp) is a relatively recent discovery, technological advances, particularly in the analysis of EEG, have been rapid and a high degree of sophistication achieved with the aid of computer assisted analyses such as Fast-Fourier transforms, Power-Spectral analysis and Brain Electrical Activity Mapping.

EEG techniques were heralded as probably the first opportunity to observe the physiological correlates of ongoing mental activity. This aim has been only partially achieved to the extent that EEG analysis has been unable to provide *sufficient* information about cognitive processes *per se*. This partly reflects the fact that the electrical activity recorded from the scalp not only reflects the activity of the neural synapses and dendrites but also glial, circulatory and metabolic processes (Monakhov 1981). Furthermore, several other biological and non-biological factors serve to constrain the interpretation of EEG records, the most notable being the influence of non-specific environmental or situational events. Notwithstanding these difficulties the continual refinements of EEG technology have supplied back important information and an essential contribution to our understanding of the dynamics of the brain.

In the studies which follow, two types of EEG recording have been utilised for subsequent analysis. The first involves obtaining an ongoing record of brain electrical activity derived from a series of scalp electrodes arranged over the scalp surface according to a standard montage system. This system allows generally for the recording of cerebral activity from the cortical areas below the electrode placement. Recording may be carried out under a variety of conditions, the most common of which are with the subject either at rest or engaged on a cognitive task. The second method covered here concerns the isolation and identification of stimulus produced brain potentials termed Event-Related Potentials (ERP's) or Average Evoked Potentials (AEP's). The procedure involves the presentation of a regular stimulus (auditory, visual or somato-sensory) and the recording of electrical potentials produced by stimulus reception. The technique relies on computer averaging and is based on the assumption that there is a relatively invariant response by the brain to a given sensory input.

The event-related responses are not observable on inspection of the ongoing EEG due to the large amount of background activity which acts as noise in which the potential is embedded. However, since this 'noise' is random and the stimulus is presented a number of times it is possible to average the EEG recording within the post-stimulus epochs, resulting in a cancellation of the background noise and the emergence of the Event Related Potential. Whilst this technique and the subsequent analysis of the components of the ERP waveform has been used extensively to determine regional brain responses in schizophrenics, we will additionally consider a modification of this technique designed to determine the integrity of transmission across the corpus callosum in schizophrenics.

ONGOING EEG RECORDING

Considering the results across studies, analysis of the resting EEG's of normal and schizophrenic samples generally supports the hypothesis that left hemisphere EEG abnormalities are characteristic of schizophrenic populations (whilst right hemisphere abnormalities are associated with affective psychosis). Thus Flor-Henry (1976), Flor-Henry *et al.* (1975) and Coger *et al.* (1979) report increased power in the 20–30 Hz frequency band (beta range) in the left temporal and frontal leads for schizophrenic patients with the reversed pattern (increased power over the right hemisphere) in manic depressive patients.

Volavka *et al.* (1981) attempted to replicate Flor-Henry's data, testing four specific hypotheses generated from that study: schizophrenic subjects would differ from a depressive group in terms of the right:left ratio in temporal power; these differences would be most apparent in the higher frequency (beta) range; schizophrenics would be characterised by an asymmetric increase in left temporal power with the depressed group exhibiting the reverse pattern. Whilst the results of Volavka *et al.*'s study confirmed the first two hypotheses, the second two relating to asymmetric power increases, were not supported. The authors point out that the discrepancy between their data and Flor-Henry's may reflect the handling of muscle artefact in the EEG recording. Thus whilst they excluded all records in which muscle artefact was apparent, Flor-Henry assumed that myogenic potentials would be randomly distributed over the scalp and hence did not exclude these data. In fact when Volavka *et al.* analysed their unedited data the results were entirely consistent with Flor-Henry's.

Whilst it is also possible that the differences in subject selection between the two studies may be an important consideration here, Volavka *et al.* themselves point out that there is a temporal relationship between the occurrence of myogenic potentials and fast EEG activity. Unable to discriminate reliably between the two, it may well be the case that by rejecting epochs containing muscle potentials they were also eliminating the most important segments of the EEG record.

EEG abnormalities in schizophrenic populations do not appear to be restricted to the high frequency ranges. Walker and McGuire (1982) report that perhaps the most consistent findings are that schizophrenics exhibit increased EEG variability recorded from the temporal lobes, more power in the high frequencies on the left hemisphere and reduced left hemisphere alpha power. Etevenon *et al.* (1979, 1982) additionally report that the EEG characteristics of schizophrenics differ as a function of diagnostic subtype. Thus their paranoid subgroup were characterised by low alpha power and more power in the theta and beta ranges, whilst hebephrenics exhibited high alpha intensity.

Furthermore, Seidman (1983) in a review of EEG studies points to interesting electrophysiological differences between the psychiatric clinical dichotomies of process-reactive and acute-chronic. Thus reactive patients exhibited normal alpha activity with focal EEG abnormalities whilst the records of process schizophrenics were more globally pathological with diffuse slowing (i.e. reduced frequency) and little or no alpha activity. EEGs from chronic patients were described as hyperstable or extremely regular (see also Shagass 1977) with diffusely abnormal recordings, variable alpha and excessive beta activity. Acute patients, on the other hand, were characterised by more focal temporal lobe abnormalities, more alpha and an increase of paroxysmal activity.

The above studies of resting EEG point to electrophysiological abnormalities in schizophrenics implicating both, but predominantly the left, cerebral hemisphere. The particular form of the abnormality may vary as a function of diagnostic subtype suggesting a possible role for the use of EEG as a diagnostic tool if the above findings are consistent.

In a series of on-task EEG studies Flor-Henry *et al.* (1979) report that when engaged on a verbal task schizophrenics show a significant reduction in the right:left temporal power ratio within the alpha range – both indicative of non-dominant hemisphere activation during verbal processing. On a spatial task, both schizophrenics and normals exhibited a reduction in bilateral parietal energy but significantly more so in the schizophrenics. These findings are interpreted by Flor-Henry as consistent with a dysfunctional left hemisphere and possibly a deficiency in interhemispheric integration during verbal cognitive activation arising as a consequence of abnormal activity in the dominant frontal-temporal circuits.

Walker and McGuire (1982) similarly report that unlike normals who show left hemisphere activation on verbal tasks, schizophrenics activate the non-dominant hemisphere irrespective of the nature of the task. Whilst these results are consistent with left hemisphere dysfunction Stevens *et al.* (1979) point out that they are also consistent with those observed in a small number of normal left-handed individuals. In such individuals there is evidence that cerebral organisation is more bilateral or even reversed. Whilst not suggesting any common heritage, it might be possible to infer that the unilateral dysfunction observed in schizophrenics reflects a similar type of alteration in functional cerebral organisation. It is difficult at this stage to offer a definitive interpretation of the functional significance of EEG abnormalities when taken in isolation. Some authors have interpreted the abnormal beta activity in schizophrenics as reflecting abnormality in focused arousal or preparedness to respond to stimuli, whilst alpha abnormalities may reflect difficulties in attention. It would seem that task-related EEG may at least hold some of these answers although difficulties inevitably arise in correlating task and environmental stimuli with brain electrical activity. Furthermore, the observation of ratio power differences between hemispheres may reflect either abnormalities in the left, right, or both hemispheres. What is clear, however, is that distinct EEG abnormalities, both intra and interhemispheric, are observable in some schizophrenics. Some of the difficulties in the interpretation of ongoing EEG records have since been clarified by studies of evoked potentials.

EVOKED POTENTIAL STUDIES

The analysis of Evoked Potentials in relation to repetitive stimulation has produced several important findings. Perhaps one reason for this is that specific components of the Evoked Potential waveform appear to be related to, or influenced by, certain environmental variables and by cognitive processing. In general, analyses of global evoked potentials indicate that in schizophrenics visual and auditory evoked potentials (VEPs and AEPs respectively) are less stable bilaterally (i.e. in both hemispheres) than in normals, but only significantly so over the left hemisphere, whilst somatosensory evoked potentials (SEPs) are not significantly altered from normal

(Shagass *et al.* 1979). Connolly *et al.* (1983) whilst concurring with Shagass' conclusions of left hemisphere dysfunction, point out that their results also indicate a more generalised impairment. Whilst the significance of waveform stability is not fully understood, it is thought to correlate with, or reflect perceptual stability (Buchsbaum 1977) or cognitive stability (Callaway 1975).

The interpretation of the EP waveform must, of course, be seen in the light of possible medication effects. Shagass *et al.* (1979) observed that visual Evoked Potential (VEP) abnormalities were more apparent in unmedicated than medicated schizophrenics. In addition, Straumanis *et al.* (1982) conclude that both AEP and VEP (but not SEP) stability is affected by tricyclic antidepressants and antipsychotic medication. To complete the picture, Saletu *et al.* (1976a,b) observed somatosensory Evoked Potential differences between medicated and unmedicated patients. That the abnormalities in Evoked Potentials were present in unmedicated schizophrenics indicates that the reduced stability may represent a neurophysiological index of the disorder. Indeed, it would appear, as Shagass (1977) points out, that the effects of medication is one of normalisation of the waveform. It would therefore be of interest to assess the same individuals pre- and post-medication whilst monitoring clinical improvements to determine the exact relationship between these variables.

Buchsbaum *et al.* (1979) recorded visual evoked potentials at occipital and temporo-parietal electrode sites during a simple visual task, in which stimuli were presented hemiretinally, and incorporating distraction and attention trials.

In addition to a global analysis of Evoked Potentials the nature of stimulus presentation enabled the investigators to analyse separately 'direct' pathway evoked potentials (right visual field – left hemisphere) and 'indirect' pathway potentials requiring callosal transmission (left visual field – right hemisphere; callosum – left hemisphere). This study is of further interest since in addition to schizophrenic, affective and normal subjects the researchers included a group comprising cases of left or right temporal lobectomy.

In global terms the schizophrenic and normal groups exhibited similar visual evoked potential amplitudes which were maximal over the left temporal-parietal lead (Wernicke's area) with affective subjects showing significantly larger amplitudes than normal and the temporal lobectomy group exhibiting the smallest potentials. Detailed analysis of the 'direct' and 'indirect' Evoked Potentials indicated that the schizophrenic group exhibited the smallest evoked potentials of all groups in the distraction/indirect pathway trials. On this analysis the schizophrenics differed significantly from all groups except the left temporal lobectomy group. These results would be consistent with at least some schizophrenics suffering specific attentional problems, with left temporal cortical dysfunction (consistent with the 'ongoing' EEG data of Flor-Henry *et al.* (1979) during verbal cognition), and with specific abnormalities of interhemispheric transfer.

Of the specific evoked potential components receiving detailed consideration perhaps the most stimulating results have arisen from analysis of the P300 component. This is a large amplitude positive wave component which peaks at between 275 to 450 milliseconds after stimulus presentation and appearing maximally over the parietal regions. Brecher and Begleiter (1983) suggest that P300 appears to be independent of the physical characteristics of the stimulus (except at very high stimulus intensities) and rather seems to be highly dependent on the subjective significance of the stimulus as well as attention on task. Saitoh *et al.* (1983) considered P300 to be an 'endogenous' potential and one which is task relevant – reflecting stimulus evaluation and task detection processes.

Roth and Cannon (1972) report that P300 amplitude was significantly lower in schizophrenics compared to normals in response to an infrequent stimulus embedded in a more frequent one. Levit *et al.* (1973) additionally observed that in normals P300 increases in amplitude when subjects are required to predict whether the next stimulus would be a tone or a light flash. This response did not occur in schizophrenics. Since it may be the case that P300 correlates with both subjective significance and attention, it might be reasonable to argue that the absence of P300 increase in this study reflects the fact that the schizophrenics were either not attending to stimuli or that the cue had no relevance for them.

In order to clarify these issues, Brecher and Begleiter (1983) attempted to manipulate the P300 by providing tangible incentives contingent upon task completion (monetary awards for correct responses and speed of responses). In this experiment the schizophrenic group were withdrawn from medication two weeks prior to testing and evoked potentials elicited under three conditions – normal stimulus reception, trials with incentives for accuracy of response, and trials with incentive for speed of response. Under all three conditions schizophrenics exhibited significantly lower P300 amplitude. Whilst in normal subjects the P300 response increased in both incentive trials (compared to the non-incentive trial) the evoked potentials of schizophrenics remained unchanged. The fact that these effects were observed, in the absence of significant differences in accuracy and speed between groups, indicates that the P300 changes do not reflect differences in subjective relevance or attention but rather may constitute a valid neurophysiological manifestation of cortical activation.

The relevance of this lower and unchanging P300 response for schizophrenia may be derived from several lines of research. Wood *et al.* (1980) postulate that P300 derives in part from the action of subcortical systems. Halgren *et al.* (1980) suggest that the recorded scalp P300 reflects the action of a cortical activator and a P300 generator in the hippocampus and amygdala. The latter suggestion is of particular interest since Scheibel and Kovelman (1981) have observed a disordered arrangement of the pyramidal cell orientation in the hippocampi of some schizophrenics at autopsy. Finally, the observation in normal populations of a correlation between reduced P300 amplitude and high 'anhedonia' scores (defined as a dulling of emotional interest or a defect in pleasure capacity) in conjunction with a negative correlation between reduced P300 and thought disorder (Simons 1982) indicates that the above findings might reflect a neurophysiological concomitant of schizophrenia characterised by an affective component. The basis of this might involve certain limbic structures known to be involved in the regulation of emotion and arousal (Milner 1971).

Morstyn *et al.* (1983) extended the analysis of P300 further by utilising BEAM (Brain Electrical Activity Mapping) in which the specific components of the evoked potential can be mapped across the post-stimulus epochs and cortical regions to provide a topographic map from which a spatio-temporal development of the potential can be derived. In general, and in support of other studies, the schizophrenics (whose main symptoms comprised thought disorder, delusional cognition, and auditory hallucinations) exhibited a reduced P300 amplitude compared to normals. In addition these authors reported a difference between groups in terms of the spatio-temporal development of P300 waveform.

Thus the development of P300 in normals was characterised by an origin in the central parietal regions spreading out in a concentric fashion to engulf both hemispheres. In schizophrenics the waveform comprised two initial components of low amplitude originating in the central parietal region and right frontal areas. Both waveforms then merged to produce an asymmetric maximum over the parieto-temporal area. Statistical analysis of all epochs by region indicated that the main difference between groups was in respect of a persistent deficiency of activity in the left middle and posterior temporal lobe in schizophrenics. Using this as a criterion for discriminant function analysis all but one of the schizophrenics were correctly classified, the exception being the only left handed schizophrenic in the group. In addition to supporting the hypothesis of predominantly left hemisphere abnormality Morstyn *et al.* consider the possibility of a more complex P300 generating system comprising a frontal cortical generator in which P300 topography is elicited by unexpected, non-attended, or non-target stimuli, and a posterior cortical generator situated in the parietal-temporal regions and associated with active target recognition. This latter system is in itself 'fired' by the limbic-hippocampal generator postulated by Halgren *et al.* (1980) (the limbic system being both close to, and linked with, the left temporal region). Since they observed no significant differences between groups in the frontal regions Morstyn and colleagues conclude that the P300 component (and its generator), responsive to unexpected stimuli, is relatively well preserved in schizophrenics, whilst the component linked to target identification is deficient.

Finally, Morihisa *et al.* (1983) utilised the facility of BEAM to analyse a wider spectrum of EEG and evoked potential data, the results of which indicate abnormal delta EEG activity and visual evoked potentials in the frontal areas and abnormal auditory evoked potentials recorded from the temporal region. Furthermore, they suggest that the abnormalities evident in the evoked potentials of schizophrenics (particularly of focal reduction in P300) and the abnormally high beta activity would be consistent with an 'irritative, if not epileptogenic cortex'. Whilst not advocating that schizophrenia represents a particular form of epilepsy, the results suggest an association between hemispheric 'irritability' and psychotic phenomena.

Whilst the majority of studies have directed their attention towards, and have supported, an hypothesis of unilateral dysfunction in schizophrenia, a small but increasing number of studies have provided evidence indicative of a disturbance of interhemispheric integration in schizophrenia. In the preceding sections we have already described certain experiments, the results of which were consistent with this hypothesis (Buchsbaum *et al.* 1979, Flor-Henry *et al.* 1979), and Shaw *et al.* (1979) provided additional evidence from their investigation of EEG power and coherence derived from resting EEGs. Coherence reflects the degree to which EEG power recorded at specific locations is similar to that recorded at another site of reference (either intra or interhemispheric) and provides an index of the shared power of two channels at each frequency. Shaw *et al.* (1979) report that for all frequency bands the schizophrenic group exhibited higher intrahemispheric and lower interhemispheric coherence than normals. The pattern of intrahemispheric coherence ratios were considered by Shaw *et al.* to be the reverse of that found for normal right handed subjects, whilst the lower interhemispheric ratios indicated a greater than normal degree of independence of the two cerebral hemispheres – an observation which might relate to the seeming impairment of function of the corpus callosum in schizophrenics described by Beaumont and Dimond (1973), Green *et al.* (1983) and Rosenthal and Bigelow (1972). In short, Shaw *et al.* argue that the results might be suggestive of a conflict between the two hemispheres of schizophrenics, a view also supported by the

EEG research of Etevenon *et al.* (1979) and Butler and Glass (1974).

The precise nature of the mechanisms underlying this phenomenon of disturbed interhemispheric integration in schizophrenics is not yet known. Flor-Henry (1983) has argued that it might arise as a consequence of left hemisphere overactivation. Weller and Montague (1979), however, argue that disruptive integration could equally arise as a consequence of a disordered right hemisphere 'driving' the left. Not only would this give rise to integration difficulties but also a disruption of left hemisphere function. This latter view, whilst contrary to the main body of evidence, accords with Venables' (1982) hypothesis that schizophrenia is characterised by a premorbid right hemisphere dysfunction which subsequently disrupts dominant cerebral function due to abnormal specialisation. A third possibility concerns the prospect that impaired interhemispheric communication arises through faulty transmission through the callosal fibres. Direct attempts to measure, electrophysiologically, the integrity of callosal transmission have been unpromising because of methodological difficulties associated with the technique.

The procedure of measuring transcallosal transmission was first devised by Salamy (1978) who argued that repetitive manual stimulation of a single hand would result in a cortical evoked potential in the contralateral hemisphere (by direct afferent transmission) followed, after a short period, by a smaller potential in the other (non-stimulated) hemisphere due to callosal transmission. The transcallosal transmission time may then be derived by subtracting the latencies between the two somatosensory potentials. Salamy originally employed this technique to estimate callosal transmission in young children and observed a decrease in transmission time with age, correlating with the known maturation of the callosal fibres. Jones and Miller (1981) were the first to use this technique to investigate callosal function in schizophrenics. They argued that if schizophrenia were associated with abnormal interhemispheric communication this might be paralleled by an abnormal delay in transcallosal transmission. However the results of this study were in the opposite direction to their hypotheses – the schizophrenics were characterised by zero delay in transmission time, i.e. a bilaterally simultaneous evoked potential was observed. The authors argued that these results would be consistent with a total absence of callosal transmission and, drawing on evidence from split-brain research, argue that the simultaneity of the response reflects the strengthening of compensatory ipsilateral afferent fibres. Whilst this *post hoc* explanation may, in the final analysis, be reasonable, other neuropsychological evidence suggests not that there is a total disconnection in schizophrenia but rather a malconnection (Green *et al.* 1983; Randall 1983). Jones and Miller's experiment has been the subject of strong criticism because of methodological difficulties apparent in their utilisation of Salamy's technique. Indeed Connolly (1982) has pointed out that the waveform potentials in Jones and Miller's normal controls were, in themselves, markedly abnormal.

Independent of this study, Gullman *et al.* (1982) carried out the same investigation. They in fact did observe an abnormal latency in transcallosal response time, but only from the left to the right hemisphere. This would not necessarily imply a primary callosal defect, but would, in fact, be most compatible with Flor-Henry's (1983) conclusions.

Finally, Shagass *et al.* (1983) attempted to replicate Jones and Miller's study taking into consideration the methodological problems. One important modification was to relocate the reference EEG lead which ideally should be placed over an electrically inert or inactive scalp site. Jones and Miller (1981) had used the standard vertex site as a reference, which is far from inert when determining somatosensory evoked potentials and may have been interpreted as an ipsilateral response. Furthermore, Shagass *et al.* (1983) interpolated into the procedure trials in which the manual stimulator was activated over the hand but without touching it. They observed clear 'auditory' evoked potentials during this trial which could have contaminated Jones and Miller's results. Under direct stimulation (and partialling out the AEP's) there were no significant differences in somatosensory waveform between groups. Clearly, in the light of this study, a more rigid methodology is required in view of the potential value of this approach.

In summary, the plethora of EEG and evoked potential studies provide a consistent and overwhelming impression that disturbance of cerebral organisation may be related to schizophrenia. These studies point to both a dysfunctional dominant hemisphere and to a disturbance of interhemispheric integration. Observable differences in EEG have been demonstrated between diagnosable subtypes of schizophrenia indicating their potential as neurophysiological markers. The next chapter discusses in more detail the behavioural and functional parameters of altered cerebral organisation and its relationship to schizophrenia.

Chapter nine

COGNITIVE PROCESSING

A glance at recent reviews of the field of cognitive functioning and schizophrenia will indicate the wealth of data which has accumulated over the last 10–15 years. A cursory examination of the data suggests that schizophrenics perform poorly on almost all tests in which they take part. Detailed inspection, however, indicates that on specialised neuropsychological and experimental procedures, specific characteristics of psychosis in general and schizophrenia in particular emerge. The focus of research has, relatively recently, swung away from general interpretations of cognitive function and styles towards a more discrete analysis in terms of lateralised cerebral organisation. A major influence in this trend has been the seminal work of Pierre Flor-Henry who stimulated an ever expanding field of enquiry when he reported clinical similarities between schizophrenics' psychosis and dominant temporal lobe epilepsy.

This is not to suggest that research focusing on attentional capacity, memory, language and information processing are merely historical antecedents to a new and better field of enquiry, but rather to acknowledge that with our growing knowledge of lateralised and specialised cerebral processes it is possible to achieve a merger of the two approaches. Thus, for example, earlier interpretations of information processing in terms of pre-attentive processing and focal attention (or controlled processing) may be considered in terms of hemispheric specialisation – pre-attentive processing being best performed by the non-dominant hemisphere and sequential, focal, processing by the verbally dominant hemisphere (Kinsbourne and Smith 1974). Similarly, the work of Dimond (1976) suggests differences between the hemispheres in respect of attentional capacity, memory, and arousal.

In keeping with this new trend, and to achieve comparability with previous sections of this book, this chapter aims to review a series of studies employing neuropsychological tests and specialised techniques of auditory, visual and manual function which have further elucidated the relationship between schizophrenic psychopathology and abnormal cerebral function.

NEUROPSYCHOLOGICAL TESTING

Since Flor-Henry's (1969) observations he and other researchers have sought to define the characteristics of schizophrenia in terms of our understanding of lateralised cerebral processes. One procedure which has made an increasingly valuable contribution to this pursuit has been that of neuropsychological assessment.

In its broadest term neuropsychological procedures encompass not only the standardised test batteries devised predominantly in America but the experimental procedures of dichotic listening and Divided Visual Field presentations. In this first section, however, we will restrict our review of neuropsychological findings to those studies utilising standardised test batteries which have been constructed and used in clinical practice and research, to investigate the cognitive and psychological sequelae of brain damage, and the most notable and widely used of which are the Halstead-Reitan Neuropsychological Battery (HRNB) and the Luria-Nebraska Neuropsychological Battery (LNNB).

Flor-Henry (1976) administered several sections from the HRNB, including the Wechsler Adult Intelligence Scale (WAIS), on groups of schizophrenics, affective psychotics and normals.

Both patient groups performed poorly on tests inferred to reflect bilateral fronto-temporal dysfunction; however, schizophrenics were most impaired on variables reflecting dominant functions (aphasia screen, oral word fluency, speech perception, Trails B of Trail Making test and signs of ideomotor apraxia), whilst the affective group displayed a predominance of non-dominant signs. Furthermore, whilst there were no differences in Full Scale IQ between groups, schizophrenics were significantly more impaired on digit span and vocabulary resulting in poorer Verbal relative to Performance IQ. Similar observations of relative verbal decrement have been reported by Gruzelier *et al.* (1979) and Gruzelier and Hammond (1976) in adult schizophrenics and children at risk for schizophrenia. The pattern of dominant greater than non-dominant impairment in schizophrenia was confirmed by Flor-Henry *et al.* (1983) in unmedicated patients. Sixty-six per cent of the schizophrenics exhibited neuropsychological profiles in which dominant dysfunction was predominant (more so for males than females) and 79 per cent showed anterior dysfunction to be greater than posterior.

Flor-Henry (1981, 1983) has considered in some detail sex differences in relation to psychopathology. He argues that in males the verbally dominant hemisphere is relatively more vulnerable but, compared to females, they have a more efficient non-dominant hemisphere. Males, therefore, will be more susceptible to dominant hemisphere dysfunction characterised by schizophrenia, autism and psychopathy. Females, however, with relative dominant hemisphere superiority and non-dominant vulnerability may be more susceptible to non-dominant dysfunction such as mood states. There does appear to be some phenomenological support for these hypotheses since males seem especially at risk for early onset, poor prognosis schizophrenia as well as autistic symptoms, whilst females are at higher risk than men for affective illness (Flor-Henry 1976).

Kolb and Wishaw (1983) completed a series of tests on schizophrenics and normals (including items from the HRNB, the WAIS and a dichotic listening procedure) designed to assess frontal, temporal and parietal function. Compared to normals the schizophrenics performed poorly on tests of frontal and temporal, but not parietal function; however, there was little evidence of specific lateralised performance decrements. These authors concluded that the results were not totally consistent with data derived from CT and other neurophysiological studies but rather were consistent with diffuse dysfunction possibly suggestive of altered cerebral organisation. The fact that the schizophrenics performed within normal limits on parietal tests may indicate either the integrity of these functions or that the tests used were less sensitive to the effects of diffuse brain dysfunction. Of interest is the fact that this schizophrenic group did not exhibit the expected relative decrement in Verbal IQ but rather their Overall or Full-Scale IQ was lower, reflecting poor performance on non-verbal tests. Taylor and Abrams (1983), using several tests from the HRNB, and an aphasia screen, also failed to observe significant and exclusive dominant hemisphere dysfunction but rather report bilateral and largely anterior dysfunction in schizophrenics.

Comparing schizophrenic patients with neurological cases characterised as having 'chronic organic syndromes', Watson *et al.* (1968) found no difference on a global index of impairment. Furthermore, using discrete subtest performance in a discriminant function analysis, a substantial proportion of the schizophrenic group were classified as organic. This finding does not, of course, raise theoretical limitations but rather suggests that the Halstead–Reitan battery is a poor discriminator between organic and schizophrenic pathology. Of course, if it is the case that schizophrenia is characterised by abnormal cerebral functioning, this result may not be too surprising. Rather then, as Watson *et al.* (1962) did, compare schizophrenia with a heterogenous group of organic cases, it would have been more useful to compare these patients with patient groups of known specifiable and focal lesion sites. In a similar study Puente *et al.* (1982) compared twenty-three schizophrenics in whom there was evidence of brain damage (including CVA, epilepsy, metabolic disorders etc) with seventeen schizophrenics with no history of neurological symptoms. Using the Luria-Nebraska the authors report that on all fourteen scales the non-organic patients performed at a significantly higher level. Since, however, Puente *et al.* did not include a normal group for comparison, or report on individual subtest performance, little can be said about the test performance of the group of interest – neurologically 'normal' schizophrenics.

The same criticism can be levelled against Moses *et al.* (1983) who report results of the Luria-Nebraska (LNNB) on schizophrenic patients and non-psychotic organics. However, they do report that, on the basis of discriminant function analysis of the fourteen scales, 90 per cent of the schizophrenics were classified as non-neurologic. Since the differential diagnosis of brain damage versus psychosis is clinically more difficult in the absence of clear motor signs, Moses and colleagues performed separate analyses excluding those neurological cases with motor deficits. Whether excluding or including this subgroup the overall rate of correct classification was 81 per cent suggesting that, compared to the Halstead-Reitan Battery, the Luria may prove useful as a diagnostic tool.

Finally, Silverstein and Meltzer (1983) report on the use of the Luria-Nebraska on a group of schizophrenic and affective patients some of whom additionally completed the Halstead-Reitan Battery. Interestingly, all schizophrenic and affective patients emerging as impaired on the Luria were also impaired on the Halstead-Reitan. No differences between groups were observed in terms of specific lateralised impairment. Thus, whilst all of the affective patients exhibited a predominance of right-sided impairment, 57 per cent of the schizophrenic group were also maximally impaired on non-dominant functions, although left-frontal functions were significantly more impaired in schizophrenics than in affectives.

The results as a whole, considered in isolation from other experimental findings, are clearly not consistent with a pure unilateral disorder in schizophrenia and do not support the conclusion that specific hemispheric dysfunction is unique to different diagnostic groups. Rather they suggest that there are degrees both of cerebral disorganisation (i.e. a continuum of increasing cerebral dysfunction) across diagnostic groups and of relative left-right hemisphere dysfunction. This view is most consistent with Flor-Henry's (1983) conceptual position that there is a bilateral dysfunction in all psychoses and that 'the severity of dysfunction is least in depression and maximal in schizophrenia with a right hemisphere emphasis in depression and a left hemisphere emphasis in schizo-phrenia' (Flor-Henry 1983: 3).

Criticisms have been raised in respect of inferring organicity or dysfunction in psychiatric populations from tests primarily stan-dardised on organic and normal samples. This criticism has two specific aspects, the first of which raises the problem of task appli-cation. Since schizophrenic patients may experience difficulties in attention and motivation, is it reasonable to assume that their poor test performance primarily reflects disturbance in these functions? This, of course, is a problem across all testing practices, whether research or clinical, and one which must be addressed before valid interpretation of test results can be made. Nevertheless, the fact that schizophrenics do not perform poorly on *all* tests (nor necess-arily on those tests susceptible to poor attention and motivation) suggests that in most reported studies test performance is not unduly confounded by such variables. The second aspect relates to the validity with which one infers organicity on the basis of test performance (Miller 1983). The essence of Miller's argument is that if a particular test is performed badly by, say, left temporal lobe cases, then any new subject who performs badly on the same test may not necessarily do so because of damage to the same locus. This of course cannot be disputed, since it may be the case that other neural systems play an intimate role in the regulation of certain functions subserved by the temporal areas. However, it does under-emphasise the main art of neuropsychological assessment which is one of convergent analysis – ruling out alternative and competing hypotheses by analysis of a wide range of individual subtests.

Taken to its logical conclusion, Miller's argument would suggest that even if this new subject were indeed a temporal lobe case, we would have no grounds for inferring temporal lobe dysfunction from his or her test performance. If this were the case it would tend to undermine the rationale of neuropsychological testing. Clearly this is not what Miller is intending but rather he is drawing attention to the complexity of neural systems in determining cognitive behaviour and cautioning against the use of over-simplistic interpretation.

AUDITORY FUNCTION

DICHOTIC LISTENING

The technique of dichotic listening relies partly on the assumption that stimuli presented to one ear are directed to the opposite, or contralateral, hemisphere by the dominant auditory afferents, and hence performance in terms of accuracy or response latency may be taken to reflect the initial operation of systems lateralised to one hemisphere. The term dichotic, however, carries with it the specific criterion that competing stimuli are presented simultaneously to each ear. Unlike the visual system in which a single visual half-field projects only to the opposite half brain, the auditory system consists of both larger crossed (contralateral) and smaller uncrossed (ispilateral) pathways and is hence not completely lateralised. Dichotic listening, therefore, relies on the further assumption that during simultaneous competition the ipsilateral pathways are suppressed and hence the contralateral pathways dominate.

Stimuli may be presented in the form of clicks, digits, words, pure tones, phonemes etc. and the basic paradigm usually requires subjects to identify stimuli without directing attention to one ear. There are however several modifications to this basic procedure (see e.g. Beaumont 1983). Generally speaking the observation of shorter response latency and/or greater percentage of correct responses in one ear (termed an ear advantage) has been inferred to reflect the superiority of the contralateral hemisphere in the initial processing of the stimuli. Thus for verbal stimuli the majority of normal right-handed individuals exhibit a right ear (left brain) advantage. Less reliable is the observation of a left ear (right brain) advantage in response to non-verbal stimuli.

Because of the nature of the auditory pathways, and the care with which stimuli must be constructed and presented, several methodological problems exist with dichotic presentations which are not as apparent in divided visual field studies. Similarly the interpretation of data derived from dichotic presentation is complex in nature. A structural interpretation relies on the superiority of one hemisphere to process incoming stimuli of a particular nature, i.e. it relies on the assumption of absolute brain specialisation. The research of Kallman (1977) and Morais and Bertleson (1973), however, indicates that attentional factors such as priming (the predictability of stimulus type and localisation, the effects of distraction etc.) and the strategy of information processing can strongly influence the emergence and magnitude of the ear advantage. Because of these difficulties some authors (e.g. Teng 1981) have suggested that ear advantages derived from dichotic procedures are unreliable indices of functional asymmetries.

Additionally, since the nature of the dichotic paradigm permits only the presentation of simple verbal or non-verbal information, the test procedure may only assess the function of discrete temporal areas involving only the primary auditory reception area (see Katz 1978). Several studies are therefore reported here in which simple and complex auditory function are assessed using monaural presentation. Whilst the ability of monaural tests to assess a single hemisphere's function has been questioned, clinical and anatomical data support the rationale of a monaural-unilateral hemisphere relationship (Katz 1978; Bocca *et al.* 1955; Rosenzweig 1951). We have laboured these methodological and conceptual issues since they obviously constrain interpretation in respect of cerebral functioning and because dichotic studies are often quoted as one of the central data bases in psychopathological research.

The present state of research findings of dichotic listening in patient populations has been cogently summarised by Bruder (1983 a,b). In reviewing the field Bruder (1983a) concludes that of eight verbal dichotic studies, two found evidence of abnormally large right ear advantage (REAs) in schizophrenics, four found normal REAs, two show no relative ear advantages, but no study reported a reversal i.e. left ear advantage. There seems little doubt that two specific factors have contributed to the disparity of these results, the first of which concerns the characteristics of test presentation.

Colbourn and Lishman (1979) report an absence of the right ear advantage in schizophrenics compared to normals and psychotic controls in response to dichotically presented consonant-vowels. Similarly, Johnson and Crocket (1982) failed to observe a REA with words and Yozawitz *et al.* (1979) report the same finding with staggered words. Gruzelier and Hammond (1980) however observe normal REAs in schizophrenics using digits. Furthermore, Lishman *et al.* (1978) observed greater than normal REAs in both schizophrenic and affective patient groups. Further analysis, however, reveals a second factor of significance – that of subdiagnostic type. Thus while Gruzelier and Hammond (1980) observed no overall differences between the schizophrenic and normal groups, non-paranoid schizophrenics performed like normals whilst the paranoid group was characterised by an abnormally large asymmetry. The right ear preference was so great in the paranoid group that increasing the intensity of left ear input by a further 20 dB produced no appreciable alteration of preference. Summarising the studies, Bruder (1983 a,b) concludes that paranoid schizophrenics stand out as the most impaired group. The results of dichotic listening are difficult to interpret since an enlarged right ear advantage is consistent with left hemisphere overactivation, right hemisphere dysfunction or deficiencies in interhemispheric integration. Partly this difficulty reflects the use of laterality indices where it is not always apparent which ear is performing abnormally. It is therefore of interest that whilst Adams (1983) observed an abnormal REA in schizophrenics this was characterised by normal right ear performance and significantly reduced left ear performance, and may more appropriately be referred to as left ear deficit. Bruder (1983a) points out that left temporal lobe damage frequently results in a bilateral decrease in performance, usually greater for the right ear and resulting either in no ear advantage or a left ear advantage. Right temporal lobe cases however are characterised by an almost total extinction of the left ear with the right ear being equal to or better than normal. Similarly Sparks and Geschwind (1968) report normal right ear performance and a virtual extinction of left ear performance in subjects after total commissurotomy. These results suggest that whilst studies reporting an absence of ear advantages in schizophrenics may be interpreted in terms of left temporal dysfunction, the observations of enlarged right ear advantages are more consistent with right-sided damage or defective interhemispheric integration.

As we shall see later, however, an abnormally large right ear advantage characterised by superior right ear performance compared to normal is not consistent with frequently reported results from divided visual field studies. Bruder concludes on the basis of this observation that the pattern of results from the dichotic literature is 'clearly *not* what would be expected if schizophrenia involved a left-lateralised lesion which impinged on the primary auditory reception (area)'. Non-verbal dichotic listening procedures, on the other hand, indicate that schizophrenics exhibit normal left ear advantages (Bruder 1983a) not consistent with right hemisphere damage – at least in terms of its ability to discriminate pitch, clicks or musical chords.

An interesting variant on the dichotic paradigm was carried out by Niwa *et al.* (1983) who addressed the problem of attentional deficits in schizophrenia by examining the attentional functioning of each hemisphere on a sustained pure tone detection task. They report that schizophrenics displayed larger reaction times with significantly more errors of omission (but not commission) in the right ear. Unlike errors of commission, which relate to stimulus analysis, the authors point out the greater frequency in omission errors of schizophrenics may relate to difficulties of response selection and organisation which become greater over extended and sustained periods particularly in the right ear (left hemisphere). Whilst Niwa *et al.* point out that these results suggest a dysfunctional left hemisphere they also consider them to be consistent with faulty interhemispheric integration.

Dimond (1976) has concluded from his research with split-brain subjects that each hemisphere has it own vigilance system; that the left hemisphere exhibits high attention which rapidly declines, in contrast to the right hemisphere which maintains a constant but lower level of performance. Since Dimond suggests that integration mechanisms between the two hemispheres play an important role in overall attentional functioning, Niwa *et al.*'s results are consistent with a disturbance of integration which reveals the characteristics of the left hemisphere's inability to sustain an initial performance level.

In general, the results of dichotic listening are consistent not so much with left-sided impairment, but, as Alpert *et al.* (1976) suggest, with anomalous cerebral functional organisation. That, however, the results may be of importance as an index relating cerebral organisation to schizophrenic pathology is evidenced by the fact that the unusual pattern of ear performance normalises after medication (Lerner *et al.* 1977, Wexler and Heninger 1979).

MONAURAL LISTENING

In an attempt to investigate other parameters of auditory function in schizophrenia, Gruzelier and Hammond (1976) determined auditory thresholds and auditory temporal discrimination in newly admitted schizophrenics taking part in a drug trial. All subjects (normal and schizophrenics) were tested on three occasions corresponding to the drug trial phases for patients of chlorpromazine, placebo, and chlorpromazine reinstatement. Using pure tone audiometry to determine absolute hearing thresholds, Gruzelier and Hammond observed a significant ear effect for both groups in phase one – with the right ear being superior. Noticeably, schizophrenics exhibited superior hearing at low frequencies (up to 1000 or 2000 Hz) whilst normals were superior at higher frequencies. This latter finding, suggest Gruzelier and Hammond, may reflect a facilitation in the rate of neural transmission and that the hearing loss at middle to high frequency ranges observed in schizophrenia is commonly seen in patients with damage to the auditory reception areas of the temporal lobe. Whilst there were no appreciable effects of drug manipulation across findings the authors report that at phase three the schizophrenics showed a highly significant hearing loss in the right ear. Since the audiometric testing in phase three was far more extensive than for the initial phase, the results suggested that the reduced right ear performance might reflect the greater susceptibility of the left hemisphere to the inhibitory effects of adaptation and fatigue with continued stimulation. In terms of auditory discrimination, schizophrenics were overall poorer than normals with significantly more right ear omissions. Performance on this test was affected by medication, with more omissions in the placebo phase and a correlation between drug dosage and omissions in phase one. Gruzelier and Hammond also report that schizophrenics were poorer on verbal subtests of the WAIS and that 50 per cent had abnormal GSR responses on the right hand. Taken as a whole, the authors conclude a left hemisphere dysfunction and 'weak' left hemisphere nervous system dynamics in schizophrenics. Kugler *et al.* (1982) also report right ear superiority in absolute thresholds for schizophrenics (but not normals) and conclude that the results are not consistent with conductive hearing loss and that the auditory and perceptual dysfunction apparent in schizophrenia is not associated with peripheral and middle ear disorders.

Kugler and Caudrey (1983) further investigated perceptual discrimination in schizophrenics using a single phonemic discrimination test under monaural conditions. Their rationale for the use of a monaural task was a practical one based on the observation that both ears tend to perform worse under dichotic than monural stimulation and hence the use of monaural presentation might minimise the expected general performance decrements encountered when testing schizophrenic populations. Following the procedure of Morais and Darwin (1974) the first of a phoneme pair was delivered binaurally and the second of each pair monaurally to the left or right ear in an unpredictable manner – subjects being asked to indicate manually whether each pair was the 'same' or 'different'. Controlling for the speed of manual movements on response (which was significantly slower in schizophrenics and depressed subjects compared with normals) the adjusted scores indicated a faster reaction time to left ear than right ear stimuli, but only for 'same' responses. Normals, but no other group, showed a significant right ear advantage in terms of reaction time for 'different' responses. In terms of errors for all groups there were more errors for 'different' responses; however group effects were only apparent for 'same' responses, with schizophrenics and normals performing equally better than depressed subjects. No ear differences were seen. This significant right ear advantage, which stands in contradistinction to the dichotic listening studies, was interpreted as consistent with left hemisphere disorder. In view of the difficulties experienced by schizophrenics under binaural compared with monural listening (see Green *et al.* 1983), it would have been desirable for Kugler's study to have included a further binaural-binaural condition.

Alpert *et al.* (1976) using binaural noise to mask monaurally presented verbal stimuli report that schizophrenics characterised by a history of hallucinations were able to differentiate semantically different stimuli in the left but not the right ear with the opposite pattern for normals and schizophrenics without hallucinations. Finally, Green and Kotenko (1980) and Green, Hallett and Hunter (1983) report a series of studies in which monaural and binaural speech comprehension was investigated in schizophrenics. In their study complex stories were delivered either monaurally to the left or right ear or binaurally (as in everyday listening) and subjects were subsequently asked to answer questions on each story. Schizophrenics, but not normals or psychiatric controls, exhibited significantly enlarged monaural asymmetries and also performed significantly worse under binaural stimulation compared to higher single ear performance. Approximately 65 per cent of the schizophrenics performed poorly in the left ear condition. The authors interpret this pattern of results as suggestive of disturbed interhemispheric communication. Gruzelier (1980) has also indicated that whilst the left ear deficit might reflect an over reliance on right ear input, a binaural deficit does suggest a disturbance of integration.

In summary, the results of auditory testing on schizophrenics are somewhat confusing. With the exception of Gruzelier and Hammonds data no *clear* pattern of auditory perceptual difficulties consistent with left hemisphere dysfunction has emerged. Whilst non-verbal dichotic listening suggests the relative integrity of right hemisphere processing in schizophrenia, the technique of dichotic listening in particular is limited in its ability to identify global temporal lobe dysfunction since performance most probably reflects only the processing attributable to the primary auditory reception areas.

Whilst abnormally large right ear advantages have been observed in schizophrenics it is unclear in many cases whether this reflects an absolute superiority of the right ear compared with normals or dysfunctional left ear performance. Should this latter prove to be the case, as was seen by Adams (1983), the results are more consistent with either a disturbance of integration or right hemisphere dysfunction. Since right hemisphere dysfunction or left hemisphere overactivation (or indeed unilateral brainstem dysfunction (Katz 1978)), would predict the same pattern of results it seems likely that dichotic listening studies in isolation may be too problematic for valid interpretation of complex cognitive functioning. However, in conjunction with monaural tests, in which more complex information approximating to everyday speech and perception may be delivered, and from audiological assessment of the central auditory nervous system, a more coherent understanding of auditory perceptual problems in schizophrenia may be achieved.

VISUAL STUDIES

DIVIDED VISUAL FIELD STUDIES

In some respects the divided visual field paradigm is less problematic than dichotic listening given the complete lateralisation of the visual system. Essentially the basic paradigm involves stimulation of a single visual half field via a tachistoscope and thus constitutes a more exacting, visual, equivalent to the dichotic technique.

In 1973 Beaumont and Dimond, the first to use the divided visual field technique with psychiatric patients, examined between and within hemisphere matching using a variety of simultaneously presented stimuli. They report that schizophrenics performed more poorly when required to match stimuli across hemispheres but were additionally somewhat poorer than normals in left hemisphere matching. This result suggested a specific deficit in interhemispheric communication, but also raised the question of lateralised dominant dysfunction. Walker and McGuire (19832) report a similar experiment by way of replication, requiring interhemispheric and intrahemispheric matching of similar stimuli presented sequentially rather than simultaneously. They report that no differences were observed between schizophrenics and normals and cite this as evidence against an interpretation of defective interhemispheric communication.

Since, however, the latter experiment did not directly replicate the procedure of Beaumont and Dimond, it is difficult to see how they arrive at this conclusion. Nevertheless, the two studies provide an interesting comparison since while, in the latter study, sequential presentation required transfer of information from one hemisphere to the other, Beaumont and Dimond's simultaneous presentation required not only transfer, but simultaneous integration of the two hemispheres (akin to the binaural condition in Green and Kotenko (1980)). Since the visual stimuli were relatively simple, transfer *per se* may not have been affected in the same way that simple auditory information such as digits, letters or words may be transferred (Kaur 1984). However, failure might occur even with simple information if simultaneous integration were necessary.

Pic'l *et al.* (1979) also offer further evidence of defective integration on two tachistocopically presented tasks of dot enumeration and letter recognition, but only in non-paranoid schizophrenics. Eaton *et al.* (1979) observed a left hemisphere advantage for verbal information in schizophrenics, however they also report that schizophrenics were overall poorer than normals suggesting a verbal deficit (there were no differences on non-verbal tests). Whilst they concluded a left hemisphere dysfunction in schizophrenia, their results were opposite to those of Gur (1978) who also interprets her results as indicating dominant hemisphere dysfunction. Gur's study is one of the most widely quoted in support of left hemisphere dysfunction. She presented to each half-field and as two separate tasks an array of dots for enumeration or syllables for recognition. Unlike normal subjects who showed a right visual field (left hemisphere) superiority for verbal information and a left visual field advantage for the spatial task, schizophrenics showed a left visual field superiority for both verbal and non-verbal stimuli suggestive of left hemisphere dysfunction. Whilst this is, in its own right, an important finding it is clearly inconsistent with the dichotic literature which suggests either left hemisphere overactivation or right hemisphere dysfunction.

Walker, Hoppes and Emory (1981) point out that unless it is the case that schizophrenics' left hemisphere dysfunction is restricted to visual stimuli, it is difficult to see how a unilateral model can account for both findings. Rather Walker *et al.* (1981) argue that the results are more consistent with deficient interhemispheric integration. First, as we suggested earlier, the exaggerated right ear advantage in schizophrenics is similar to the results from commissurotomised patients. Second, the key to understanding Gur's results in terms of an integration model lies in the configuration of the verbal stimuli, which were presented in vertical format.

Walker *et al.* (1981) argue that at degraded, tachistoscopic rates of presentation the identification of nonsense syllables must initially be visually or spatially analysed and then phonetically processed, i.e. it is primarily a non-verbal task. If the callosum is intact the left hemisphere's phonetic abilities are likely to benefit from the superior spatial skills of the right hemisphere and then manifest its own superiority for phonetic analysis. If, however, problems exist with callosal integration the left hemisphere would be at a significant disadvantage in performing the initial visual analysis of the sensory input. Thus under tachistoscopic viewing the right hemisphere would be at a significant advantage. Since the schizophrenics performed with a left visual field (right hemisphere) advantage on the spatial presentation, a task requiring little interhemispheric communication, the results are entirely consistent with a model of degraded interhemispheric communication.

LATERAL EYE MOVEMENTS

Bakan (1971) and Gur (1975) have suggested that the direction of eye movement (lateral eye movement or LEM) may indicate activation of the cerebral hemisphere contralateral to the direction of gaze. Indeed Kinsbourne (1972) has observed that right LEM's are associated with verbal processing while left LEM's occur preferentially during spatial tasks.

Very few studies of lateral eye movements have been carried out with schizophrenics; however, Schweitzer *et al.* (1978) observed that schizophrenics preferentially look right when thinking of spatial or emotional material and exhibited an overall increase in activity compared to normals. Schweitzer (1979) concludes that this indicates an inappropriate pattern of left hemisphere activity but additionally suggests a more overall and diffuse abnormality in hemispheric activity. A further interpretation might be that the preferential right eye movements reflect a lack of right hemisphere reciprocal inhibition. Schweitzer's results are somewhat confounded by the observation that females, regardless of diagnosis, exhibited preferential right LEMs as compared to males.

MANUAL STUDIES

HANDEDNESS

The relationship between handedness and cerebral organisation remains one of the most important questions to be resolved. Rasmussen and Milner (1975) report that over 95 per cent of right handed individuals have speech lateralised to the left hemisphere; 70 per cent of left handers show the same pattern; of the remaining 30 per cent half have reversed specialisation and half have mixed or bilateral speech representation.

These data were derived from individuals for whom there was no evidence of early brain injury involving the left hemisphere. Including those subjects with evidence of early left hemisphere damage, the percentage of right handers with left hemisphere speech was 81 per cent (6 per cent bilateral speech, and 13 per cent with right sided speech) whilst for left or mixed handers 30 per cent had left hemisphere speech, 19 per cent bilateral and 51 per cent right sided.

Carter *et al.* (1980) and Satz (1979) analysed from several studies the incidence of aphasia following focal brain lesions. These authors observed that the best fitting model of speech representation was that in which 76 per cent of left handers had bilateral speech, 25 per cent with left hemisphere speech and hence none with right sided speech, whilst for right handers 95 per cent had left sided speech and 5 per cent lateralised to the right. Whilst these two studies appear consistent for right handers, there is some degree of disparity for left handers partly accounted for by the difference in method used to infer speech representation, different ways of classifying handedness and different criteria for infering 'bilateral' representation. The relationship between speech lateralisation is also influenced by the presence of familial dextrality and by sometimes minor, and often unrecorded, early CNS injuries. Whilst the issues surrounding this relationship are complex, it seems an important one to resolve given the ease with which handedness may be determined. Whilst one cannot necessarily infer an individual's speech lateralisation just by knowing that person's hand preference, it is often used to provide additional evidence for normal or abnormal cerebral organisation.

Observations of a relative incidence of left and right handedness in schizophrenics have varied as a function of the characteristics of the schizophrenic group. Gur (1977) and Dvirskii (1976) both report an increase in sinistrality in schizophrenia whilst Oddy and Lobstein (1972) report no excess. Alternatively, Bolin (1953), Fleminger *et al.* (1977) and Taylor *et al.* (1980) report an excess of dextrality in schizophrenics. Lishman and McMeekan (1976) whilst reporting no differences between groups did find a significant excess of left handers in young male psychotics with delusions. Both Gur (1977) and Nasrallah *et al.* (1981a) report an excess of full dextrality in chronic schizophrenic populations and Nasrallah *et al.* (1982d) also noted that paranoid, but not non-paranoid, schizophrenics exhibited excess sinistrality. This group of paranoids was also characterised by left-eyedness, a result which led the above authors to conclude that paranoid, but not non-paranoid, schizophrenics exhibited impaired lateralisation. Since there was no familial history of left handedness in these groups, Nasrallah and colleagues suggest that the excess may reflect early cerebral insult. An equally plausible hypothesis, however, might be that left handedness may represent an index of abnormal cerebral laterality associated with the development of schizophrenia. That this may be the case is suggested by the work of Hallett and Green (1983), who observed an excess of left handedness in male children at risk for schizophrenia, and of Boklage (1977).

Boklage's analysis of monozygotic twins, one or both of whom were diagnosed as schizophrenic, has suggested that discordance for schizophrenia may be due to anomalous lateralisation in the schizophrenic twins (observed as either left handedness or incomplete handedness in the non-schizophrenic twin). Thus whilst concordance for schizophrenia was present in twenty-three out of twenty-four same handed pairs, only eight out of twenty pairs of different handedness were concordant. This work has since been replicated and supported by Luchins *et al.* (1979).

In summary there appears overall, little evidence that handedness as an index of cerebral laterality is significantly altered in schizophrenics except perhaps in paranoid subgroups. This may not be surprising since evidence suggests that more complex cognitive and integrative functions are deficient in schizophrenia which may not be apparent by assessing simple and gross variables. However, the observation of Hallett and Green (1983) and Boklage (1977) and the difficulties in simple manual co-ordination seen in children at risk for schizophrenia (see Ch. 10) suggests that handedness might be a useful index of abnormal cerebral laterality earlier in life.

MOTOR FUNCTION

Walker and Green (1982) employing a neuromotor examination on schizophrenic, non-schizophrenic psychiatric and normal subjects observed no lateral differences between the hands across groups. Rather they reported that on certain tests schizophrenics were poorer in co-ordination and speed. Nasrallah *et al.* (1982b) also report that on thirty motor tests, designed to detect 'soft' neurological signs, schizophrenics were significantly impaired on nineteen. These signs, indicative of neuro-integrative deficits, were however not specific to the schizophrenic patients.

On a series of motor and sensory tests Torrey (1980) found few differences between schizophrenics and normals except that schizophrenics were poorer on two sensory tests – face-hand tactile suppression and palm graphaesthesia involving the right hand.

Ritzler and Rosenbaum (1974) in a methodologically elegant study explored possible problems of proprioceptive feedback in schizophrenics. They argued that, since proprioceptive feedback requires central integration, the performance of schizophrenics on such tasks might provide clues for a possible link between central integrating disturbances and the higher order integrating problems evident in schizophrenic symptoms.

Using a manual pursuit rotor task, subjects were engaged on a five minute practice with the non-dominant hand, a post-test again with the non-dominant hand with an interpolated trial using the dominant hand. In normals, the interpolation of a task with the other hand after minimal rest produces an inhibitory effect on the post-trial which can be alleviated with rest. By using two groups with and without rest and a third control group which performed only at pre- and post-trials, the authors were able to provide pure measures of the effects of an interpolated task and of the effects of inhibition. Unlike the normals without rest who exhibited the inhibitory effect there was no evidence of bilateral transfer of inhibition in the schizophrenics. In conjunction with this deficit, the observations of positive learning effects for both schizophrenics and normals suggest a proprioceptive deficit involving impairment of central integrating mechanisms. Since this task is essentially intermanual in nature the results also suggest specific problems of inter-hemispheric integration.

Studies by Dimond *et al.* (1979, 1980), Green (1978), Carr (1980), and Hatta *et al.* (1984) also indicate specific difficulties with intermanual transfer. Dimond *et al.* (1979) found that schizophrenics have difficulty naming objects placed in the left but not the right hand. Newlin *et al.* have suggested that since this task was verbal in nature, these results are consistent with dysfunction of the verbally dominant hemisphere; however, since schizophrenics had

123

no difficulty in naming objects in the right hand this seems unlikely. Furthermore, Dimond *et al.* (1980) carried out a series of tasks in which subjects were requested to indicate a part of the hand, forearm or body touched by the experimentor with the same-side or opposite-side hand. Overall, the authors report more errors when schizophrenics were required to respond with the hand opposite to the side of the body touched.

In a more robust design Green (1978) reports marked deficits in schizophrenics' abilities to perform an intermanual shape discrimination task. Familiar objects presented to one hand could be selected from a group of objects presented to the opposite hand with no difficulty. However, when the task was made more complex, with the use of unfamiliar objects, defective inter-manual but not intra-manual performance was observed in the schizophrenics. Similar problems were evident when schizophrenics were required to learn to place a number of unfamiliar objects in a certain order and then reproduce that order with the same or opposite hand. Again, schizophrenics had little difficulty when required to complete both operations with the same hand, but showed significant errors when required to reproduce the order with the opposite hand. In summary, the results of a wide variety of manual and motor tasks do not, on the whole, support a model of lateralised dysfunction in schizophrenia, but rather point to a disorder of central organisation possibly reflecting defective inter-hemispheric integration.

SCHIZOPHRENIC LANGUAGE AND APHASIA

Since many of the primary problems associated with schizophrenia are language based, it is not surprising that researchers have sought to investigate similarities between language disturbance in schizophrenia and the problem of language processing and production related to known organic lesions – the aphasias. Using, as part of their test battery, a short aphasia screen, Scarone *et al.* (1983) observed that schizophrenics were more impaired than controls on tests of copying, naming and spelling – a pattern of performance similar to that observed in patients with bilateral damage. Similarly, Taylor and Abrahms (1983) infer bilateral dysfunction from their aphasic testing but report that the schizophrenics performed particularly badly on tests implicating the dominant temporo-parietal areas. The use of neuropsychological tests (reviewed earlier in this chapter), which contain aphasia subtests, have also pointed to problems both of receptive language (such as phonemic discrimination) and expressive language (verbal fluency) in schizophrenics (Flor-Henry 1979, 1983).

Utilising the token test as an assessment of language comprehension Adams (1983) reports that schizophrenics perform significantly worse than normals. Overall weighted scores indicated that 73 per cent of the schizophrenics performed within the upper range of an aphasic population. Detailed linguistic analysis of performance, however, indicated that whilst aphasic patients begin to perform badly in the early parts of the test (since the test involves many of the basic elements of linguistic structure such as nouns, adjectives and verbs on which aphasic subjects perform badly) the schizophrenics performed badly only at higher levels in which new grammatical elements, such as prepositions, conjunctions and adverbs, appear. In particular, schizophrenic patients exhibited significant errors on prepositions denoting spatial and temporal relationships (under, before, behind, in front of etc).

Portnoff (1982) points out that whilst there is little commonality between elements of schizophrenic speech, such as word salad, and jargon aphasia, there are similarities between agrammatism in schizophrenia and semantic aphasia. Furthering this analysis Andreasen (1982) has begun an extensive investigation of the relationship between schizophrenic and aphasic language disturbance. Phenomenologically, the disturbance in schizophrenic language includes pressured speech, tangentiality, incoherence, derailment and illogicality as positive symptoms, and negative symptoms include poverty of speech and poverty of content. In Andreasen's analysis neologisms, once thought to be common in schizophrenia were, in fact, rarely encountered. Similarly incoherence was only observed in 16 per cent of cases. Andreasen's (1982) analysis of the syntactic, semantic, discoursive and pragmatic components of speech is still in its initial phase, but indicates that whilst schizophrenics perceive and process language normally in terms of syntactic and semantic components, they exhibit deficits in language production involving discoursive and pragmatic components. In attempting to define the neurologic and anatomic correlates of such impairment, Andreasen notes similarities between these problems in schizophrenic language and to those experienced in transcortical aphasia and semantic (Wernicke's) aphasia.

In summary, whilst there are obvious similarities in style between aphasic and schizophrenic language, there is no absolute comparability. Such similarities as there are do not, of course, imply similar neural mechanisms. Such an interpretation would be as problematic as earlier interpretations of 'regression' derived from observed similarities between the speech of schizophrenics and of normal young children. Since there seems to be little evidence from other investigations of discrete cortical lesions in schizophrenia, it

seems reasonable to infer that the abnormalities of cortical activation and integration apparent in schizophrenics impair cortical
efficiency which in turn gives rise to symptomatically similar, but
pathogenically dissimilar, language disturbance.

ATTENTION, MEMORY AND SCHIZOPHRENIA

It is well known that schizophrenics have difficulty in recalling
verbal information. Brief viewing of letter displays, for example,
indicates that schizophrenics process less information than normals
and that this deficiency increases as a function of the number of
units of information presented (Neale 1971). Evidence from the
research of Davidson and Neale (1974) suggests, however, that
whilst schizophrenics are slower in visual searching they do use the
same form of processing as normals. In terms of visual searching,
studies of smooth pursuit eye tracking with schizophrenics suggests
a problem in non-voluntary attention. Holzman and Levy (1977),
for example, found impairment of smooth pursuit eye movements
in 50–80 per cent of schizophrenics, in a lower but still significant
percentage of affective psychoses and in 8 per cent of normals (as
well as in 50 per cent of the first-degree relatives of schizophrenics
and 10 per cent of relatives of non-schizophrenics). Holzman and
Levy relate those disorders to CNS disruption superior to the brain
stem. Spohn and Larson (1983) have classified the eye movement
impairments in schizophrenics as consisting of saccadic intrusions
(back and forth movements) and abnormal saccadic smooth pursuit
(compensatory) movements. These abnormalities appear to be
unaffected by medication and are not an effect of simple
inattentiveness (Lipton *et al.* 1983). However, they are not exclusive
characteristics, and hence not pathognomic of schizophrenia since
they appear to be present in a wide range of psychiatric and neurological populations.

Behavioural studies suggest little difference in basic processing
between schizophrenic and normal subjects, but rather that the
operation of levels of processing beyond the sensory scanning stage
are primarily responsible for schizophrenics' impaired performance.
Schneider (1976), for example, has indicated that schizophrenics
have particular problems with selective attention, making more
errors when relevant task stimuli are embedded within irrelevant
information. Since selective attention may be impaired, the
difficulties in memory recall experienced by schizophrenics may, in
part, reflect difficulties in separating, or distinguishing between,
relevant and irrelevant stimuli. The exact locus of these attentional

problems is as yet not fully known. Koh *et al.* (1973) and Nachmani and Cohen (1969) have, however, observed that whilst schizophrenics' recall is significantly impaired, their recognition of stimuli is relatively intact, suggesting that selective attention is not a sufficient explanation. Recognition is considered by many to be a relatively passive process compared to recall – which requires additional organisation processes, such as the chunking and coding of individual items of information for longer term retention. Koh *et al.* (1972, 1973) and Bauman (1979) provide persuasive evidence that whilst schizophrenics can recognise and encode stimuli's attributes in a normal fashion, they experience considerable difficulties in higher order organisation of this information.

In general terms, the possibility that attentional and recall processes may be impaired in schizophrenics may have implications for the interpretation of test results in terms of lateralised cerebral processes. Similarly the potential effects of affect, arousal and effort on these processes must be considered, since they may reflect controlling factors governing their mobilisation and allocation (Gjerde 1983). However, evidence does suggest that these general factors may in themselves reflect the operation of lateralised processes.

SUMMARY AND SYNTHESIS

It is a difficult task to provide a definitive synthesis of the overwhelming, and on occasions, apparently contradictory findings presented in this chapter; and the research field has become further confused by the development of several 'second generation' hypotheses. One specific issue contributing to this confusion has been in respect of inferring dysfunction from asymmetric performance. Such asymmetries lend themselves to alternative hypothesis in terms of under- or over-activity such that underactivity in one hemisphere or overactivity of the opposite hemisphere would both predict the same pattern of performance on certain tests. Additionally different test procedures have generated results which suggests both under- and over-activity within the same hemisphere system – inferences which are clearly incompatible. There seems little doubt that some of these contradictory findings reflect differences in sample characteristics and test procedures. In addition part of the difficulty in establishing a coherent conceptual framework reflects the reliance on a small number of studies which are often quoted as providing a factual basis for subsequent investigation without due consideration of their limitations.

Beaumont and Dimond's (1973) study is, for example, often quoted exclusively for its implications within an interhemispheric model without also giving equal consideration to results from the same study consistent with unilateral dysfunction. Similarly Gur's (1978) study is heavily quoted in support of unilateral dysfunction whilst the results are equally compatible with an alternative hypothesis – that the right hemisphere of schizophrenics may be more effective on some aspects of language processing (since the schizophrenics performance on the verbal task in the left visual field display was comparable to the right visual field performance of normal controls).

Similarly, the fact that the schizophrenics exhibited a bilateral reduction on the spatial task, compared with normals, is rarely considered. Lastly, the general interpretation of dichotic listening studies, investigations of lateral eye movements, and divided visual field studies is also problematic in the absence of a clear understanding of the role of attentional asymmetries, response strategies, and retrieval strategies.

In spite of these difficulties the evidence reviewed here does suggest that CNS disorganisation, maximally implicating the dominant hemisphere, and a disturbance of interhemispheric integration may constitute important cerebral determinants of schizophrenia. Whilst Marin and Tucker (1981) have concluded that the research has not clearly delineated the neural mechanisms crucial to schizophrenia it may well be naive to look for specific and highly localised damage on the basis of the nature of schizophrenic symptomatology, specific performance decrements on task, and comparisons with discrete organic populations. The fact that schizophrenic-like symptoms have been observed in certain neurological cases with circumscribed lesions has obviously spurred research into the neural mechanisms of the schizophrenic process. This should not, however, lead us necessarily to believe that these neural systems are simple and discrete. We have already seen that schizophrenic symptoms are apparent in some cases of dominant temporal lobe epilepsy. However, Elliot (1969) has observed a high rate of schizophrenic symptoms in patients with damage to the corpus callosum. Nasrallah (1982) also reports that delusions and hallucinations appear as significant features in patients with tumours involving the anterior part (genu) of the corpus callosum, suggesting that interruption of interhemispheric frontal lobe connections may be associated with schizophrenic symptoms.

Despite the similarities between left temporal lobe epilepsy, callosal damage and schizophrenia and the ability of derived models to explain schizophrenic symptoms it has to be remembered that there are also important *differences* in symptomatology between these disorders. Furthermore, several alternative cerebral loci may also play an important role. Thus Ross and Mesuram (1979) observed that right temporal lobe damage can affect the emotional components of verbal communication leading to a state akin to blunted affect. Damasio and Maurer (1978) also point out that the problems of motor-perceptual control exhibited by schizophrenics are more comparable to the aphasic based defects associated with the lesions to the cingulate gyrus than to dominant temporal lobe lesions. Also, the possibility that subcortical systems, such as the limbic system and the brain stem, might also contribute to the problems evident in schizophrenia suggests that future research needs to adopt, more so than at present, a three-dimensional approach to CNS function rather than an 'up-down' or 'left-right' perspective.

Whilst it is apparent that far fewer studies have been designed to investigate interhemispheric processes the hypothesis of a disturbance of interhemispheric communication and integration in schizophrenics has a certain heuristic appeal since it raises the possibility of a mal-functional interaction between the two hemispheres which may be positive in nature. A profound absence of connection, or disconnection, is not implied since this is usually accompanied by a loss of function rather than the presence of qualitatively unusual phenomena. Green, Hallett and Hunter (1983), Nasrallah (1982, 1985) and Randall (1983) have attempted to describe the phenomenology of Schneiderian First Rank Symptoms in terms of an interhemispheric model. They postulate that, in the presence of faulty interhemispheric communication, the right hemisphere's activity may interfere with and intrude into the left hemispheres awareness leading to a subjective interpretation of the intrusions as hallucinations, feelings of control, thought insertion, etc., arising from an independent source. This may then lead to delusional constructs in order to rationalise these perceived external and independent influences.

Ultimately, as Flor-Henry (1979) has pointed out, major disturbances of mood may not be explicable without reference to disturbances of interhemispheric processes; and it would seem reasonable to argue that the same applies to disturbances of language. This is highlighted in Flor-Henry's (1983) review of the research field where he states that it seems likely that unilateral dysfunction and transcallosal disturbance arise together and that schizophrenia may be a state dependent on loss of lateral cognitive specialisation. This statement and the suggestion that schizophrenia may be characterised by abnormal cerebral organisation is possibly one of the few inescapable conclusions to be drawn from the data.

Contrary to most interpretations, several authors have raised the possibility that the primary defect state in schizophrenia is one of right hemisphere dysfunction (e.g. Venables 1982). Schweitzer (1982) for example, has argued that left hemisphere overactivation observed in schizophrenics may represent a compensatory reaction to a fundamental right hemisphere defect, a view supported by Weller and Montagu (1979). Whilst some of the data presented here could be interpreted to reflect right hemisphere damage, the proponents of a primary right hemisphere defect state have tended to suggest that this occurs prior to the onset of schizophrenia, and that symptoms only become apparent when left hemisphere processes become involved. There is, however, little evidence in support of this contention. One of the most widely quoted studies in support of this view is that of Itil *et al.* (1974) who observed right sided EEG abnormalities in high-risk children. As we shall see later, these results are somewhat anomalous and require independent replication. In contrast, the overwhelming impression from studies of children at risk for schizophrenia is one of disturbed CNS integration and primarily verbal deficits (see Ch. 10).

Two further areas for development may help to clarify the relationship between abnormal cerebral organisation and schizophrenia. The first suggests the utility of adopting appropriate and multiple measures of laterality in the same groups, an approach already underway (Gruzelier 1983). Multiple assessment of the same processes, perhaps incorporating measures at different levels of analysis (e.g. regional blood flow, EEG, and a behavioural test) would seem to be a necessary avenue to determine the specificity and the precise CNS parameters of schizophrenic pathology. The second promising area involves studying samples of children considered at higher-than-average risk for schizophrenia by assessing neuromaturational parameters and applying methods which have revealed impairment of hemisphere function in adult patients. It is to this second area which we now turn our attention.

Chapter ten

HIGH-RISK RESEARCH

One of the most constant problems of research into adult schizophrenic patients concerns the degree to which the difficulties observed in patients reflect crucial and pathognomic signs, or whether they are consequent upon primary deficits characterising the disorder; whether they represent non-specific effects of psychosis or whether they reflect the effects of hospitalisation and medication. In our review of adult investigations it is evident that certain abnormalities appear to be specific to schizophrenia and are apparent in unmedicated patients and across a wide spectrum of patients (outpatient, long stay etc). Nevertheless it would be highly desirable to state definitively that a specific abnormality characterises schizophrenia and is of aetiological significance. Perhaps the only way of unravelling this problem is to study pre-schizophrenic individuals.

Having said this it is unlikely, given the complex nature of the disorder, that a single simple abnormality will be isolated which will invariably predict schizophrenia in 'marked' individuals. Nevertheless it may be feasible to identify types of abnormality which act as biological and psychological 'risk factors' and the potential importance of these discoveries justify the extensive methodological problems associated with this type of investigation. There are a number of ways in which this issue has been addressed: follow-up, follow-back and high-risk designations.

Follow-up studies involve scrutinising the historical records of, for example, a child guidance clinic and attempting to trace these individuals into adulthood. The aim is to identify specific problems in childhood requiring professional attention and to examine their relationship with adult psychiatric status – specifically schizophrenia. This approach has several shortcomings. First, retrospective research indicates that many adult schizophrenics are not seen in child guidance clinics and thus any schizophrenics identified may be unrepresentative of this population as a whole. Second, whilst the data obtained from clinics are not retrospective they are likely to be sketchy for research purposes and would be subject to differences in clinical interpretation, diagnosis and information-gathering procedures.

Follow-back methods initially identify adult schizophrenics and then attempt to recreate their 'pre-schizophrenic' life history, either by asking the subject or relatives to recollect the individual's history, or by tracing archival records (medical, social and school reports, etc). The former approach to recollection is considered to be extremely unreliable since any data are not only retrospective but are additionally biased by the knowledge of adult outcome. Data derived from archival records are free of this bias, but suffer from the problems of availability, reliability and validity. Most importantly, whilst the follow-back approach may be able to identify certain consistent characteristics in 'pre-schizophrenic' groups, it can be by no means certain that these are of any aetiological significance.

The third approach, the *high-risk* method, whilst also subject to several methodological problems, offers perhaps the only viable way of addressing the issue of aetiology. The follow-up and follow-back approaches are unable to provide sufficiently reliable information but may be of importance in identifying potential variables for study by the high-risk methodology; by identifying populations of children, assessing them on these variables, and then following them up longitudinally into the high-risk period.

This chapter concentrates only on the high-risk approach. For those readers wishing to pursue the other methodologies, we refer them to Neale and Oltmanns (1980) for an excellent review.

HIGH-RISK METHODOLOGY

The high-risk or prospective approach begins with the identification of children considered at risk for schizophrenia. High-risk may be defined in two specific ways. Some researchers have identified risk populations on the basis of subjects attaining high scores on tests of specific psychological characteristics known to be elevated in adult patient populations. Thus Claridge (pers. comm.) has identified at-risk populations on the basis of attaining high scores on the psychoticism scale of the EPQ. Venables (pers. comm.) has also identified such populations characterised by high anhedonia scores, and Coursey *et al.* (1979) defined their sample on the basis of biochemical assay – the observation of low blood levels of monoamine oxidase. More traditionally, high-risk has been defined in genetic terms and refers to the elevated risk for inheriting the disorder. The offspring of schizophrenics (who have a morbidity risk of some 10 per cent compared to the general population risk of 1 per cent) have therefore been the main target group for research. Of these two criteria, logistically the latter is more realistic since the former approach entails the follow-up of a general population sample in whom the average risk is only 1 per cent and would therefore require the inclusion of vast numbers of subjects to identify, for analysis, a large enough group of individuals who subsequently break down.

The ideal high-risk project might comprise the assessment of children of schizophrenics (as well as the schizophrenic and non-schizophrenic parents) at various stages before the risk period (beginning at approximately the fifteenth year), and on several measures, to attempt to isolate abnormalities which might predict later psychopathology (such as the identification of abnormalities previously observed in adult schizophrenics), and then to follow the children regularly through into the risk period identifying any individuals who break down. Furthermore, ideally, follow up should continue until the *end* of the defined risk period, particularly if the rate of breakdown is to be utilised as evidence for a specific model of genetic transmission. The enormity of this task is only too apparent given the length of time and resources needed for the research and the number of potential variables one might wish to assess.

High-risk research carries with it many advantages. For example, since data are collected currently and in an unbiased fashion neither the experimenter nor the family know who will eventually break-down. The approach also offers the potential of including an additional control group over and above the inclusion of psychiatric and normal controls. Thus at follow-up the high-risk children can be subdivided into those who remain well and compared with those who exhibit evidence of psychopathology. Such an approach has been an important component of the Copenhagen project initiated by Mednick and co-workers (although such comparisons with a 'well' group must remain tentative since some of these may break down eventually at a later stage in the risk period).

Whilst superior to other methodologies there are, of course, several distinct drawbacks. Thus whilst it may be possible to identify differences between high-risk and control groups, these differences may be due to the operation of a large set of variables and several alternative hypotheses need to be ruled out before specifying the locus of an effect. Similarly, identifiable differences in the 'here-and-now', whilst being of interest in their own right, are only of importance from an aetiological perspective if they predict important characteristics in the future. Whilst this problem is alleviated to some degree if these differences are comparable to those demonstrated in adult patients, the issue can only be definitively resolved by long-term follow-up of some ten to twenty years. The length of time required for this approach may be associated with demoralising consequences since, during the intervening twenty years, fresh data may effectively rule out the initial observations as valid precursors and consequently severely weaken the foundations of the research. It may also be the case in the absence of the above that the premorbid abnormalities do not, in the final analysis, predict breakdown.

A third problem concerns the definition of high-risk in terms of parentage. Since only 10 per cent of schizophrenics have parents who are themselves schizophrenic, it may be argued that the at-risk offspring of schizophrenic parents and the parents themselves are unrepresentative of the groups as a whole. Finally, several practical problems confront the high-risk researcher, the most notable of which concerns the issue of matching across groups. The task of matching samples, firstly by matching parents and then children is an enormous one and often results in the exclusion of a large number of potential subjects and variables of interest. For example, handedness may be controlled in studies investigating cerebral functioning, usually by restricting one's sample to right handers. However, if handedness is an important index of cerebral organisation it would be an important variable to observe. As an example, Hallett and Green (1983) observed an excess of left handedness in the male offspring of schizophrenics, but not females or controls. This would seem to be an interesting observation, and the exclusion of left handers might effectively have excluded an important subgroup.

This raises two general issues regarding matching. First, what should we match for? Most researchers would agree that age, sex, and socio-economic status should be matched across groups. There is, however, disagreement as to whether intelligence, social stability and emotional functioning should be matched, particularly as high-risk children seem to perform badly on tests designed to measure these functions (Gruzelier *et al.* 1979; Weintraub *et al.* 1978).

The second issue relates to the effects of matching across groups. Whether we begin the matching process with the high-risk or the control sample it is possible that matching on a number of variables results in one or both groups becoming unrepresentative of the population it seeks to define. Some authors have attempted to rectify this problem by including a second normal control group which is either modestly matched, or not matched at all, to the other groups (e.g. Neuchterlein 1983). It is of interest that in Neucherterlein's study his tightly matched normal controls did, in fact, perform more poorly on a vigilance task than his loosely matched or stratified normal controls.

To summarise, high-risk research essentially comprises two phases: a cross-sectional phase in which the children and controls are compared on various tasks, and a longitudinal phase in which the children are followed up over a period of some years to observe breakdown. These two phases may be accelerated by testing several groups of children in definable and overlapping age ranges (e.g. 3–7, 5–9, 7–11 etc). This accelerated longitudinal approach evaluates a vast age range (including well into the risk period) assessed at the same time. Its major drawback is achieving continuity across the groups and in equating test procedures such that they measure the same variables within each group. So far most studies have either completed, or have restricted themselves to, the cross-sectional phase. The notable exceptions to this are the studies by Fish and Mednick who have now followed up their samples well into the risk period.

CROSS-SECTIONAL STUDIES

In an attempt to discover the antecedents of schizophrenia, most researchers have either explicitly or implicitly assumed the primacy of a neurobiological abnormality in schizophrenia. We agree with this assumption and we would argue that this primary neurobiological state serves to constrain learning experiences and might itself be modifiable by the opportunities for learning interpersonally, in other words, a transactional approach. Following these assumptions it would seem rational to vary one's assessment battery as a function of the child's age. Thus, as Garmezy (1978) points out, it might be more fruitful to investigate neurobiological indices during infancy and early childhood but to increase the scope of the assessment procedures to include assessment of personal and interpersonal indices during late childhood and adolescence. Certainly the techniques employed to investigate neurobiological states may have to be modified according to age, particularly if the primary defect is 'soft' in nature and reflects developmental delay or deviation and hence may be masked during later childhood.

Most studies within the high-risk paradigm have concentrated on neurobiological variables and this review will largely restrict itself to those investigations. For reviews of purely 'sociological' studies we refer the reader to Wynne *et al.* (1978) and Neale and Oltmanns (1980).

A number of cross-sectional studies have utilised, as their sample, individuals from the cohort identified by Mednick and colleagues in Copenhagen. We begin our review with this sample and with Mednick's own research. Mednick considered that schizophrenia was a learned thought disorder produced by autonomic hyperactivity. He regarded tangential and irrelevant thoughts as reinforced avoidance responses which serve to reduce autonomic arousal by diverting an individual's attention away from anxiety producing stimuli. Mednick thus hypothesised that schizophrenics' skin conductance levels (as in index of autonomic arousal) in response to auditory stimuli (as an experimental analogue of stress) would be characterised by autonomic hyperresponsivity, excessive generalisation and slow recovery from states of autonomic imbalance. These hypotheses were formulated some twenty years ago, since when independent research has offered little consistent support for them.

Mednick and Schulsinger (1968) demonstrated that compared to normal children the high-risk offspring of schizophrenics exhibited higher GSR amplitude and shorter latency responses to stress stimuli, greater responsivity to generalisation stimuli and less habituation to stress stimuli. Whilst these results were in accord with the general hypothesis of autonomic hyperactivity, a further finding, that the high-risk group recovered *more* quickly than controls, was not. Independent attempts to replicate these findings have produced inconsistent results. Garmezy (1978) reports that Erlenmeyer-Kimling's initial investigations observed no differences between high-risk and normal children although her sample size of 29 is somewhat modest compared to Mednick's sample of 207. Furthermore, the Rosenthal study (Van Dyke *et al.* 1974) provided no evidence of autonomic hyperactivity in at-risk individuals and the Rochester group were able to replicate only two of Mednick's findings, neither recovery time nor habituation differed between groups (Salzman and Kelin 1978).

Gruzelier *et al.* (1979) report IQ differences between a subsample of the Copenhagen high-risk group and controls which were similar to those observed in adult schizophrenics. Their sample of seventy high-risk children aged between ten and thirteen years, matched for age, sex, race and social class with normal and psychiatric controls, were required to complete subtests of the Wechsler Intelligence Scale for Children. Whilst no differences were apparent on performance, or non-verbal, subtests (Block Design and Object Assembly) the high-risk children performed at a significantly lower level on the verbal subtests of Vocabulary and Similarities compared to both control groups, the effect being to produce an overall reduction in Verbal IQ. Gruzelier *et al.* (1979) also report that the high-risk sample performed badly on the Mazes subtest, a test which has been shown to be of discriminative importance in the identification of temporal lobe cases and has additionally been used to measure impulsivity related to hippocampal involvement.

The authors conclude that these results are consistent with dominant hemisphere involvement, particularly implicating the dominant temporal-hippocampal systems. The results are also similar to those obtained from adult patients (Gruzelier and Hammond 1976) who exhibited WAIS deficits on the Vocabulary, Similarities and Comprehension subtests relative to Block Design and Object Assembly. In global terms, however, the psychiatric control children performed midway between the high-risk and normal controls on verbal subtests (and significantly different from both) raising the alternative explanation that the effects may reflect adverse environmental factors which may be more severe in schizophrenic than 'other' psychiatric families.

Itil *et al.* (1974) and Simeon and Itil (1975) report EEG findings on high-risk children, adult schizophrenics, normal controls and psychotic children – the high-risk sample being derived from the Copenhagen cohort. Computer analysis of ongoing EEG records indicated that the high-risk children exhibited more slow delta, more fast beta, less alpha and higher average frequencies, similar to the EEG abnormalities evident in adult patients. In contradistinction to the adults, however, the most significant difference between the high-risk and controls was between the right parietal and temporal leads. Analysis of Auditory Evoked Potentials indicated shorter latencies in the adult schizophrenics, high-risk children and unmedicated psychotic children (for the psychotic children the abnormalities became 'normalised' after pharmacotherapy). Amplitude differences observed between adult patients and normals in this and other studies were not observed in the high-risk population. Itil *et al.* (1974) conclude that shorter latencies 'may indicate a potential for schizophrenia whilst amplitudes are only affected when the disease is clinically manifest in adulthood'. More generally, they suggest that the abnormal EEG findings are consistent with a hyperarousal which is highly variable and suggest that they reflect deficiencies in hemispheric specialisation well before the onset of illness. Erlenmeyer-Kimling *et al.* (1982) have however pointed out a number of discrepancies in Itil's findings. Perhaps the most important and irreconcilable difficulty concerns the fact that, whilst computer analysis of their data indicates less fast waves and alpha, more fast beta and higher average frequencies in the high-risk group, visual inspection of the data points to the exact reverse of this pattern. Furthermore, Hermon *et al.* (1977) report few EEG differences between high-risk and control subjects engaged on a sustained visual attention task with only a slight but non-significant increase in beta activity over the left hemisphere. Other studies utilising evoked potentials have also failed to replicate the clearcut findings of Itil.

Friedman *et al.* (1979) and Hermon *et al.* (1977) both report *longer* latencies in high-risk children to auditory and visual stimuli respectively. The latter also observed larger amplitudes at 100–200 milliseconds post-stimulus and Friedman *et al.* (1980) observed smaller late positive amplitudes (P350 + P400). This latter finding of reduced late-positive amplitude is similar to the observations in adult schizophrenics. Erlenmeyer-Kimling (1968, 1977) suggest that this latter finding and her own observations of longer latencies may reflect poor attentional span and concentration.

Marcus (1974) reports on two separate and ongoing high-risk studies in Israel in which general indices of cerebral function were ascertained in the offspring of schizophrenics and normals. The first study, initiated in 1965, comprised fifty high-risk and fifty normal controls matched in terms of age, sex and social background. Each group was further divided into those children reared in city-based nuclear families and those reared in kibbutzim. Several tests including GSR, IQ and attainment tests, decision making, and a neurological examination were carried out. Test results were interpreted individually and in combined fashion to provide a cumulative record of cerebral functioning. For each type of analysis both groups were divided by age into a 7–11 age range and 11–15. Whilst no significant differences emerged in the older age groups, on the cumulative record a clearly defined proportion of the younger high-risk group achieved high scores, indicative of non-optimal functioning and delayed CNS maturation. Fully 50 per cent of the high-risk group fell within the maximal range of non-optimal functioning whilst the other 50 per cent and most of the normal children fell within the optimum range.

Marcus considers this as additional evidence for the operation of a single dominant gene for schizophrenia (which 50 per cent of the offspring would receive). The lack of significant differences on the cumulative scores between the older groups may reflect either a masking of the 'soft' maturational delays or the fact that the tests used, which were largely developmental examinations, may have been relatively insensitive when used with the older children. On individual subtests, the high-risk group as a whole were characterised by some degree of delay in general motor development and in right-left orientation, perception and intersensory (auditory-visual) integration – these differences being more significant in the younger group. Finally, within the high-risk group the 'city-reared' children were described as more pathological than kibbutz-reared children both in terms of the cumulative score and on specific tests of motor development, reflecting the ability of environmental rearing conditions to constrain or ameliorate the manifestation of neuromaturational abnormality. Marcus' second study on an infant population is still in its initial phases, however preliminary analysis (Marcus *et al.* 1984) is suggestive of neurointegrative disturbances in motor and sensorimotor processes in a subgroup of the high risk children.

A similar investigation of neuro-motor performance was undertaken by Hanson *et al.* (1976) on children aged 0–7 years. As well as high-risk children this study contained psychiatric controls and two normal controls – matched and unmatched. On a variety of physical and neurological tests they found no significant differences between groups except on three indices, poor motor skills, large intrapersonal test score variance and schizoid behaviour at ages 4–7 years. On a combination of these three indicators, 17 per cent of the high-risk children compared to none of the controls were identified. It was observed that on all three indicators taken in isolation the non-matched normal controls were superior to matched controls. Thus, 21 per cent of the matched normals exhibited poor motor skills compared to 7 per cent for the non-matched group; 28 per cent versus 19 per cent on test score variance; and 10 per cent versus 0 per cent exhibiting schizoid behaviour. A final point of interest was that the authors observed no significant differences between groups in terms of the prevalence of pregnancy and birth complications.

There is, overall, a considerable degree of disparity between studies investigating neurological development and maturation in young high-risk samples. Erlenmeyer-Kimling (1982) reviewed eight such studies and concluded that four provided evidence of abnormal delays, three provided negative findings, and the results of one was inconclusive. In all studies, however, discrete abnormalities are found, the single most consistent sign being an impairment of fine motor co-ordination.

Recently Hallett and Green (1983) reported on a relatively small scale investigation of high-risk children to determine whether at risk children might exhibit similar deficits to adult schizophrenics on tests inferred to assess interhemispheric integration (Green and Kotenko 1980; Green, Hallett and Hunter 1983). On a test of complex auditory comprehension delivered under monaural and binaural listening conditions, the high-risk children (matched on age, sex, and verbal intelligence to a normal control group) displayed significant binaural deficits, larger but statistically non-significant monaural asymmetries and poorer overall performance than the normals, similar to the problems exhibited by adult patients. Additionally, the high-risk children performed significantly worse on a test of phoneme discrimination and the group as a whole were characterised by an excess of left-handers. The authors considered these results to provide initial evidence of defective interhemispheric integration prior to the onset of illness and suggest that these may indicate abnormal developmental cerebral maturation and specialisation.

More recently, Hallett *et al.* (1986) confirmed the above findings on a larger but independent sample of high-risk and normal children. In addition to the observation of significant binaural performance, the high-risk group displayed an absence of the normal right ear advantage on a Verbal Dichotic Listening Test. As a whole these results were taken as indicative of abnormal interhemispheric integration and abnormal language lateralisation in children at risk for schizophrenia. Statistical analysis indicated the interhemispheric abnormality to be the primary variable and it was suggested that results reflected a primary abnormality in corpus callosum maturation which subsequently interferes with the process of functional lateralisation of language.

Finally, a number of cross-sectional analyses have investigated attentional processes in high-risk children. Many of these studies have used a variation of the continuous performance test. The results have been somewhat varied and this probably reflects the slight alterations in test procedure and additional methodological and sampling practices. The results of both Erlenmeyer-Kimling *et al.*'s (1982) investigations and of Neuchterlein (1983) indicate that high-risk children perform more poorly than controls. The application of signal detection theory suggests that this performance decrement reflects reduced perceptual sensitivity and attention to stimuli in contrast, for example, to hyperactive children who respond poorly because of reduced motivation.

The overall results of cross-sectional investigations point to abnormalities of arousal and attention (demonstrated electrophysiologically, psychophysiologically and behaviourally), poor fine motor performance and possible specific delays or abnormalities in the maturation of the central nervous system. At this stage, however, it is impossible to determine the relationship between observed difficulties and adult pathology since these projects have not been in progress long enough to identify schizophrenic breakdown. In fact relatively few studies have achieved this longer term goal, the most notable exceptions being the studies of Mednick and of Fish.

THE LONGITUDINAL PERSPECTIVE

In their 1973 review of the Copenhagen study, Mednick and Schulsinger report that twenty of the high-risk group had suffered severe psychiatric breakdown. Thirteen had been admitted to a psychiatric hospital 'with many diagnoses of schizophrenia' and the seven not admitted 'included some who were clearly schizophrenic'. Matching these twenty 'sick' children to a further twenty high-risk individuals who remained well, Mednick and Schulsinger (1973) report that the 'sick' group were characterised by abnormalities in autonomic functioning consistent with hyperactivity. In more global terms, however, it is pertinent that whilst roughly 10 per cent of the high-risk group had broken down, as a whole the GSR measures were unable in any systematic way to distinguish between this 10 per cent and the remaining 90 per cent who remained well. Furthermore, Schulsinger (1976) reports on a small group who had 'definitely' become schizophrenic, and it is interest that only four of these came from the previous 'sick' group.

One specific issue which Mednick focuses on in great depth is that within the 'sick' group 70 per cent had suffered one or more serious pregnancy or birth complications (PBCs) compared to 15 per cent in the 'well' group and 33 per cent of the normal controls, and that the presence of PBCs strongly correlated with the electrodermal differences reported by Mednick and Schulsinger (1968). Mednick concentrated on the fact that anoxia at birth might impair hippocampal functioning which is first, selectively vulnerable to anoxia and secondly, plays a significant role in conditioned autonomic behaviour – lesions of the hippocampus resulting in the sort of autonomic abnormalities observed in the high-risk children. However this report of increased PBCs and Mednick's subsequent observations have not been replicated by recent studies, notably those of Gottesman and Shields (1977) and Hanson *et al.* (1976). Whilst there is some evidence that lowered birth weight may be associated with future breakdown and might in some cases represent a 'risk increasing' factor, the problem with Mednick's analysis was that he combined a number of PBCs (anoxia, prolonged labour, breech presentation, prematurity, mother's illness in pregnancy) as if they were a single category and as if they all had the same effect. Both Hanson *et al.* (1976) and Fish (1975) additionally point out that developmental delays resulting from such pregnancy and obstetric complications rarely continue after the first year of postnatal life, whereas genetically determined lags are more persistent. Furthermore, Mednick's interpretation of these data in terms of neonatal damage to the hippocampus is, to a large extent, based on animal studies (Kessler and Neale 1974; Neale and Oltmanns 1980). The results of more contemporary animal investigations suggest that there is no reason to believe that the hippocampus of the human neonate is *selectively* vulnerable to anoxia.

The second study to incorporate a longitudinal perspective is that of Fish. This study began in the early 1960s and comprised a small group of high-risk and normal children. Fish's studies were essentially clinical in nature, the subjects being identified through her own clinical network.

Only very recently (Fish 1984) has information been reported on adult breakdown. Prior to that Fish was concerned with childhood breakdowns and, in particular, with childhood schizophrenia. Fish (1977) has argued for a continuity between childhood and adult schizophrenia on the basis of three observations. First, on the basis of similarities in clinical phenomenology between the two disorders; secondly in terms of a genetic continuity, that the rates of schizophrenia in the parents of childhood schizophrenics are as high as the rates in parents of adult schizophrenics (and that adult schizophrenia tends to cluster in the families of childhood schizophrenics); and thirdly on the basis of diagnostic continuity – children diagnosed as schizophrenics are frequently and independently diagnosed as schizophrenic in adulthood.

In a series of investigations of neurological maturation in high-risk infants, followed through initially to the age of ten, Fish (1977) observed evidence of major disorganisation in neurological maturation involving postural-motor, visual-motor, and physical development. Rather than being of 'fixed' neurological status Fish regarded these abnormalities as being a defect in the timing and integration of neurological maturation and has referred to this complex of defects as 'Pandevelopmental Retardation', or PDR (and, more recently, Pandysmaturation [(Fish 1984]). PDR was significantly related to psychiatric morbidity at ten years of age, perhaps the most significant observation being the relationship between a failure at four months to achieve intermanual integration and severe to moderate psychopathology at ten years (all children rated as having severe/moderate psychopathology had experienced delays in hand-hand integration). Fish argues that these delays of neurological integration are the analogue of disorders of higher integrative functions seen in older children and adult patients. In addition, since none of the children with PDR had experienced pregnancy or birth complications (and none of the children with PBCs had shown PDR) Fish argues that the reported difficulties in integration reflect genetically determined developmental delay. Recently Fish (1984) has reported a similar relationship between psychopathology at ages 20–22 and PDR attesting both to the significance of her observations at the fourth month of life and to her own assumptions of a relationship between childhood and adult psychosis.

Regrettably, at present, there are few other significant results to emerge from the ongoing high-risk projects. Overall the results indicate that specific electrophysiological, neurological and cognitive difficulties may characterise high-risk populations and may be important precursors to adult illness. Fish's study, whilst subject to criticism, has provided perhaps the most important link between neurobiological abnormalities in early life and later psychopathology.

It is evident that high-risk research has both enormous costs but also the potential of vast rewards. Most studies have addressed the question as to whether it is possible to predict the development of schizophrenia from premorbid characteristics. Garmezy (1978) has however raised a more fundamental issue; that we should be tracking the complete development of children born to schizophrenics through infancy, childhood, adolescence and early maturity. As we have seen, some researchers are addressing this issue with the additional cost of adding a further 10–20 years to the life of a project. Unlike other research where studies may be conceived, planned and completed within a few years, the risk researcher must achieve a compromise between the excitement of potential results and the patience, and perhaps diffidence to await them. One can only agree with Garmezy's observations that:

> These ills beset all risk investigators – the long journey to disorder, the restricted samples, the difficulty of ascertainment of offspring, the uncertainty of parental diagnosis, the absence or elusive presence of signs of disorder in the offspring, the difficulty of data analysis, the absence of psychiatric registries and the limitations of case record data. These are limitations that are the way of the research lives of those of us who study risk for schizophrenia. Diffidence is not in and of itself a virtue, but I believe that it can keep us from leaping to too rapid a conclusion that the resolution of the enormously complex problem of the aetiology of schizophrenia is just around the risk researcher's corner (Garmezy 1978: 471–2).

Whilst not around the corner, we await with anticipation the results of these labours.

Part three

ENVIRONMENTAL FACTORS

Chapter eleven

THE ENVIRONMENT AND AETIOLOGY

TWIN STUDIES FROM AN ENVIRONMENTAL PERSPECTIVE

The twin study paradigm is a favoured approach for the testing of genetic hypothesis as it represents the only naturalistic means of varying gene dosage under conditions where environmental factors are theoretically held constant (see Ch. 4). Equally, the paradigm can provide information on the extent of the environmental (i.e. non-genetic) contribution, this being in proportion to the overall *discordance* for schizophrenia between genetically identical twins where one co-twin has developed the disorder. In addition, a comparison of discordant MZ twins might identify environmental variables responsible for the triggering of schizophrenia in genetically vulnerable individuals. Thus, although environmental variables are not directly manipulated (unlike the adoption studies – p. 33) the technique is, potentially, highly informative from an environmental point of view.

Doubts have been raised about the validity of the twin-study method which will naturally constrain the above prospectus. The strongest criticism has come from environmentalists who argue on the basis of firm empirical evidence from normal twins that MZ twins tend to be managed in a similar fashion by their parents (vs DZ twins) and tend to have the same friends (Lytton 1977) thereby invalidating the assumption that environment is held constant. However the only reason why MZ twins should be treated similarly is because either they are perceived as similar by virtue of their monozygosity or parents respond to pre-existing behavioural similarities in the twins. Regarding the former, studies exist of twins whose zygosity has been misclassified and in these cases behavioural similarities result from *true* zygosity rather than *perceived* zygosity (Scarr, Carter and Saltzman 1979). Lytton (1977 op. cit.) has

147

confirmed in an ethological study of forty-six normal male twins that similarities in parental management represent *responses* to similar behaviours and that *parent-initiated* behaviours were similar among MZ and DZ twins.

Thus the available evidence from normal twin pairs suggests that the rearing environment of MZ twins is more similar than those of DZ pairs but that this is the result of behavioural similarities of MZ twins.

Gottesman and Shield's (1983) presentation of the twin study data, standardising diagnoses across studies, find the concordance rates average 46 per cent (range 35% to 58%) for MZ twins and 14 per cent (range 9% to 27%) for DZ twins, thus clearly high-lighting a genetic factor. There is also of course an equally large *dis*cordance in the MZ twin (54%) suggesting that an environmental factor protects against the full expression of the genotype or, alternatively, acts in conjunction with the necessary genotype. It would appear on the surface that non-genetic factors are of equal importance in their contribution to the overall liability to the development of schizophrenia.

There is unfortunately no simple equation between concordance rates and the relative contribution of genetics and environment. The overall population incidence of a disease will have a considerable bearing on the expected MZ concordance rates. Smith (1970) has calculated theoretical concordance rates in relation to the overall heritability of liability and population incidence, on the assumption that genetic and environmental contributions are normally distributed. Thus, if a disease has no heritability, then the MZ co-twin will develop the disease with equal probability to other members of the population (i.e. the concordance rate = population incidence); if the liability is 100 per cent heritable then the concordance rate will be 100 per cent independent of population incidence. In between these extremes the predictions are surprising. Assuming a life-time risk for schizophrenia of 1 per cent, if the heritability (see Ch. 4 for definition) is 50 per cent then the predicted MZ concordance rate will be as low as 13 per cent; a heritability of 80 per cent will yield a concordance rate of 37 per cent. The implication is that the observed 46 per cent MZ concordance rate suggests a very major contribution of genotype to the overall liability (see Ch. 4). One further consideration to be borne in mind is that in those twin studies which have reported on the characteristics of the discordant MZ twin, between approximately one quarter and one half were diagnosed 'schizoid' or evidencing 'character/neurotic' disorders. Thus only 23 per cent of Gottesman and Shields' (1972) discordant sample and 33 per cent of Kringlen's (1967) were considered 'normal'. If a broader definition of the psychopathology were adopted, the MZ concordance rate would be even higher.

How then are we to evaluate the significance of environmental factors in the light of these findings? First, of course, the twin study results do support a contribution of environment to the overall liability, amounting to some 20 per cent of the variance. However estimates of heritability will vary according to the level of environmental variability: with little environmental variation, genetic factors will appear to predominate in individual differences and conversely the greater the environmental variability. For this reason heritability estimates for IQ derived from twin studies for example have been criticised as they do not permit the widest possible variation in environment thereby spuriously increasing heritability; when relevant environmental variables are allowed to vary (e.g. social class), IQ heritability is significantly affected (Clarke and Clarke 1974). The same argument might equally apply to twin studies in schizophrenia; that is, the relevant gene dosage is systematically varied whereas relevant environmental factors are unknown and presumably not varied to their greatest extent. Therefore studies such as these do not provide an accurate picture of the influence of environment, and, in particular, the estimation of a 20 per cent contribution of environment to the overall liability must be considered a minimum figure.

Furthermore, under certain models of the genetic-environmental interaction, a situation can be conceived where the environmental influence might outweigh other factors. If it is assumed that normally distributed genetic and environmental factors operate additively in some way to achieve a threshold of liability for the expression of the schizophrenia phenotype, then it is plausible that a sub-group of schizophrenics exist whose liability principally comprises the environmental pathogen. Support for this possibility comes from studies of perinatal complications and season of birth in schizophrenia which are reviewed later.

In summary, the twin studies unequivocally point to a major genetic contribution; however they point also to an essential environmental component, which could well be underestimated and in some cases outweigh genetic factors.

DISCORDANT MONOZYGOTIC TWINS

The elegance and simplicity of this method of isolating environmental factors through comparisons of differences between discordant MZ twins is balanced by some difficult methodological problems. First, any attempt to study *ongoing* socio-environmental differences between twins is confounded by the likelihood that any such differences will, to an unknown degree, *reflect* differences between the twins (see previous section). Realistically, the investigator must concentrate on retrospective data which preferably should be archival (i.e. written records prior to the illness onset) as parental retrospective accounts may again be influenced by knowledge of the twins' adult status. As archival data on familial, interpersonal and social variables are rare and idiosyncratic, the method is really only suited to quasi-objective data such as birth, developmental and school records.

Undoubtedly the most comprehensive analysis has been undertaken by Pollin and colleagues in the USA, who located eleven discordant pairs, rising to seventeen by 1974 (some pairs were later excluded because the discordant twin later developed schizophrenia). A range of variables were studied, but by and large the results were disappointing. Mosher *et al.* (1971) found no differences between twins in closeness or identification with parents but did find that parents report a poorer self-image in the affected twin. In a different sample Gottesman and Shields (1972) also find that affected probands were more submissive or withdrawn as children but, as this tends to be both a characteristic and a premorbid trait of schizophrenia, its environmental significance is uncertain. No differences were found by the Pollin group in MOA activity (Wyatt *et al.* 1973) or in neurological soft signs (Mosher *et al.* 1971). Clear differences did emerge in birth weight. Of the twelve clearly discordant twins with good birth records, ten showed a pattern of lower birth weight in the affected twin. This suggests that some intra-uterine experience associated with lower birth weight may be involved. A meta-analysis of birth weight data by Gottesman and Shields (1983) from five twin studies suggest that this observation may be chance as only 49 per cent of the eighty-seven discordant twin pairs showed this pattern, although when it does occur there can be up to a 20 per cent difference in birth weight.

Perhaps the most striking result was reported by Boklage (1977) who examined the correlation between the concordance for handedness and schizophrenia using the British sample of Gottesman and Shields (1977). He found that in the twelve pairs concordant for right handedness, eleven were concordant for schizophrenia; of the sixteen pairs not concordant for right handedness, only four were concordant for schizophrenia. The degree of concordance for schizophrenia found in the subgroup concordant for *right* handedness is unparalleled in twin study research. This group may represent that theoretical part of the distribution of genetic risk where only a minimal environmental contribution is required to trigger schizophrenia. It would have been interesting if the concordant and discordant groups were contrasted for the level of genetic risk (i.e. family history of schizophrenia) as one might anticipate a lower risk in the handedness-discordant group as clearly some environmental factor has intervened in one co-twin to produce a schizophrenic breakdown.

What kind of environmental factor may lead to differences in the cerebral organisation underlying handedness in genetically identical individuals? One possibility is that the twins' embryonic development might have differed. This can often occur in normal MZ twins sharing the same chorionic membrane where, as a result of transfusions of blood between the twins during their development, one twin can be lighter and generally frail. This might account for discordance and also for the observations of greatly reduced birth weight in some affected MZ twins. Another possibility relates to the well accepted finding that early cerebral insult can lead to a compensatory reorganisation of cerebral function. Pre or perinatal trauma with cerebral sequelae may have affected one twin, leading to cerebral reorganisation and a greater risk for schizophrenia (perinatal problems are more prevalent among twins).

There are two findings which lend strong support to this second possibility. First, pregnancy and birth complications, known correlates of brain damage, are more frequently found among the schizophrenic member of MZ twins discordant for schizophrenia (Pollin and Stabenau 1968). More direct support comes from recent studies in the UK of CT scans of the brain performed on twenty-one MZ twin pairs including twelve discordant and nine concordant for schizophrenia, compared with matched normal twin controls. Reverley *et al.* (1982) found little or no intra-pair difference in cerebral ventricular size in normal twins, but among MZ twins discordant for schizophrenia the intra-pair difference was significantly greater and the schizophrenics had consistently larger ventricles than either the normal co-twins or normal controls. This was followed up (Reveley *et al.* 1984 by a related study examining the relationship between the level of genetic risk, ventricular enlargement and complications of birth in a group of twenty-one schizophrenics from twenty one MZ twin pairs. Their major finding was that ventricular size was very much greater among those with a *low* genetic risk p < 0.01). There was also evidence of birth complications in association with low-risk schizophrenia but unlike the normal controls, where ventricular size correlated strongly with birth complications, this did *not* replicate in the schizophrenics, suggesting that enlarged ventricles *and* birth complications are independent risk factors in schizophrenia. One weak aspect of the Reveley's study is that birth history was assessed retrospectively by interviewing mothers who were, of course, aware of their offspring's adult status.

The studies of discordant monozygotic twins have provided valuable insights into a possible environmental agent in schizophrenia. On the basis of the two studies by Reveley *et al.* which controlled for genetic risk it may be inferred that a high genetic risk requires little in the way of an environmental event to raise the liability above a threshold necessary for the expression of the phenotype. In those of lower genetic risk the requirements are greater in that the environmental event(s) needed to trigger the disorder is such as to lead to some subtle form of CNS dysfunction and, more speculatively, an abnormal cerebral organisation of function. Two environmental agents are suggested: birth or prenatal injury and embryonic malfunction (the latter being sometimes viral in origin and season related). These possibilities have been tested in numerous studies of singleton births to which we now turn.

SEASON AND PLACE OF BIRTH

Barry and Barry (1961) were among the first to demonstrate an excess of winter births among individuals later emerging as schizophrenic. This finding was later replicated by Hare and Price (1968) who confirmed that the phenomenon is confined to schizophrenic and not neurotic individuals. Patterns of reproduction in normal populations are never even across the seasons and generally there is a sinusoidal rise and fall in births throughout seasons of the year which can vary with each quinquennium. A stratified control group is therefore essential to compare with natural variations in birth rate. Subsequent large scale population studies in Sweden (Dalen 1974), Norway (Ødegard 1974), Japan (Shimura *et al.* 1977), Britain (Hare *et al.* 1974) and the USA (Torrey *et al.* 1977) have replicated the effect, demonstrating a winter excess of schizophrenic births averaging 15 per cent. The months with the excess vary from study to study, but generally fall in the December to April period. Parker and Neilson (1976) and Jones and Frei (1979) have replicated the effect in Australia – where of course winter falls in the middle of the year – and find an excess in the months of June, July and August.

What might account for this unusual phenomenon? The obvious explanation which comes to mind is that parents of schizophrenics simply show a different pattern of procreation; however this is disproved since the pattern is not shown in respect of their non-schizophrenic siblings. Lewis and Griffin (1981) have offered an explanation for the effect in terms of a methodological artefact.

They argue that those born *later* in any given year will be younger and therefore will, on average, have had fewer months at risk, whereas those born earlier in the year (i.e. the winter months) will have been at risk longer and therefore show a greater incidence of schizophrenia. They support this by an analysis of the births of over 10,000 schizophrenic patients in Missouri, USA. Lewis and Griffin found the usual winter excess but when they corrected for the excess period at risk, the effect disappears. This simple demonstration appeared to have invalidated a great deal of previous research. However the 'age prevalence' effect cannot account for the replications in the southern hemisphere (i.e. excess in June, July and August) nor for observations in some studies of excesses in December. Watson *et al.* (1982) and Shur and Hare (1983) both attempted to replicate Lewis and Griffin's study using different data. Both studies replicated the birth-season effect but in neither case was the effect influenced by the age prevalence correction. Indeed Shur and Hare analysed data separately for those under twenty-one years, for whom the impact of up to twelve months additional risk period should be greater, and again the birth-season effect remained.

The effect itself is quite modest but there is a possibility that it is much greater in subgroups of the schizophrenia spectrum. This was suggested initially by Dalen (1974) who found that a subgroup selected for a relatively good prognosis (less than three years' hospitalisation) showed a more pronounced birth-season effect than his 'chronic' group. This hypothesis was supported by Pulver *et al.* (1983) in a young sample divided into good and poor prognosis on the basis of length of hospitalisation; they found a very marked winter excess only in the 'good' prognosis group. This research team also found a more pronounced effect for females (Pulver *et al.* 1981) but of the seven studies examining a sex difference, four find the season effect more marked in females, one finds males more pronounced and two find no sex difference.

Another subgroup with a more marked birth-season effect could be the early onset group: Pulver *et al.* (1983) find a 36 per cent excess of winter births in their young (17–23 years) schizophrenic group which is over twice that found in other studies which use a broader age range.

Genetic risk is a further possible interacting factor. Kinney and Jacobsen (1978) in a sample of thirty-four adopted schizophrenic patients found that a winter excess was present only in those with a low genetic risk (i.e. no family history of the disorder). Shur (1982), in a much larger study in London finds a trend towards a winter excess in his low-risk group but conversely a winter deficit in the high-risk group, although his study did not find a significant overall winter excess. Machon *et al.* (1983) find genetic risk an interacting factor when *overall* psychopathology is the dependent variable but in this case it is the *high-risk* group which is more prone to the winter-birth effect. The significance of this genetic risk effect is severely weakened as, in using subjects from Mednick and Schulsinger's (1968) prospective Danish study, their low-risk group was still young at follow-up and only one (out of 104) was schizophrenic, which represents the population average. These authors do find a birth-season effect in their high-risk group when the dependent variable is the presence or absence of schizophrenia.

Overall then the finding of an excess of winter births in schizophrenia seems to be a reliable phenomenon and to be most marked in the better prognosis group and possibly in females and those of early onset.

The principal reason for the intense interest in this phenomenon is the possibility that season-related environmental agents might be responsible for the elevated risk. One such source of influence are, of course, the viral infections which are highly prevalent in winter. Several viral illnesses peak in the winter and spring including rubella, measles and influenza. Indirect evidence for this comes from studies showing elevated levels of cerebrospinal fluid antibodies to common viruses in a large subgroup of schizophrenics compared to normal and medical patients (Tyrell *et al.* 1979; Albrecht *et al.* 1980) although the possibility of an impaired immune response has been suggested (King *et al.* 1985). Population studies of normals suggest that maternal viral infections are associated with congenital abnormalities particularly involving the CNS (Coffrey and Jessop 1959). To complete the circle, pregnant schizophrenic women were shown by Rieder *et al.* (1975) to produce an unexpectedly high level of still births and foetuses with congenital abnormalities. These strands of evidence suggest that the foetus at risk for schizophrenia is susceptible to viral insults (susceptible in the terms of raising the liability to schizophrenia and to the sequelae of viral insult) and that the perinatal deaths and anomalies in pregnant schizophrenic women may represent the worst outcome of an infective process.

Since exposure to viral infections is likely to be increased in crowded conditions such as exist in cities, one might suppose that schizophrenic women living in urban environments would be more susceptible. This possibility was tested by Machon *et al.* (1983) using the Danish high-risk prospective sample of Mednick and Schulsinger. The sample of 207 high-risk offspring were divided up according to whether they were born in winter or other seasons and in an urban or non-urban environment. Their results were striking and are reproduced in part in Table 3.

In contrast to the population base rate of 1 per cent and the high-

TABLE 3 Per cent high-risk subjects diagnosed schizophrenic by place and season of birth*

	Winter	*Non-winter*	
Urban	23.3% (7/30)	8.4% (8/95)	(12.0%)
Non-urban	0.0% (0/16)	6.3% (2/32)	(4.2%)
	(15.2%)	(7.8%)	(8.9%)

* Adapted from Machon *et al.* (1983)

risk rate of 8.9 per cent nearly one-quarter of those born in urban-winter conditions developed schizophrenia, which was statistically significant. The same result was found for severity of psychopathology. The *interaction* between *place* and *season* of birth makes alternative explanations of either place *or* birth-season effects difficult to sustain.

These data are suggestive but the point is immediately raised as to why children are susceptible at birth and not apparently in the first trimester of pregnancy. Machon *et al.* argue that after birth the neonate is much less dependent on the mother's immune system and infection can lead to subtle CNS damage unlike infections of the first trimester which are more profound (e.g. rubella). No study has yet ascertained whether these mothers actually contracted a viral infection or whether the winter-born have more viral antibodies or are less immune; clearly this is the next line of investigation.

The viral hypothesis suggests that a form of brain damage may raise the schizophrenic liability which links in nicely with the results of Reveley *et al.* (1982, 1984) that discordance in low genetic risk MZ twins was correlated with cortical abnormalities (ventricular enlargement) in the affected co-twin. A further source of possible CNS insults are those derived from the various complications of pregnancy and birth which one might anticipate on this hypothesis to be in greater evidence in schizophrenics.

PREGNANCY AND BIRTH COMPLICATIONS

Mention has already been made of the finding of Pollin and Stabenau (1968) that birth complications were more frequent among the schizophrenic members of discordant MZ twin pairs. In addition to this, three other research strategies have been reported: retrospective studies of known schizophrenics, studies of the birth experiences of schizophrenic women and studies of the offspring of schizophrenic women, later emerging as schizophrenic.

The first overall finding is that pregnant schizophrenic mothers do not experience appreciably more complications than other mothers. An initial positive finding by Mednick and Schlusinger (1968), particularly regarding long labours and placental dysfunction, was not replicated by Mednick (1973) in respect of birth weight, pregnancy or delivery using eighty-three schizophrenics and matched controls whose psychiatric and pregnancy data were independently collected. Several further studies failed also to find any association (e.g. McNeil and Kaij 1973; Mirdal *et al.* 1974). Thus a 'schizophrenic' genotype, the mother or the foetus, itself does not predispose towards pregnancy complications. Any relationship between schizophrenia and pregnancy complications must arise as a reaction to 'naturally occurring' complications.

Retrospective studies of known schizophrenics show that their births are unusually complicated but no single complication distinguishes schizophrenic from control groups (e.g. Pollack *et al.* 1968). Interestingly, Pollack *et al.* (1968) also reported a relationship with adult schizophrenia and birth records of minimal brain damage. Although retrospective in nature and therefore subject to the idiosyncracies of different recording methods and of individuals, there is no possible way in which data such as these could be contaminated as their future diagnosis would not have been known at the time of the birth.

Once again the Danish long term prospective high-risk study of Mednick and Schlusinger provides the best available data on this issue. Their follow-up of 207 high-risk children made use of the fact that nearly all births in Denmark are attended by a midwife who completes a standardised form about the delivery and the condition of the neonate and mother.

In 1970 Mednick reported a follow-up of the sample at age twenty and found that when all pregnancy and birth complications were combined, 70 per cent of those who had a psychiatric breakdown (including schizophrenia) experienced at least one of these complications. The matched high-risk and low-risk groups (with no breakdowns) showed figures of 15 per cent and 33 per cent respectively.

A ten year follow-up of his sample (Schulsinger 1976) was undertaken when the average age was twenty-four years, i.e. part way through the maximum risk period. The results with respect to perinatal complications (Parnas *et al.* 1982) make fascinating reading. These authors divide the sample into schizophrenia (N = 13), 'borderline' schizophrenia (N = 29) and no mental illness (N = 55). As before no differences emerged on individual complications except for abnormal foetal position which was more common in the schizo-phrenics (p < .03); however as there were nineteen listed compli-cations this would be a change expectation. Nevertheless, for all complications combined the schizophrenic group showed a greater frequency and severity of complications than the borderline group (p = 0.008). Some two-thirds of the schizophrenics experienced at least one complication whereas few of the borderline group did so. The group without mental illness lay midway between these two groups and was not different from either. One might predict that once the sample are through the major period of risk then some of the non-mental illness group will join the psychiatric groups.

The importance of these findings is that if one accepts the adop-tion study results suggesting that schizophrenia and borderline schizophrenia are phenotypic variants of a similar genotype (Kety's 'schizophrenia spectrum') then clearly Parnas *et al.* have made an important discovery in isolating one class of environmental factors which is responsible for the differential expression of the same genotype. Aside from this study by Parnas *et al.* no study has found clear interaction with subgroups such as by sex, prognosis or genetic risk.

It is not clear what pathological mechanism underlies this relationship as the very disparate birth complications do not obviously give rise to a common effect except in respect of a broad notion of brain dysfunction (which is of course a common obser-vation among at-risk children (Fish and Hagen 1972)). It is conceiv-able that there may be a link with the season of birth and the viral hypothesis discussed previously. The Parnas study used the same sample as Machon *et al.* in their study of birth-season and the clear effects of both obstetric complications and birth-season in the *same sample* must overlap and correlate to some degree. For example, the effects of viral events may cause 'obstetric' complications such as asphyxia, placental dysfunction, abnormal foetal turning or position and subsequent use of forceps, prematurity/low birth weight and so on. In other words, might the studies of birth-season/viral agents and obstetric complications be measuring the same phenomenon?

Future research programmes might therefore look at the relation-ship between obstetric complications, season of birth, cerebrospinal antibodies, neurological dysfunction and their interaction with genetic risk and subsequent subtypes of schizophrenia.

THE REARING ENVIRONMENT

Between the 1940s and the 1960s the literature was dominated by the view that schizophrenia arose as a result of deviant socialisation or communication processes within the family. Family theories were most prominent in the USA where, under the influence of the psychiatrist Harry Stack-Sullivan, the ascendancy of Freudian theory inevitably focused attention on families which were regarded as the pre-eminent influence on psycho-sexual development.

THEORIES OF FAMILY INFLUENCE

Early conceptualisations of the role of family life focused exclusively on the mother-child relationship, as developmental theorists viewed this as the most important element in socialisation. A number of clinical observations of these relationships characterised the mothers as cold, overprotective and domineering. 'Schizophrenogenic mothers' were thought to have arrested the development of the child's ego (the sense of self and reality) and that upon encountering the 'real world' in adolescence and early adulthood, the demands were such that the adult is forced to eschew reality and to retreat into a form of thinking characteristic of early childhood. This form of thought, termed 'primary process' thinking is, according to Freud, characterised by narcissism and fantasy, which was felt to bear some relationship to schizophrenic thought processes.

The approach was broadened in the 1950s to include the family as a whole and theories were developed on the assumption that the family should be viewed as a psycho-social system obeying natural laws. Empirical studies of family life in schizophrenia began therefore to emerge.

These more formal theories stemmed from the work of three research groups based in the USA; two of these (Bateson *et al.* 1956; Singer and Wynne 1963) specifically addressed the nature and style of communication between family members and the third, (Lidz *et al.* 1957) that of family structure and relationships.

Bateson proposed that communication between parents and offspring was frequently contradictory and placed the child in a 'double-bind'. This consisted of three components: the first is a 'primary negative injunction' prohibiting certain actions; the second, a 'secondary negative injunction' conflicted with these prohibitions and third, a 'tertiary negative injunction' indicates that a choice must be made, that there are no means of escape and that the child is prevented from clarifying the inconsistency. According to Bateson, the inconsistent secondary communication need not conflict at a verbal level, thus the tone of voice, facial expression or posture with which the primary negative injunction is delivered may be inconsistent with the content of the verbal communication. These incompatible communications were thought to affect the acquisition of an internally coherent construction of reality (or ego development in Freudian terms) and Bateson suggested that patients might thereby generate fallacious constructions such as delusions, and show extreme mistrust of all communications as is sometimes exhibited by paranoid schizophrenics.

Wynne and Singer's theory suggested that parental communication was not inconsistent but rather vague and fragmented lacking coherence and purpose. According to this theory, the child's cognitive and social development is impaired through the absence of coherent messages and a focus of attention which is essential for learning. Wynne and Singer saw a direct relationship with this fragmented communication and the disordered thinking characteristic of many schizophrenics.

The family socialisation theory of Lidz (Lidz *et al.* 1957) argues that schizophrenic families fail to provide a cohesive, stable and supportive environment for the developing child and may fail to provide role appropriate models. Two abnormal family structures were identified by Lidz. 'Schismatic' families are those in which the conflicts between parents lead them to compete for the loyalty and affection of family members as a means of undermining the other's influence and control over family affairs. 'Skewed' families display abnormal dominance patterns: bizarre and psychopathological behaviour of one marital partner is complemented and supported by the submissive needs of the non-dominant partner. The children are encouraged to support and acquiesce to the abnormal views of the dominant partner thereby impairing cognitive and social development. According to Lidz, in both kinds of family the divisions between the generations are blurred and parents fail to act in role-appropriate ways. This arouses anxiety about incestuous feelings and schizophrenia is seen as one way of handling the conflicts and distortions of family relationships.

RESEARCH EVIDENCE

Communication deviance

Two major studies have cast strong doubt on the validity of Bateson's double-bind concept. The first was that of Ringuette and Kennedy (1966). Five groups of judges, including experts on the double-bind concept, were given letters written by parents to their children in order to assess which of these letters were written by schizophrenics. It was assumed that elements of the double-bind would appear in written communications. It was found that not only were the experts (including Bateson himself) unable to agree upon what constituted a double-bind communication (coefficient = 0.19) but also none of the judges were able to distinguish between schizophrenic and non-schizophrenic families. Using an obser-vational technique, Haley (1968) set parents the task of instructing their offspring to select eight cards from an array of twenty-four arranged in front of them through provision of a verbal description. Schizophrenic offspring and their parents performed poorly on this task; however when parents of schizophrenic offspring instructed normals, their performance was unaffected, suggesting that the deficit lay in the schizophrenic offspring rather than their parents. Ethological studies would, of course, be the most valid test of this (or other) communication hypotheses; however, these have their own methodological problems which will not be discussed at length here. Nevertheless it is not unreasonable to expect that such a supposedly powerful mode of communication would appear in contexts other than in the home.

Wynne and Singer, in contrast to Bateson have attempted rigor-ously to define and operationalise communication deviance. They obtained a sample of speech by administering the Rorschach test and defined large number of categories of communication deviance (e.g. 'odd use of words', 'unstable percepts') which were summed to provide a deviance score. These workers have successfully managed to distinguish between parents of schizophrenics, neurotics and normals under blind conditions. Hirsch and Leff (1975) partly replicated these results but found that the differences between groups was accounted for simply by the verbosity of schizophrenics' parents. Wynne *et al.* (1976) in a remarkable study, obtained protocols of Rorschach tests administered to 'normal' parents and biological and adoptive parents of schizophrenics and scored them for communication deviance, blind as to the identity of the parents. Singer was then asked to classify the parents according to whether they had reared a schizophrenic child on the basis of the communi-cation deviance data. Singer correctly classified all (adoptive and biological) parents of schizophrenics and all adoptive parents of non-schizophrenics. Wynne subsequently reported that the biological and adoptive parents of schizophrenics were indeed more verbose (as Hirsch and Leff suggested) but that this did not account for the qualitative group differences.

A number of investigators have observed family interactions in the laboratory under artificial conditions. These techniques seem to be sensitive to the parameters of the experimental procedure with the result that the numerous studies using the paradigm are often conflicting. On balance, these data suggest that schizophrenics' parents lack clarity, are not attentive and tend to be verbose in communication with their offspring (Jacob 1975). This conclusion bears strong similarities to Wynne and Singer's theory of 'amorphous' and 'fragmented' communication styles.

Overall, the evidence converges towards the conclusion that

parents of schizophrenics, as a group, communicate in an abnormal manner.

Dominance and conflict

Lidz and his colleagues report only a series of single case investigations without the use of control groups rendering a scientific evaluation of this theory impossible. However other investigators have attempted to evaluate Lidz's theory.

A questionnaire technique commonly used to ascertain family dominance patterns is the 'Revealed Difference technique' where a number of hypothetical family problem situations are posed requiring management decisions; those situations where parents disagree are analysed to discover which parent's solution gains eventual ascendancy. Cheek (1965) and Ferreira and Winter (1965) failed to find differences in dominance patterns between schizophrenic and non-schizophrenic groups. Similar results have been obtained using small group interaction techniques using measures such as each parent's total talking time, statement length and frequency of interruptions (Jacob 1975). Sharan (1966) specifically tested Lidz's hypotheses about the blurring of sex and generation boundaries by examining whether the patient and dominant parent were of the opposite sex in interactions involving ill and well offspring and their parents. No differences between dominance patterns with ill or well offspring emerged.

The research into conflict has revealed a number of positive findings. Using the Revealed Difference Questionnaire, Ferreira and Winter (1965) found more disagreement in decision-making in schizophrenic parents compared to those with offspring having some other psychiatric condition, although the father's choice predominated in all groups contrary to Lidz's formulations. Cheek (1967) found that there was much more disagreement between parents about standards of behaviour in 'schizophrenic' families. Small group interaction studies tend to find conflict on measures such as 'interruptions' and 'simultaneous' speech among families of schizophrenics with a poor premorbid history (Hirsch and Leff 1975). The presence of disturbance in the affected offspring may be a factor in the genesis of parental conflict, as Ferreira and Winter (1965) found that families with either schizophrenic or maladjusted (but non-psychiatric) offspring produced similar levels of disagreement about standards of behaviour. The evidence is therefore equally consistent with the possibility that deviant offspring produce or highlight parental discord.

The latter point reflects a general problem of methodology in all these studies, which is that these observations of family life are made *after* the onset of schizophrenia and it is difficult therefore to disentangle cause from effect. The conflict, instability and communication problems present in many families of schizophrenics cannot therefore easily be ascribed a causal influence. It may even be that the abnormalities observed in parents and their affected offspring may simply be a marker of a common genetic background, in itself bearing no aetiological significance.

If these studies of parents and families of schizophrenic patients have proved equivocal there is a body of data which can, in theory, answer the fundamental question as to whether families play any role in the genesis of schizophrenia. These data come from the Danish adoption studies of Kety and Rosenthal.

IMPLICATIONS OF THE ADOPTION STUDIES FOR FAMILY THEORIES OF SCHIZOPHRENIA

It is known that schizophrenia tends to run in families over generations. The average risk to a child of a schizophrenic parent is about 14 per cent (vs 1 per cent in the general population) and where both parents are schizophrenic, the risk rises to 46 per cent (Slater and Cowie 1971). It is important to note that there will be greater discontinuity over two or more generations and that a majority of schizophrenics do not have schizophrenic parents or siblings.

Family theorists argued that these observations were consistent with a familial genesis because the presence of a schizophrenic parent represented an extreme manifestation of disordered family relationships (child rearing, interpersonal relationships or dominance patterns) responsible for the appearance of schizophrenia. The demonstration of an inherited component in the early 1960s, by virtue of the twin studies, did not refute the family hypotheses because it was considered that a disordered family environment was a necessary condition for the emergence of schizophrenia in genetically vulnerable individuals and furthermore that in certain extreme cases this could be sufficient on its own (such as being reared by a schizophrenic parent). Indeed, as we have already seen, the substantial discordance for schizophrenia in MZ twins suggests an environmental component. Thus the transmission of schizophrenia within families would arise as a juxtaposition of the inherited genotype and, through rearing by a schizophrenic parent, the negative influence of the family.

One way of testing this special case of the family hypothesis would be to rear the offspring of schizophrenics in a normal environment, the prediction being that the incidence of schizophrenia should fall to chance levels or at least to the level found in adopted children.

A natural form of this ideal experiment can be conceived if a sample of offspring of known schizophrenics adopted away early in life could be traced. Such studies have been undertaken with major implications for the family theories. The first was reported by Heston (1966) in London who assembled a sample of forty-seven offspring of schizophrenics adopted away within three days of birth. He discovered that 10.5 per cent had developed schizophrenia and a further 17 per cent borderline schizophrenics compared to 0 per cent for his controls, i.e. the risk remained unchanged for a high-risk offspring.

This study was then followed up by better controlled studies in Denmark matching the national adoption registers with the Danish psychiatric registers, in addition to follow-up psychiatric interviews. Two kinds of adoption methodology have been employed. In the Kety-led studies (Kety *et al*. 1971, 1975), thirty-four children adopted within a month of birth and later emerging with schizophrenia served as the index cases. Their adoptive and biological relatives' psychiatric status was assessed and compared with those of a normal (adoptive) control group. There has been some debate about the methodology of these studies (Lidz *et al*. 1981), particularly about diagnostic practices, but which has been responded to by Kety (1983) who noted in particular that the original data have stood up to an independent analysis using modern operational criteria as embodied in DSM III (Kendler *et al*. 1981). The results of these studies were: (1) the adoptive relatives show no elevation of schizophrenia whereas (2) the biological relatives show a concentration of schizophrenic disorders. These data point strongly to a genetic factor but for present purposes demonstrate that schizophrenia in the rearing family is not a necessary factor in the familial transmission of schizophrenia.

Using a different methodology, Rosenthal and his colleagues assembled a sample of thirty-nine offspring of schizophrenic parents adopted away at an early age. An average of eleven years elapsed between the birth of the thirty-nine adoptees and the first hospitalisation of the index parent. Neither the adoptive families nor the adopting authorities had any knowledge that the biological parent had or could develop schizophrenia. A control sample of adopted children of parents without any history of psychiatric disorder served as the comparison group. Rosenthal *et al*. (1968) discovered an 8 per cent incidence of schizophrenia in the index adoptees compared to 0 per cent for the controls. With the inclusion of borderline schizophrenia and subsequent additional cases the figure rose to 18.8 per cent for the index cases (vs. 10.1 per cent for controls). Once again these data were reanalysed using DSM III criteria (Lowing *et al.* 1983). These authors found the same effect but with stricter operational criteria, a heavier concentration of borderline schizophrenia in the index sample.

Rosenthal's results, even more so than Kety's, show how difficult it is to break the cycle of schizophrenia from one generation to another through immersion of the genotype in a normal rearing environment. However as Lidz and Blatt (1981) and others have intimated, no measurement has ever been taken of the *adoptive* family environment and have suggested that there may exist some 'schizophrenogenic' influences to account for the high incidence of schizophrenia. However, given the 18.8 per cent incidence of schizophrenia in index adoptive families, this then implies that at least one in five (adoptive) families are sufficiently pathological to trigger schizophrenia. The true figure will need to be much higher as this assumes a most fortuitous pairing of genotype with the pathological family environment. In other words, a pathological rearing environment would need to be so prevalent as to call into question the meaning of the term 'pathological' and 'schizophrenogenic'.

Some further predictions relating to the role of rearing environments can be tested using the adoption data. Families with a schizophrenic member should evidence schizophrenogenic influences. Thus one would predict that the siblings of the affected individual should show an increased risk even though one might not expect all siblings to be affected. This has been confirmed but the result confounds genetic and environmental influences. However, *adoptive* full siblings should show an increased risk and the biological siblings a lesser one if rearing factors are important. This prediction is not borne out. Karlsson (1966) in Iceland traced eight schizophrenics raised in foster families with twenty-eight foster siblings, none of whom became schizophrenic; this compared with twenty-nine full biological siblings (reared apart) which included six schizophrenics. A similar result was obtained in the Danish adoption study.

Comparisons of fostered children of schizophrenics reared in different environments were reported by Heston and Denny (1968). They found no difference in the incidence of schizophrenia (or other psychiatric disorder) between those reared in foster families or foundling institutions (N = 22, 25 respectively). Higgins (1966) studied fifty young adults born of schizophrenic mothers, twenty-five of whom were reared by their mothers and twenty-five in foster homes or institutions, in both rearing situations approximately 10 per cent emerged with schizophrenia.

Wender *et al.*'s (1974) remarkable study of twenty-one children with no family history of psychiatric disorder who were reared by a schizophrenic parent, provides a means of testing whether such rearing is sufficient alone to precipitate schizophrenia. Wender did not find an increased risk for schizophrenia in these adoptive individuals, although it must be pointed out that some parents developed serious psychopathologies other than schizophrenia and did so when the average age of the adopted child was eleven years – past the time when rearing practices might be considered to have had a formative effect.

In summary, the adoption studies have shown that the likelihood of developing schizophrenia in genetically high-risk individuals does not vary in spite of sometimes profound changes in the rearing environment. The adoption technique is naturalistic and prone to bias, for example the incidence of borderline schizophrenia in the normal adoptees is higher than chance possibly reflecting psychopathology in their (normal) biological parents being partly responsible for their adoption. At the very least the results show that rearing by the schizophrenic parent is not a necessary (and certainly not a sufficient) condition for the emergence of schizophrenia in genetically high-risk individuals. As this form of rearing has to be considered by family theorists as an extreme manifestation of 'schizophrenic' influences, then the basis for believing that the family in general has an independent role in the aetiology of schizophrenia must be seriously brought into question.

THE FAMILY AND SCHIZOPHRENIA: A SYNTHESIS

The adoption studies have seriously undermined a model of family influence in which the independent occurrence of genotype and family pathology, when juxtaposed, trigger the schizophrenia phenotype (Fig. 1).

This does not prove that families play no part in the emergence of schizophrenia – much depends on how the role of family life is modelled. The model outlined in Figure 1 assumes a unidirectional, continuing influence (a 'main-effect' model, see Fig. 2a). However, families could still exert an effect through a 'transactional' process (Fig. 2b).

Transactional models originate in the child development literature and assume that the child is not a passive recipient of parental behaviour but is an active agent in his own development. Samerof and Chandler (1975) invoked a transactional model to explain some child development data which might have a relationship to schizophrenia. Their review demonstrated that disturbances of childhood temperament and cognitive function resulting from perinatal trauma (e.g. anoxia) can be ameliorated or worsened according to the quality of the 'caretaker' (family) environment, in this case as

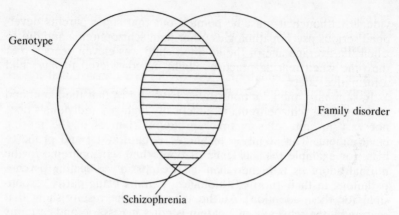

Fig. 1 A simple ('main effect') family model of schizophrenia

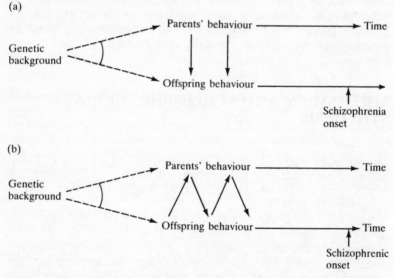

Fig. 2 The (a) 'main-effect' and (b) 'transactional' family models of schizophrenia

indexed by social class. It was suggested that the families' reaction to or management of these disturbances reciprocally influenced the offspring's behaviour, in turn affecting parental behaviour and so on. Such cumulative transactional influences serve to bring the child towards a homogeneity of developmental outcomes; an extreme of perinatal disorder and/or poor family adjustment serve to bring the child outside these modal outcomes.

It is quite feasible that this might operate in schizophrenia and would be consistent with the adoption data because family effects are postulated to emerge as a failure of these long-term transactions to bring the child within 'normal' limits, which biological and adoptive parents might equally fail to do. For the transactional model to apply it would require to be demonstrated that disturbance exists in the pre-schizophrenic and is primary. There is some evidence to support this:

1. As a group pre-schizophrenics, particularly males, tend to be recorded at school as dull, low achievers (Orford 1975), unstable, poorly behaved or quiet (Watt 1978). An unusually large number are seen at child guidance clinics (Waring and Ricks 1965). Progeny of known schizophrenics frequently display these characteristics (e.g. Mednick and Schulsinger 1965).
2. Where abnormalities in parents of schizophrenics have been discovered they are predominantly in patients of poor premorbid history and in the case of communication disturbance (observed after onset) this is specific to the affected offspring and can also be observed in adoptive families (see previous section).
3. Perinatal complications and neurological signs are associated with schizophrenia (see previous section).

The specific function which biological *or* adoptive parents may have is that, as a result of a long-term, deviant, transactional process, the liability to schizophrenia is increased through exacerbation of cognitive and social neurologically-based deficits. Additionally, a stressful relationship could develop with the disturbed pre-schizophrenic, thus precipitating the onset (stress is a known precipitant of psychotic episodes – see (Ch. 12).

Under the transactional model many of the abnormalities in adoptive and biological parents of schizophrenics noted previously will be emergent qualities, unrelated to genetic factors, as highlighted by Singer's compelling report of the efficacy of measures of communication deviance to identify which adoptive parents reared a schizophrenic. Nevertheless, the model proposed here is highly speculative and will necessitate a truly prospective design to examine it.

THE SOCIAL ENVIRONMENT: THE CORRELATES OF SOCIAL CLASS

The study of social class in relation to schizophrenia has until recently, proved a popular method among researchers of varying theoretical persuasions, by which the potential influence of the environment can be observed. For the sociologists it is a convenient reflection of the role of power and status in society; for the ecologists social class correlates with features such as crowding, deprivation and health; for the psychologists, child-rearing practices, access and response to education, parental communication etc are known social class correlates with possible pathological importance. It is thus the *correlates* of social class which could provide a rich source of hypotheses if a link with schizophrenia can be demonstrated.

A link between social class and schizophrenia has, in fact, now been well established. Since the classic study of Faris and Dunham (1939) showing the preponderance of low social status schizophrenics living in dilapidated, inner city areas of Chicago, numerous further investigations have confirmed their findings in many countries including the USA, UK and Holland (e.g. Hollingshead and Redlich 1958, Turner and Wagonfeld 1967, Hare 1956, Wiersma *et al*. 1983). Doubts were raised, however, about the methodology of these studies but subsequent attempts to correct for these found that the effect remained whether the diagnosis was broad or narrowly defined; whether the frequency of schizophrenia was measured in terms of the number of new cases (incidence) or the total number of cases (prevalence) or whether social class was measured by education, occupation or a mixture of these (see Kohn 1973 for review). An important finding in many of these studies is that the relationship between social class and schizophrenia is not a linear one: the effect is particularly noticeable in social classes IV and V (unskilled manual) where a 100 per cent excess of schizophrenics has been observed (Goldsberg and Morrison 1963).

The excitement generated by these data began to evaporate as alternative, non-causal explanations were suggested. A clinical observation often made by those having day-to-day contact with schizophrenics is that many fail to meet the expectations of their parents' social class and that prior to the first episode patients have difficulty maintaining stable employment and relationships, and tend to drift apart from their families. The link with social class may simply have arisen because patients 'drift' into the lower social strata as part of a premorbid decline. Indeed, the preponderance of schizophrenics in inner city areas was later found to be due to patients living *alone* in cheap 'rooming-house' or 'bed-sit' districts and the incidence of schizophrenia among those living with families were distributed evenly in all city areas. It is possible that such premorbid decline may arise from two overlapping processes: the first being a passive downward drift in social status; the second, one of social segregation in which schizophrenics actively segregate themselves and seek anonymity in inner-city areas without necessarily incurring social decline. The latter may, perhaps, be more in evidence among 'inner-city' schizophrenics (Hare 1956). The drift hypothesis is consistent with the non-linear relationship with social class noted above, as, by definition, drift must stop at the lowest social class.

Empirical investigations have broadly confirmed these speculations although no study has explicitly distinguished between 'drift' and 'segregation'.

One line of investigation has compared the social status of schizophrenics with their fathers, on the basis that the social class distribution of fathers should resemble the normal population if schizophrenics are in reality drawn randomly from all social groups. In a British sample, Goldberg and Morrison (1963) find no difference between the population social class distribution and that for the patients' fathers. Turner and Wagonfeld (1967) find only a modest difference in a sample drawn from the USA. Both of these studies looked at individual father-son comparisons, finding that downward social mobility was the rule rather than the exception. Goldberg and Morrison showed that where there was an insidious onset starting in adolescence, patients did not reach the social status of their fathers; where the onset was sudden and in early adulthood many had done so but dropped in social status prior to admission. These results were confirmed in a subsequent Dutch study (Wiersma et al. 1983).

A second approach to this issue has employed data from the Danish adoption studies. In those studies where the index cases were known schizophrenics raised by foster parents (Kety et al. 1968) it was found that their social class was indeed lower than adopted controls and when compared with their adoptive fathers, the schizophrenics were of lower occupational status. The adoptive controls had in contrast reached the occupational status of their adoptive fathers. The other adoption paradigm in which children of schizophrenics raised in foster homes are followed up over time (e.g. Rosenthal et al. 1968) finds a social class relationship with the adoptee's adult status but not with the status of their adoptive family.

The balance of evidence suggests that the 'true' incidence of schizophrenia is evenly distributed throughout the social classes and that the observed relationships are the results either of premorbid cognitive handicaps affecting patients' future occupational adjustment and/or of a social decline (segregation) following the onset of schizophrenia. The evidence does not eliminate the possibility of a sociogenic influence but any such class-related effect is unlikely to prove substantial. Clearly a design is required in which the social class distribution of schizophrenics who have not drifted is assessed and compared with the general population.

Other socio-economic indices have been studied in addition to social class. The most notable was that of Brenner (1973) who studied rates of mental hospitalisation in New York State from 1852 to 1967. He showed that rates of admission were closely linked with unemployment, changes in the latter having a delayed effect of up to twelve months. The relationship was particularly strong for the functional psychoses. However, Brenner failed to distinguish first from readmissions. If the relationship held up only for readmissions then given that schizophrenics tend to occupy the lowest social class, they are likely to experience unemployment first and some may therefore find hospitalisation attractive. Alternatively, if the relationship were demonstrated to be causal, this would provide evidence that economic factors influence the *course* but not the *inception* of schizophrenia. If the relationship held with first admissions a causal hypothesis would be strongly supported, but nevertheless it would have to be demonstrated that periods of high unemployment do not simply affect the *timing* of the schizophrenic onset rather than its probability.

It is disappointing that the prodigious research effort into social class and schizophrenia has not yielded more substantial findings. The results of Brenner have suggested that stresses associated with economic hardships may bear some influence on the course of schizophrenia, a hypothesis reviewed in the next chapter.

CONCLUSION

The ascendancy of genetic theories in recent years must now give way to the acceptance that environmental factors play a vital role in raising the overall liability to schizophrenia and in triggering the disorder itself. The twin study data themselves provides the clearest evidence for this assertion. The most convincing evidence for environmental agents comes from the studies of the *interaction* of genetics and environment. Many of these results lend support to what Shields (1978) termed a 'stress-diathesis' model in which a continuum of liability to schizophrenia is postulated. The liability is assumed to have a threshold of expression and can be contributed to by genetic and environmental factors in inverse proportions: a high genetic risk requiring little environmental contribution and a low genetic risk requiring more. Low genetic risk schizophrenics have been observed to have a greater incidence of ventricular enlargement, perinatal complications and winter births. In one study an environmental factor (perinatal complications) appeared to determine the severity of the schizophrenic phenotype in a high-risk group, i.e. definite vs. borderline schizophrenia.

It is uncertain how these disparate effects could have a common pathway: it is possible that perinatal complications and winter births/viral agents may actually be tapping the same phenomenon and give rise to a subtle form of brain damage, possibly leading to a compensatory cortical reorganisation of function. Future environmental research clearly needs to take into account the interaction of genetic risk and the ultimate form of the disorder.

The rearing and broader social environments as *independent* influences would appear to be minimal; however, in both cases crucial studies have yet to be performed, in particular those based on a transactional model. It is feasible on the basis of parallels with the child development literature that these socio-environmental effects may actually raise the schizophrenic liability as the outcome of such a transactional process. However, in view of the known role of these factors in relapse (see Ch. 12), they may well determine the timing rather more than the probability of schizophrenia.

Chapter twelve

THE ENVIRONMENT AND PROGNOSIS: SOCIAL OUTCOME

THE COURSE AND OUTCOME OF SCHIZOPHRENIA

In this and the following chapter we will explore the influence which environmental factors have on the outlook for schizophrenia once the disorder has appeared. The degree of such influence will be constrained by the homogeneity in the 'natural history' of the disorder; if the course and outcome of schizophrenia with or without treatment is subject to little variation then the opportunity for effects of variations in the social environment will be reduced. The first task then is to answer the question 'Is there a natural history of schizophrenic disorders?'

Before examining this issue a word of caution is in order. There is a pervasive belief in psychiatry that schizophrenia is *by definition* a chronic disorder without *restitio ad integratum*. Thus Kendall *et al.* (1979) write 'Kraeplin's original concept . . . was founded on the assumption that complete recovery was unusual and . . . is the main justification for distinguishing schizophrenia from other psychoses' (1979: 30). Although, as we shall see, schizophrenia is prognostically distinct from other disorders, Kraeplin's doctrine has been largely unquestioned to the point that different diagnostic systems for schizophrenia have been evaluated in terms of their efficacy in predicting a poor outcome (e.g. Kendall *et al.* op. cit.). Such a view represents the wholesale application of the techniques of medicine where prognoses of illnesses are usually homogeneous; this assumption should not, in our view, be made in psychiatry where the subject matter is qualitatively different (i.e. thoughts, emotions, behaviour) and about which relatively little is understood. Although there is no reason why the course of a disorder cannot in part validate the concept itself, rationally the concept should first be defined, then the issue of its predictive efficacy treated as an empirical question.

VARIABILITY VS. CONSISTENCY

Long term follow-up studies of schizophrenia are legion – by 1961 Zubin listed over 800 such studies (Zubin *et al.* 1961). We will not attempt to review all such studies but instead attempt to draw some general conclusions (see WHO 1979 for a detailed review). It is in fact difficult to draw conclusions which are anything other than general because the studies vary in diagnostic practices, follow-up period, measurement and criteria of symptomatic course etc.

In spite of these differences, however, long term follow-ups of schizophrenic patients consistently provide a picture which is marked more by variability than by a homogeneous overall process. Bleuler's (1978) Swiss follow-up study is considered by many to be seminal because he employed first admissions, used a long follow-up period (over twenty years) and personally examined all patients using defined criteria and with no attrition. He reports that 30 per cent of his sample were fully recovered (no symptoms and in gainful employment), 38 per cent were mildly chronic (definite symptoms but behaviour normal and living outside the institution); 13 per cent were moderately severe (institutionalised with many symptoms but faculties preserved and 'normal behaviour possible') and 15 per cent severe chronic (thought-disordered, confused, constant care required). Ciompi (1980) reports a very long term follow-up and although a large proportion had died, it would be assumed on the basis of Kraeplin's doctrine that those who outlived the natural course of the disorder so to speak would be chronic; in fact only 19.7 per cent were so, the remainder sharing a similar spread of outcome comparable with Bleuler's sample.

The routes by which these long term end-states are achieved are similarly variable. Undoubtedly the most methodologically sophisticated follow-up study, the International Pilot Study of Schizophrenia (IPSS), found that in a two year cross-cultural follow-up of over 1,000 patients the course of over 70 per cent of their patients was marked by time-limited episodes of psychosis followed by complete or partial recovery. Bleuler also noted that nearly 50 per cent of his sample were rehospitalised on more than one occasion and subsequently released.

Certain patterns in the course of schizophrenia have consistently emerged (WHO 1979; Ciompi 1980, Watt *et al.* 1983) and can be summarised as follows:

Pattern 1. One episode, full recovery (25 per cent).
Pattern 2. Episodic course, full remission (20 per cent).
Pattern 3. Episodic course, partial remission (25 per cent).
Pattern 4. Episodic course merging into chronicity (15 per cent).
Pattern 5. Chronic deterioration (15 per cent).
The quoted figures are averages of very different studies but do

illustrate the prevalence of the episodic pattern and underline the heterogeneity in the course as well as the long-term outcome of schizophrenia.

Some of this heterogeneity in course and outcome is undoubtedly due to the introduction of major tranquillisers as comparisons before and after their introduction suggest that schizophrenia has become much more benign with fewer entering into chronic deterioration and with more full recoveries but at the expense of a more punctuated episodic course with more persisting symptoms between major episodes (Achte 1967; Brown *et al.* 1966, Bleuler 1978). Even before the neuroleptics, however, variability in course and outcome was the rule (Bleuler 1978).

PREDICTION OF OUTCOME A DIAGNOSTIC ISSUE?

Most studies do indeed show that schizophrenia has a poorer outcome compared to the other psychoses (e.g. WHO 1979). This has suggested to some workers that more refined diagnostic criteria for schizophrenia might well predict a homogeneously poor outcome group as Kraeplin suggested. Some studies have therefore attempted to compare different diagnostic systems in terms of the ability to predict a poor outcome.

In a comparison of 'broad' and 'narrow' diagnostic systems Strauss and his co-workers (Strauss *et al.* 1974; Hawk *et al.* 1975) could find no difference in outcome over a five year period between three diagnostic systems (Schneider, Langfeldt, DSM III) using eighty-five patients. Kendell *et al.* (1979) compared six definitions using clinical and social outcome measures and found that although some definitions were better than others in identifying a greater proportion of chronic patients (but on different measures) the *proportion* of poor outcome patients in each diagnostic system was little greater than 50 per cent.

Helzer *et al.* (1981) in a further analysis of data presented by Brockington *et al.* (1979) again diagnosed patients according to different operational criteria including the new and more restrictive North American definition as embodied in DSM III. The DSM III definition requires six months of continuous psychosis to elapse *before* the final diagnosis is applied. It is not surprising therefore that this definition succeeded in defining very few psychotics as schizophrenic and, of those that were selected, a much poorer prognosis compared to other definitions was observed. In terms of prognosis the definition is circular as clearly DSM III is attaching the label 'schizophrenia' primarily to those who show signs of heading for a chronic outcome rather than by the nature of the disorder itself. Also, in view of their finding that 30 per cent of their DSM

III schizophrenics had recovered on six year follow-up there seems to be no logic whatsoever to this circular definition. This study, although providing the best prediction of (poor) outcome using DSM III criteria, cannot provide any information about the natural history of the broader spectrum group except perhaps to underline the fact that chronicity is one outcome for some and is apparent usually after six months of unremitting psychosis.

Schizophrenia is symptomatically heterogeneous and therefore it is not unreasonable to speculate that there may be valid subgroups of schizophrenia, of differing natural histories, thereby accounting for the apparent variability in outcome.

The classical subtypes of schizophrenia (paranoid, simple, catatonic, hebephrenic, latent, schizo-affective) are difficult to discriminate reliably (Kendall 1975) and are symptomatically indistinct with the exception of the distinction between 'simple' schizophrenia (predominantly negative symptoms) and schizo-affectives (mainly positive and affective symptoms) – WHO 1973. Prognostically, schizo-affective disorders do seem to have a superior outcome to schizophrenia (Harrow and Grossman 1984) and simple schizophrenia a poorer one, but the remaining subgroups do not appear prognostically distinct (WHO 1979).

'Simple' schizophrenia is characterised by the so-called 'defect state' (flat and incongruous effect, apathy, poverty of speech) and as such its poor prognosis has been noted in other guises. Thus males of early onset (15–25 years) are usually associated with poor premorbid adjustment, negative symptoms and a gradual onset, and tend to have a very poor outcome (WHO 1979; Salokangas 1983). As we have seen, there is now evidence that some of those with severe negative symptoms tend not to respond to neuroleptic medication, have enlarged ventricles and possibly a lower genetic risk (Andreasen *et al.* 1982b). This group could therefore be considered a distinct group with a unique underlying pathology. Similarly the schizo-affectives are regarded by many as a variant of the affective disorders because (a) they tend to respond to treatment appropriate for affective patients (e.g. lithium carbonate) and (b) their first-degree relatives show a preponderance of affective rather than the usual schizophrenia spectrum disorders (Welner *et al.* 1974).

CONCLUSION

The course of schizophrenia is characterised by between-subject variability rather than consistency, and, particularly since the advent of the neuroleptics, the modal pattern is an undulating episodic one. No one has yet succeeded in predicting significantly the prognosis of schizophrenia on the basis of the symptomatological picture alone as witnessed by the finding of the IPSS that symptom information accounted for only 15 per cent of the variance in outcome. Two schizophrenia subgroups have been identified of contrasting prognoses, the simple and schizo-affective groups, the former being largely male of early onset with predominant negative symptoms. These constitute a minority of the schizophrenia spectrum but there is a suggestion that these groups have a unique pathology and do not easily fit into the schizophrenia spectrum. By and large therefore it is extremely difficult to characterise the 'natural history' of schizophrenia because it is so variable. We shall argue in the coming pages that there are so many environmental influences on its prognosis as to render the concept of 'natural history' meaningless.

SOCIAL DISABLEMENT IN SCHIZOPHRENIA

THE SOCIAL FUNCTIONING OF SCHIZOPHRENIC PATIENTS

The results of numerous studies support the impressions of those in close contact with schizophrenia that, as a group, they show a greater degree of difficulty in adapting to the demands of community life than normals and other psychiatric patients (Wallace 1984). Thus Serban (1975) found that his large samples of acute and chronic schizophrenics experienced greater difficulty across a range of life skills – employment, financial matters, socialisation etc, than the normal population, a result previously found by Hogarty and Katz (1971) in the course of their standardisation of the Katz Social Adjustment Scales. There is in addition, evidence that among those patients where the symptoms become chronic, community functioning becomes increasingly problematical; this in addition to the psychosis itself, generates a need for institutionalisation or semi-independent living such as accommodation in hostels or remaining with families. Birchwood (1983) reported that his sample of seventy-seven chronically ill but non-institutionalised patients (mean duration of illness eleven years) were significantly *less* well adjusted in independence, recreational, pro-social activities and employment than fifty-three young schizophrenics followed up in the community two years after the onset. He also found a significant correlation between duration of illness and social impairment in the chronic group.

There is also evidence that schizophrenic patients generally fare less well in life than **other** psychotic patients, particularly compared to those with an affective element (Brockington *et al.* 1979, WHO 1979).

The inability to develop and maintain relationships with other people is generally regarded as characteristic of schizophrenia, a view fully supported by the literature. Observations of hospitalised symptomatic patients suggest that they spend less than 10 per cent of their time in social interaction (e.g. Paul and Lentz 1977); that this does not vary with duration of illness (Goffman 1963) and that schizophrenics interact less than other psychotic or affectively disordered patients (Rosen *et al.* 1980). A limited number of studies have examined the level of social contact among schizophrenics which has usually been found to be quite poor and tends to centre around their relatives (Pattison *et al.* 1975; Tolsdorf 1976). Brockington *et al.* (1979) found that some 50 per cent of schizophrenics were rated as 'socially isolated' with a tendency for schizophrenics to be more isolated than non-schizophrenic psychotics.

In summary, many persons developing schizophrenia will face considerable difficulty surviving adequately in the community, a problem exacerbated by self-imposed social isolation. For those that leave home the problem may be further compounded by a downward social drift and a decline in their quality of life. It is known from epidemiological research that schizophrenics, particularly males, are less likely to marry and that up to two-thirds of first episode schizophrenics will return home (see Ch. 1). However, even in these environments where material deprivation will be lessened, a great many will be unemployed, isolated and dependent on their relatives (Creer and Wing 1973). In the region of one-third will eventually require institutional or semi-independent accommodation, and according to one estimate only a third of those who develop schizophrenia will return to an 'average' level of social functioning (Keith *et al.* 1976).

VARIABILITY VS. CONSISTENCY IN THE SOCIAL OUTCOME

As we noted in our discussion of the symptomatic course and outcome, an overall poorer outcome for schizophrenia does not imply an homogeneously poor outcome. The few studies which have measured the social outcome in schizophrenia seem to come to a similar conclusion. Manfred Bleuler's (1978) long-term follow-up in Switzerland has already been referred to; with regard to social functioning he reports that 40 per cent of his first admissions had a 'good' outcome (self-supporting outside an institution), 13 per cent a 'moderate' outcome (partly self-supporting outside an institution, e.g. with parents or in a hostel) and 41 per cent a poor outcome (rarely self-supporting, hospitalised frequently or constantly). A five year follow-up of schizophrenia in Finland (Achte 1967) revealed that 51 per cent were 'socially recovered', 41 per cent were 'not socially recovered'. In England Brown *et al.* (1966) followed up a sample of acute schizophrenic patients over five years and using combined symptomatic and social criteria, found that 49 per cent were functioning well and not handicapped by symptoms, 23 per cent were handicapped by symptoms and functioning at an impaired level and 28 per cent were severely ill at follow-up and hospitalised. These data, particularly the Bleuler study where symptomatic and social functioning were clearly separated, show that in the short or long term variability in the social outcome is, once again, the rule, that symptomatic and social outcome are correlated and that social decline is by no means universal.

PRIMARY AND SECONDARY HANDICAP

In characterising the overall nature of the handicaps which schizophrenia can generate in an individual Wing (1978) draws an important distinction between the primary and secondary handicaps (see Table 1).

To what degree are the social (secondary) handicaps underpinned by these intrinsic problems?

It was noted earlier that schizophrenics are often socially isolated. Sokolovsky *et al.* (1978) and Cohen and Sokolovsky (1978) studied the social networks of schizophrenic and non-schizophrenic ex-patients living in single room occupancy hostels in New York. They found that for those persons *without* residual symptoms there was no difference between schizophrenics and non-schizophrenics in their social networks; those schizophrenics with moderate to severe symptoms had smaller networks with more dependent relationships than those without symptoms. This would suggest that schizophrenic symptoms are entirely responsible for social impairments. However, this study was conducted mainly on older, male and generally isolated patients and of course it is difficult to judge whether the asymptomatic patients were socially impaired or not relative to the general population. A better approach to this issue would be to study the inter-correlation between symptomatic and social functioning variables in a random sample of patients.

Strauss and Carpenter's (1974, 1977) two and five year outcome study present data on the inter-relationships between outcome measures. They found that the severity of positive symptoms correlated $r = -0.63$ with quality and quantity of social contacts $r = -0.49$ with ability to meet basic needs, $r = -0.47$ with employment status and $r = -0.8$ with 'fullness of life'. In a two year follow-up of fifty-three first admission schizophrenics Birchwood (1983) found that severity of positive symptoms (derived from the PSE) correlated −0.54 with interpersonal functioning, −0.55 with social activity, −0.48 with performance of independence skills and −0.51 with employment. (A correlation of 0.63 implies that approximately 40 per cent of the variance in one variable is accounted for by variation of another.)

Two studies have reported data relevant to the relationship between negative symptoms (flattened affect, motor retardation, poverty of speech) and social adjustment. In an institutionalised population Wing and Brown (1970) found that the negative symptoms of flat effect and poverty of speech correlated in the range $r = 0.4$ to $r = 0.6$ with indices of social functioning, such as degree of outside contact, level of occupation and social interaction, Birchwood (op. cit.) reported a correlation of −0.44 between overall social adjustment and negative symptoms, and a correlation between social adjustment and combined positive and negative symptoms of $R = 0.55$. Positive and negative symptoms are clearly associated with social impairments.

It is not hard to see why these symptoms could lead to social impairment. Preoccupation with hallucinations or persecutory delusions will directly inhibit social interaction; psychomotor retardation and apathy will reduce motivation to maintain social contacts for example.

Apart from the symptoms of schizophrenia, the associated cognitive deficits in schizophrenia might well undermine the integrity of social interaction. Thus studies have demonstrated that schizophrenics' attentional functions are poor (Schwartz 1978), that they show difficulty in accurately discriminating emotions from facial expression (Walker *et al.* 1980) and appear to be unable to generate relevant solutions to interpersonal problem situations (Platt and Spivack 1972). There is also evidence that schizophrenics show either deviant or unstable constructs of people (e.g. 'timid', 'friendly', 'trustworthy') particularly patients whose thoughts are tangential and not goal-directed (Bannister and Fransella 1966). Clearly these problems in social cognition will undermine social communication.

This evidence suggests that persisting symptoms and cognitive deficits exert a depressing effect on patients' social functioning although there is considerable (50 per cent) variation in social level which is unaccounted for by symptoms. Two caveats must be borne in mind here. First, the fact that symptoms appear to have this depressive effect under 'natural' conditions does not necessarily mean that social functioning is not amenable to intervention and change, but that persisting symptoms will probably *constrain* the extent to which pre-existing social functioning can be restored.

Second, it is possible that some of the association between symptoms and social status might arise from a *reciprocal* influence of social functioning on the ambient level of symptoms.

PSYCHOSOCIAL INFLUENCES ON THE SOCIAL OUTCOME IN SCHIZOPHRENIA

PREMORBID STATUS AND SOCIAL DRIFT

The level of social readjustment achieved following the onset of schizophrenia will be limited by the level of adjustment achieved prior to the onset. To what degree, then, are the post-onset social impairments a continuation of impairments pre-dating the illness onset?

Studies of archival records of schizophrenics, those made during their school attendance for example, have been reviewed earlier in this book and showed that there was an excess of predominantly male pre-schizophrenics who were reported either to be anti-social and poorly behaved or passive and introverted. This was generally confirmed in studies of adolescents at high risk for schizophrenia. This overlaps with studies previously reviewed which demonstrated that downward social drift and social alienation beginning at puberty and often leading to migration into inner-city areas, was commonly observed among pre-schizophrenic males. It was also concluded that this group with an insidious onset will tend to show a poor prognosis.

The question immediately arises as to whether this subgroup accounts for the social impairments generally observed in schizophrenics *after* the illness onset. It has been estimated that about one-third of schizophrenics will return to an average level of functioning (Keith *et al*. 1976). Clausen and Kohn (1966) estimate that up to one-third of schizophrenics will be 'isolates' or 'partial isolates' as a result of premorbid decline. Thus it may be estimated that 50 per cent of social impairments post-onset arise *de novo* following the onset of schizophrenia.

Another view on this comes from the use of scales of premorbid adjustment. These point to a correlation between social outcome and premorbid status as measured by the Phillips Scale (Phillips 1953). These correlations tend however to be modest: Strauss and Carpenter (1974) report a significant correlation of only 0.27 between the Phillips Scale and social relations after two years. However, when Strauss and Carpenter divided up their sample into 'Schneiderian' schizophrenics (predominantly positive, florid symptoms) and 'non-Schneiderian' (more negative symptoms) only the latter showed a significant (and strong) correlation, even though the two groups did not differ in premorbid status. The implication of this is that premorbid status is predictive in part because poor premorbid adjustment is associated with a distinct subgroup of (predominantly male) schizophrenics of insidious onset who will move into immediate chronic deterioration. Even so the best estimate suggests that this subgroup accounts for no more than 50 per cent of those with future social impairment. By and large, therefore, poor social outcome reflects, in part, a continuation of social disability existing before the onset, but such disability is probably in many cases a harbinger of schizophrenia itself.

NORMAL PSYCHOSOCIAL PROCESSES

One further reason why premorbid status is predictive of social outcome may simply be that the relationship reflects a developmental consistency over time much as might be found in any *normal* population assessed on two occasions. Construed in this way the social outcome in schizophrenia might in part reflect the 'ordinary' psychosocial processes which are brought to bear on normal individuals and which determine the variety of normal outcomes.

Various considerations support this view. First of all, the full range of social functioning is observed in schizophrenia as that for the normal population. Second, 'normal' psychosocial factors dictate that the various components of social adjustment would be far from perfectly correlated – one would not anticipate for example that those in the best paid jobs would necessarily have numerous social contacts or engage in a wide variety of social activities, a view confirmed in the normative data of the Katz Social Adjustment Scales (Katz 1963). A similar degree of discordance between components is found in the social functioning of schizophrenic patients: Strauss and Carpenter (1974) report a 0.53 correlation between employment and social contacts and Birchwood (1983) reports an average correlation of 0.44 between the six subscales of his social adjustment scales. The temporal consistency which undoubtedly exists in normal social functioning has also been found in the social functioning of schizophrenics: thus Strauss and Carpenter found that the best predictor of each social outcome variable after five years was a measure of the *same* characteristic made three or five years previously.

In view of these parallels there is every reason to suppose that the 'normal' psychosocial processes which give rise to (a) a variety of social outcomes (b) temporal consistency in social functioning and (c) a linked but loose relationship between components of social adjustment, operate in schizophrenia also. Such 'normal' processes might include personality, modelling, family influences, schooling and so on. Seen in this context the onset of schizophrenia might best be viewed as an additional 'life factor' bearing upon the temporal consistency in overall social development and influencing some components (e.g. employment) more than others (e.g. independence skills).

SOCIAL OUTCOME IN SCHIZOPHRENIA: A MULTIFACTORIAL ISSUE

The social outcome in schizophrenia, or more appositely the quality of life, is a complex issue and is grossly misunderstood when it is characterised as one outcome variable of a disease process. It is undoubtedly true that the onset of schizophrenia acts like a 'main-effect' reducing *on average* levels of social functioning (especially employment) and that this is particularly so in those patients with persisting symptoms of schizophrenia, both positive and negative. However, again one is struck more by the variability in the social outcome of schizophrenia rather than by its homogeneity. The exact prediction of social outcome depends in part on premorbid levels which will obviously set a limit on the level of social recovery. The level of premorbid adjustment will vary as a function of prodromal schizophrenia (e.g. social drift), characteristic of a minority subgroup of patients, but also in large part will be determined by 'normal' life processes. Such life processes, the influence of family, school, personality, intelligence and opportunity, will lead to a moderate linking of the components of social adjustment and to its overall temporal consistency in normals which are both evident in people suffering from schizophrenia. In addition to premorbid status and symptomatic level, *social recovery* factors will finally interact to produce a stable outcome: these will include family and community support, the availability of active psychosocial interventions and, in those prone to relapse, compliance with maintenance medication. In short, the social outcome in schizophrenia can be construed as the developmental outcome of a dynamic interaction of intrinsic impairments, normal psychosocial processes and social recovery factors. Seen in these terms, the margin of influence of environmental intervention on the social outcome is considerable.

Chapter thirteen

THE ENVIRONMENT AND PROGNOSIS: CLINICAL OUTCOME

STRESSFUL LIFE EVENTS

The hypothesis that life stress could have some causal role in schizophrenia originated from the results of social intervention studies where it was discovered that intense efforts to stimulate chronic, withdrawn patients as part of a rehabilitation programme led in some instances to a re-emergence of positive, florid symptoms (Wing *et al.* 1964). This phenomenon has also been observed in studies of the token economy (Kazdin 1977) and in 'sociotherapy' with young patients (Goldberg *et al.* 1977).

The possibility that life stress might precipitate psychotic episodes in acute patients has been intensely researched (Rabkin 1980) but conclusions are difficult to draw as the studies have not been explicit about the possible functions of life stress. The following possibilities should be clearly distinguished:

1. Schizophrenia arises as a specific consequence of severe stress associated with life events, or crises, without the presence of any underlying vulnerability.
2. The timing of schizophrenia, the first or subsequent episodes, is influenced by the experience of stressful life events. Thus the *probability* of the first, or of other episodes developing is determined by other factors.
3. The probability of an episode is influenced by the experience of stressful life events.

It is also important to keep in mind that the experienced level of stress may vary as a function of (a) the number or severity of life events and (b) greater vulnerability to the impact of life stress.

As to the first hypothesis, it is required to be demonstrated that schizophrenics experience more stress than other psychiatric or normal groups. In fact, when the period immediately prior to onset is examined (Beck and Worthen 1972; Jacobs *et al.* 1974) depressed patients report substantially more stressful life events, and in general both depressed (Brown and Harris 1979) and neurotic disorders (Cooper and Sylph 1973) are associated with severe personal stress. Thus the notion that schizophrenia represents a *specific* response to stress receives no support.

The strongest evidence for the role of stressful life events in schizophrenia comes from the research of Brown and Birley (1968). These authors retrospectively measured the frequency of life events during the period leading up to an acute episode of schizophrenia and compared this to the average of a normal British sample. They found that 60 per cent of the schizophrenic sample experienced at least one stressful life event in the three weeks prior to onset compared to 19 per cent of the normal sample. Looking further back in time, Brown and Birley found that the proportion of patients reporting events declined sharply and was found not to differ from their normal sample.

There have been many criticisms raised regarding the interpretability of these (and similar life events) data. Perhaps the most frequent criticism is that patients themselves are agents in the precipitation of these life crises due in some part to the disorder itself. Brown and Birley compared events which could legitimately be ascribed to the disorder with those which could not (e.g. death in the family) and found that the results were unaffected. Two further problems are the possibilities of retrospective bias and selective sampling. Regarding the former, it is possible that informants' perceptions may, in their desire to rationalise the patient's disorder, have distorted the timing of an event. As Brown and Birley interviewed at least two informants separately, this effect is likely to be minimal. The possibility of selective sampling is perhaps the most serious problem. Brown and Birley specifically excluded patients for whom the timing of the onset was unclear or gradual. The proportion of patients eliminated amounted to some 60 per cent. A second sampling issue is that inherent in all retrospective studies; how many patients face similar life crises *without* incurring an emergence of symptoms? An answer to this question will not only indicate the potency of environmental stress to bring about a psychotic episode, but more importantly a comparison of those who do and those who do not relapse can provide some insights into the processes involved. This issue will be considered at the conclusion of this section.

Two further research groups have attempted to examine the same hypothesis as Brown and Birley. Jacobs and Myers (1976) using the Social Readjustment Rating Scale (Holmes and Rahe 1967) failed to find any excess of life events in the twelve months prior to onset in sixty-two first admission schizophrenics compared to a sample of matched normal controls. However, this does not contradict the Brown and Birley findings as they found an excess of events in the three weeks prior to onset, an effect likely to be masked over a twelve month inclusion period. Harder *et al.* (1980) measured life events in 217 first admission psychiatric patients of whom thirty-five were schizophrenic. Using the same measure as Jacobs and Myers, but measuring 'independent' events only, they found that overall stress in the year prior to onset was not related to the severity of schizophrenic and psychotic symptoms whereas there was an association with increases in life event stress in the twelve weeks before admission thus providing support for Brown and Birley (1968).

Brown and Birley (1970) suggest that the impact of life events is greatest on those receiving maintenance medication, a view subsequently confirmed by Leff *et al.* (1973) who found that the rate of independent life events in the five week period before relapse was 44 per cent in the drug-relapsed group compared to 21 per cent for the placebo-relapsed group. The implication of this finding is that severe stresses are required to precipitate relapse when medication is taken regularly. Thus medication might be regarded as having a stress-buffering function.

The findings of Brown and Birley are consistent with the notion that the timing of episodes is influenced by life stress (hypothesis 2); whether such episodes would not have occurred without life stress (hypothesis 3) cannot be concluded from these designs. An ideal design to test hypothesis 3 would be to follow up prospectively a cohort of schizophrenics over a two or three year period, to measure the incidence of life events in a regular fashion and to relate this to symptomatic changes over this period. An alternative is retrospectively to compare matched patients with a high versus low rate of relapse for their experience of life events over a given period. Such experiments have yet to be performed. Schwartz and Myers (1977) came nearest to this in their comparison of 132 community based schizophrenics with a history of multiple relapses, and community controls. They found that the schizophrenics were experiencing life events of all kinds ('controllable' and 'uncontroll-able'; 'dependent' and 'independent' of the illness) at a high level compared to controls.

The evidence for the role of life events in schizophrenia is sugges-tive but not conclusive. At best the research supports the hypothesis that the timing of schizophrenic episodes can be influenced by independent and dependent stressful circumstances impinging upon the patient. The possibility of a more influential role awaits the results of more sophisticated research methodology in which a random unselected sample of patients are followed up and the relationship between stressful life events and relapse observed for all patients, including those who do *not* relapse.

The evidence we have reviewed does not suggest that schizophrenic patients are exposed to unusually high levels of acute stressful events; in fact, in the Brown and Birley study most of the patients relapsed in response to a *single* event. Analysis of the reasons for the patients' apparent vulnerability to such events could shed light on the underlying processes involved and highlight potential therapeutic implications.

One possibility is that the vulnerability is somatic in origin: it has been observed, for example, that some schizophrenics show a high level of autonomic arousal or sensitivity to aversive stimuli (Dawson and Neuchterlein 1984) and it may be this which mediates the impact of stressful experiences. Another possibility is that schizophrenics' resources to cope with stressful experiences are impoverished in some respect. These coping resources fall into two categories. The first includes the actual strategies adopted to alleviate the impact of the stressors at both the cognitive and behavioural levels. Knowledge of patients' deficiences in this area could have practical therapeutic implications. However, there has been no research into the nature of such strategies in normal populations which would be an essential prerequisite if we are to discover whether schizophrenics are, in fact, deficient in such coping resources (Marzillier and Birchwood 1981). It is widely accepted (see Ch. 12) that many schizophrenics fail to develop or lose appropriate social and life skills and one might reasonably suppose that this would have an important bearing on the manner in which they adjust to life changes and stresses. Clearly, this is an area ripe for further study and raises the issue of the significance for the patient of his social readjustment following the onset of schizophrenia, an issue discussed in further detail below.

A third factor which may increase vulnerability is the lack of support and ties with other people, including the patients' family. This may influence stress either by depriving the patient of a source of stimulation and models for coping with stress or more directly by increasing the appraisal of personal threat (Lazarus 1966). The limited amount of research which has addressed this issue has reached the conclusion that many schizophrenics lack the social support of a normal population and follow-up studies of schizophrenia have indeed shown that social isolation is a significant prognostic indicator (WHO 1979).

A major problem is that poor social support is confounded with social incompetence and social withdrawal, which are themselves prognostically significant. It will need to be demonstrated that social support and social ties, independently of social competence and withdrawal, increases vulnerability to stress and hence adversely influences outcome. In view of the well established findings that the peak incidence for schizophrenia lies within the 18–30 age group, it may be that as this represents a period of major role transition with consequent changes in social relationships, this could be seen as a manifestation of the impact of weakened social support networks, particularly as the effect is unlikely to be accounted for entirely by social incompetence or social withdrawal. Once again there is suggestive evidence that low social support may act as a vulnerability factor, but more sophisticated research designs are required to disentangle the complexities involved.

FAMILY LIFE AND THE COURSE OF SCHIZOPHRENIA

Our discussion of the role of the family environment will centre around a research programme originating in the UK which has achieved a level of prediction unparalleled in psychiatry. These are the studies of 'Expressed Emotion'.

THE STUDIES OF EXPRESSED EMOTION

The impetus for this long and successful series of studies was founded on some results reported by Brown et al. (1958) showing that schizophrenics returning to parents or spouses fared worse than those returning to lodgings of siblings in terms of community survival. This effect has not since been replicated (Blumenthal et al. 1982) although Brown's initial finding that the amount of face-to-face contact between patient and family was an interactive variable does suggest that close relatives may place patients at risk for relapse. This was hypothesised to be relatives' 'emotional over-involvement'.

Brown et al. (1962) operationalised this in terms of the amount of emotion, positive or negative, hostility and domination rated during the course of a factual interview about the patient. Using a prospective design they found that homes rated high in emotional involvement (a composite of all measures) were strongly associated with clinical deterioration over twelve months. Following the methodological refinement of emotional involvement to include critical comments rated in terms of tone of voice as well as content (Brown and Rutter 1966; Rutter and Brown 1966) a replication was attempted (Brown et al. 1972). Relatives rated as 'high expressed emotion, mainly those making more than seven critical comments, were associated with a much higher rate of relapse over nine months

compared to the low EE group (58 per cent vs 16 per cent) statistically independent of patients' level of disturbed behaviour. This
interacted with the overall level of weekly relative-patient contact
time. A further successful replication with refinements in measurement by Vaughn and Leff (1976) included a meta-analysis of these
two studies (N = 128) suggesting that risk factors of high EE,
contact time and use of medication operated in a hierarchical
additive fashion such that, for example, patients in low contact (less
than thirty-five hours per week) with a high EE relative and taking
medication reduced the relapse rate to 15 per cent, comparable with
the low EE group. On the other hand, high contact with a high EE
relative without medication predicted almost certain relapse (97 per
cent).

Subsequently Leff and Vaughn (1980) using the same sample,
demonstrated that low EE patients who relapse were much more
likely to experience an undesirable life event, suggesting that
relapse is precipitated either by high EE, stressful life events or
more likely a combination of both. The effect has been replicated
in the USA (Vaughn *et al.* 1985) and in Britain the predictive
efficacy of high EE has been demonstrated over two years (Leff and
Vaughn 1981). Leff and Vaughn found that although maintenance
medication was beneficial in preventing relapse in high but not low
EE homes over nine months, this was reversed over two years (i.e.
medication became protective in low but not high EE homes)
presumably as extra-familial stressful experiences impinge on the
low EE patients, prompting relapse in those not on medication.

In spite of efforts to control for relevant variables, the designs
are essentially correlational and it is quite possible that poor prognosis schizophrenics provoke high EE rather than vice versa. The
causal role of high EE and indeed the therapeutic significance of
these data was demonstrated by Leff *et al.* (1982) who managed to
reduce high EE through a comprehensive intervention package
which contained relapse to 9 per cent (versus 50 per cent for the
no-intervention control group) over nine months. This was
essentially replicated by Falloon *et al.* (1982) using a similar
design but not all patients in their groups were from high EE homes
(these interventions will be discussed in more detail in Ch. 15).

The high EE index is essentially a measure of relatives' interview
behaviour and is, therefore, remote from actual family life. This
immediately raises two important questions: what is the basis of
high EE in actual family interactions and what is its mode of action?
In view of Leff and Vaughn's (1980) finding that high EE *or* life
events are associated with relapse in those not on medication, but
in those protected by medication, a sufficient condition for relapse
was high EE *and* a life event, then high EE and life events would
appear to be functionally equivalent. That is, high EE could be

considered to act as a form of chronic psychological stress whose impact may be mitigated by medication.

There is evidence that such psychological stress may be mediated autonomically. Evidence for this comes from psychophysiological studies. Tarrier *et al.* (1979) found that among remitted patients, those who came from high EE families *maintained* a high level of autonomic arousal in the presence of their relative compared to low EE patients whose arousal level dropped in the presence of their relative. Sturgeon *et al.* (1984) found a higher level of autonomic arousal in acutely ill patients with high EE compared to low EE relatives independent of the presence of the relative during recording or of maintenance medication. These results on the surface suggest that high arousal is a direct response to a high EE relative and in view of the known abnormalities of autonomic arousal (Dawson and Neuchterlein 1984) may represent an interface of the bio-social interaction. Sturgeon *et al.* (1984) report data which suggest a more complex picture. First, high EE patients show higher electrodermal activity than low EE patients, and those who subsequently relapsed showed an elevation of electrodermal activity in the presence of the key relative. Second, Sturgeon and his colleagues retested high EE patients subject to a family intervention (Leff *et al.* 1982) and found that a change from high to low EE was *not* accompanied by a lowering in arousal after nine months.

One possible explanation is that it might require more than nine months for this hyperarousal to reduce to the level of low EE patients. An alternative, but not necessarily incompatible, explanation is that the high EE group is intrinsically more vulnerable to relapse (i.e. as indexed by hyperarousal) and that the effect of the environment is to raise it above a threshold necessary for relapse. Sturgeon *et al.* also show that within the high EE group those who *increase* arousal in the presence of a relative are the ones who are particularly prone to relapse. Thus, although the possibilities need to be further explored, it seems possible that high EE represents a chronic psychosocial stress on patients who are intrinsically more *vulnerable* to relapse and that even if high EE is reduced the vulnerability may remain, possibly permanently.

A second issue concerns the nature of family life in high EE homes and how it differs from low EE homes. Answers to these questions are important in themselves but are crucial for those attempting to develop effective and efficient intervention strategies; hitherto family interventions have been intuitive and 'scattershot' in nature as there has been no descriptive or functional basis on which to draw.

One line of enquiry has hypothesised that the high EE families are more isolated from social support systems which might help to ameliorate the stress associated with a schizophrenic member. The original study of Brown *et al.* (1972) found that where the high EE relatives were parents they tended to be more often living alone compared to the low EE group. Where patients were married the *presence* of others (mainly children) in the household was associated with high EE presumably because other dependents only add to the stress. Fewer social contacts were reported by all the high EE families. However, Anderson *et al.* (1984) failed to replicate this in respect of either quality or size of social networks using more sophisticated measurement techniques. In a study concerned with relatives' coping behaviour, Birchwood (1983) reports that families which provide support to the principal care-givers ('cohesive families') tended to have greater success in managing a schizophrenic patient at home. Given that the immediate family is the most consistently and readily available support, it is perhaps this network which will be the dominant influence and should be investigated in relation to EE.

Another approach has been to observe directly the interactions of family and patient. Kuipers *et al.* (1983) in a laboratory family interaction situation found that high EE relatives tended to spend more time talking and less in listening to the patient compared to low EE patients. Miklowitz *et al.* (1984), using a similar procedure, found that high EE relatives make more critical remarks and that the high EE-overinvolved relatives make more intrusive remarks such as telling the patient how he thinks or feels. These observations strongly support the validity of the EE measure and indicate that relatives' behavioural propensities in interviews are similar to those in laboratory interactions but give only a limited insight into actual family life and why some families behave in this way.

A fresh perspective is provided through consideration of some of the fundamental data reported by Brown *et al.* (1972) and Vaughn and Leff (1976):

1. There is close relationship between behavioural disturbance and EE. Patients in the high EE group are, compared to the low EE group, more behaviourally disturbed or work impaired ($\gamma = 0.8$) and have had more previous admissions ($\gamma = 0.51$). As behavioural disturbance declines from its peak at acute admission so do the number of critical comments and the proportion of families classified high EE (Brown *et al.* 1972).

2. Leff and Brown (1977) report that for first admission patients 38 per cent of high EE families relapsed compared to 69 per cent for readmissions. It may be inferred that *with time* high EE families become more powerful in their influence or that families are 'incorrectly classified' following first admission. Whichever is correct, it would seem that there are some developmental changes within these families.

One interpretation of these data is that families *emerge as high EE as chronicity advances*. This is not to dispute any causal significance of family variables but to suggest that high EE is a *visible* sign of pathological family disturbance which emerges as the outcome of a developmental process, often in the context of a more advanced disorder.

These data show that high EE is closely related to patients' disturbed behaviour. It would seem reasonable to conclude therefore that high EE represents a *differential* response to patient behaviour. Perhaps the most apposite issue then is why families seem to differ in their response to patients' behavioural disturbance. It has long been a complaint of families that managing a disturbed family member can prove extremely taxing, placing pressures on both patient and family (see Ch. 1) and anecdotal observations suggest that low EE families fare better in this respect (Kuipers 1979).

A hypothesis explored by Birchwood (1983) argued that negative family influences emerge as a result of relatives' failure to cope adequately with schizophrenics' persisting behavioural disturbance (which is often quite marked). In other words, high EE might be synonymous with coping failure.

Birchwood (1983) specifically explored the role of relatives' coping styles in relation to a variety of characteristic behavioural changes observed in the home setting (e.g. withdrawal, loss of independence, talking to 'voices' etc). Using relatives' self-reports of their coping behaviour, cued by a video role-play technique, it was found that coercive, punitive styles of management, which were associated with high stress and poor perceived control, were associated with relapse in a retrospective follow-up design. The negative symptoms were particularly subject to coercive responses. The specific implication of this study is that stressful interactions between family and patient occur mainly in the context of patients' disturbed behaviour and that the relatives' management of persisting 'schizophrenic' disturbance should be the principal focus of family interventions. Indeed, most high EE relatives in the intervention of Leff *et al.* (1982) spontaneously solicited discussion and advice on these issues.

The British studies of expressed emotion have provided the most convincing and methodologically sophisticated demonstration that the environment to which the discharged schizophrenic patient is exposed has a crucial bearing on whether the disorder re-emerges or not. The full clinical implications of this research has yet to be realised and among other things requires fuller elaboration of the meaning of the EE construct.

SOCIAL AND COMMUNITY ADJUSTMENT

Follow-up studies of schizophrenia consistently find that indices of patients' social-interpersonal functioning are associated with outcome including social isolation, poor premorbid interpersonal functioning and unemployment (WHO 1979). It is usually assumed that the social outcome is the direct result of the symptomatic outcome. The reverse is also possible i.e. 'To what degree does successful social readjustment reciprocally benefit the symptomatic course of schizophrenia?'

Hogarty and colleagues (1973, 1974a,b) studied the effect of maintenance medication (active vs. placebo) and a social therapy (present vs. absent) in a double blind multi-clinic trial. 'Socio-therapy' consisted of a '. . .problem solving method designed to respond to the interpersonal, social and rehabilitative needs of study patients' (1975:604). They describe one young female schizophrenic whose social therapy consisted of support in the management of a 'difficult' family relationship, practical instruction in budgeting, cleaning and cooking, help in securing stable employment and accommodation with the effect of improving her abilities to cope with the 'day-to-day realities of life' (1975:604). As anticipated, by twenty-four months 80 per cent of placebo patients relapsed compared to 48 per cent of drug treated patients. For those who 'survived' beyond the seventh month (60 per cent of the placebo and 80 per cent of the drug group) there was a significant benefit of sociotherapy on the relapse rate, particularly for males and after two years 53 per cent of the drug only group had relapsed compared to 37 per cent of the drug plus social therapy group.

Some 10 per cent of the sample were lost to follow-up and it is not clear whether this was random or not, nor was it clear whether those who relapsed in each condition were drawn randomly from that group. Also, as medication was self-administered orally, it is not clear whether the apparent subtle interaction of drug and social therapy and survival beyond seven months was due to improved drug compliance as a result of intensive professional contact with the sociotherapy group. However, Hogarty *et al.* (1974b) report that the social adjustment of those surviving in the community beyond eighteen months was much improved, clinically and statistically, with combined drug and sociotherapy which is what one would expect if the combined prophylactic benefit of drugs and socio-therapy were achieved through improvements in social functioning.

In another study Liberman *et al.* (1981) assigned twenty-eight medicated schizophrenics at high risk for relapse to receive either intensive social skills training and family therapy or intensive health therapy (yoga, jogging etc). After one year, interpersonal functioning was substantially improved in the social skills group of whom 21 per cent relapsed vs. 50 per cent for the control (non-significant).

These two studies support the notion that improvements in social functioning can lead to reciprocal benefits in the course of schizophrenia but only in the context of maintenance medication, but that their effects may take some time to appear. From Hogarty's work it seems possible that the effect of improved social functioning may be to improve patients' ability to meet the demands of daily life which otherwise might prove excessively stressing. These studies are suggestive but require considerable methodological improvement if definitive conclusions are to be drawn.

NEGATIVE SYMPTOMS AND THE SOCIAL ENVIRONMENT

The negative symptoms, poverty of speech, blunted affect, apathy, motor retardation, are traditionally considered features of the chronic end state in schizophrenia. Negative symptoms which often co-exist with positive symptoms (Andreasen 1985), tend to persist between major episodes (as they often do not respond to medication) and in recurring or chronic disorders may gradually in time come to dominate the clinical picture. Thus in view of their relationship with positive symptoms, environmental factors which retard (or accelerate) relapse will probably also have a similar effect on negative symptoms although this is speculative.

There has been a recent revival in interest in negative symptoms with some taking the view that their presence is indicative of a progressive underlying pathology (Crow 1981b). Eve Johnstone and colleagues for example (1981: 202) argue that the negative symptoms '. . . are due to the disease process and not to the circumstances of its treatment'.

Three studies provide a contrasting view. El-Islam (1979) compared the status of matched schizophrenics in rural and urban areas of Qatar in the Middle East. He found that those in rural areas had milder negative symptoms which he ascribed to their more supportive extended family structure.

A study by Wing and Brown (1970) examined the role of the institutional environment on (a) indifference to discharge, i.e. institutionalism, (b) social withdrawal, and (c) negative symptoms. They did so by relating the social measures of conditions in three UK hospitals (e.g. per cent of time unoccupied, nurses' attitude, level of outside contact, personal possessions, etc.) to measures of psychiatric status, *within* each of the hospitals studied, *between* hospitals (the three hospitals being very different in their social conditions and rehabilitative facilities); *within* and *between* hospitals over time as the hospital environments improved over a four year period through the improvement of ward regimes and the advent of social and industrial therapies. Patients and environments were measured independently. The results of this study were clear and are worth enumerating in detail:

1. Measures of hospital conditions were highly intercorrelated and all correlated strongly with patients' level of negative symptoms within hospitals;
2. The differences in social conditions between the three hospitals was strongly related to the differences in the negative symptoms of patients in these hospitals;
3. Improvements in social conditions over time was matched by a reduction but not an elimination of negative symptoms; the biggest reduction came in the hospital which made the greatest improvement in social conditions;
4. With increasing length of stay, patients became more indifferent to discharge.

Two further results are worthy of mention. First, patients differed with respect to their vulnerability to understimulating conditions. Those with coherently expressed delusions were apparently less vulnerable. Second, withdrawal and negative symptoms often predominate when the patient becomes preoccupied with inner experiences such as auditory hallucinations. This study suggests that the 'flattening-out' process may be the result of a vulnerabilty to negativity which may be fully realised when the environment is an understimulating one and where attention is drawn to inner ('schizophrenic') experiences. This can happen in settings other than hospitals, for example it is a common observation among patients who live alone in lodgings or hostels in the community (Lamb and Goetzel 1971).

The Wing and Brown study demonstrated that although negative symptoms are not entirely a secondary (social) phenomenon, a pre-existing vulnerability may be expressed or exacerbated by the degree of activity and stimulation provided by the social environment.

CULTURAL FACTORS

The similarity in the form of schizophrenia in culturally heterogenous countries has been noted earlier in this book. Cross-cultural studies have also sought to discover whether the prognosis for schizophrenia is also similar. Common sense suggests that the outcome will, if anything, be somewhat better in western countries due to superior medical practice. In fact, the research consistently points in the opposite direction (Warner 1983).

The first well-controlled study was reported by Murphy and Rahman (1971). These authors followed up British and Mauritian first admission samples (N = 90, 100 respectively) over five and twelve years. The groups were matched on important variables, including diagnostic characteristics. They found that the same proportion (30 per cent) of each sample developed a chronic, unremitting disorder; however, whereas 68 per cent of the Mauritian sample showed no further relapse after the first episode, only 32 per cent of the British sample did so. In an attempt to control for genetic differences, Murphy and Rahman located a genetically similar population inhabiting the westernised Virgin Islands and found that they too showed an inferior course compared to the Mauritians. In 1979, Waxler followed up a sample of first admission schizophrenic patients in another developing country, Sri Lanka, finding that after five years nearly half had had no further episodes of schizophrenia. Kulhara and Wig (1978) in a four-and-a-half to six year follow-up in rural India also found that 41 per cent of their sample did not relapse. However, this study showed a high rate of attrition of the sample at follow-up (43 per cent).

The most reliable cross-cultural comparisons have come from the International Pilot Study of Schizophrenia (IPSS) in which over 1,000 patients from nine countries were followed up using standard assessments, diagnostic criteria and follow-up procedures. Their results are summarised in Table 4.

On all the measures the developing countries show superior outcome. Once again the difference mainly occurs as a result of the large proportion of patients who do not relapse in the developing countries. Indeed, so strong was this (unpredicted) effect that the well established prognostic distinction between schizophrenic and affective psychoses did *not* materialise in the developing countries.

The explanation for these differences are potentially numerous. The methodological rigour of the IPSS and the systematic elimination of artefacts such as high family tolerance for disturbed behaviour and sampling errors (see Waxler 1979) suggests that the effect reflects a genuine difference between cultures. However further work is required to ascertain whether the samples of schizophrenics in developing countries truly match the developed ones.

In view of the number of countries contributing to this effect it seems reasonable to suppose that the answer lies within the culture

TABLE 4   Course of schizophrenics over two years in nine countries (Data from WHO, 1979)

Country	No further episodes (%)	No remission (%)	Time in psychotic episode(s) (%)	'Severe' social impairment (%)
'Developing'				
Nigeria	58	7	16.3	5
Columbia	19	26	34.5	22
India	51	20	28.7	18
Mean:	42.7	17.7	26.5	15.0
'Developed'				
UK	23	30	46.8	38
USSR	7	18	29.6	21
USA	21	47	46.4	32
Czechoslovakia	17	30	49.4	33
Taiwan	27	27	43.3	20
Denmark	6	50	53.2	33
Mean:	16.8	33.7	44.7	29.5

itself and its response to schizophrenia, rather than an intrinsic characteristic of the patients themselves. Study of societal structure of developing countries and their response to mental disorder has been examined by social anthropologists (Murphy 1978; Waxler 1979) and may be summarised as follows:

1. Societal structure is predominantly rural and agrarian and the functional economic unit tends to be the village rather than the family and indeed the boundary between family and village life is often blurred. Thus roles are assigned within the village to maintain its functional integrity, independence and economic viability.
2. Families are able to reintegrate the individual back into community life through the provision of a useful social role and are assisted in this because their relatives have greater influence over the means of economic production. In contrast, socio-economic features of western countries, such as the view of labour as a marketable commodity, the prevalence of unemployment and the technical sophistication required of workers, places schizophrenic patients with residual symptoms at a grave disadvantage.
3. Abnormal behaviour is tolerated to a greater degree although

families are aware that they *are* tolerating disturbance (i.e. families' reports of 'abnormal' behaviour concord with professional evaluations). Such tolerance does not prevent them seeking treatment however (see Waxler 1979).

4. Families retain greater control over the treatment of the individual and may terminate it if they are dissatisfied. Support for the patient from family and community is strong.

5. Long-term residence in institutions is rare, the average length of stay over a five year follow-up period in a sample of Sri Lanka patients being forty-five days compared to the Brown *et al.* (1966) figure for a comparable British sample of 366 days. It is the view of Waxler (1979) that families and mental health professionals in developing countries strongly resist long term institutionalisation.

Evidence for the first two observations comes from the IPSS study where it was found that, on all indices of social functioning, patients in developing countries fare better; for example, 'severe' social impairment is twice as common in developed countries.

In seeking an explanation for this apparently powerful cultural influence Murphy (1978) and others have argued that the prevalent view in developing countries of the 'curability' or transience of schizophrenia does not lead to the inculcation of an illness or sick role which the patients act out. This view has its origin in labelling theory which holds that labels assigned to individuals (e.g. 'psychiatric patient') carry with them certain expectations of behaviour which the recipient carries out once he has accepted the label. Labelling theory itself has been questioned as a coherent account of schizophrenia (Cochrane 1983); however, the belief in the transience of the disorder must surely enhance the confidence and self-image of patients, which in turn may have consequences for their psychological readjustment.

In the light of anthropological observations an explanation could be sought in the different experiences of patients following discharge from hospital, particularly the superior support and social reintegration available in developing, rural countries. One might speculate that a more accepting, tolerant environment with the availability of a useful but perhaps undemanding occupational role is much less likely to place excessive stress on patients, a factor known to influence relapse. Indeed the environmental factors which have been observed to influence outcome *within* cultures i.e. life stress, family reactions, community or social reintegration, institutionalisation and social support, seem to be most favourable in the developing countries and, collectively, contribute to the superior outcome for schizophrenia. Statistically speaking, a developing country could be regarded as a 'Multiple R' of these favourable microsocial factors.

A transcultural study of schizophrenia measuring directly these features of their *environments* needs to be undertaken to establish the validity of these speculations. The opportunity for such a study exists in the UK where there is a large population of Asian immigrants who strongly retain their cultural identities and maintain close extended family networks. A comparison of the prognosis for schizophrenics between native and immigrant cultural groups, and its relationship to their respective responses to schizophrenia, would be instructive.

CONCLUSION

It is often assumed that the modal outcome pattern in schizophrenia is a chronic one and that variations in the course and outcome of schizophrenia is associated with endogenous illness (and treatment) factors. As far as the first assumption is concerned, long-term follow-up studies, notably Bleuler's (1978) classic investigation, show that chronic deterioration, even prior to the introduction of neuroleptics, is a pattern characteristic only of a minority.

It is sometimes argued that even if the positive symptoms are not permanently expressed, the cognitive deficits underlying the disorder lead to chronic social disabilities. However, follow-up studies point to a variety of outcomes including many who are restored to 'normal' social functioning. Why does there seem to be so much variation in outcome? This is, in part, probably due to intrinsic factors: there are known prognostic differences between schizophrenics with predominantly negative symptoms ('simple' schizophrenics) and those with affective symptoms ('schizo-affectives') which may have a different underlying pathology. This is only part of the story.

Observations of how schizophrenics fare in non-Western cultures suggest that even without the full benefit of western treatment, their outlook is more favourable. We have argued that this cannot be accounted for by the 'camouflaging' of the most severely disturbed, but could derive from the superior socio-cultural re-integration afforded to individuals with schizophrenia in these societies. Many of the components of socio-cultural reintegration- work availability, societal acceptance, life stress and social functioning and familial assimilation- are factors known to predict outcome *within* western cultures.

Within and cross-cultural evidence suggests therefore that a close relationship exists between socio-environmental factors and the clinical outcome of schizophrenia which is supported by a number of social intervention studies which have been conducted in recent years (see ch. 19). In the final chapter we shall attempt to model the nature of this 'bio-social' interaction.

Chapter fourteen

MICRO-ENVIRONMENTAL FACTORS

TRADITIONAL MODELS OF PERSONALITY

The last century has witnessed numerous attempts to develop psychological models of human behaviour, and to extrapolate from such models hypotheses concerning the emergence of behavioural and experiential dysfunction. The study of personality has of course proved to be a multifaceted field of enquiry, with no agreed demarcation of the phenomena that should form its proper and distinctive concern, the proposal of many different personality theories, and the use of numerous constructs varying in their level of complexity and hypothetical inference. Many theorists have however adopted an 'intrapsychic' approach to personality, in which behaviour is assumed to be the fairly consistent product of some underlying personality structure, and in which behavioural explanation requires analysis of the structures' nature and organisation, its determination and development, and the dynamic processes and intrapsychic forces through which it finds behavioural expression. Within this model, whose structural and dynamic constructs are hypothetical and inferred, psychopathological behaviour is typically considered representative of some disturbance in the normal process of personality development. Viewed as a symptom, abnormal behaviour is therefore of interest only in so far as it indicates dysfunction in the underlying personality structure or its dynamic forces. Probably the best known exponent of this sort of model was Sigmund Freud, who in considering the problem of psychosis suggested that schizophrenics have regressed to a state of primary narcissism as a result of an increase in the intensity of id impulses. Since primary narcissism is described as a phase early in the oral stage of psychosexual development before the ego differentiates from the id, it is suggested that there is no separate ego to engage in reality testing and the schizophrenic therefore loses contact with the world.

Personality theories and intrapsychic models of human behaviour have however encountered major difficulties in terms of the scientific and empirical establishment of their theoretical propositions, the validity and reliability of the measures they have employed to tap underlying personality dispositions, the prediction of behavioural consistency across settings (e.g. Mischel 1968, 1973) and the inferential, and often apparently circular status of their hypothetical constructs. In respect of the latter for example, it is not uncommon for theories to explain abnormal behaviour in terms of some inferred intrapsychic abnormality, and then to justify the inference of the abnormality by reference solely to the behaviour it is posited to explain. Intrapsychic models of abnormal behaviour in general, and psychosis in particular, have also lacked clear and specific treatment implications associated with diagnostic findings, and have not given rise to interventions with schizophrenics of established utility or demonstrable efficacy (Eyzenck 1966; Paul 1969). In terms of Freud's model for example there is clear support neither for the speculation that ego impairment arising from increased id impulses produces regression to a childhood state, nor for the utility of psychoanalytical therapy in the amelioration of schizophrenic symptoms.

THE BEHAVIOURAL APPROACH

An increasingly influential and widely accepted alternative to the intrapsychic model has however been represented by the 'behavioural approach' to the explanation of human behaviour. Like the study of personality itself, the approach has found expression in diverse lines of enquiry and theoretical emphases, rather than through a single unified theoretical model. Most contemporary behavioural psychologists however share certain working assumptions that give the approach a distinctive identity. In the first instance it is agreed that behaviour should be studied in its own right, not as the mere exemplar of more important processes located in some mental dimension, and that its causes should be determined through rigorous scientific analysis and experimentation. At a methodological level therefore the task of explaining behaviour is considered to be that of discovering and describing lawful relationships between behaviour as an dependent variable and those independent variables of which it might be a function. Such a task, which if successful permits behavioural prediction and behaviour change, demands an experimental methodology characterised by the careful definition of behaviour and related concepts, the use of

201

objective procedures of observation and measurement, the application of research designs permitting the isolation of dependent-independent variable relationships, an emphasis on data collection and replication, and so on.

Secondly, behavioural psychologists are broadly united in their conviction that the most important causes (independent variables) of behaviour are to be found in a person's social and physical environment. The roots for such a conviction are several, and may be traced well before J B Watson propounded the behaviourist tradition emphasising behaviour, environmental circumstances and stimulus-response relationships. Of particular influence however have been those attempts to determine general principles of learning through which behaviour changes as a result of experience and interaction with the environment. One of the earliest methodological research programmes of this type was of course that of Ivan Pavlov, who described the principles of classical conditioning through which new responses of the autonomic nervous system could be acquired by the process of pairing neutral and unconditioned eliciting stimuli. Similarly important programmatic research was undertaken by E L Thorndike, whose principles of instrumental conditioning describe the effects of environmental consequences on the emission of complex behaviour, and whose Law of Effect suggested that behaviour followed by satisfying or dissatisfying states of affairs is respectively more or less likely to be learned and maintained. Perhaps most influential however has been the work of B F Skinner, who has attempted to reach laws of behaviour inductively through observation, and to elaborate how environmental consequences influence behavioural probability. On the basis of an extensive body of research therefore Skinner has argued that behaviour is strengthened or weakened as a function of the events that follow it, and described the effect through the operant conditioning principles of positive and negative reinforcement, extinction, punishment, schedules of reinforcement and stimulus control. Skinner's particular emphasis on functional relationships between behaviour and environmental conditions represents a significant departure not only from the intrapsychic model itself, but also from Watson's methodological behaviourism, contemporary neo-behaviourists such as Hull, and such philosophical traditions as logical positivism and operationism. While the intrapsychic model for example views behaviour as the product of an inner personality, and assumes that people can behave independently of their environment, Skinner's stimulus-response-reinforcement model is interactive, transactional and regards people as 'beings in the world' rather than as autonomous and isolated entities. Similarly in contrast to Watson, Skinner does not consider stimuli to mechanically elicit responses, but suggests they 'set the occasion' for behaviour which is to be reinforced, and make behaviour more likely only through a process of differential reinforcement in their presence. The model does not therefore reify situations, predict cross-situational consistency, ignore the person or deny the existence of a private (as opposed to mental) world within the skin. It instead emphasises the total (private and public) person as the 'behaver' and suggests variable discriminative responding as a function of their previous learning history and current environmental circumstances.

Following on from the above, a third major characteristic of the behavioural approach is its contention that the environment plays a major role in the determination of behaviour described as abnormal. Specifically, it is suggested that abnormal behaviour, the labelling of which is itself considered a learned, societally determined behaviour, develops and is maintained according to the same principles of environmental influence and learning that apply to normal behaviour. Dysfunctional responding is viewed therefore not as the linear product of some underlying abnormality which has causal properties independent of an environmental context, but as the result of certain learning experiences or the failure to profit from environmental experience. The understanding of such behaviour is accordingly considered to demand an analysis of the environmental events to which it is systematically related, as well as of the person's environmental and learning history.

In its strongest form this thesis suggests that not only the development and maintenance, but also the emergence, acquisition and hence aetiology of abnormal behaviour can be explained solely by reference to environmental experience. The main 'risk' factor for the development of abnormal behaviour is therefore considered to be exposure to particular and unusual sorts of learning and environmental experiences, which promote dysfunctional responding and/or fail to provide the conditions for the development of normal and appropriate behaviour. In its weakest form, the thesis focuses its attentions not on aetiology but on the role of the environment in shaping and maintaining behaviour already labelled as abnormal. In this version of the model it is suggested therefore that the form, occurrence and fate of abnormal behaviour will depend upon its environmental consequences, whatever unknown factors might give rise to its initial emergence and acquisition. Perhaps the most common form of the thesis however suggests that while some types of abnormal behaviour arise and are maintained solely through learning, the likelihood of others, including psychosis, is influenced by the interaction of biological 'predisposing' factors and environmental experience. While emphasising the role of environmental factors in the maintenance of abnormal behaviour, and suggesting that it is in the last analysis acquired through a process of learning, this version of the model therefore acknowledges that biological factors may influence the probability of its emergence.

The contention that biological factors represent an important class of independent variables which set limits on the possibilities of behaviour is of course not inconsistent with the claim that behaviour is ultimately learned, and even Skinner stresses the importance of an individual's genetic make-up. At a very simple level for example it is obviously accepted that the behavioural differences between humans and animals reflect not merely exposure to different contingencies of reinforcement, but also the different possibilties of behaviour afforded by their respective biological characteristics. It is acknowledged therefore that biological dysfunction may constrain the ways in which a person can interact with the world around them, and that they may accordingly limit the possibilities of behaviour and make certain types of behaviour more or less likely. Biological abnormalities may for example limit the ways in which a person can receive, integrate or process sensory information from the world around them; or they may limit the possibilities of complex and enduring learning; or they may restrict the ways in which a person is physically capable of responding to or acting upon their environment; or they may give rise to internal stimuli which interfere with a person's response to relevant external events. Such abnormalities are not in themselves considered to cause abnormal behaviour in a singular or linear manner, since the expression of behaviour still depends upon the person's interaction with their environment, and their learning experience. By disturbing the person-environment relationship, and by limiting the ways in which the person and environment can act upon each other, such dysfunction may however influence behavioural probability, and make the acquisition of abnormal and normal behaviour respectively more or less likely. Of overriding importance therefore is the contention that principles of environmental influence and learning apply to the development and maintenance of abnormal behaviour, even if only within the limits set by a person's biological defect. Since in many instances of abnormal behaviour strong and consistent evidence of biological abnormality is lacking, an entirely environmental model of their genesis and maintenance is in principle feasible. Even models of psychopathology which posit some biological abnormality must however still consider the acquisition of abnormal behaviour within an environmental context, and the ways in which it is shaped and maintained by environmental experience. In short the behavioural approach contends that the role of learning and the environment in abnormal behaviour cannot be ignored.

THE BEHAVIOURAL APPROACH AND SCHIZOPHRENIA

METHODOLOGICAL IMPLICATIONS

The behavioural model outlined in the previous section has a number of implications for the study and understanding of schizophrenic behaviour, and has served to guide several lines of methodological observation and descriptive and theoretical enquiry.

Several authors have in the first instance observed that the effects of environmental consequences on behaviour carry significant methodological implications for the study of schizophrenia in general, including research guided by the assumption of an underlying biological abnormality. As noted elsewhere in this book, biochemical research for example has focused in the main not on dependent and independent variables which are both organic in nature, but on the relationship between some biochemical parameter and schizophrenic behaviour. While such research has been therefore implicitly organic-behavioural in nature, it has been characterised by immense sophistication at the level of biochemical assay, and typically poor methodology at the level of behavioural definition, subject description, the measurement of behavioural change, and notably control and consideration of environmental factors that might influence either the subject's behaviour or their biochemical functioning. To the extent that the behaviour of subjects will vary as a function of their differential learning histories and current contingencies of reinforcement, attempts to isolate reliable biochemical correlates of behaviour, to predict the universal effect of drugs and so on, will be subject to inevitable confounds. Salzinger (1973) has similarly noted the methodological rationale for considering principles of environmental influence in the study of motor, cognitive and verbal functioning in schizophrenics, and has emphasised the difficulties in determining differences between schizophrenics and other groups if contingencies of reinforcement are ignored.

In considering work on motor functioning for example, Salzinger notes the dangers of inferring a basic motor defect from the responses of schizophrenics on a reaction time task without reference to the conditions under which measurements are made, a difference between schizophrenics and normals being absent when a powerful reinforcement contingency was in effect and appearing only when the contingency was eliminated. Similarly, research on verbal conditioning (e.g. Inglis 1966; Salzinger 1973; Ullmann and Krasner 1975) has indicated the extent to which verbal reports of schizophrenics can be modified by interviewer reinforcement even within a brief interview, as well as the rapidity of response extinction when the contingency is removed. Even the clinical interview, often the main source of information upon which diagnosis is based, may therefore be subject to confounds if subtle environmental influence is not considered. The behavioural approach accordingly suggests that even research focusing on a presumed biological disease state should increasingly acknowledge its organic-behavioural status, recognise the effects of contingencies of reinforcement, adopt improved methodologies for defining and assessing behaviour, use more powerful experimental designs to determine variables to which schizophrenic behaviour is related, and so on.

DESCRIPTIVE STUDIES

Other behavioural psychologists have pursued a descriptive line of enquiry through which they have sought to develop an empirical data base concerning characteristics of schizophrenics' learning and response to environmental conditions. The work of Skinner and Lindsley in the early 1950s for example represented an attempt to chart the laws of behaviour for the schizophrenic patient, and a number of reports (see Inglis 1966; Lindsley 1960) have described characteristic operant response rates, responses to a wide range of potential reinforcers, the effects of different schedules of reinforcement, the effects of other people or treatment on response rates under particular schedules of reinforcement, characteristics of stimulus generalisation, extinction and other conditioning phenomena.

Several other workers have examined conditioning phenomena in an effort not merely to compile an empirical data base, but also to test theories of schizophrenia which posit some crucial abnormality in responding or learning, or which suggest other types of primary dysfunction of which disturbed learning might be a consequence. Learning experiments have for example been used to explore descriptive models of schizophrenia which take as their starting point some critical abnormality in the ways schizophrenics respond to antecedent and consequent stimuli. Thus Garmezy (1966) has tested the suggestion that schizophrenics are characterised by withdrawal from aversive stimuli, and lessened responsivity to conditioned reinforcers, by studies of the stimulus generalisation gradient. Similarly Salzinger (1973) has interpreted various response and conditioning characteristics of schizophrenics in terms of his 'immediacy hypothesis', and the suggestion that schizophrenics are abnormal in their greater susceptibility to control by immediate stimuli. In contrast to those sharing Skinner's distrust of hypothetical constructs, several other investigators have used learning paradigms to test hypotheses involving such concepts as nervous system disorganisation, cortical inhibition, drive, arousal, attention or motivation. Pavlov's hypothesis that psychoses involve abnormal cortical inhibition (see Ban 1964) has for example been investigated by studies of unconditioned responses and such classical conditioning phenomena as conditionability, delay and trace reflex formation, responsivity to various forms of conditioned stimulus, stimulus discrimination and extinction (Ban 1964; Astrup 1962). Rates of conditioning, stimulus generalisation, performance on discrimination tasks and so on, have similarly been used to test models of schizophrenia positing abnormalities in anxiety, arousal or drive (e.g. Broen and Storms 1967; Mednick and Schulsinger 1968).

BEHAVIOURAL MODELS OF AETIOLOGY

The above studies have assumed that abnormalities in the probability of responding to different sorts of stimuli, in drive levels controlling the emission of responses, and so on, play an important causal role in the determination of schizophrenic behaviour. As noted previously however, a major characteristic of the behavioural approach has been its contention that behaviour labelled as abnormal develops and is maintained according to the same principles of environmental influence and learning that apply to normal behaviour. In its strongest form this thesis in fact suggests that dysfunctional behaviour may be explained solely in terms of its consequences and environmental experience, without reference to hypothetical abnormalities in the mechanism of learning, drive or neural functioning. Even its more conservative expression, which acknowledges the possible importance of predisposing factors or biological constraints, similarly emphasises the environment's critical role in shaping and maintaining abnormal responding. Perhaps more characteristic of the contemporary behavioural approach to schizophrenia therefore have been those attempts to describe the development and maintenance of schizophrenic behaviour in terms of the direct influence of contingencies of reinforcement and environmental experience. In the main the focus of such work has been the moulding and maintenance of schizophrenic behaviour within institutional settings, rather than on its initial acquisition and development. Some speculations have been offered however to suggest how learning might in principle at least account for the acquisition of certain schizophrenic symptoms (e.g. Salzinger 1968, 1973). Salzinger (1973) suggests for example that 'lack of contact with reality' may arise as a function of 'superstitious conditioning' (Herrnstein 1966) whereby an irrelevant response is acquired through its chance occurrence with a non-contingent reinforcer. Similarly Salzinger suggests that delusional ideation may represent a form of superstitious conditioning in which stimuli accidentally present when a response is emitted acquire the property of stimulus control (Herrnstein 1966). Thus it is suggested that some stimulus, accidentally present when a person is for example working badly, comes to increase the likelihood of working badly, and is then considered by the person to possess supernatural powers which prevent him from working well. Such ideas may then be negatively reinforced by removal of the aversive thought that he is incapable of work. Salzinger further speculates that hallucinations may represent the outcome of classical conditioning, whereby a conditioned stimulus comes to serve as a discriminative stimulus for seeing or hearing something that is not there, or by the simple reinforcement of 'recognition responses' which may be emitted in the presence of a discriminative stimulus even when the stimulus to be recognised is removed.

While such suggestions are offered as speculative illustrations of principle rather than probable mechanisms through which symptoms actually arise, Salzinger (1973) has gone on to argue that contingencies of reinforcement in conjunction with the abnormality described in his 'immediacy hypothesis' may offer a heuristically useful explanatory framework for the disorder's development. Perhaps the most thoroughly elaborated social learning model of schizophrenia however is that offered by Ullmann and Krasner (1975). The lynchpin of their thesis, from which the development of schizophrenic behaviour is deduced, is the premise that through a 'failure of reinforcement' (1975: 357), discriminative stimuli no longer signal the occasions when behaviour will have reinforcing consequences, and the behavioural act of attending to conventional cues and social stimuli is extinguished. It is suggested therefore that through no longer attending to stimuli common to people in the core culture (that is stimuli to which 'normal' people respond) and through attending instead to other cues, the influence of other people is reduced and the person may appear to display poor social judgement, to show blandness of affect and indifference, to be abstracted, preoccupied, aloof, emotionally withdrawn, to be apparently disorganised and irrelevant in thinking and so on. To other people the person may appear lazy, and perhaps therefore being the subject of criticism and disapproval, may develop increasing feelings of alienation and persecution. At this stage the person may try various ways of returning to acceptable behaviour, such as seeking medical assistance for somatic complaints, or thinking their situation through to find its explanation. The latter may however involve the development of elaborate philosophical schemes, or the idea that their predicament is caused by some 'plotter', and these and other delusional ideas gain ground simply as false beliefs lead to reinforcement while 'normal' beliefs do not. As attention to meaningful societal stimuli is extinguished, hallucinations may also arise as internal stimuli, lying along the continuum of dreams and illusion, which have equal import, may be equally worth attending to and provide stimulation. The person may, moreover, learn of hallucinations as part of the enactment of the psychiatric patient role, from for example reading the mass media, observing others or the questions of professionals.

The latter suggestion highlights Ullmann and Krasner's appeal not merely to principles of learning and contingencies of reinforcement, but also to ideas derived from labelling theory and role enactment. In considering the developing course or 'career' of the schizophrenic, Ullmann and Krasner suggest therefore that the person may increasingly adopt the mentally ill role as a solution to the extinction of alternative ways of obtaining reinforcement. Such a role may not only provide positive consequences for the person themselves, but also be encouraged by significant others and particularly by the expectations and selective reinforcement of professionals encountered during the process of assessment, diagnosis and treatment. Ullmann and Krasner consider the learning of patient role enactments and secondary deviations to be particularly powerful within the hospital setting, wherein attention to appropriate social cues is even further extinguished. Thus while the ability to be attentive and behave appropriately is not itself lost, the institution further reinforces quiet, passive, compliant patient behaviour, and provides little incentive for attending to relevant cues or emitting differential responses. It is more likely therefore that the person will become withdrawn, and without reinforcement for attention to external cues, that hallucinatory and illusory behaviour will increase. Behaviour labelled as thought disordered may also increase, since efforts at logical thought and speech in the societally expected mode are not reinforced. Associations may therefore be made on the basis of physical (e.g. sound) or functional characteristics of words, rather than on an appropriately abstract-logical basis, while in adopting the line of least resistance set phrases, neologisms, word salad, automatic obedience, and negativism may also develop. In short Ullmann and Krasner in line with many others (e.g. Goffman 1961) consider most of the problems of the chronic 'deficit' state to be the iatrogenic products of institutional treatments.

In support of their model, which emphasises not an inability to attend or behave, but the extinction of attention to culturally important stimuli, Ullmann and Krasner cite several lines of evidence. In the first instance they suggest that an environmental model of schizophrenia gains strength from both anthropological and epidemiological research, and those studies suggesting significant variability in the emission of schizophrenic behaviour depending upon environmental demands and specific aspects of the persons social situation (see Ullmann and Krasner 1975: 353–356). The main source of supportive evidence however is considered to be the several experimental studies in which core behavioural indicants of schizophrenia have been modified through direct environmental manipulation and the judicious management of contingencies of reinforcement. In respect for example of disorganised thinking, emotional blandness and bizarre verbalisation, Ullmann and Krasner note several studies in which verbal operant conditioning procedures have improved logical thought evident in proverb interpretation, increased the frequency of 'emotion' words and affective responses during conversation, and respectively increased and decreased healthy and 'sick' verbal behaviour. Similarly, several studies are cited to suggest that motoric apathy, operationally defined as the absence of 'concomitant behaviour' and social withdrawal, may be significantly modified through shaping and contingent reinforcement for appropriate behaviour and social interaction. As acknowledged by Ullmann and Krasner, such experimental studies are of course essentially demonstrational in nature. Thus while suggesting the potential influence on schizophrenic behaviour of direct environmental manipulation, they have not themselves provided evidence of durable, generalised and clinically significant therapeutic change. As a further line of supportive evidence, Ullmann and Krasner however also cite several clinical studies in which therapeutically useful changes in symptomatic, personal and social behaviour have been reported through the application of individualised behavioural programmes and such ward wide systems of contingency management as token economies. Taken together, Ullmann and Krasner suggest such lines of evidence to provide persuasive support for a sociopsychological formulation of schizophrenic behaviour.

As one of the few well developed behavioural accounts of schizophrenia, Ullmann and Krasner's thesis deserves attention as an important counterbalance to those models whose exclusive focus is some biological disease process or hypothetical underlying abnormality. Certainly those aspects of the theory addressing the shaping and maintenance of schizophrenic behaviour in institutional settings, if rather radically expressed, seem both plausible and persuasive, and carry significant implications for both intervention and rehabilitation. The attempt to additionally provide a purely psychosocial account of the acquisition and initial development of psychotic behaviour must however be considered less convincing, unsupported by direct evidence, and in certain respects of only limited face validity. The main source of support for the general thesis is, as noted, evidence of behaviour change in chronic, institutionalised schizophrenics following environmental manipulation. As described later in this book, recent evidence does indeed suggest the value of psychosocial and behavioural interventions in ameliorating such 'negative' symptoms of schizophrenia as withdrawal, apathy and loss of volition, and in promoting improved levels of personal, social and independent functioning. Attempts to control 'positive' symptoms by behavioural techniques, while promising, have however yet to provide strong evidence for clinically significant amelioration, let alone elimination, of such core features as auditory hallucinations, or delusional beliefs. In this respect Marziller and Birchwood (1981) have noted that reductions in verbal reports of 'voices' or delusions following positive reinforcement, time out, response cost and so on, cannot be considered demonstrative of reduction in the hallucinatory or delusional beliefs that gave rise to the verbal expressions. Wincze *et al.* (1972) for example note that in spite of reductions in delusional talk following operant procedures, each of their ten patients still presented paranoid ideas on psychiatric examination. Thus while environmental manipulation can modify certain aspects of schizophrenic behaviour, the ability of behavioural techniques to change core symptoms in a fundamental manner is not yet proven. Even however were behavioural procedures demonstrably effective in this respect, rigorous extrapolation from treatment effect to cause cannot be made without further direct evidence (a problem which as noted similarly limits biochemical theories whose support is based on the therapeutic effects of drugs). The behaviour change data cited by Ullmann and Krasne can therefore at best provide indirect evidence concerning the variables and mechanisms involved at this stage of acute problem acquisition. In principle, consideration of different or additional independent variables may be necessary to understand the probability of symptomatic acquisition in comparison with the maintenance of such behaviour in institutional settings.

Other evidence cited by Ullmann and Krasner is similarly indirect in nature, including that derived from anthropological enquiry, and those reports of situational behavioural variability. Moreover, anthropological evidence other than that cited suggests that schizophrenia is probably not in fact culturally relative. Thus the form of deviance subsumed within the category 'schizophrenia' shows an impressive degree of cross cultural consistency (WHO 1979), while the adoption of more consistent definitions of schizophrenia gives rise to similar figures for incidence and prevalence between cultures (Jablensky and Sartorius 1975).

Perhaps even more problematic however is the failure to specify in a convincing manner the environmental conditions under which the basic non-responsivity to culturally important cues might actually arise, and the related failure to address the theories' core premise in terms of even indirect supportive evidence. Thus it is suggested only that attending behaviour is extinguished through a 'failure of reinforcement', the types of familial, social or other circumstances through which abnormal contingencies might be expressed, and the precise ways in which such a failure might occur, being left unarticulated. Since Ullmann and Krasner's exclusively psychosocial perspective eschews consideration of predisposing factors of a biological nature, it must be assumed that attention might be extinguished, and schizophrenic behaviour emerge, in potentially any individual subject to sufficiently unfortunate and peculiar learning experiences. Given the gross, and often bizarre form of deviance typical of schizophrenia, the credibility of such a contention must however depend upon a clearer specification of the uniquely peculiar environmental conditions through which attending responses can be so dramatically and destructively extinguished. Similarly deductions from the basic premise, concerning the development of for example hallucinations, lack convincing face validity. While environmental factors may play a crucial role in their development, form and expression, and while inattentiveness to external cues may increase the possibility of attention to internal events, the suggestion that hallucinations may be simply learned as part of role enactment, or that they represent the end point of a continuum of internal events such as dreams, cannot be considered a persuasively adequate or complete account of those factors promoting hallucinations in one person and not another. In the absence of a clearer specification of the ways in which attention is extinguished, it is also uncertain how the thesis might account for other reportedly characteristic aspects of schizophrenia's course. One feature of the disorder increasingly prevalent since the advent of neuroleptic medication is for example its episodic nature, a pattern of remission and relapse, whether partial or complete, being commonly observed. In this respect, it is difficult to envisage exactly what environmental conditions would be necessary for the irregular but repeated lapsing in and out of an enacted 'patient' or 'mental illness' role, or the episodic regaining and then extinction of attention to culturally important cues. The suggestion that remission and relapse can itself be construed as merely role appropriate behaviour seems unlikely since double blind placebo studies of neuroleptics suggest that relapse can be reduced by about 50 per cent over a twelve month period with administration of a psychoactive compound. Again it is not improbable that environmental factors play an important role in remission and relapse, nor indeed is it inconceivable in principle that their role is primary. If the latter position is to be maintained, however, strong direct support evidence must be presented.

AN INTEGRATED MODEL OF AUDITORY HALLUCINATIONS

As noted elsewhere in this book, studies of genetics, neuro-psychological functioning, the effects of neuroleptic medication, and so forth, do in fact provide fairly strong suggestive, if not conclusive, evidence for the role of biological factors in schizophrenia's aetiopathology. Perhaps the greatest difficulty with Ullmann and Krasner's model therefore is not its attention to learning, environmental pressures and social influence, but its failure to acknowledge the potential importance of independent variables of a biological variety, and its exclusively environmental rather than interactive status. As noted earlier, the more liberal behavioural approach to behaviour fully accepts that biological factors influence the nature of person-environment interactions and thereby influence the probability or limit the possibility of behaviour. Such a position does not invoke biological causality, and indeed suggests that given either normal or impaired biology, behaviour can in the main be satisfactorily predicted through observation over time of its environmental history and current controlling stimuli. Knowing that people have the biological capacity for speech for example is not sufficient for predicting when they will talk, or what they will talk about. The latter will depend upon environmental histories and current circumstances and in many respects verbal behaviour can be understood and predicted without knowledge of biological circuitry necessary for speech. Equally however, a full explanation of how and why humans talk and animals do not demands analysis of neurophysiological differences between the species. Similarly, in the case of an individual who suffers brain damage following an accident, their relationship with their environment, and the probability of certain of their responses, will be altered. Through direct observation of this changed person-environment relationship over a period of time, it may again become possible to understand and predict the individual's behaviour in terms of environmental circumstances, even if the exact nature of the brain injury is not known. Knowledge of the damage and its effects however may facilitate behavioural prediction without such extensive direct observations, and may in particular be necessary to understand why the person does not react in a 'normal' manner to, for example, material presented in a visual-spatial modality. It is therefore entirely consistent to argue both that schizophrenic behaviour, like normal behaviour, is a function of its consequences, but that the possibility of its acquisition particularly in respect of such bizarre and qualitatively unusual responses as 'voices' is influenced by unusual biological characteristics and abnormal patterns of person-environment interaction. In contrast therefore to Ullmann and Krasner's 'strong' behavioural thesis, a more heuristically useful behavioural approach to schizophrenia is an interactive one, which accepts the necessary predisposition of constitutional and perhaps inherited biological deficits which modify the possibilities of interaction with the environment. As noted elsewhere in this book, such deficits at one level of analysis may involve impaired integration of the cerebral hemispheres, and perhaps the development of unusual patterns of hemisphere functional specialisation. Such abnormalities may for example constrain the effective integration of environmental input, limit the possibilities of complex or enduring learning or increase the likelihood of internally generated stimuli which compete with external events for responses. The emergence of schizophrenic behaviour may thus involve the interaction of such constraints with particular sorts of reinforcement contingencies and environmental pressures (expressed through unusual familial influences, life events, life crises, social and work stresses etc), its subsequent course reflecting their continuing dual presence, as well as the social and personal consequences of breakdown, the adoption of a patient role, negative aspects of treatment, and the deleterious effects of institutional practice and social policy.

The greater conviction that can perhaps be attached to an interactional perspective may be exemplified by consideration of the problem of hallucinatory voices. The investigation of auditory hallucinations has of course been hindered by their essentially private status and inaccessibility to direct observation, as well as disagreement concerning the positive criteria necessary for their distinction from other types of non-veridicial perceptual experience (see Slade 1976a). In contrast to Ullmann and Krasner's suggestion that they lie on a continuum including dreams and illusions, schizophrenic voices as first-rank symptoms (Schneider 1959) are however characterised by the percipient's attribution of their source to a third person, their provision of a commentary on the percipient's behaviour and reference to the percipient as he or she, and other qualitatively unusual features through which they are differentiated from pseudo-hallucinations, illusions or imagery. Ullmann and Krasner do however make the important point that voices may be viewed as responses, citing in this respect McGuigan's (1966) reports of increased chin muscle amplitude, respiration and faint whisperings immediately prior to a patients' reports of hallucinatory experiences. McGuigan's speculations that hallucinatory voices might therefore be initiated when a person 'talks to himself' had in fact been suggested earlier by Parrish (1897), Lagache (1935) and Gould (1948), the latter reporting increased lip and chin EMG activity in a far higher percentage of hallucinated than control subjects. Using a stethoscope Gould also noted correlated respiratory changes and even indistinct words in some subjects, and in a subsequent case study (Gould 1949) reported that the otherwise inaudible speech of an hallucinated paranoid schizophrenic could be detected by a microphone as variably rapid and indistinct words whose content corresponded closely with the self reported content of the hallucinatory voice. Concluding that the subject was in fact experiencing as voices her own faint whisperings, Gould (1950) like McGuigan contended that auditory hallucinations are primarily a disorder of speech rather than perception, reliably reflected in most cases by EMG activity and in some by actual subvocal speech. More recently Green and Preston (1981) have reported a case study in which sensitive throat microphones were used to record a schizophrenic's faint whispering, previously observed at times his self reports and non-verbal behaviour suggested him to be hallucinated. Analysis of audio and video tapes made during two experimental interviews suggested that the patient alternated between normal speech, during which he made appropriate eye contact and spoke with a normal mouth opening, and whispered speech, during which he lowered his gaze and vocalised through the right side of a partly open mouth; that his reports of hearing an hallucinatory female voice were reliably preceded by detectable episodes of whispering; and that when amplified, the whispers could be reliably detected as words, phrases and sentences whose content corresponded closely to the patient's reports of what the voice had said. In several important respects the whispers heard by the experimentor conformed to Schneiderian first-rank hallucinations, being 'heard' by the patient as arising from a third person, referring to the patient as 'he', commenting on his actions, giving him instructions, using vulgar phrases untypical of the patient's usual speech, and being the source of amusement. When recordings were played back to the patient however he expressed surprise, but maintained his delusional framework with which the source of his voice was a 'real' female with whom he was in love.

Such single case studies cannot of course in themselves demonstrate the generality of a correspondence between hallucinatory experience and abnormal subvocal or whispered speech, nor establish a causal link between the two. They do however provide at least suggestive evidence that voices may indeed be usefully viewed as behavioural responses, and that they may be expressed by a person talking to themselves. If this is indeed the case, what role might learning, environmental influence and biological abnormality play in their determination? At one level, voices as internal speech must of course be learned, their content varying between different individuals, and clearly reflecting particular and idiosyncratic personal experiences. It also seems however that environmental circumstances play an important role in providing various setting conditions under which voices are more likely. Slade (1976b) has for example emphasised the role of stress and resulting anxiety as precipitating factors, noting previous case studies (Slade 1972, 1973, 1975) in which there was evidence for a build up of mood state disturbance prior to hallucinatory occurrences, and in which behavioural interventions producing improved mood state were associated with reduced hallucinations. In this respect it is perhaps interesting that Cooklin *et al.* (1983) reported an increase in spontaneous skin conductance fluctuations in association with hallucinatory onset in a group of schizophrenic subjects, while Toone *et al.* (1981) noted elevated skin conductance responses in hallucinated subjects of varying diagnostic classification.

Results of the latter study do not however clearly establish that skin conductance changes were related specifically to hallucinations or to psychopathology in general, while in respect of the former Cooklin *et al.* acknowledge that their results may reflect increased arousal as a consequence of voices rather than an antecedent. Indeed on introducing an interviewer in the hope of decreasing arousal and thereby reducing the level of voices, Cooklin *et al.* noted a reduction in the proportion of time hallucinated from 55 per cent to 9 per cent (chance probability 0.001) without any significant change in arousal. Similarly it is not certain that Slade's single case studies (e.g. Slade 1973) clearly establish the status of stress induced anxiety as an antecedent rather than consequent or concomitant product of hallucinatory voices, nor as noted below, that the reduced voice frequency reported with desensitisation reflects the direct influence of lowered arousal.

While stress, difficult environmental demands or excessive stimulation and hyperarousal (see Falloon and Talbot 1981) may be important precipitants of voices in some, and perhaps several instances, they do not therefore appear to be unique or singularly necessary antecedent conditions. Indeed in the experience of the present authors and others (see Falloon and Talbot 1981), several other more benign environmental conditions may promote hallucinatory voices, including the content of other peoples' conversation, being asked about voices, being in situations previously associated with voices, and particularly lack of environmental stimulation and reduced levels of ongoing behaviour that demand attention to and interaction with the external environment. The potential importance of limited external stimulation, and reduced amounts of meaningful input to which a person may attend and overtly respond, has of course long been suggested by the occurrence of hallucinations in normal subjects under conditions of sensory or perceptual deprivation (see Zubeck 1969). Several experimental studies suggest however that such factors also influence the probability of hallucinations in schizophrenics, Slade (1974) for example noting reductions in hallucinatory voices as a function of the amount of external task information to be processed and the necessity of making an overt verbal response. More recently Margo *et al.* (1981) have reported substantial variability in the duration, loudness and clarity of voices in schizophrenic subjects when conditions of auditory input are systematically manipulated. Investigating seven patients under nine experimental conditions, Margo *et al.* noted that voices were most markedly reduced in comparison with control levels when subjects were required to actively monitor external material by reading a simple prose passage aloud, and by then describing its content. Smaller, and progressively less notable voice reductions were observed under passive conditions involving listening respectively to interesting speech, boring speech, vocal music, regular electronic blips, foreign speech and irregular blips, while increases in voices were reported when subjects were placed in a quiet room wearing earphones and dark goggles, or were exposed to white noise. Margo *et al.* suggest therefore that hallucinatory voices are influenced not by absolute levels of stimulation *per se*, but by the extent to which input is structured, engages attention, and importantly necessitates an overt response.

On the basis of such observations Slade (1976b) has suggested that the conscious experience of voices will depend upon the prevailing level of stimulation to which the individual is responding. Proposing a 'limited channel capacity' model of consciousness, Slade argues therefore that an increasing information load imposed by activity reduces the amount of spare capacity for the hallucinatory experience. The concept of 'limited channel capacity' would however appear to afford little additional explanatory power over the more parsimonious observation that one response occurs infrequently in competition with another, or that a response is more likely in the absence of incompatible behaviour. It seems reasonable to suggest therefore that hallucinatory responses are less probable in the presence of externally directed attention and behaviour, and more likely in their absence. What is perhaps more interesting is the possibility that the nature of the ongoing activity is itself significant. Several studies suggest that probably any incompatible operant or motor behaviour will inhibit hallucinatory voices, Lindsley (1963) noting for example their reduction when nonpathological behaviour is strongly reinforced. The suggestion that voices are in fact internal speech however gains strength from the numerous direct and indirect observations of reduced voice frequency in the presence specifically of overt speech. Thus Gould (1949), Erickson and Gustafson (1969), Errickson *et al.* (1978), Field and Ruelke (1973), Green and Preston (1981), and others have all noted that verbal behaviour, and even gargling, singing or gross movements of the mouth can inhibit hallucinatory voices, while Falloon and Talbot (1981) have observed that schizophrenics in naturalistic settings frequently seek out the opportunity to talk to others to control their voices. It is perhaps interesting therefore that as noted earlier, Cooklin *et al.* (1983) found voice reduction in the absence of changes in arousal when subjects spoke to an interviewer, while in Slade's (1973) case study the subject failed to improve with imaginal desensitisation but reported voice reductions when they were exposed *in vivo* to more people with whom they were encouraged to talk. Similarly Margo *et al.* (1981) note the most significant reduction in voices when subjects were required to read out aloud, and it is perhaps interesting that of the passive listening conditions the most consistently inhibiting influence was exerted by auditory input demanding verbal processing. Slade (1976b) does in fact consider the possibility that overt speech responses may block a 'common motor pathway' and it seems extremely plausible that speech inhibits abnormal internal verbal behaviour by preventing access to the vocal musculature.

The identification of environmental consequences of hallucinations that might reinforce their maintenance is however more problematic. Several clinical studies do of course suggest that verbal reports of voices may be maintained and increased by external reinforcers such as staff attention, but there is little reason to believe that such consequences significantly influence hallucinatory experiences themselves. A number of workers have in fact noted that voices do not appear modifiable by the direct application of reinforcement contingencies (e.g. Lindsley 1963), and others (e.g. Haynes and Geddy 1973; Green and Preston 1981) have been unable to identify obvious external reinforcers for hallucinations of subjects in their case studies. One possible source of reinforcement for voices may however be the person's own response to their occurrence, including for example talking back to the voices, looking for their source, laughing at their content, talking to others about what they say, doing what they suggest or command, and so on. Such 'post-voice' responses may be viewed as analogous to the conditions of reciprocal control exerted in a normal conversation between two different people, or as elements of a complex behavioural chain maintained by some more remote and intermittent reinforcer. In respect of the latter it may be noted that voices are seen by at least some percipients as pleasant (e.g. Arieti 1967; Alford and Turner 1976; Al-Issa 1978), being sources of advice, encouragement, compliments, reassurance, amusement and friendship. Following the voice's advice may for example enable the percipient to gain access to a source of external positive reinforcement, while talking to the voice might be negatively reinforced through avoidance of demanding or aversive circumstances, escape from lack of stimulation or social isolation, and so on. At a related level voices may also be reinforced by the positive effect and mood they promote, and in instances where they are preceded by stress or anxiety, by the negative reinforcement afforded by anxiety reduction and mood state improvement (Slade 1976b).

Evidence that voices may be influenced by environmental circumstances and the percipient's other behaviour does not in itself however provide an adequate explanation of their development in some people and not others. Thus many individuals are subject to stressors, inactivity, low levels of prevailing stimulation and so on without developing third person voices with whom they talk and which they actually 'hear'. In this respect, purely learning or environmental models of hallucinations have yet to provide a convincing account of the uniquely peculiar conditions through which they might be differentially acquired. In the absence of such an account it does seem therefore necessary to adopt an interactional framework within which predisposing factors of some sort are considered potentially important independent variables influencing the probability of voice acquisition. In this respect a number of authors have reported certain aspects of cognitive functioning which might differentiate hallucinating from non-hallucinating psychotic patients. Asking subjects to imagine the words and music of 'White Christmas', Mintz and Alpert (1972) for example noted that 85 per cent of hallucinated schizophrenics reported either 'hearing' the record and believing it was playing, or at least imagining its sound very clearly, while only 5 per cent of non-hallucinated subjects reported hearing it with any vividness. On a second test in which subjects rated the accuracy of their verbatim repetitions of partially intelligible sentences, hallucinated patients were observed to judge their accuracy more poorly, and according to Mintz and Alpert to have therefore poorer contact with reality. The authors accordingly suggest that the likelihood of hallucinations is greater given a predisposition for vivid imagining and an impaired perception of reality. On the basis of administering cognitive, personality and imagery tests to groups of hallucinated and non-hallucinated psychotics, Slade (1976c) similarly suggested that vivid mental imagery in combination with poor reality testing in the auditory modality provides a predisposition for voices, and further that this predisposition may be genetic (Slade 1976b). A role for disturbed cognitive processing in voice production has also been suggested, Hemsley (1977, 1978) for example proposing that voices represent adaptions to defective filtering and information processing, and Margo *et al.* (1981) arguing that voices are related to an inability to utilise and perceive structure in presented information. Other workers have proposed however that a necessary condition for the emergence of schizophrenic hallucinations is some sort of neurophysiological abnormality. Dysfunction of the temporal areas involved in speech perception and analysis has been frequently suggested in this respect (e.g. Bazhin *et al.* 1975), a possibility supported by the observation of 'schizophrenic' type symptoms in a small proportion of temporal lobe epileptics (Slater and Beard 1963), by the induction of hallucinations in epileptics by direct electrical stimulation of the brain (Penfield and Perot 1963) and by other evidence marshalled to support the dominant temporal dysfunction model of schizophrenia (Flor-Henry 1979). Electrical stimulation of the temporal lobes however rarely produces auditory hallucinations of a schizophrenic type, more typically eliciting non-auditory hallucinations, non-verbal sounds such as buzzing or ringing, or repetitive sequences of words recalled from memory (Halgren *et al.* 1978, Penfield and Perot 1963). Indeed in Penfield's series of over 500 patients less than 8 per cent reported meaningful hallucinatory experiences on electrical stimulation. Halgren *et al.* (1978) have noted therefore that studies of electrical stimulation suggest not that complex mental phenomena are elicited by direct activation of the neuronal substrata of some conscious experience, but rather that medial temporal stimulation alters the ongoing activity in the rest of the brain. In the light of evidence suggesting voices involve abnormal internal speech, Green and Preston (1981) have therefore speculated on their association with abnormal activity of areas of the frontal lobes concerned with speech production, in addition to or instead of dysfunction in the temporal lobes, while Freeman and Williams (1952) have suggested amygdaloid dysfunction as a basis for complex temporally patterned movements of the vocal musculature experienced as auditory hallucinations. Recent consideration has also been given to the indirect role in symptom production of temporal dysfunction which occasions disturbed inhibition of one hemisphere by the other, or other forms of functional hemisphere asymmetry (see Gruzelier and Flor-Henry 1979; Flor-Henry and Gruzelier 1983). In this respect it is perhaps interesting to note Budzinsnki's (1977) suggestion from a cognitive perspective that voices reflect right hemisphere processing normally unavailable to consciousness but manifest because of failure in the dominance of the left hemisphere.

A full understanding of such new and qualitatively unusual phenomena as schizophrenic voices may however demand models appealing not to organic deficit or the effects of unilateral neurological impairment, but to qualitatively abnormal patterns of brain organisation and unusual types of interaction with and between the cerebral hemispheres. Perhaps the most intriguing and provocative thesis concerning the biological predisposition for voices is therefore that recently offered by Green and his colleagues (Green *et al.* 1983). As noted elsewhere in this book Green *et al.* (1979) have argued that schizophrenics are characterised by an impairment of interhemispheric integration, and that symptom production may be associated with disturbed information transfer or abnormal interaction and perhaps competition between the cerebral hemispheres. Green *et al.* (1983) have however gone on to suggest that impaired integration is present from early in life (being perhaps genetically based), and that it gives rise to abnormal patterns of hemisphere specialisation and laterality of function, and in particular to the bilateral representation of such normally lateralised functions as language comprehension and speech production. Auditory hallucinations it is suggested, therefore correspond to the operation of an abnormal bilaterally duplicated language system, through which one hemisphere is capable of subvocalisations or whispers which are experienced by the other as alien thoughts or voices. While at this stage speculative in nature, Green *et al.*'s thesis is of considerable interest as one of the few attempts to provide a neuropsychological basis for the peculiar duality of consciousness that typifies the experience of auditory hallucinations. As Green *et al.* note such duality has long been observed, Wigan (1844), suggesting that hallucinated patients exhibit 'two distinct and opposing trains of thought', and the subject of Preston and Green insisting that his own whispers were produced by somebody else. Since the phenomenology of disturbed consciousness in schizophrenia has only been poorly addressed by models of organic deficit, the involvement of impaired interhemispheric integration as a mechanism for the division of consciousness seems a fascinating possibility.

In contrast to the purely social learning approach of Ullmann and Krasner (op. cit.), an interactive account of voices might therefore suggest that they are indeed responses involving perhaps abnormal internal speech, that they are, like normal behaviour, importantly influenced by learning history, current setting conditions and the person's ongoing and consequent behaviour, but that their emergence is probable only given some predisposing characteristic such as impaired interhemispheric integration. The latter, and its associated division of self-consciousness, may also be an important pre-requisite for the emergence of other first-rank positive symptoms of schizophrenia, such as thought insertion and withdrawal, feelings of influence by alien forces and so on. Attempts to understand their development and maintenance in terms of environmental influence may similarly therefore gain credibility with acknowledgement of the potential importance of biological independent variables which modify the person-environment interaction and make the learning of qualitatively unusual behaviours more probable. Certainly, as noted later in this book, recognition of the role of biological constraints and predispositions has given rise to more fruitful learning based approaches to the amelioration of positive symptoms.

BEHAVIOURAL APPROACHES TO INSTITUTIONALISATION

An interactional perspective may in general terms provide a more heuristically useful framework for examining schizophrenic behaviour at any stage of its development, not merely at the level of initial acquisition. Thus in the 'chronic' long stay patient characterised by such predominantly negative symptoms as apathy, inactivity, lack of initiative, dependency and so on, biological independent variables may again act to constrain the possibilities of behaviour and limit the usual impact of environmental influence. Indeed it seems entirely plausible that to some extent at least the probability of negative symptoms is increased by changing and additional biological abnormality arising iatrogenically through prolonged neuroleptic medication. It does seem however likely, as suggested by Ullmann and Krasner (op. cit.) that many of the behavioural deficits and excesses typifying long-term institutionalised schizophrenics may be best understood in terms of deleterious environmental circumstances and contingencies of reinforcement. Indeed, if purely behavioural accounts of positive symptoms have lacked conviction, far more credibility may be attached to those addressing the institutional extinction of self care, social, occupational and independence skills, and the reinforcement of such inappropriate behaviours as nonsense talk, shouting or hoarding. Ullmann and Krasner's critique of hospital practice is not of course unique, Barton (1959), Goffmann (1961), Zusman (1967) and many others describing the insidious and destructive process of 'institutionalisation', 'disculturation', 'disengagement' and 'social breakdown'. Like Ullmann and Krasner such authors have emphasised the patients' loss of contact with the outside world, their exposure to only limited meaningful stimulation, their gradual adoption of a passive, functionally arresponsible and anonymous patient role, and so on.

The analysis offered by Ullmann and Krasner and other behavioural psychologists however focuses not on the hospital as a physical or social structure, but on the role of reinforcement contingencies and those environmental and learning mechanisms through which the social factors described by others actually influence the behaviour of the individual. It is important therefore in providing a functional rather than a formal analysis, which can help specify and operationalise the precise ways in which hospitals exert their effects, and which can accordingly afford clearer guidelines for environmental change which might ameliorate or prevent institutionalised behaviour. Indeed, in the absence of such an analysis, attempts to restructure institutional practice may involve no more than the introduction of arbitrary stimulation programmes which are merely time consuming, lack clear purpose, have little relevance to the idiosyncratic needs of the individual, and carry little rehabilitative significance. The advocacy of community care predicated on a purely sociological critique of institutional practice may similarly miss the point that contingencies of reinforcement in group homes, hostels or family dwellings may in fact be functionally similar to those operative in large psychiatric hospitals. The behavioural approach is therefore valuable for emphasising not the formal characteristics or necessarily deleterious effects of hospitals *per se*, but those contingencies which may typify institutional settings and of which impoverished behaviour is a function. It is accordingly also valuable in explaining that changes in the formal aspects of hospital practice will be useful only in so far as they give rise to reinforcement contingencies through which 'normal' adaptive behaviour is consistently followed by meaningful consequences.

In broad outline, a functional analysis of the antecedent and consequent conditions surrounding institutionalised behaviour highlights the relative lack of discriminative stimuli and reinforcers for appropriate behaviour, the presence of discriminative cues, opportunities and reinforcers for 'patient', arbitrary and inappropriate behaviour, the non-contingent availability of certain reinforcers, and the presence of punishers contingent upon behaviour considered appropriate beyond a hospital setting. In fleshing out the antecedent side of this stimulus-response-reinforcer model, behavioural psychologists have for example noted that institutionalised settings may provide few opportunities for a resident to cook for themselves, to do their own shopping, to budget, to choose their own activities, to make constructive use of leisure time, to plan, to make decisions, to carry responsibility or to learn or engage in many other domestic, independent and social behaviours necessary for effective adaption in the world beyond the hospital. Such settings, particularly long-stay hospital 'back-wards' may however provide abundant cues and setting conditions for passive role-appropriate patient behaviour, for compliance with rules and routines, for engaging in arbitrary and repetitive behaviours such as washing bottles, and for the behaviour which facilitates the smooth running of the institution but has little relevance to the demands of the outside world. Many have also noted that given the lack of provision for structured activity, for use of leisure, for appropriate social interaction and other normal behaviour which has significant consequences, far more opportunities exist for symptomatic, problem and inappropriate behaviour. While noting the importance of such antecedent conditions, behavioural psychologists have however paid particular attention to the environmental consequences of which institutionalised behaviour might be a function and in this respect have emphasised the critical role of hospital personnel as the main source and controllers of reinforcement in the hospital setting. As suggested by Ullmann and Krasner and others, overstretched staff may for example have little time to attend to and offer social and other reinforcers for the maintenance of behaviour necessary for extra-hospital adaption, and may in fact view such appropriate behaviour as assertiveness, making requests or taking decisions as disruptive, undesirable and in need of a programme to reduce their occurrence. Appropriate behaviour may therefore decrease in frequency because it is ignored, produces no significant positive consequences or is actively discouraged and punished. On the other hand however more non-demanding, compliant and co-operative role appropriate patient behaviour may be viewed as 'good', may be consequated by such reinforcers as staff have at their disposal (e.g. material incentives, access to see a doctor, attention), and may increase. At other times reinforcers such as cigarettes may be dispensed on a purely time-related, non-contingent basis, accentuating the residents' arresponsibility and belief that those incentives still of interest do not depend upon the emission of appropriate responses as might be the case in the 'real world' outside. Behavioural psychologists have also suggested a major role for staff administered positive and negative reinforcers, particularly social attention, in the development and maintenance of inappropriate behaviour such as destruction of property, verbal aggression, bizarre verbalisation, hoarding and so on. Thus it is contended that where there are few discriminative stimuli for appropriate behaviour, where normal behaviour has few significant effects and where staff attention and other incentives are in scarce supply, inappropriate behaviour may well prove a 'key' to gaining access to functionally important consequences and may accordingly increase. A resident who is ignored when making a reasonable request to see a doctor may, for example, break a window, be attended to by concerned staff, see a doctor and be therefore reinforced for destructive behaviour. Similarly, verbal aggression may be reinforced and learned in an individual whose rational requests to be excused from a group activity are ignored, but whose outbursts have as a consequence staff attention and avoidance of the activity. Again, a resident whose attempts at normal conversation receive little response from staff or other patients may learn to emit bizarre verbalisation since these are functionally more effective in gaining the interest of others. The behavioural approach suggests therefore that many instances of odd behaviour in chronic schizophrenics are the product not of some disease process or intra-psychic conflict, but of observable contingencies of reinforcement.

As noted earlier, Ullmann and Krasner (op. cit.) have cited several lines of evidence in support of a functional analysis of this type, drawing in particular on experimental studies in which disorganised thinking, apathy, social withdrawal and bizarre verbalisation have been modified through environmental manipulation. Another important line of evidence has however been provided by Ayllon and his associates (e.g. Ayllon 1963, 1965; Ayllon and Michael 1959) on the basis of work with long stay residents of Saskatchewen Hospital in Canada. In an early paper entitled 'The Psychiatric Nurse as a Behavioural Engineer', Ayllon and Michael (1959) for example suggested as above that apparently intractible problems such as repeatedly entering the nurses' office, nonsense talk, hoarding magazines and so on, were in fact products of their functional consequence and might be altered if such consequences were removed. Since observations suggested staff attention to be probably the most important reinforcer involved, ward personnel were requested to consistently ignore defined inappropriate behaviour and to reinforce instead more appropriate alternatives. In each instance this simple operant strategy resulted in notable reduction in the previously persistent odd responses. Thus one subject of the study, Helen, had caused problems with a three year history of persistent 'delusional' talk about an illegitimate child and the men pursuing her – a behaviour so annoying to others that she had on several occasions been assaulted by other patients. Typically nurses had responded to such talk by listening and by attempts through discussion to understand it and uncover its roots. On the basis of ignoring talk about the child or her suitors, and of attending instead to more sensible speech with social interaction and discussion, the proportion of inappropriate talk was reduced to less than one quarter of its previous level. Interestingly, after this reduction was achieved, the proportion of Helen's problem talk suddenly increased again to about 50 per cent. On investigation it was discovered that Helen had been visited by a social worker, who had unknowingly reacted to the delusional talk with concerned attention and had again reinforced its occurrence. The role of attention was similarly demonstrated in the later report of Ayllon and Haughton (1964) concerning a subject with a fourteen year history of such bizarre sentences as 'I'm the Queen . . . how's King George?' During the first phase of the study staff ignored neutral, non-psychotic verbalisation and paid attention to bizarre speech, and in the second the procedure was reversed. Results were dramatic, psychotic talk increased markedly compared to baseline when reinforced, and dropped well below baseline when ignored, with normal speech similarly decreasing and increasing depending upon the attention it received. In another study Ayllon and Haughton (1962) reported on the use of simple operant procedures to increase self feeding and use of utensils in a group of chronic patients, noting interestingly that as self feeding improved, delusional statements that the food was poisoned, and that God had ordered them not to eat it, decreased. Ayllon (1963) similarly described the use of operant procedures to modify the behaviour of a long-term psychotic patient whose weight of 250 lbs was maintained by stealing food, who hoarded towels in her room and who wore about 25 lbs of excess clothing. Subsequent to the programme the patient's relatives, previously embarrassed by her bizarre appearance, visited her and offered to take her home, for the first time in nine years. Many other reports of the use of operant procedures in institutional settings are described by Kazdin (1975b).

While such evidence cannot, as noted earlier, be readily extrapolated to the emergence of positive symptoms at the acute stage, it does appear to support the contention that reinforcement contingencies play an important role in the development and maintenance of many behavioural excesses and deficiencies in long-term residents of psychiatric institutions. The strength of such a contention is moreover supported by the frequent use of methodologies and research designs through which the role of environmental consequences can be demonstrated in a direct manner (e.g. ABAB reversal designs, prolonged baseline designs etc). It may of course be noted that many of the relevant studies were completed in the early 1960s when 'backwards' and, to use Ullmann and Krasner's phrase, an 'aide culture', were common in hospital settings. While circumstances have changed, and many hospitals now adopt a far more explicitly rehabilitative philosophy, the behavioural analysis however remains important for highlighting the ways in which subtle and inadvertent contingencies of reinforcement can produce behavioural impoverishment and problems. It also remains crucially important for affording guidelines for the development of social intervention and rehabilitation strategies.

Part four

TREATMENT AND REHABILITATION

Chapter fifteen

PHYSICAL AND PSYCHOSOCIAL APPROACHES TO TREATMENT

Attempts to characterise and explain schizophrenia are of interest ultimately in so far as they offer clues to the development of effective remedial, and perhaps even preventative, therapeutic interventions. In practice, however, most treatment innovations have owed less to hypothesis and data concerning the disorders' causation than to a process of empirical, and often serendipitous discovery. Indeed, it has been less common for treatment to follow logically from established models of pathology, than for evidence concerning the *modus operandi* of empirically determined interventions to guide and bolster explanatory hypotheses themselves.

Nineteenth century attempts to treat what we would now call schizophrenia by various non-specific physical techniques were, inevitably, devoid of rationale, ineffective, and rooted firmly in the pre-scientific tradition which had seen patients with disorders of unknown aetiology '. . . purged, puked, poisoned, punctured, cut, cupped, blistered, bled, leached, heated, frozen, sweated and shocked' (Shapiro 1971). Empirical experimentation with radical somatic interventions however continued well into the present century, the 1930s in particular witnessing the advent of insulin coma therapy (Sakel 1938), prefrontal leucotomy (Moniz 1935) and bilateral electroconvulsive therapy (Cerletti and Bini 1938). Despite the absence of detailed knowledge of the parameters of their physiological and psychological effects, understanding of their mechanism of action, or even unequivocal evidence of their efficacy, such techniques remained in fairly common employment over the next twenty years. Their use was however superseded in the 1950s with the advent of neuroleptic drugs, whose apparently specific antipsychotic efficacy, predictability, convenience and relative safety ensured their rapid adoption as the first line 'treatment of choice'. The discovery of even these drugs was however largely accidental, the prototypic neuroleptic chlorpromazine being initially developed as an antihistamine, being utilised with schizophrenics because of its powerful sedative effects, and being thus observed by chance to possess specific antipsychotic properties. In recent years attempts have of course been made to develop and re-examine other forms of treatment in line with current explanatory thinking. The dopamine hypothesis has for example encouraged the development of various neuroleptic derivatives, as well as the use of other substances thought to act upon dopaminergic systems. Similarly, hypotheses concerning transmethylation, prostaglandins, endorphins, wheat gluten and so on have encouraged clinical trials with for example nicotinic acid (vitamin B), primrose oil, zinc, penicillin, opiate antagonists such as naloxone, haemodialysis, gluten free diets, etc. In even these cases however the process of exploration has been essentially empirical, and it remains the case that existing medical treatments for schizophrenia are not logically derived from known pathology. The selection of drug treatments is therefore based not upon identified biochemical abnormalities, but upon the formal characteristics of symptoms suggested by empirical observation to be associated with therapeutic response.

Notwithstanding the above, it is however clear that the last thirty years have witnessed very significant advances in the availability of more effective therapeutic techniques. Notable in this respect, of course, has been the introduction of neuroleptics and depot derivatives thereof, their use having improved the prognosis of those suffering their first episode, reducing the necessity for prolonged hospitalisation, and facilitating the discharge of many long-term patients previously considered incapable of successful community adjustment. At the same time, chemotherapy (see Ch. 16), has not proved effective for all schizophrenics, rates of relapse and non-remission still run at around 50 per cent within two years (WHO 1979), and growing concern has been occasioned by such possible correlates of chronic neuroleptic toxicity as dementia and tardive dyskinesia (Famuyiwa *et al.* 1979). Such problems have therefore encouraged not only a continuing search for drugs which are more effective, less toxic and capable of rational administration, but also an increasing emphasis on the development of non-physical, psychosocial interventions which can augment chemotherapy, and in some instances afford therapeutic relief in their own right.

Early investigations of the potential utility of psychosocial intervention strategies involved the application of psychotherapeutic procedures developed from the traditional, intrapsychic model of personality described in an earlier chapter. While Freud himself had little contact with schizophrenic patients, the use of psychoanalytic techniques for example was pioneered by Harry Sullivan in the 1920s, and later extended and elaborated by Sullivan's associate Frieda Fromm-Reichmann (see Fromm-Reichmann 1952). Psychodynamic procedures were also employed by John Rosen (1946), although in contrast to Fromm-Reichmann's patient and gentle probing of her clients' 'defences', Rosen sought to establish communication and foster insight through a far more confrontational and controversial approach known as 'direct analysis'. More recently Carl Rogers (1967) has suggested the potential value of genuine, empathic listening within the context of client-centred therapy, while other workers have explored a variety of existential and humanistic techniques. Despite the success claimed by such workers, the few available experimental and methodological evaluations of insight and personal growth psychotherapies have however failed to provide substantive evidence to suggest their efficacy or widespread utility with schizophrenic clients (e.g. Corey 1977; Feinsilver and Gunderson 1972; May 1974; May *et al.* 1976). Indeed, given the sophisticated cognitive demands inherent in, for example, facing the existential realisation of one's ultimate isolation, gaining insight into one's self or one's past experience, and so on, the very feasibility of employing such techniques with the majority of schizophrenics must be considered uncertain. While the establishment of an empathic therapeutic relationship itself is of undoubted value in the delivery of any therapeutic technique, there is as yet therefore little strong evidence to suggest that fully developed insight or growth orientated approaches have clear value as either alternatives or adjuncts to conventional chemotherapy.

A range of rather more promising psychosocial procedures has however emerged over the last twenty-five years on the basis of work undertaken in the fields of social, cognitive and in particular behavioural psychology. The clinical approach within which such procedures have found application is now commonly known as broad based 'behaviour modification', the key features of which include (after Craighead *et al.* 1976):

1. The use of an experimental and functionally analytic approach to clinical data, which focuses on relationships between objectively defined and potentially measurable overt and covert behaviour, and the potentially observable and manipulable determinants of such behaviour;
2. The use of a broadly defined set of clinical procedures whose description and rationale rely on the experimental findings of psychological research, and in particular on principles of learning, social influence and cognitive change;
3. An emphasis on the evaluation of intervention effects, the goal of which is to assess efficacy and provide data upon which alternative strategies may be designed if appropriate,

As emphasised by Craighead *et al.* (op. cit.) behaviour modification is therefore best characterised not as a specific theory or set of principles, nor as a 'cook book' of techniques whose use depends upon the formal characteristics of problem behaviour, but as an experimental methodology in terms of which tools of behavioural influence are selected on the basis of a functional problem analysis. In its early development behaviour modification of course owed much to the behavioural approach described in an earlier chapter, particularly in respect of its emphasis on behaviour, objectivity, evaluation and functional analysis in terms of dependent-independent variable relationships. Perhaps not surprisingly therefore the earliest, essentially demonstrational, examples of behaviour modification with schizophrenics were based upon principles of operant conditioning, Ayllon and his associates (e.g. Ayllon and Michael 1959) for example analysing such problems as hoarding and delusional talk in terms of their environmental consequences, and attempting their modification by such operant strategies as extinction and reinforcement of alternative behaviour. Such early investigations encouraged the application of more varied operant principles with more complex cases, and in particular prompted attempts to pursue a constructive policy of generating normal patterns of behaviour using reinforcement procedures (e.g. Ayllon 1963). This work in turn gave rise to the development of remotivating environments in the form of token economies, and during subsequent years varied operant procedures (including positive reinforcement, prompting, shaping, chaining, fading, stimulus control, extinction, response cost, time out, overcorrection, satiation, etc) have been applied to many behavioural excesses, deficits and core schizophrenic symptoms. Behaviour modification with schizophrenics has not however been confined solely to the application of operant techniques, and in recent years the range of tools upon which the approach has drawn has been substantially broadened to include other principles of learning such as classical conditioning and observational learning, methods of cognitive change and techniques of self regulation. While their selection is still based upon the adoption of a functionally analytic methodology, techniques utilised with schizophrenic clients now therefore include counter conditioning procedures including desensitisation, skill training techniques (e.g. modelling, role play, rehearsal, feedback), the systematic provision of information and instruction, cognitive restructuring procedures, problem solving techniques, self management training (e.g. self instruction, self monitoring, self reinforcement, thought stopping) and so on. Such procedures have already been the subject of a considerable body of clinical research, and their use is reviewed in some detail in later chapters in this section.

Chapter sixteen

PHARMACOLOGICAL MANAGEMENT

Drug treatment for schizophrenia is now a widespread practice. The era of anti-psychotic drugs (described as 'major tranquillisers' or 'neuroleptics') began with the discovery of the phenothiazines. Phenothiazine was first synthesised in 1883 and made its medical debut in 1934 as a urinary antiseptic and insecticide; a chemical derivative promethazine ('Phenergan') was discovered to possess antihistamine and sedative properties, but attempts to sedate agitated patients with it were unsuccessful. Charpentier in Paris synthesised a further derivative, chlorpromazine, which the French surgeon Laborit used in combination with other drugs to improve the action of analgesics. Laborit discovered that chlorpromazine ('Largactil') seemed to tranquillise without sedating his (normal) patients. In 1952 Delay and Deniker in Paris found that chlorpromazine had a potent therapeutic influence on disturbed, agitated patients, alleviating hallucinations and delusions. This compound and its variants – notably trifluoperazine and fluphenazine – were widely adopted in clinical practice. A chemically similar group of drugs, the thioxanthenes, were later synthesised in Copenhagen by Petersen (e.g. Flupentixol). A further but chemically distinct group, the butyrophenones, were developed in Belgium by a pharmaceutical company but now only one of these is marketed (Haloperidol).

Each of these groups of compounds later became available in injectable form and are widely known by their trade names: Modecate, Depixol and Haldol Decanoate. These oil-based compounds are administered by deep intramuscular injection into the gluteal muscle every two weeks or so. They diffuse slowly into the bloodstream and ensure continuity of drug-taking and are not subject to metabolism by the liver (unlike tablets).

These drugs have three clinical functions: the treatment of acute episodes of schizophrenia; as a maintenance treatment to prevent the re-occurrence of further episodes (prophylaxis) and as a means of managing symptoms in chronic, unremitting schizophrenia.

233

ACUTE TREATMENT

The control of acute symptoms with neuroleptics is relatively uncontroversial and boasts a high clinical efficacy (Freeman 1978). Many psychiatrists continue to use chlorpromazine in acute patients as this has some sedative properties which can help to quell severe agitation. It is usually administered in doses of 100–300 mg three times daily. Once the disturbance is controlled, the medication might be changed to one without sedative properties (e.g. trifluoperazine). In general, improvement is visible within four weeks.

Electroconvulsive therapy (ECT) has been advocated by some as an adjunct to neuroleptics, particularly in those with depressive features. Brandon *et al.* (1985) compared two groups of medicated schizophrenic patients: those given real ECT and those given simulated ECT. They found that real ECT led to a much quicker improvement of schizophrenic (and depressive) symptoms, although by twelve and twenty-eight weeks follow-up there was no apparent benefit from real ECT. The sample used by Brandon *et al.* were highly selected (the majority had previous ECT and had a significant depressive component) and it is far from certain whether the results would generalise. Any benefit from ECT appears to be short-lived, and any long-term advantage has yet to be demonstrated. In view of concerns expressed about the negative effects of ECT, its use should be subject to caution.

MAINTENANCE TREATMENT

The continued use of neuroleptic medication following discharge from hospital was advocated because of the high rate of relapse which in one study was reported as high as 80 per cent within two years (Hogarty *et al.* 1974). The prevention of relapse is critical: it can lead to irreversible social consequences and increases the likelihood of symptoms persisting between major episodes (Johnson 1985). Continued regular medication is of proven efficacy in the prevention of relapse. Hogarty (1984) shows that they are particularly effective in those who manage to survive for one year. After a year the average relapse rate is 65 per cent on placebo versus 15 per cent on drugs, whereas during the first year after the onset, the figures are 68 per cent on placebo versus 41 per cent on drugs. Those who continue to take medication even though asymptomatic are at risk for relapse if medication is discontinued: Hogarty (1984) reports that if drugs are discontinued, two- thirds will subsequently relapse. Thus drugs control the symptoms but do not resolve the underlying process.

Maintenance regimes are now common practice in psychiatry but it is clear that not all patients benefit equally: there are those who relapse *in spite of* medication and those who remain well *without* medication. In double-blind trials of maintenance medication some 20 per cent of patients receiving a placebo are consistently shown *not* to relapse over two years whereas between 30 and 40 per cent will relapse on medication. As we have argued earlier in this book it is extremely difficult to predict on the basis of clinical variables which individuals will fall within 'good' and 'poor' outcome groups and available research on the characteristics of 'drug responder' and 'drug-resistant' patients has proved contradictory (Johnson 1985). The ability to identify those who will receive maximum benefit from maintenance regimes is important because it might offer one means of reducing the numbers of individuals exposed to long-term treatment with its attendant risks and side-effects (see below). We would argue that better prediction of individual response and indeed the ability to *reduce* the need for medication can be derived from attention to psychosocial variables as there is evidence that medication acts as a stress-buffer: those individuals on medication seem to require higher levels of stressful experiences to trigger an episode than those not protected by medication (Leff *et al.* 1983). This issue will be returned to in a later chapter and its therapeutic implications will be considered in the concluding chapter.

SIDE EFFECTS

The neuroleptics produce a range of frequently distressing side-effects. Prominent among these are those affecting motor control. These fall into four subgroups.

- *Acute dystonic reactions* include muscle spasms involving the head and neck and may affect vision.
- *Akathisia* consists of restlessness and agitation where the individual might pace up and down, fidget or rock repetitively.
- *Parkinsonism* includes stiffness, tremor, shuffling gait and dribbling.
- *Tardive dyskinesia* is a side effect which emerges some twelve months or more after the start of long-term treatment and consists of involuntary movements of the head and tongue and can affect speech, posture and sometimes breathing. Tardive

dyskinesia can be a permanent handicap as it persists in up to 50 per cent of patients when the drugs are withdrawn (Johnson 1985).

These motor anomalies can occur in up to 40 per cent of cases (Johnson 1985) and the usual practice has been to prescribe anti-cholinergic drugs such as Orphenadrine to control them. These drugs have their own side-effects (including dyskinesia itself) and doubts have been raised about their clinical utility. Studies have, for example, examined the emergence of these side-effects on discontinuation of anti-cholinergic drugs, and their results show that '. . . a conservative estimate is that fewer than half the patients on these drugs would develop (motoric) symptoms if they stopped taking them' (Johnson 1985:12).

In many cases, the motoric side-effects may be due to an unnecessarily high dose of neuroleptic. Johnson (1977) reports that in at least half of his patients, side-effects could be abolished by dose reduction without prejudicing therapeutic efficacy. However, very low-dose maintenance regimes do carry an increased risk of relapse, although with lower doses fewer early signs of tardive dyskinesia have been observed and relapse can be aborted by prompt increases in medication (Kane *et al.* 1983). Low dose strategies clearly need further examination. However, there is evidence (Johnson 1985) that drug dosages are unnecessarily high in clinical practice and that maintenance doses can drop to one-third of that used in acute treatment over the first 1–3 years after discharge thus reducing the need for anti-cholinergics to between 10 and 33 per cent of cases, compared to the present prescribing level of around 60 per cent (Edwards and Kumar 1984).

Chapter seventeen

AMELIORATION OF POSITIVE SYMPTOMS

AUDITORY HALLUCINATIONS

The majority of people diagnosed as schizophrenic report the experience of auditory hallucinations (WHO 1979), their presence in the form of third-person voices and running commentaries being in fact viewed by many as highly discriminatory first-rank symptoms. Like other positive features of schizophrenia, voices are generally considered fairly responsive to antipsychotic medication, particularly to such neuroleptics as haloperidol and trifluorperazine (e.g. Kruse 1959; Anderson *et al.* 1976). It has however become increasingly clear that a significant proportion of both young acute and long-term chronic schizophrenics continue to experience persistent hallucinations despite pharmacological interventions. Birchwood's (1983) sample of first onset schizophrenics followed up after two years for example contained 40 per cent with psychotic symptoms of varying severity, including 20 per cent reporting or showing behavioural signs of hallucinations (e.g. talking to an imaginary person). The studies of Johnston (1976) and Falloon and Talbot (1981) have similarly suggested that persistent hallucinatory voices may be quite common in longer term patients characterised by a predominant 'defect state'.

The extent to which voices occasion their percipient distress, or disrupt adaptive social functioning, is not in fact entirely clear. Thus some patients at least appear to find their voices fairly reinforcing (e.g. Arieti 1967; Erickson and Gustafson 1968; Alford *et al.* 1982) and contrary to expectations Lewinsohn (1967) found no particular relationship between auditory hallucinations and decreased social interaction or competence, length of hospitalisation, or rate of relapse. Similarly in a behavioural survey of 560 in, day and outpatients at the present authors' hospital, perceptual-ideational problems, including hallucinations were found to correlate only

−0.05 with total 'assets' (basic self help, independence and social-
leisure skills). For many schizophrenics however the experience of
voices is clearly unpleasant (e.g. Alford and Turner 1976; Al-Issa
1978), their bizarre and often threatening nature being especially
distressing to acute patients whose insight is intact and who know
they are unreal. It also seems that in many instances persistent
voices can impair social and community adaption (Wallace 1984),
that their presence may interfere with treatment compliance (e.g.
Alford *et al.* 1982, Erickson and Gustafson 1968, Weingartner
1971), that they may underpin delusion formation (Wallace 1984),
and that they may instruct the percipient to engage in various sorts
of inappropriate and dysfunctional behaviour. In one case known
to the present authors for example, a schizophrenic was admitted
to hospital having attacked a neighbour with a machete on the
instructions of his voices. Moreover, in contrast to the results of
Lewinsohn (op. cit.), several sources of evidence cited elsewhere
in this book suggest that persistent symptoms do significantly predict
future major episodes of schizophrenic breakdown. Any means of
bringing them under control are likely therefore to have considerable therapeutic and rehabilitative utility.

One approach to the problem of refractory voices, based on
biological formulations of their origin, has involved the use of
physical treatment techniques such as frontal lobotomy (see Kalinowsky and Hoch 1952), amygdaloidectomy (Freeman and Williams
1952), insulin-coma treatment (Kalinowsky and Hoch op. cit.) and
electroconvulsive therapy (El-Islam *et al.* 1970). At best however
such procedures are reported to afford only temporary relief for
some subjects, or to influence the quality rather than frequency of
hallucinatory experience, and even these unimpressive results have
not been replicated. In the absence of any convincing or agreed
theoretical rationale for their use, the employment of invasive
psychosurgical procedures in particular must at this stage be
considered entirely unjustified. More recently the use of drugs other
than neuroleptics has also been explored, some success being
reported with tranquillising agents such as diazepam (Beckman and
Haas 1980), and opiate antagonists such as naloxone (Watson *et al.*
1978). The efficacy of such procedures has however yet to be established by replicable supportive evidence, and increasing attention
has therefore been paid to the development of non-invasive, non-
pharmacological methods of hallucinatory management. In this
respect the utility of procedures based on social learning theory and
principles of behaviour modification have received substantial recent
investigation.

As a methodology drawing its tools from many areas of psychological research, behaviour modification approaches to voice control
have taken several forms and have variously utilised principles of

respondent and operant conditioning, methods of cognitive change and procedures of self-management.

COUNTERCONDITIONING AND ANXIETY REDUCTION TECHNIQUES

One line of enquiry has been predicated on the possibility that voices are, in some instances at least, precipitated by stress and anxiety (Slade 1976b), and that counterconditioning and anxiety reduction techniques such as systematic desensitisation might therefore reduce their occurrence. Alumbaugh (1971) for example described the use of desensitisation in conjunction with self management procedures in a subject whose voices seemed to be associated with anxiety about smoking cigarettes, reporting a significant reduction in hallucinations that was maintained at one year follow-up. In the first of two published case studies Slade (1972) similarly reported that imaginal desensitisation to anxiety associated with being alone or interacting with family members was successful both in improving the subject's mood state and in reducing the frequency of voices, although in this instance the subject did subsequently relapse and require rehospitalisation. In the second case study (Slade 1973) the initial use of imaginal desensitisation over thirteen sessions had little effect on voice frequency, but significant improvements in mood and reductions in hallucinations were observed when *in vivo* desensitisation procedures were introduced. Voice reductions following a two-stage desensitisation hierarchy were also reported by Siegal (1975), although the subject remained unable to function satisfactorily in a work setting despite maintenance of hallucinatory improvement at twenty-one month follow-up. Similarly Lambley (1973) reported initial success with the use of desensitisation to disturbing thoughts, but noted the re-emergence of both hallucinations and uncomfortable thoughts within a six month period. Counterconditioning procedures other than desensitisation have also been described by some workers, Nydegger (1972) for example reporting a reduction in hallucinatory and delusional reports through assertion training and verbal conditioning in a subject who experienced anxiety when making decisions in social situations. Follow up at two and a half years suggested that the reduced frequency of hallucinatory reports and associated behaviours had been maintained.

Despite the at least encouraging nature of some of this research, the utility of counterconditioning procedures as vehicles for voice control must still be considered rather uncertain. As yet the results of only a few studies are available for consideration, and while some have reported reasonably durable hallucinatory reductions, the changes in others have been shortlived, have not apparently promoted generalised clinical improvement or social adaption, and have in some instances (e.g. Lambley 1973) been associated with an exacerbation of other abnormal behaviour. Moreover, in those instances where improvement has been noted, methodological confounds and the concomitant use of other behavioural treatment techniques preclude any definite assessment of the specific influence of anxiety reduction *per se*. While as noted earlier in this book there is evidence of an association between arousal and voices in at least some subjects (Toone *et al.* 1981; Cooklin *et al.* 1983), it is not clear that anxiety precedes voice production or whether it is a collateral or even consequent product of the hallucinatory experience itself. Slade's (1972, 1973) case studies for example cannot therefore establish that the observed voice reduction was a direct function of mood improvement, and it is in fact perhaps notable that the most marked changes in the second study were reported when the subject 'was being exposed to more people to whom he was being encouraged to talk' (Slade 1973: 296). In the light of evidence discussed earlier it seems possible therefore that the critical component of the therapeutic procedure was not anxiety reduction but the encouragement of incompatible social and particularly vocal behaviour. Methodological confounds are even more clearly present in Alumbaugh's (1971) study in which the effects of desensitisation are uncertain given the subject's simultaneous cessation of smoking, while the role of assertion training in Nydegger's (1972) study is similarly confounded by the apparently powerful effects on hallucinatory reports of verbal conditioning contingencies. The extent to which counterconditioning and particularly desensitisation techniques have application in schizophrenia has moreover been questioned by the frequent reports of patients' inability to select or imagine anxiety-inducing stimuli, to reliably report changes in anxiety, to attend and concentrate during sessions, or to completely relax (Gomes-Schwartz 1979). In the light of evidence for deficiencies in schizophrenic cognitive processing, Gomes-Schwartz has suggested therefore that successful desensitisation may in fact require sophisticated cognitive skills beyond the ability of most schizophrenic patients. Notwithstanding such reservations it however remains possible that anxiety reduction techniques do have a useful role to play in affording at least some relief to those schizophrenics whose voices are anxiety related and who are able to comply with therapeutic task demands. Particularly in view of evidence that some schizophrenics in naturalistic settings seek to modulate arousal as one self determined means of hallucinatory control (Falloon and Talbot 1981), results of those case studies available may be considered sufficiently promising to merit further investigation.

OPERANT CONDITIONING AND CONTINGENCY MANAGEMENT

A second group of behavioural studies has been based on the premise that voices are operant responses, whose occurrence is a function of their reinforcing consequences, and whose frequency might therefore be modified by contingency management and other procedures based on principles of operant conditioning. Adoption of this premise has encouraged the employment of a wide range of specific techniques, and despite some variability in outcome, improvement has now been reported with such diverse procedures as extinction by removal of the social reinforcers thought to maintain the hallucinatory behaviour, differential reinforcement for reductions in voice frequency, punishment by the contingent delivery of aversive stimuli, removal of reinforcers and time out, and satiation. Exploring the effects of differential social reinforcement, Rutner and Bugle (1969) for example required their subject to monitor daily voice frequency, and reinforced reported reductions by social attention while withholding attention if voices increased. Under such conditions the frequency of self reported voices declined from 180 per day to zero over a sixteen day period, the extinction of hallucinatory reports and concomitant improvements in other aspects of the subject's presentation being maintained at six month follow up. As noted earlier, Nydegger (1972) similarly used verbal conditioning, in conjunction with assertive training, to influence the hallucinatory behaviour of a young paranoid schizophrenic who reported voices and a rigid delusional framework. The subject was told that voices were thoughts for which he was unwilling to take responsibility, and that in future he should talk about thoughts rather than voices. Thereafter talk of voices was ignored, while reports of thoughts, decisions, or anything involving personal responsibility was attended to with social reinforcement. Reports of hallucinations and delusions were noted to cease after two months of treatment, the improvement being maintained at two and a half year follow-up. Ayllon and Kandel (1976) have also reported that the content, as well as frequency of hallucinatory behaviour can be controlled through differential social reinforcement, and that these effects can be generalised to a ward setting.

Other investigators have developed intervention strategies within a punishment paradigm, whereby reports of voices are consequated by the delivery of an aversive stimulus such as electric shock or white noise, by the contingent loss of a reinforcer or by time-out from reinforcement. Results of studies employing faradic punishment techniques have however been mixed. Bucher and Fabricatore (1970) for example reported a reduction in voice frequency in a

241

subject who was required to self-administer shock whenever voices were experienced, although faint murmurings were still reported and the voices reappeared when the patient was discharged. Comparing groups of patients who used a self-shock device, were exposed to a placebo-shock condition or formed a no treatment control, Weingaertner (1971) moreover reported significant reductions in voice frequency within two weeks in all groups, but observed no significant difference between the three conditions. Although Weingaertner concluded therefore that placebo effects were the primary agents of change, Ullmann and Krasner (1975) note that the results at least suggest voices to be amenable to social influence techniques. While noting a reduction in voice frequency, similarly- rather uncertain effects of shock were reported by Anderson and Alpert (1974) who used faradic aversion to punish button press responses indicating an hallucinatory experience while reinforcing competing behaviour. More durable, and apparently specific improvements following experimenter administered shock have however been reported by Alford and Turner (1976) and Turner *et al.* (1977) in their comparison of the effects of faradic stimuli and 'stimulus interference'. While interference conditions, including engaging the subject in conversation or sounding a loud bell, were observed to reduce reported voice experience, effects were temporary and did not generalise to baseline periods or beyond the laboratory. The use of contingent shock was however noted to have a more permanent suppressive effect, with maintenance of improvement being reported at one year and six month follow-up respectively.

The employment of aversive stimuli, other than electric shock has also been described, Fonagy and Slade (1982) for example reporting on the use of eighty decibel white noise in a cross-over design whose conditions included white noise presentation following indicated termination of an hallucinatory incident (termed punishment), the presentation of noise during reported hallucinations and its withdrawal after voices ceased (termed negative reinforcement), and a control of random noise presentation. It is in fact uncertain why in this study the punisher was delivered at 'voice offset' rather than is more usually the case immediately contingent upon hallucinatory onset, while in respect of the noise escape and avoidance condition it may be noted that the term negative reinforcement is more usually considered to apply to an increase in behaviour contingently consequated by the removal of a stimulus. Nonetheless Fonagy and Slade report a voice reduction in all, and particularly two of the three subjects in the study, observing some generalisation of treatment effects beyond the experimental situation and noting white noise presented concurrently with hallucinatory reports to be the most effective condition. The utility of imaginal and covert aversive stimuli has also been reported, Moser (1974) for example employing a covert sensitization procedure whereby a young schizophrenic was taught to evoke imaginal feelings of nausea contingent upon hearing voices. Results suggested that the use of the strategy effected an immediate and lasting reduction in self-reported hallucinatory experiences.

Other investigators have employed punishment procedures in which reinforcers are contingently removed following hallucinatory onset. Richardson *et al.* (1972) for example reported a reduction in hallucinations concerning electricity through the contingent removal or privileges, the specificity of the contingency being illustrated by the continuing presence of other voices to which it did not apply. Haynes and Geddy (1973) have also noted the successful reduction in voices following time out from reinforcement (brief isolation in a small room), although Davis *et al.* (1976) observed the effects of time out to be only temporary, with initially suppressed voices later returning to baseline. Other conditioning-based intervention studies ʰᵃᵛe investigated the use of satiation and massed practice on the grounds that a repetitively overproduced response may lose its re-inforcing properties, become ultimately aversive and cease to be produced. Liberman *et al.* (1974) have for example reported some success with a massed practice programme in which two young schizophrenics listened to repeated taped presentations of sentences associated with their voices until they became fatigued or bored. More recently Glaister (1985) has described the successful use of what the author terms 'satiation therapy' in a long-term patient who was frightened by his unpleasant voices and who occasionally responded to their demands by shouting back at them, breaking furniture and refusing to comply with staff instructions. Voice rate was reported to decline to virtually zero after eighty five half hour homework sessions in which the subject sat in a quiet room and recorded the time, content and 'demandingness' of his hallucinatory experiences, concomitant improvements in his general behaviour also being observed by ward staff. While remaining an inpatient, long-term follow up at five years suggested the therapeutic gains to be maintained.

In evaluating results of this group of studies, it must again be noted that interpretational confounds and limited data preclude any as yet definite conclusions about the general utility and efficacy of procedures developed within the operant framework. Thus while several studies have reported apparently encouraging, and in some instances generalised and durable improvement, others have noted clinical effects which are limited in scope or duration, and which have not clearly generalised beyond the treatment setting. More-over, the predominance of single case reports allows no more than cautious evaluation of the relative efficacy of different techniques, a problem compounded by the evident variability in subject characteristics across studies, by the use in some investigations of multiple component interventions, and by the failure of others to provide adequate control conditions or to describe interventions in sufficient detail. Even in those reports where clinically significant outcomes have been noted, it is often therefore difficult to isolate those components of treatment critical to the effect observed. A further problem with published studies is their reliance on patients' self reports, which as both Gomes-Schwartz (1979) and Marzillier and Birchwood (1981) have observed leaves open the question of whether hallucinatory experiences themselves are influenced or merely the overt verbal report of their occurrence. As Marzillier and Birchwood have emphasised, the problem is particularly acute in contingency management studies where there is a clear incentive to deceive the experimenter (access to reinforcers), and in punishment studies where the report of voice reduction can lead to the avoidance of shock or other aversive consequences. Indeed, Marziller and Birchwood suggest that punishing patients for reports of what might be distressing symptoms may not only be ineffective in respect of hallucinations themselves, but may in fact have deleterious effects. In considering this problem in relation to his own study however Nydegger has noted:

> . . . some members of staff . . . asserted that the patient had not been purged of his hallucinations, but had merely been taught not to speak them. Thus it could not be said that he was not hallucinating. When I asked the critics how they knew that S had hallucinated in the first place, they promptly reeled off these behavioural indicators: he talks to himself; 'listens' to things no one else hears; withdraws to isolated corners; and says that he hallucinates. I then pointed out that all of these indicators were observable behaviour – a point which they reluctantly conceded. I then asserted that since none of the indicative behaviours existed any longer, it could be maintained that S no longer hallucinated (Nydegger 1972: 227).

Clearly the problem is difficult to resolve in the absence of more reliable and independent indices of hallucinatory occurrence, and while Nydegger's (1972) appeal to behavioural correlates is a reasonable attempt to go beyond the mere operational equation of voices with their reports, there is often poor agreement between nurses' observations and patients' self reports of hallucinatory experience (Falloon and Talbot 1981). One important avenue for future research is perhaps therefore suggested by the work of Gould (1950), McGuigan (1966) and Green and Preston (1981), whose results suggest that covert hallucinatory behaviour may be externalised by means of EMG recordings or even the use of sensitive throat microphones. In conjunction with more sensitive and carefully defined measures of collateral behaviour (e.g. lip movements, eye gaze, posture etc) such indices may permit more reliable voice identification and help clarify the effects of reinforcing and punishing contingencies on hallucinations themselves.

At this stage therefore the utility of operant procedures in voice control must remain an open question. It may be emphasised however that their potential role is not dependent upon the ultimate verification of a purely operant approach to the aetiology, acquisition and development of hallucinatory occurrence. As noted in an earlier chapter, a pure social learning model of the type proposed by Ullmann and Krasner (1975) lacks conviction, is unsupported by strong evidence for the critical role of external social reinforcement such as staff attention, and fails to consider the fairly strong evidence for necessary predisposing biological characteristics of an unusual type. On these grounds attempts to extinguish voices by removing their presumed social reinforcers may well be ineffective in relation to hallucinations themselves and influence only their reports. As noted earlier however, there seem persuasive grounds for viewing hallucinations as covert responses rather than ill defined 'experience', and also for suggesting that as behaviours they may be influenced by antecedent stimuli, by ongoing behaviour, by concurrent environmental conditions, and by consequent events other than staff attention, including perhaps the percipients' own responses. The facts that some sort of biological abnormality is a precondition for voice emergence, or that social attention plays a minimal role in their maintenance, do not logically preclude the possibility of their modification by social influence, environmental manipulation or such operant conditioning procedures as differential reinforcement of incompatible behaviour, punishment or satiation. Indeed biological preconditions exist in relation to all behaviour since it is only biological organisms which behave. Abnormal biology is however expressed in an environmental context and the behavioural literature is replete with examples of behaviour change in individuals whose biological characteristics are unusual or impaired, and for whose abnormal behaviour immediate environmental consequences cannot be determined. Thus while at the very least operant conditioning may control the acting out of hallucinations, a goal itself of importance to the maintenance of community tenure, they may also in principle have a role to play in the control of voices themselves.

COGNITIVE RESTRUCTURING

A third, and as yet sparsely employed behaviour modification approach to voice control has involved the use of cognitive restructuring procedures, whereby attempts are made to modify belief systems and delusional frameworks considered to be associated with the hallucinatory occurrence. In one of the few published studies in this area, Alford *et al.* (1982) have described the use of cognitive procedures with a forty year old chronic paranoid schizophrenic who presented with a ten year history of hallucinatory-delusional verbalisations and who was considered particularly resistant to intervention in view of her apparently positive evaluation of the voices themselves. Utilising a multiple phase treatment-baseline-treatment design, Alford *et al.* therefore compared the effects of social interference, in which the subject was actively engaged in conversation, self control, in which the subject was asked to stop the voice in any way she could, and cognitive restructuring. In the latter the subject was engaged in religious and philosophical discussions in which verbal shaping and simple syllogistic reasoning were used with the specific objective of altering the intrinsic value of the beliefs and voices from positive (rewarding or reinforcing) to negative (aversive or punishing). In this respect attempts were made to lead or shape the patient to arrive at her own conclusions, but to explicitly encourage her adoption of a negative evaluation of voice occurrence which might prompt efforts to resist and stop their emergence. Results suggested that frequency of voices in relation to baseline decreased substantially during both social interference and self-control treatment sessions, (in respect of the latter the subject being unable to describe the strategies she had used), but such changes did not generalise to the ward setting. Marked and rapid decelerations in on-ward voice frequency were however observed following the cognitive restructuring procedure, the patient's husband also reporting that hallucinatory behaviour was 'amazingly less' in the first few weeks after discharge. Voice frequency however subsequently returned to baseline levels, in part the investigators suggest because of the patient's reinvolvement in a mail order mystical sect, and in part because she was unable to attend for regular outpatient follow-up therapy. The results may nonetheless be considered sufficiently interesting to merit further investigation to determine the magnitude, utility and comparative efficacy of operations designed to modify the intrinsically reinforcing valence of some hallucinatory sensations.

SELF-MANAGEMENT PROCEDURES

Alford *et al.*'s (op. cit.) reports of the suppressive effects of social interference and self control interventions are of additional interest in respect of other attempts to teach self control techniques through which schizophrenics might modify hallucinatory behaviour on their own initiative. That self control strategies might be usefully employed has been suggested in particular by their fairly common use by schizophrenics in naturalistic settings (Falloon and Talbot 1981). In a fascinating attempt to identify spontaneously employed methods of voice control, Falloon and Talbot interviewed forty persistently hallucinating schizophrenics living in community settings, and collected information on tactics adopted and their comparative degree of success. Of three broad categories of response emerging, the first and most commonly employed tactic involved changing ongoing behaviour by for example engaging in leisure or work activities (87 per cent) and initiating interpersonal contact (98 per cent). The second category involved manipulation of sensory input or arousal, strategies utilised including relaxing or sleeping (73 per cent), putting hands over ears (15 per cent), physical exercise (15 per cent) or listening to loud music (15 per cent). In this respect the authors suggest that increases or decreases in sensory input or arousal depend upon conditions of prior hyper- or hypoarousal, the product being establishment of an equilibrium between internal arousal and external stimulation. The third category of coping techniques identified were cognitive in nature, primarily involving reduction in attention to voices by, for example, generating alternative thoughts. Such a strategy was apparently more successful in terms of reducing patients' distress then directly responding to voices overtly or covertly. Comparing those subjects in whom community adjustment was 'good' or 'fair' with those whose adaption was impaired, Falloon and Talbot noted that inter-personal contact, reduced attention and relaxation were more likely to be employed by the good adjustment group, and that the latter also used their strategies more consistently and were more aware of the stimuli associated with voice onset.

Clearly several of the behavioural treatment procedures reviewed earlier in this chapter have included components of self control (e.g. self-monitoring), and the potential utility of some, such as those aimed at reducing arousal, would appear to gain strength from the employment of similar tactics by some schizophrenics in natural settings. A number of studies have however focused directly on the teaching of self control procedures, Samaan (1975) for example describing the use of thought-stopping combined with flooding and reciprocal reinforcement in a female patient with hallucinations of her mother shouting threats. Teaching the patient to respond sharply to voice occurrence with the words 'Stop it, stop it!', Samaan reported a reduction in voices from twenty-three to zero per day over ten weeks, including four weekly training sessions. Errickson *et al.* (1978) however reported little success with thought stopping combined with covert assertiveness training in a young schizo-affective female, while Lamontagne *et al.* (1983) noted no statistically different voice frequencies between groups of chronic, persistently hallucinating patients receiving either phenothiazine with thought stopping or phenothiazines alone. In the latter study however Lamontagne *et al.* observed that most patients failed to use thought stopping after the four session treatment period.

Perhaps the most interesting of Falloon and Talbot's (op. cit.) observations however concerns the apparently common use of alternative behaviour, interpersonal contact and particularly talking as naturally learned methods of voice self-management. As noted earlier, several experimental and clinical studies have similarly observed significant suppressions in hallucinatory occurrence when patients are engaged in conversation (e.g. Alford *et al.* 1982; Alford and Turner 1976, Cooklin *et al.* 1983, Margo *et al.* 1981, Turner *et al.* 1977). Such strategies would of course be expected to reduce hallucinations if they were indeed behaviour, and specifically if they were equivalent to abnormal subvocal speech. That this is a strong possibility is suggested both by the experimental studies of Gould (1949), McGuigan (1966) and Green and Preston (1981) and by observation of the behaviour of subjects in case studies. Alford *et al.* (1982) for example noted that:

> The hallucinatory-delusional verbalisations in the present case appeared to entail a form of subvocal speech for which the patient ascribed an external control. That the patient's mumblings appeared to reliably parallel her reports of the Holy Spirit talking to her does suggest that subvocal speech was an active contributor to her hallucinatory-delusional behaviour (Alford *et al.* 1982:432).

Similarly Field and Ruelke (1973:640) observed that '. . . hallucinating patients frequently have movements in their throats, suggesting they may be physically as well as mentally creating the auditory hallucination'.

Field and Ruelke therefore taught their subject to obstruct voices by making incompatible vocal responses such as singing, while in an earlier report Erickson and Gustafson (1968:328) similarly described teaching a patient to reduce voices by 'using his vocal cords for something else' such as talking, or even gargling with water. Although Errickson *et al.*'s (1978) use of thought-stopping had little effect, they also reported an immediately effective and durable change when the subject was encouraged to engage in incompatible verbal activity.

A potentially useful self-control technique would therefore appear to involve teaching patients to interrupt voice occurrence and to engage in alternate vocal behaviour, the intention of such a procedure being to both physically block voice production and perhaps also to promote their extinction by removing the patient's own normal responses which might act as reinforcers. A preliminary investigation of this approach has been reported by Green and O'Callaghan (1980) who worked with a forty-nine year old schizophrenic whose voices persisted throughout the day, interfered with his daily activities and caused him to commit several destructive acts to both himself and property. In the first stage of treatment the subject was required to indicate the immediate onset of a voice, upon which the experimenter shouted 'Stop', pointed to objects in the immediate environment, and asked the subject to describe them out aloud in very specific detail. The subject was then shaped to himself shout, say, whisper and finally subvocalise 'Stop' on hallucinatory onset, and similarly to point to and describe objects aloud, to whisper descriptions and finally to subvocalise without pointing. Throughout emphasis was placed on externally directed attention and on very detailed ongoing verbal description, the subject also being encouraged to practice the techniques outside therapy sessions. Results suggested that while voices were present on 100 per cent and 90 per cent of days during baseline and placebo phases of the study respectively, they were reduced to 64 per cent of days during the treatment period and 48 per cent of days in the following two months. On the basis of the subjects self monitoring over the next twelve months voices were noted as present on only 27 per cent of days, and only 20 per cent of days during the last three months records were kept. At the two and a half year follow-up the subject reported that voices only very rarely occurred, that he no longer listened to them or attached significance to their content, and that he could readily remove them with the 'stop and name' technique. The technique has subsequently been applied with two schizophrenics by James (1983), who has similarly noted an immediate sharp decrease in hallucinations and an improvement in social behaviour and mood.

The generalised utility of self-control procedures, like the generality of an equivalence of voices with subvocal speech, is clearly as yet unestablished. Moreover such techniques clearly demand substantial co-operation on the part of the patient, and may find their most useful application with acute onset cases wherein a degree of insight is retained. Like other procedures described however, they appear to offer sufficient promise to merit more detailed investigation, particularly within the context of attempts to develop voice control programmes individually tailored to the circumstances of a given case. It in fact seems unlikely that any single technique will prove to be effective across all cases, and multicomponent programmes based on analyses of idiosyncratic setting conditions, precipitating stimuli, concurrent behaviour, reinforcers and motivation to change, may be necessary.

COMPENSATORY TECHNIQUES

In considering psychological approaches to hallucinatory management, mention may however also be made of recent and intriguing speculation concerning the possible utility of a compensatory (as opposed to behavioural) procedure empirically derived from neuropsychological investigations of interhemispheric integration. As noted in an earlier chapter, Green and his associates (e.g. Green *et al.* 1983) have reported that when listening to complex speech with either their right ear only, their left ear only or both ears, schizophrenics show larger than normal asymmetries in monaural comprehension between the two single ear conditions, and a relative deficiency in binaural comprehension compared to that of the best single ear. Green *et al.* (1979) have interpreted such results in terms of an impairment of interhemispheric integration, and suggest as one practical implication the possibilities of improving speech comprehension in functional terms by occluding auditory input to the 'deficient', ear by an ear-plug (and hence raising comprehension from its normal binaural listening level to that of the best single ear). In the course of investigations using the speech comprehension task Green (1978) however observed that in some instances reports of voices seemed to be precipitated by complex speech input to the ear suggested by testing as 'deficient', and in one instance at least by rapid alternation of speech input from one ear to the other. In the absence of a well-articulated theoretical rationale, Green (1978) reasoned on empirical grounds therefore that occluding auditory input to the 'deficient' ear might serve to reduce the precipitation of voices, and reported a number of informal single case observations in which this indeed seemed to be the case. Interestingly in the following year McGuffin (1979) reported observations of a young schizophrenic who of his own accord wore an ear-plug to 'hear things clear', and of two other hallucinated patients who showed improvement with self instigated use of ear-plugs.

The explanation of such effects remains of course unclear, although speculation concerning an association between voices and possible bilateral language representation in schizophrenia has encouraged Green (1984) to suggest that auditory input via the 'inferior' ear precipitates voices by activating the subordinate hemisphere's linguistic capabilities. Unfortunately, the generality and clinical significance of ear-plug effects must also remain uncertain, given the absence of any large scale clinical investigations and the availability of only a few single case reports. In respect of the latter James (1983) has reported the successful suppression of hallucinations in two schizophrenics by the concurrent use of an ear-plug and the verbal distraction technique described above, although he questions the role of the ear-plug since reversal of its side of insertion after treatment had begun 'made no apparent difference to the decline in auditory hallucination once it had started'. The study's design does not however permit a clear separation of the effects of the two treatment elements, and it is of interest both that voices suppression was reported as 'immediate', and that improvement after ear-plug reversal was slower. Moreover, James did not employ the test of monaural and binaural speech comprehension to determine the presence of a monaural deficit or to guide selection of the ear for plug insertion. Green's (1984) Auditory Comprehension Test was however employed by Birchwood (1986) with a thirty-eight year old schizophrenic whose monotonous and unpleasant voices occurred over 300 times a day. On the basis of a 50 per cent reduction in comprehension of complex speech in the left ear compared to the right, an ear-plug was inserted into the left ear with an immediate 50 per cent reduction in voice frequency. A further slow improvement was observed following the addition of the verbal distraction technique, and while still experiencing voices at follow-up the patient reported them to be still less frequent, less audible and less troublesome. Further validation of the patient's improvement came from ward staff who noted his greater animation and sociability. Interestingly temporary removal of the ear-plug during follow-up contact produced a 25 per cent increase in voice frequency which was reversed on the plug's reinsertion. Morley (1985) has also reported on a case of persistent voices in which hallucinatory frequency and clarity were transiently reduced while listening to music, but in which voices were totally abolished by the unilateral placement of a wax ear-plug. In view of the convenience of the ear-plug technique, the potential of its use with even some schizophrenics clearly merits further investigation.

DELUSIONAL IDEATION

Delusional beliefs are considered by many to be a further core feature of the peculiar duality of consciousness that characterises the central schizophrenic syndrome (WHO 1979), and like auditory hallucinations are usually thought to respond fairly well to neuroleptic medication and to such drugs as pimozide (e.g. Falloon *et al.* 1978). In some patients however, persistent delusions of external control, reference, persecution or grandeur, often in association with hallucinatory voices, prove resistant to medication and continue to interfere with adaptive social and community functioning. Such persistent and dysfunctional beliefs have therefore been the subject of several intervention programmes conceived in terms of the principles of behaviour modification.

OPERANT CONDITIONING AND CONTINGENCY MANAGEMENT

Most commonly behavioural programmes have operationally equated delusions with their verbal expression, have considered their maintenance to be a function of external reinforcers such as attention, and have attempted their control through extinction and the contingent use of social interest, tokens or privileges to differentially reinforce rational and non-deluded talk (e.g. Ayllon and Michael 1959; Ayllon and Haughton 1964; Kennedy 1964; Liberman *et al.* 1973; Nydegger 1972, Patterson and Teigan 1973; Rickard *et al.* 1960; Wincze *et al.* 1972). Some attempts have also been made to reduce the frequency of delusional verbalisations by the use of punishment procedures such as time-out (e.g. Davis *et al.* 1976). The reduction in deluded talk effected by such interruptions has been often dramatic, has been in some instances at least of apparent durability, and in view of the experimental designs employed, has been clearly attributable to the contingency procedures themselves. In some cases however change has been shortlived, and interpretation of positive results is again confounded by the operational equation of delusions with verbalisations and by the reliance on self reports of delusional occurrence. As emphasised by Marziller and Birchwood (1981), 'saying is not believing', and it remains unclear whether contingency procedures have influenced the experience of delusional beliefs themselves or merely their verbal reports. That the latter might be the case is for example suggested by the observation of Wincze *et al.* (1972), who noted that of the patients in their study showing reduced delusional talk following operant procedures, all continued to present with paranoid delusions on psychiatric examination. Similarly Davis *et al.* (1976) noted that when overt delusional references were consequated by time-out, the patient in their study was observed with her hand over her mouth muttering what ward staff presumed to be statements of a delusional type. A reduction in delusional talk may itself of course be an important goal which carries important consequences for community and social adaption (see Paul and Lentz 1977), and several of the studies noted above have reported generalised improvements in behaviour and particularly in interpersonal adjustment. The extent to which contingency procedures may influence delusional beliefs themselves however awaits further evaluation.

COGNITIVE RESTRUCTURING

A second group of behaviour modification studies have attempted the direct modification of delusional ideas by applying cognitive restructuring and change procedures which address the evidence upon which an individual's cognitive evaluations are based, and the person's interpretative assumptions. Some success on measures of belief strength has for example been reported by Watts *et al.* (1973) and Milton *et al.* (1978), who required their deluded schizophrenic patients to systematically evaluate the evidence for their beliefs and to generate alternative explanations. In a study investigating the interactive effects of cognitive techniques and pimozide, and the effects of cognitive change alone, Hartman and Cashman (1983) have similarly reported some improvement in delusional thinking and thought disorder in three patients encouraged to identify, evaluate and change irrational belief systems, maladaptive self statements and dysfunctional styles of information processing. As noted earlier, at least temporarily beneficial effects of cognitive procedures involving verbal shaping and syllogistic reasoning were also reported by Alford *et al.* (1982) in the case of a schizophrenic with delusional-hallucinatory verbalisation of a religious nature. At this stage however insufficient evidence is available to judge the likely generalised utility of such procedures or the durability of their effects, particularly since they make substantial demands on a subject's cognitive capabilities and treatment cooperation.

SELF-MANAGEMENT

The use of self-control procedures in the modification of delusional thought has as yet received little systematic investigation, although as with voices, anecdotal evidence suggests that some schizophrenics in naturalistic settings have learned self-management coping strategies to combat delusion formation. Marzillier and Birchwood (1981) have for example described informal observations of a patient who learned to avoid arguments on religious and political topics which precipitated the recurrence of delusional ideas, of another who used distraction and relaxation to interrupt ideas that other people's eyes were 'radiating', and of a third who learned to check with his wife before reacting to ideas that the idle chatter of others involved personal abuse. In one of the few experimental studies in the area, Lamontagne *et al.* (1983) have reported a significant improvement in the frequency of persecutory thoughts in a group of schizophrenics taught a thought-stopping procedure, therapeutic gains being apparently maintained at six month follow up. Clearly investigation of other self-control procedures, such as externally directed attention combined with relevant vocal activity, would seem to be advised.

DISORGANISED THINKING

In addition to attempts to control delusional ideation, a number of other investigators have utilised behavioural procedures to modify the disorganisation of thought and cognitive processing observed in many schizophrenic patients. Some studies have for example described the experimental manipulation of 'disorganised thinking' by simple verbal shaping, and have reported significant improvements in the appropriateness and abstraction of verbal responses on measures of proverb interpretation and word association (e.g. Little 1966; Meichenbaum 1966; True 1966; Ullmann *et al.* 1964). The clinical utility of such experimental demonstrations has not however been established, and of perhaps greater interest have been those attempts to teach schizophrenic patients self-control techniques through which they can monitor and regulate their own thinking and cognitive processes. A fascinating study in this respect has been described by Meichenbaum and Cameron (1973) in a paper entitled 'Training schizophrenics to talk to themselves'. Utilising a variety of procedures including instruction, modelling, shaping, chaining, rehearsal and reinforcement, subjects were trained over eight forty-five minute sessions to monitor their own behaviour and thinking, to be sensitive to the interpersonal signals of others that indicated they were emitting bizarre, irrelevant or incoherent speech, and to use such self instructions as 'be relevant and coherent, make myself understood', or 'I'm not making myself clear', 'try again'. The early stages of training focused on the performance of simple structured sensory-motor tasks such as the Porteus Maze and Digit Symbol Tests, subjects being taught to monitor and evaluate their behaviour by self-questioning and the use of self-controlling and self-instructional statements to attend and behave in a task relevant manner. Teaching was effected by the experimenters first modelling the task, talking out aloud while the subject observed, then by the subject performing the task while the experimenter provided instructions, then by the subject instructing himself aloud, whispering to himself and finally using self-instruction covertly. Later stages of training focused on more demanding tasks involving greater cognitive effort and interpersonal interaction, subjects being for example required to self-instruct during proverb interpretation and interviews, while in the final sessions they were taught the concept of extracting information from the expression and behaviours of others. As the authors noted therefore:

> The schizophrenic was trained to 'listen to himself', to monitor his own thinking and if his cognitions were maladaptive, to produce incompatible self-statements and behaviours. The focus of therapy shifted from manipulating external environmental consequences to

directly influencing how the client perceives, evaluates and reacts to the environment (Meichenbaum and Cameron 1973:531).

Results of the study suggested the programme to be superior to placebo-control on measures of thought disorder and distractibility, although the generalisation of such improvements were unfortunately not evaluated. Similar self instructional training procedures were however employed by Meyers *et al.* (1976) who taught a forty-seven year old chronic hospitalised schizophrenic with persistent psychotic speech to emit such covert self-instructions as 'I must talk slowly; remember to pause after a sentence; I must stay on the topic; relax, take a few deep breaths'. Results of the study were extremely encouraging, the subject being discharged, improvements being reported to spontaneously generalise, and the therapeutic gains being maintained at six months follow-up. Perhaps surprisingly however the initially positive findings appear to have encouraged little in the way of replication or extension, and the widespread utility of self-instructional training, like many other techniques, awaits firmer establishment.

Chapter eighteen

AMELIORATION OF BEHAVIOURAL AND SOCIAL IMPAIRMENT

BEHAVIOURAL DEFICITS AND EXCESSES

It is evident from the preceding chapter that social learning approaches to the control of 'positive' schizophrenic symptoms are still in the early stages of development and evaluation. The utility of behaviour modification procedures is however far more clearly established and widely acknowledged in respect of the behavioural deficits and problems which characterise many chronic residents of psychiatric institutions, and which typically prove refractory to the effects of medication. As noted in an earlier chapter, the social-learning approach to institutionalised behaviour and 'negative' symptoms suggests a critical role for environmental conditions which fail to cue and reinforce appropriate self care, independence, social interaction or occupation, but which do provide setting conditions and inadvertent incentives for 'patient', arbitrary or maladaptive behaviour. The approach accordingly suggests that significant amelioration of the negative features of chronicity might be effected by the judicious application of procedures of contingency management, and particularly by ensuring that adaptive behaviour is consistently cued and reinforced.

Much of the evidence for this position has been provided by those studies considered later in which ward or unit wide contingency systems have been developed in the form of token economy programmes. Additional support has been however forthcoming from several other investigations of the employment of contingency procedures with individual and groups of schizophrenics in institutionalised settings. A number of studies have for example reported significant improvements in grooming, personal hygiene, use of utensils and mealtime behaviour, independence skills and work performance with contingent reinforcement of appropriate behaviour by social, tangible, activity or 'high probability' behaviour incentives (e.g. Ayllon and Haughton 1962; Di Scipio and Trudeau 1972; Esser 1967; Glickman *et al.* 1973; Hollander and Horner 1975; Mertens and Fuller 1963; Mikulic 1971; Mitchell and Stoffelmayer 1973). Reductions in such inappropriate behaviour as stealing food, hoarding, wearing excessive clothing, somatic complaints and 'sick talk', and destructive behaviour have also been described with the employment of such procedures as extinction, punishment and the reinforcement of more appropriate alternative behaviour (e.g. Ayllon 1963; Allyon and Michael 1959; Liberman *et al.* 1974; Meichenbaum 1969; Ullmann *et al.* 1965). The systematic provision of antecedent cues in the form of specific instructions for appropriate behaviour has also been observed to facilitate the development of personal skills such as grooming (e.g. Suchotliff *et al.* 1970) and to promote the reduction of maladaptive behaviour of various types (e.g. Fraser *et al.* 1981) in some schizophrenics. Exploring the effectiveness of instructional training with a group of nine deteriorated long-term inpatients, Fraser *et al.* (1981) for example reported significant reductions across work, recreational and meal-time settings in such inappropriate behaviours as unprompted laughing, posturing, mannerisms, incoherent speech, smearing food, picking up food from the floor, chewing cigarette butts, body rocking and demanding cigarettes. The potential use of counterconditioning procedures in reducing excessive levels of anxiety in at least a few schizophrenic subjects has also been suggested by some (e.g. Cowden and Ford 1962; Weidner 1970; Zeisset 1968), although not all (Serber and Nelson 1971; Wienman *et al.* 1972) studies of systematic desensitisation.

In conjunction with evidence from token economies (Kazdin 1977) and indeed from the vast number of studies employing behaviour modification procedures with other clinical groups (Kazdin 1975b), such results provide strong support for the role of psychosocial change procedures in reducing the debilitating effects of long-term institutionalisation, and in combatting at least some of the inappropriate behaviours which have proved refractory to other interventions. It is probably fair to say therefore that such procedures are fairly commonly employed by clinical psychologists, nurses, occupational therapists and other professional groups in psychiatric settings, and that their potential utility is increasingly recognised. It is important to emphasise however that while demonstrating the possibilities of behaviour change with various social learning techniques, clinical and research studies have not provided a cookbook from which procedures can be drawn simply in terms of the formal characteristics of a presenting problem. The literature does not therefore suggest that a given behavioural deficit should be necessarily approached by merely reinforcing its occurrence with some predetermined tangible reinforcer, nor that bizarre

257

speech for example be necessarily ignored, or that destructive behaviour be dealt with by time out, or that hoarding be subject to satiation. Indeed, the literature does not even suggest that a presenting problem should be itself the necessary focus of attention, other functionally related behaviours being in some instances more appropriate intervention targets. Instead, the results of clinical studies suggest the utility of behaviour modification as a methodology which adopts an experimental and functionally analytic approach to clinical problems, and which selects procedures based on social learning and psychological research in the light of the idiosyncratic characteristics of a given individual's case. Since the functional determinants of topographically similar problems in two individuals may differ, different intervention programmes may be required in each case. Thus in terms of a given problem behaviour, analysis of its development over time, of its current antecedent and consequent circumstances, of functionally related behaviours and so on, may indicate a programme which utilises stimulus control procedures to minimise its environmental precipitants, or a programme using some direct procedures such as extinction, response cost, overcorrection, time out, punishment or satiation, or an intervention involving the reinforcement of incompatible behaviour, or one teaching the patient more effective and acceptable ways of responding to a situation, or one teaching skills of self-control and self-management. Similarly analysis of a given behavioural deficit (deemed specifically relevant to the individual's adaptive functioning) may indicate the necessity of providing appropriate setting conditions for appropriate behaviour to occur, or ensuring that its emission is consequated by idiosyncratically relevant reinforcers, or of teaching the skill from a rudimentary level.

Even given such an individual approach to behavioural excesses and deficits, there are of course practical and theoretical limitations to the degree of change behavioural procedures can be expected to produce in many schizophrenic patients. As noted in an earlier chapter biological factors may again serve to impair cognitive processing, to limit the rate or possibility of complex processing, to limit the rate or possibility of complex learning, to increase the likelihood of internal stimuli competing with external events for the patients' attention, and to thereby influence the probability and constrain the possibilities of certain sorts of behaviour. In this respect some patients exposed to behavioural procedures may show marked and clinically important improvements in personal and adaptive functioning, but remain incapable of independent adjustment in a complex, advanced and demanding extra-hospital environment. Moreover the effects of time limited behavioural interventions are unlikely to be durable unless specific attempts are made to programme generalisation, by for example selecting targets likely to be naturally reinforced in the post-treatment setting, or by teaching the patients to reinforce themselves. In some instances however it is likely that long-term or even permanent systems for reinforcing adaptive behaviour may be necessary, either within the hospital or in discharge environments such as hostels or family homes.

Notwithstanding such constraints, it remains clear that psycho-social procedures do have a role to play in reducing negative symptoms of schizophrenia, and that their sensitive and considered employment by suitably skilled personnel should be encouraged. Perhaps the most important avenue for future research however lies not in further investigation of their role in chronic institutional settings, but extrapolation of the lessons they provide to the design of care settings which promote adaptive behaviour and prevent the deterioration into dependent institutionalisation.

SOCIAL WITHDRAWAL AND SOCIAL SKILLS

A commonly observed area of deficit in schizophrenia concerns the adequacy and extent of interpersonal interactions, many patients showing reductions in the frequency and quality of social behaviour, and some regressing to a state of extreme withdrawal in which they prove unresponsive to social approach and offer little or no spontaneous speech.

OPERANT CONDITIONING PROCEDURES

Early behavioural approaches to the problem explored the use of operant procedures in redeveloping speech in markedly withdrawn long-term institutional residents, most of whom were considered of extremely poor prognosis and who had proved refractory to any form of therapeutic intervention. King *et al.* (1960) for example compared the utility of recreational therapy, verbal psychotherapy and operant procedures with groups of mute and near mute patients who had undergone extensive therapy in their average of nine years' hospitalisation with little beneficial effect. Using modelling, praise and tangible reinforcers, King *et al.* gradually shaped speech during the course of teaching a simple operant response, simple and complex problem solving, and finally a cooperative problem solving task. Pre and post measures of adjustment based on both ward observations and interview assessments clearly indicated the superiority of the operant procedures over control conditions, improvements being noted in levels of verbalisation, motivation to leave the ward, transfers to better wards, more interest in occupational therapy, and reduced resistance to treatment. The patients undergoing verbal therapy were in contrast observed to become even more verbally withdrawn.

Similarly successful shaping of speech in mute or near mute patients with modelling and reinforcement of successive approximations has been reported by Baker (1971), Sherman (1965), Thomson *et al.* (1974) and Wilson and Walters (1966). While the resultant self-initiated speech has been sometimes noted for its automaton-like quality, limited extent and modest generalisation, the achievement of any change at all must be considered impressive and of potential importance in establishing a point of contact with regressed patients otherwise impervious to treatment. Other early behavioural approaches to the social behaviour of chronic but less regressed schizophrenic patients have employed positive reinforcement procedures to increase the frequency of emotion and affect words in speech (see Ullmann and Krasner 1975) and to improve interpersonal awareness and the frequency of social interaction (e.g. Bennett and Maley 1973; Di Scipio *et al.* 1973; Kale *et al.* 1968; Ravensborg 1972; Stahl *et al.* 1974).

SOCIAL SKILLS TRAINING

On the assumption that social behaviour comprises basic component skills which may be lost or never learned, more recent research has examined the use of elaborate social skill training programmes (SST) through which elements of interpersonal skills are taught by instruction, modelling, prompting, rehearsal, feedback, practice and reinforcement, and are then meshed into more complex interactional behaviour. Initially employed with shy, non-assertive and isolated individuals presenting with anxiety or dysphoric mood, SST or variants such as assertion training in fact enjoyed little success when first applied to schizophrenics. Thus in the first reported use of assertion training with schizophrenic subjects, Serber and Nelson (1971) were able to report modest improvement in only two of fourteen patients some six months after treatment. More encouraging improvements with a training variant termed structured learning therapy were however noted by Gutride *et al.* (1973) and generally positive results have been reported in a subsequent spate of well designed and executed studies employing social skill training techniques (Wallace *et al.* 1980). Several controlled within-subject investigations have for example used multiple baseline across behaviour designs, in which specific micro-social skills are trained singly and sequentially with performance assessed on standard role-play interaction tests. Such studies have clearly demonstrated that psychotic patients can be trained in such basic verbal and non-verbal skills as eye contact, smiling, posture, gesture, speech duration and latency of response on both an individual (e.g. Edelstein and Eisler 1976; Fredericksen *et al.* 1976) or group basis (e.g. Williams *et al.* 1977), as well as suggesting that specific skill changes can generalise to role-play interactions not used in training (e.g. Bellack *et al.* 1976; Edelstein and Eisler 1976), and be maintained for several weeks after training has ended (Bellack *et al.* 1976; Hersen and Bellack 1976). Further support for a specific skill training effect on role-played interactions has emerged from a number of well controlled between-group comparisons (e.g. Eisler *et al.* 1978; Finch and Wallace 1977; Goldsmith and McFall 1975; Hersen *et al.* 1979; Jaffe and Carlson 1976).

Issues in social skills training research
Confident conclusions about the generalised clinical utility of SST are however as yet constrained by uncertainty concerning those programme elements critical to its therapeutic effects, reports of individual variability in response, limited generalisation of change to 'real life' social settings, and inadequate follow-up data. Comparison of results across settings has for example been limited by the employment of variously elaborate and multi-component SST programme variants, and relatively few investigations have examined the specific impact of different treatment elements. Of those that have, the majority (e.g. Edelstein and Eisler 1976; Eisler *et al.* 1973; 1978; Hersen *et al.* 1979), although not all (e.g. Hersen and Bellack 1976) have suggested the particular importance of at least the inclusion of modelling procedures. Thus Eisler *et al.* (1973) showed modelling to be an effective component of an assertion training package for a mixed group of patients, while Hersen *et al.* (1979) reported both covert and live modelling to be equally effective procedures which were not enhanced by the addition of rehearsal. Examining the impact of SST on different clinical groups, Eisler *et al.* (1978) similarly reported that modelling represented a critical supplement to instruction and feedback with schizophrenic subjects, although with the non-schizophrenics its addition was unnecessary. Particularly in view of possible constraints imposed by cognitive limitations, further research is however clearly required to determine those procedures of specific value in promoting skill acquisition, maintenance and generalisation, with schizophrenic subjects.

Evaluation of the utility of SST is however most importantly constrained by the current lack of convincing evidence for change which is durable and which generalises to the natural environment.

In view of doubts about the validity of role-play measures as indices of social performance in naturalistic settings (Bellack *et al.* 1979), short-term changes in micro-communication skills restricted to role-played interaction on completion of treatment can be considered an only limited demonstration of the clinically significant efficacy of SST. Moreover several studies have noted both variability in individual outcome and a lack of significant generalisation of skill improvements to real life situations (e.g. Bellack *et al.* 1976; Furman *et al.* 1979; Hersen *et al.* 1974; Jaffe and Carlson 1976; Shepherd 1977). Other investigations have however described at least some generalised change in spontaneous non-role played interactions (Finch and Wallace 1977), extended conversations (Eisler *et al.* 1978), spontaneous participation in group therapy (Shepherd 1978), behavioural observations of homework assignments (King *et al.* 1977) and observations of ward-based social behaviour (Frederickson *et al.* 1976; Matson and Zeiss 1978).

More encouraging generalisation has also been reported in a recent pilot study by Liberman *et al.* (1984) who employed an elaborate SST variant termed 'personal effectiveness training' (PE) to strengthen the communication and community survival skills of three chronic schizophrenics considered at risk for relapse. In a multiple baseline design involving the sequential training of interpersonal behaviour relevant to hospital, family and community settings, daily PE training was provided over a ten week inpatient period during which patients were stabilised on neuroleptic medication, participated in the milieu activities of their ward, and were in some instances joined by their parents for joint problem solving and communication training sessions, and for education on the nature and treatment of schizophrenia. A number of interpersonal behavioural assignments formed the foci for basic and complex skill training in each of the three behavioural domains, targets within the hospital including for example requesting a change in the behaviour of another person in a group therapy meeting or engaging a nurse in 10 minutes conversation, those in the family setting including initiating conversation with parents, requesting privacy and inviting parents to recreational events, and those in the community including arranging and attending an interview with a vocational counsellor, obtaining information on housing from a citizens' advice bureau, exchanging an item bought from a shop, or visiting a sports centre. All patients were discharged home on completion of the ten week inpatient phase, and PE training was gradually faded out over a five week outpatient period. The specific and proximal impact of training was assessed by sequential changes in the completion of 'real life' behavioural assignments, and in the verbal and non-verbal micro elements of communication evident on the Behavioural Assertiveness Test, while more general changes in symptomatic status, social adjustment, family emotions and interpersonal skill were assessed by pre and post applications of an elaborate battery of social response measures. Results suggested that all patients improved in most areas of social behaviour assessed, there being in particular clear and specific evidence of change in interpersonal assignment completion as a temporal function of the introduction of training, and specific programme effects being similarly evident through changes in micro social skills rated blind from videotaped role play interactions. A number of homework assignments were moreover completed without prior rehearsal in a training session, all patients showed statistically significant improvements in conversation skills in naturalistic, untrained situations, nurses' ratings of ward behaviour and parents' ratings indicated modest improvements in two of the three patients, two patients reported self-rated increases in assertiveness and decreases in social discomfort and all showed remission of positive symptoms of schizophrenia. Results suggest therefore that relatively complex social and survival skills, as well as such micro components as eye contact or speech latency, can be trained during therapy sessions and subsequently emitted in naturalistic settings.

The extent and clinical significance of post-treatment generalisation following even such an intensive and comprehensive PE programme must however be considered uncertain. Thus the several indices of generalisation noted by Liberman *et al.* were observed primarily at completion of the ten week inpatient training period. It is not clear however that following discharge, skills taught in sessions were spontaneously emitted in natural community settings, that the skills were employed by patients to handle situations other than those specifically targetted in training, that response generalisation occurred through the emergence of related social and survival skills, that skills were integrated into higher order strategies of effective social interaction, or that patients enjoyed a more extensive, enriched and satisfying social life. A priority for further research is clearly therefore the demonstration that SST can effect meaningfully generalised improvements in the effectiveness of social performance and the quality and satisfaction of interpersonal interaction. Such a demonstration will demand more than evidence of statistical changes in micro or even complex skills on completion of treatment, and must address the extent to which patients can be equipped to make and retain friends, to use hospital or community leisure, recreational and information facilities, or to handle novel and demanding interpersonal situations in a confident and effective manner. A similarly important priority for further research is the demonstration that SST can effect temporal generalisation in the sense of promoting long-term and durable changes in social behaviour. Of the as yet relatively few long-term follow-up studies, most have in fact reported results which are poor or equivocal (e.g. Goldsmith and McFall 1975; Jaffe and Carlson 1976; Serber and Nelson 1971). Even following Liberman *et al.*'s (1984) complex programme a degree of deterioration in the skill levels of all three patients was observed on the Behavioural Assertiveness Test only five weeks after discharge, and of the two patients available for one year follow-up both showed a return of pre-treatment signs of secondary impairment such as apathy, slowness and social withdrawal. Neither of these patients however presented with a recurrence of positive symptoms, and one patient followed up over three years continued to live at home with his father and attend a social club for ex-patients. The subject of Hersen *et al.* (1975) was also discharged following treatment and reported to be maintaining a job at twenty two week follow-up. Nonetheless the assumption that newly learned and often initially imperfect skills will be naturally reinforced and maintained after treatment clearly requires examination. Indeed the promotion of lasting improvement may demand the incorporation into SST perhaps of specific maintenance techniques, the provision of long-term support arrangements through which nurses, social workers, parents or others in the patient's environment are encouraged to prompt and reinforce effective social function, and the availability of booster training sessions if a decline in social performance is evident.

Refinements of the social skills training approach
While the focus and initial results of SST suggest the approach to be of direct relevance to one of the central problems of schizophrenia, it is evident from the above that increasing attention must be paid to the issues of variability, limits, generalisation and durability of training effects. As with other applications of behaviour modification procedures to schizophrenic problems, it seems probable that SST techniques will become increasingly refined as further evidence emerges concerning biological and cognitive features of the schizophrenic process which may constrain the person's interaction with their environment, and the possibilities of change through social influence. To date most SST programmes have been developed on the assumption that interpersonal skills have been lost or never learned, a plausible hypothesis in the light both of evidence for the extinction of social behaviour through lack of opportunity and reinforcement, and the presence of social withdrawal as a frequent premorbid trait. In some patients however interpersonal problems appear to emerge in conjunction with cognitive deficits and hallucinatory or delusional symptoms which limit and interfere with normal behavioural function, while in even those who have never acquired relevant skills cognitive and symptomatic problems may constrain the impact of intervention

programmes. Thus effective interpersonal behaviour demands not merely the emission of a behavioural response, but the prior perception and appraisal of a social situation and the cognitive generation of an appropriate response. Attentional, memory and conceptual deficits in schizophrenia may therefore constrain the perception and processing of interpersonal information, and require definition and remediation as a pre-requisite to the acquisition of higher order skills. In this respect Liberman *et al.* (1984) noted defective judgement of social cues, poor timing of response initiation, and difficulties in selecting responses to problem situations to be major limitations on the function of their subjects, the authors urging therefore greater emphasis on the teaching of cognitive 'receiving' and 'processing' skills in addition to an 'expressive' behavioural repertoire. Cognitive and learning deficits may similarly limit the rate and possibilities of skill acquisition, the suggestive evidence concerning the specific importance of modelling with schizophrenic patients perhaps emphasising the necessary role of clear, highly structured and gradual teaching conditions. To the extent that loss of motivation and apathy reflect in part at least biological aspects of the schizophrenic process, the importance of incentive provision to facilitate the retention of learning is perhaps also suggested. In some cases a pre-requisite for the development of appropriate social behaviour may moreover involve attempts to reduce preoccupation with auditory hallucinations, to teach more rational thinking, or to combat other problems functionally related to social withdrawal.

As a further refinement in the SST approach it also seems desirable that increasing emphasis be placed on the development of highly individualised programmes, which involve not merely functional analyses of the type described in the previous chapter, but importantly seek to select targets for change which are idiosyncratically relevant and meaningful to the patient in question. To date most social skill programmes have focused on increasing preselected verbal and non-verbal micro-skills considered to be generally important components of 'normal' social interactions such as holding a conversation or asserting one's point of view. It is perhaps important to note however that such a focus was originally developed to address the problems of motivated people who had difficulty in initiating conversations in parties, in asking a member of the opposite sex for a date, in asserting themselves at work, or expressing their feelings to a spouse. In such cases, where typically the clients wanted to initiate conversations or be more assertive, the microskill targets were clearly relevant to effective performance in specific situations in which difficulty was encountered, and improvement in their emission was a functional means to an end. In respect of work with schizophrenics however it is uncertain that micro-skill emissions or formal aspects of conversational style can in themselves be considered relevant targets unless they are related to performance in idiosyncratically important situations, or represent a means to a defined and personally relevant end. Few studies have in fact sought to integrate basic skills into more relevant higher order social order strategies, and their focus on micro-skill targets must by default be considered fairly arbitrary. Even those studies which have sought to train more complex social and survival skills have in the main pre-selected essentially arbitrary targets on the strength of the experimenter's conception of what constitutes important social behaviour. While perhaps relevant to some people in some settings, such arbitrarily selected targets may be irrelevant to the individual schizophrenic patient. Indeed it is not even certain that all of the typically taught micro-skills are important in all situations. This point was highlighted for one of the present authors who accompanied a young and rather dull schizophrenic to a run down pub in a deprived inner city area. In an effort to model appropriate behaviour to the patient, whose social skills in conventional terms were lamentable, the smartly dressed experimenter and a colleague entered a pub with confident posture, smiles and assertive eye contact, and were greeted by the sudden and immediate descent of silence, suspicion and threatening stares. The patient however took the situation in his stride, staring at the floor with slouched posture and mumbling that the therapists were with him and were 'OK'. Clearly in this instance the therapists' social skills were situationally inappropriate, while those of the 'unskilled' patient were essentially normal!

Given the relatively arbitrary and personally irrelevant nature of many targets in SST studies, it is perhaps unsurprising that they decline on completion of treatment. It seems important therefore that target selection be based on consideration of both the clients' social and cultural backgrounds and potential areas of interest, and of the social norms and demands of the post-treatment environment. As noted by Liberman *et al.* (1984), the minimally sufficient repertoire of social skills required to sustain community functioning is not known, but what is appropriate is likely to anyway vary across environments and demand local research. Thus broadly 'normative' behaviour in a deprived inner city area may differ from that observed in a rural community or middle class suburb, and target selection must be based on local circumstances. Similarly social targets should reflect the particular sorts of demands in the post-treatment setting, and the social, recreational, leisure, transport and other facilities available. Thus it might be pointless teaching skills related to the use of a cinema if none exist locally, or, if the client expresses a definite interest to attend, additional training in the use of public transport, using bus timetables and so on may be essential.

Equally important to target selection are of course the person's individual social and cultural background and idiosyncratic (even if historical) interests. Thus while visiting a restaurant may be a relevant target for one patient, spending an evening at a dog race meeting may be more appropriate for another. Similarly during conversational training a patient whose performance is poor when discussing current events may be more animated and alert if talking about a previous interest in steam railways. Obviously interview or observation of some patients will fail to elicit information on potential interests, although in many cases discussions with relatives or significant others will provide useful hints, and if necessary reinforcer sampling may be explored. Perhaps in many instances the initial stages of SST should focus not on microskills which it is hoped will later generalise to natural settings, but on accompanying the patient on a number of occasions to one or more relevant social situations in which interest may be kindled, and motivation to change be engendered. Specific micro skills required for later independent completion of the activity may then be determined by observation and trained with the greater guarantee they will be reinforced in the natural setting.

While much further work is required, SST perhaps in combination with other treatment techniques, would appear an extremely promising approach to the rehabilitation of at least several schizophrenic patients. Moreover, while as yet applied in the main to chronic patients, its potential role in arresting the process of social withdrawal in young acute patients seems an important area for further investigation.

Chapter nineteen

SOCIAL INTERVENTIONS

PREVENTING LIFE STRESS

As noted earlier, a number of studies have suggested the onset and relapse of schizophrenia can be precipitated in many instances by life events and stressors which are 'undesirable' in nature (Paykel 1978) and which tax the individuals' limited resources for producing an adaptive coping response (Serban 1975). Brown and Birley (1968) and Birley and Brown (1970) have for example noted that in comparison with controls, a group of acute admission schizophrenics reported a marked increase (up to 60 per cent) in the incidence of significant life events (e.g. moving house, starting or leaving a job, marriage, death etc) during the three week period immediately preceding illness onset. Similar increases in life crises were observed immediately prior to relapse, and Brown *et al.* (1973) suggest available evidence to strongly support a causal 'triggering' role for stress in schizophrenic breakdown. A number of studies have also suggested particular sorts of stressors in the home environment to be directly related to relapse in acute schizophrenics after discharge from hospital (Brown *et al.* 1972). While in respect of the latter substantial headway has been made in reducing the risk of relapse through family interventions (Leff *et al.* 1982), relatively few other attempts have been made to explore the utility of minimizing exposure to stress or improving adaptive and coping resources.

LIFESTYLE COUNSELLING

Since many sources of stress (e.g. bereavement, loss of employment due to economic recession) lie beyond the individual's control, the opportunities for limiting exposure to some categories of life event are clearly constrained. In some respects however difficult life circumstances may arise as a function of longstanding maladaptive patterns of behaviour or lifestyle, and may moreover be compounded by the secondary consequences of the onset of schizophrenia itself. One potentially useful avenue for research might therefore involve counselling against lifestyles which are constantly changing, as is the case with patients who drift from job to job, or who are geographically mobile (Dunham 1965). Similarly careful assessment of for example occupational skills, and placement of a patient in employment suitable to his level, might help in the prevention of job stress and reduce the likelihood of losing a job. The utility of such an approach is as yet however uncertain, and clearly any such 'lifestyle' counselling should guard against the possibility of condemning patients to lives which are in fact dull and unfulfilling.

THE PROMOTION OF COPING SKILLS

The possibilities of teaching more adaptive and effective styles of coping are also unclear, particularly in view of uncertainty about the way in which people in general handle crises in a successful manner, and the availability of only limited data on the extent to which schizophrenics are specifically deficient in such coping skills. The coping process is however generally considered to comprise phases of cognitive appraisal and problem solving, the generation and emission of an appropriate behavioural response, and in many instances the recruitment of social support. At the cognitive level 'coping' appears in the first instance to involve the initial appraisal of a situation as stressful or otherwise, and the subsequent active process of evaluation and reappraisal of the threatening implications of an event in the light of available coping alternatives (e.g. Lazarus *et al.* 1970; Luckof *et al.* 1984). Some evidence at least suggests that cognitive appraisal may be defective in some schizophrenics, Fitts (1972) for example noting that poor self-image and lack of self-worth to be pervasive in his sample, and Luckof *et al.* (op. cit.) reporting that many partially recovered schizophrenics are sensitive to the behaviour of others and inappropriately perceive their behaviour as rejecting. Inappropriate stressor appraisal, the self-perception of inability to resolve problem situations, and perhaps the underestimation of actual available coping resources, may suggest the potential utility of application of cognitive change methods such as those used by Beck *et al.* (1979) in the treatment of depression. Some evidence also suggests that schizophrenics may be relatively poor in using cognitive problem solving strategies to generate and evaluate solutions to ameliorating or removing a source of stress, Spivack *et al.* (1976) for example noting many of the patients in their sample to be unable to produce and evaluate effective solutions on a problem solving task. The extent to which such difficulties reflect cognitive skill deficits or the disorganisation of available skills due to cognitive dysfunction (e.g. distractibility, slowed thinking, ineffective assimilation of meaning (Neuchterlein and Dawson 1984)) is unclear. Nonetheless exploration of the utility of suitably configured and structured problem solving training programmes would seem worthwhile.

The generation and emission of behavioural responses to a problem situation of course demands the prior availability of a suitably elaborate repertoire of life skills and competence in their performance. Since many schizophrenics present with marked deficits in several areas of behavioural function, a pre-requisite to the development of general problem solving skills may be the teaching of social skills, specifically relevant independence skills, specific types of occupational skill and other survival skills identified as of idiosyncratic relevance to the individual's environmental circumstances. Attempts in this direction are described elsewhere in the previous chapter, and to the extent that life difficulties and stressors are more probable in the absence of important life skills, such skill training programmes may also of course serve a preventative function.

In respect of the third commonly acknowledged component of the coping process, the recruitment of social support, many schizophrenics are at an obvious disadvantage in view of their relative social isolation and limited interpersonal skill. While social skills training is therefore again suggested as an important form of intervention, it seems clear that for many patients active attempts must be made to provide a stress-buffer in the form of an effective social support network to which they have ready access. In some instances such a network may be provided by professional personnel or volunteers, but for many the most realistic source of close support is their immediate family. The family intervention programmes described later therefore have a potentially critical role to play in transmuting a possible source of stress into a focus for positive, non-intrusive social support.

COMPLIANCE TO NEUROLEPTIC MEDICATION

Evidence that neuroleptic drugs may possess specific antipsychotic and prophylactic properties has encouraged their routine and virtually ubiquitous administration to schizophrenics on both an acute treatment and continuing maintenance basis. As noted else-where, neuroleptics have of course guaranteed neither symptomatic remission nor prevention of relapse in all cases, nor have they ensured the promotion of adaptive social function or effective environmental adjustment. Thus despite variation in the type of compound and diagnostic criteria employed, most drug trials report rates of non-remission and relapse of around 50 per cent within two years (WHO 1979), coupled with poor adjustment for many survivors. There is nonetheless convincing evidence that in comparison with placebo, antipsychotics can significantly reduce the occurrence of florid symptoms and rate of relapse in many patients (Hogarty *et al.* 1974).

Irregular or total medication non-compliance however occurs in as many as 50 per cent of discharged schizophrenic patients, such non-compliance being associated with elevated rate of relapse (e.g. Vaughn and Leff 1976; Hogarty *et al.* 1979). Identification of factors generally related to non-compliance (e.g. poor doctor-patient com-munication, lack of knowledge, drug side-effects, family pressures, etc) and discrimination of patients 'at risk' for non compliance (e.g. Hogan *et al.* 1983) and the development of procedures to enhance compliance (e.g. Liberman and Davies 1975) would appear there-fore to be important areas for further investigation. Hogan *et al.* (op. cit.) have for example described a thirty item self-report ques-tionnaire covering positive and negative subjective experiences, attitudes and knowledge about medication, and report the scale (particularly items concerning feelings such as tiredness and poor concentration) to reliably classify 88 per cent of known compliers and non-compliers. Interpretation of Hogan *et al.*'s data is in fact confounded by their report of a moderate correlation (0.43) between a rating of psychiatric symptoms and 'critical' subjective feelings, perhaps suggesting the latter to be symptoms of the disorder rather than medication side effects. However it appears that some 'at risk' individuals may be identified, and perhaps in conjunction with their relatives or other significant care agents, be the subject of special attention and intervention. Emphasis might for example be placed on providing clear information concerning the likely experiential effects of medication, the nature of prophy-laxis, the importance of balancing the benefits versus costs of drug maintenance, and so on, although in some instances it may be additionally necessary to involve care agents as monitors, to address the organisational aspects of drug delivery or to provide incentives for compliance. The possible utility of such an approach is perhaps suggested by the enhanced drug compliance accompanying some psychosocial intervention which include educational components (Falloon and Liberman 1983).

It is however becoming increasingly clear that great care must be taken in balancing the potential benefits of maintenance medication against its actual and potential risks. In the light of evidence that perhaps as many as 20 per cent of patients do well without medication (Hogarty *et al.* 1974), a critical area for investigation is the elucidation of personal, social and familial factors which predict good outcome irrespective of maintenance drug regimes. In this respect the results of Leff and Wing (1971) and Carpenter and Heinrichs (1981) suggesting that patients with good prognosis, irrespective of medication, were characterised by acute onset, 'good' premorbid adjustment and a pronounced affective component. Improved quantification of these characteristics and the development of high-risk behavioural prototypes is required if it is to be possible to consider only those patients above a certain level of risk as suitable for long-term neuroleptic treatment.

An additionally important focus of attention is the potential use of intermittent drug regimes. While drug dose reductions may occasion increased visibility of psychotic symptoms, interventions timed at the point of relapse in relatively symptom-free patients may be capable of sustaining prophylactic effects without the side-effects of continuous medication. Hogarty *et al.* (1973) have for example noted that while 66 per cent of stabilised patients in their sample relapsed in the year following withdrawal of medication, the need for rehospitalisation was reduced to only 15 per cent by the prompt reinstatement of drug therapy. The possibility of an even earlier intervention is promised given that a prodromal period prior to relapse has been reported (Herz and Melville 1980). In nineteen carefully selected patients Herz *et al.* (1982) successfully controlled relapse through reinstatement of their drug regime once prodromal symptoms (e.g. anxiety, agitation, restlessness) emerged. Similarly in a comparison of twenty-seven patients who received continuous medication over twenty-five weeks with fourteen on 'early intervention' medication prior to relapse (this group receiving medication for nine weeks in total), Carpenter and Heinrichs (1983) observed no differences at six month follow-up between the groups in clinical or social functioning. While an early intervention strategy may be inappropriate for those with persistent serious psychoses and the few without prodromal signs, its use may be particularly acceptable to drug non-compliers who prefer medication only at times of evident need. Again it would therefore seem important to develop improved operational criteria for prodromal signs, and to incorporate them in psychometrically validated instruments which care agents and particularly relatives could be trained to use.

In the light of evidence described elsewhere that psychosocial intervention may reduce the rate of relapse, their increasingly widespread application may of course also reduce the need for medication among patients living in high-risk environments. In this respect it is interesting to note that a large scale family/psychosocial intervention in California (Falloon 1984, personal communication) is currently exploring an innovative method of 'titrating' the need for medication with the level of psychosocial risk, so that a balance of 'relapse inducing' and 'relapse protecting' measures is achieved at a low level of relapse risk. Future clinical practice may therefore witness an increasing use of 'titration' and 'early intervention' drug treatment in combination with comprehensive psychosocial interventions, with those at risk for non-compliance being provided with additional educational and compliance enhancement procedures.

FAMILY INTERVENTIONS

In recent years there have been a number of attempts to apply the knowledge which has accumulated concerning the role of family factors in schizophrenia, the results of which have proved very promising and give considerable cause for optimism.

The first such study of family intervention was conducted by Goldstein and his colleague in California (Goldstein and Kopeiten 1981). Their intervention consisted of helping families identify stressful circumstances which might have precipitated the psychotic episode, to develop more effective stress-reducing strategies and to anticipate future ones. This was done to enable patients' return to the family environment particularly with the first six weeks in mind as they argue that this is the maximum risk period for relapse. This intervention took place over six weekly sessions involving the individual, his family and therapist. Interestingly the focus of intervention frequently concerned the provision of realistic expectations about recovery so as to 'discourage premature efforts to pressure the patient into activities beyond his functional capacity at the time'.

The intervention was structured as a sequence of four steps with later steps depending on the successful completion of earlier ones. Initially the family and the individual were provided with a clear understanding of the breakdown itself from both the individual's and the family's perspective. This step was largely educational, to highlight the role of stress in its onset and improve family cohesion. The first therapeutic objective was to arrive at concrete descriptions of two or three stressful situations within the family (e.g. arguments about the individual's inactivity). The second step involved developing strategies for managing or avoiding these situations. The third step involved evaluating and refining these strategies. Finally, future difficulties were anticipated and planned for. Goldstein and

Kopeiten reported a controlled trial over a six week post-discharge period varying drug level (moderate vs. low) and family therapy in a 2 × 2 factorial design; 104 young (mean age twenty-three years) people with schizophrenia entered the trial and were randomly assigned to the groups.

The high dose/family therapy group showed a much lower rate of relapse compared to the lose dose/no family therapy group at both six weeks (0 per cent vs. 24 per cent) and six months (0 per cent vs. 48 per cent). No differences emerged between the remaining groups.

In spite of variable management regimes after the six week intervention – which would randomly and not selectively alter the treatment received by the two groups – Goldstein reported significant effects of drug (p > .01) and family therapy (p > .05) over six months but does not report the results of their interaction or data for all group comparisons. One is struck by the absence of relapse in the high dose/family therapy group and the ability of family therapy to halve the rate of relapse in the low dose treatment groups (48 per cent vs. 21 per cent) over six months. The study suggests that high dosage of medication and family intervention are functionally equivalent in forestalling relapse and when both are present (or absent) an extreme of outcomes is obtained. This study suggests that the very early adjustment of families to schizophrenia (two thirds were first episode patients) may be crucial and a brief, six week intervention can correct this before relatively permanent response characteristics set in. Thus the generalisability of this brief intervention to an older sample and also the durability of its effects remain uncertain.

The research team in London that were largely responsible for the renewed interest in family therapy as a result of their work on 'expressed emotion', reported the results of their intervention programme four years later (Leff *et al.* 1982).

Their study was a simpler comparison of two groups (N = 12) both stabilised on maintenance medication with one receiving the family intervention. In contrast to Goldstein their subjects were selected *a priori* as being at high risk of relapse (i.e. high contact with a 'high EE' family) and were also much older (35 yrs vs. 23 yrs). The intervention consisted of three components. The first was an educational package in which the relatives were informed about the nature, course and treatment of schizophrenia. The second was a relatives group in which high and low EE families met together and the therapists facilitated interactions between them. The rationale for this was that low EE families had found ways of coping with the everyday problems of living with schizophrenia which high EE families might learn from.

Berkowitz *et al.* (1981) report three themes that recurred in their relatives groups. The first was a need for more information. Relatives were not concerned with knowledge for its own sake but rather the *consequences* of the information for them (e.g. 'how will I cope with relapse?') The second concerns relatives' negative emotional reactions including stigma, guilt, worry about the future, worry about leaving the individual alone for a while and guilt about enjoying a social life. The third and major theme brought up by relatives were problems relating to the management of disturbed behaviour within the home environment.

The third component of the intervention comprised individual sessions with families using 'dynamic interpretations or behavioural interventions'.

At nine months follow-up there had been only one relapse (9 per cent) in the family intervention group compared with 50 per cent of the control group, although one of the intervention group was not available to follow-up. This was maintained over two years (Leff *et al.* 1985) although this held only when patients who defaulted on medication were excluded from the analysis. The intervention led to a significant reduction in criticism which accounted for a reduction of EE in five of the eleven families and in five families there was a reduction in face-to-face contact; overall the social intervention was successful in 73 per cent and in these families there was no relapse.

The results of this study are impressive and give considerable cause for optimism; however the content of the intervention was intuitive, without clear rationale and largely exploratory in nature, which is not surprising given that little is known about what life is like in a high EE family.

The appearance of the Leff *et al.* report was closely followed by a study undertaken by Ian Falloon and colleagues in California. In contrast to the intervention of Leff *et al.* their family intervention was more structured and well-defined (Falloon *et al.* 1984), thus enabling replication. The intervention aims to train family members to recognise and resolve sources of environmental stress from within and outside the family. The first stage involves a sophisticated assessment of the family as individuals and as a system. A list of 'problems' is drawn up from the perspective of each family member, personal and family related. Falloon *et al.* assess the families' problem-solving by interview and observation in a group context as well as their specific response to each problem behaviour and its possible reciprocal effect.

Falloon's approach to intervention is predicated on the assumption that high risk family environments are stressful because families' 'negative' response patterns are a result of these *endemic* characteristics which are inappropriate to deal with schizophrenia: (a) communication disturbance (b) poor family problem solving and (c) disturbed family relationships.

The participants of the study were defined using the same criteria as Leff but were some ten years younger. Most came from high EE households, but individuals from low EE households were included who were considered at high risk of relapse on the basis of 'poor premorbid adjustment, multiple previous admissions or evidence of extreme family tension'. They compared the family intervention (N = 18) with the best available individual community after-care (N = 18) including education about schizophrenia and vocational rehabilitative counselling. The contrast group therefore received an intensive psychosocial intervention.

Follow-up over nine months showed a 6 per cent relapse rate in the family group (vs. 44 per cent), matched by a low readmission rate (11 per cent vs. 50 per cent) and lower (blind) monthly ratings of target symptoms, which replicated over two years (Falloon *et al.* 1982). Falloon also reports a greater tolerance of their families for social deficits, improved problem solving effectiveness and improved family well-being. We are, however, not informed of any changes in EE. Falloon *et al.* found that the family intervention led to improved compliance with medication regimes; however given maximum compliance, the relapse rate is far lower than would be expected with drugs alone and also the dosages of drugs required were much lower in the family group. Falloon's intervention, although clear and systematic, went beyond the family itself and advised on stress reduction strategies in relation to external events impinging on the family (including the patient). Also families were given basic information about early warning signs of relapse which might itself have led families to alert their therapists, with whom they were in constant contact, of an impending relapse, which might have been averted with medication. Thus it is not clear how much the resolution of intra-familial 'stress' was responsible for the effects although it was subsequently reported that experimental families improved in problem-solving effectiveness (Doane *et al.* 1985). This observation does not invalidate the conclusion (that an intensive family-oriented social intervention is superior to individual after-care in medicated schizophrenics), but suggests that the results were achieved by means in addition to modifications of the family interior.

There is one further study which we shall briefly mention here. This is the large scale intervention of Hogarty and colleagues in the USA involving a random sample of 374 clinically diagnosed schizophrenics randomly assigned to one of four groups in a 2 × 2 factorial design (Drugs × Social Therapy). The social intervention was described as intensive individual casework and rehabilitative counselling often involving work with families. Beyond discussion of cases the intervention was not operationalised, nor was there any means of showing that it had succeeded. However there is an indication that the cumulative relapse rate over two years was lower in those receiving medication and social therapy, particularly if the patient was asymptomatic. Hogarty also reported that this combined treatment group showed superior community adjustment, but this conclusion must be disregarded as it is based on a subsample of non-relapsers (relapsers were withdrawn from the study).

This group of psychosocial interventions have been presented in some details as they appear to represent a potentially significant advance in the management of the symptoms of schizophrenia.

While the importance of such findings is widely recognised a number of crucial questions must however be addressed if the research is to achieve maximum clinical benefit.

FOR WHOM AND IN WHAT RESPECT ARE THESE INTERVENTIONS EFFECTIVE?

Two of the interventions were conducted on patients who were *a priori* at high risk for relapse as defined by the high EE index. In the Leff study this was further restricted by including those only in high contact with relatives which may have accounted for the age difference between Leff's and Falloon's samples (high contact may be associated with chronicity (see Ch. 13). Given that low contact with high EE is associated with a rate of relapse, which, even over nine months, is double that of low EE families (28 per cent vs. 13 per cent), then many more patients and families might profitably benefit if *all* high EE families are regarded 'at risk'. This might thereby reduce the dosage of medication required for low contact/high EE patients who appear much more 'drug sensitive' than their low EE counterparts (Vaughn & Leff 1976). In a similar vein, these studies do not need to be unnecessarily restricted by restrictive diagnostic practices. Given that the original study of EE included many with 'possible schizophrenia' as well as definite ('Schneiderian') schizophrenia, then there seems little reason to restrict this now. Leff *et al.* noted that their recruitment criteria led to two-thirds of schizophrenic admissions being rejected: this could be substantially reduced with benefits to patients and families without compromising methodological rigour.

In two of the studies reviewed the investigators did not restrict their sample to high EE patients and in a further study (Falloon *et al.*) a small number of low EE families were included who were considered to be at risk for relapse. Goldstein in particular took no account of EE and obtained good results. It may be argued that in so doing he was 'wasting time' with 'low EE' families and that without balancing the high EE patients between contrast groups, this may have biased the outcome (the latter is unlikely in view of the relatively large 'N' involved and his efforts to match groups on other prognostic indicators). This then begs a major question: is high EE sufficient to define all the important needs and risks associated with schizophrenia? The index appears to be a good short term predictor of relapse; however it remains to be seen whether these interventions can alter the course of schizophrenia in the long term, with or without longer term family intervention. Falloon *et al.* (1981) argue that clinical exacerbations (but not 'relapses') occurred at a moderate level in their successful family therapy group, so perhaps the amplitude rather than the frequency of symptom exacerbation is the 'real' dependent variable, leaving the *underlying* course unaffected. The point to be emphasised is that the prevention of short symptom exacerbation may turn out to be of only limited value in contrast to patients' quality of life which these interventions generally have not emphasised. This brings us to a second point: does high EE select patients and families with other needs or risks, such as social disabilities? The needs of low EE families have not been analysed, however it is known from follow-up studies (e.g. Watt *et al.* 1983) that there are numerous patients who are marginally maintained in the community with considerable psychiatric or social problems who are not regularly readmitted and would be overlooked in the EE assessment procedure. It has also been suggested that low EE families may reduce relapse risk by reinforcing patients' social withdrawal, thus alleviating stressful confrontations (Birchwood 1983). In some instances low EE may represent a conflict of needs or risk. For these reasons it is argued that high EE may define a short-term, narrow band of need.

In summary therefore family interventions might be applied usefully to a broader range of patients and their families than can be presently achieved with EE, so as to capture as many needs and need groups as possible. The important questions would then be within-group ones: what kinds of interventions help what kind of patient in what kind of family and with what kind of effect? For example, certain patient variables may have some bearing on their responsiveness to social intervention: premorbid functioning, genetic risk, time since onset and nature or degree of persisting symptoms. In addition to relapse, multiple measures of outcome should be used including social functioning and measures of family well-being.

WHY ARE FAMILY INTERVENTIONS EFFECTIVE, WHAT ARE THEIR ACTIVE INGREDIENTS AND WHAT INFORMS THEIR DESIGN?

It has been suggested that family interventions enhance compliance with medication, thereby moderating relapse, and in one study evidence for this was presented (Strang *et al.* 1981). This cannot wholly account for the results as in the Leff and Goldstein studies medication was carefully controlled, and in the Falloon study the family intervention group required *lower* doses of medication (cf. Strang *et al.* 1981). In Leff's and Falloon's interventions changes in family variables were observed concomitant with the control of relapse (changes in EE and problem-solving ability respectively). Notwithstanding the need for replications, it may be assumed for the moment that a crucial intra-familial factor has been changed. The term 'stress' is often used to summarise this for which there is intuitive appeal but it is a notoriously difficult concept to define and measure. Traditionally stress has been defined either in terms of its stimulus characteristics (including the recipients' perceptions of the stressfullness of the stimulus) or in terms of the response it has on the individual. There have been some successful attempts to monitor patients' psychophysiological functions: this demonstrated a high level of autonomic activity in patients from high EE families. However, the apparent failure to find any changes in patients' autonomic functioning among families who were reduced from high to low EE suggests that these patients were *intrinsically* vulnerable to relapse (Sturgeon *et al.* 1983) and that these measures cannot presently be assumed to represent a stress response *per se*.

We are left then with defining stress in stimulus terms. In the case of life-events which are acute forms of 'stress' known to precipitate relapse, the definition of the stressor and its subjective qualities are more straightforward to define and measure (e.g. death of a spouse). Thus in this case, a reduction in stress could be argued if a patient experienced fewer life events or perceived them as less stressful and easier to cope with as in the case of depression (Brown and Harris 1978).

Defining the stressors within the family environment poses a difficult problem. Unlike life events which are brief, discrete and readily quantifiable events, family life is an ongoing complex dynamic of relationships in which the patient himself plays an active part. The definition of stress in the family environment (EE) relies on a binary classification derived mainly from a count of critical comments made by relatives during the patients' admission to hospital.

The EE classification clearly has a predictive value and a function in its own right. However as a direct measure of stress in stimulus terms it has a number of drawbacks. In the first place EE is a typology and construes family characteristics as 'traits' in the same sense as personality or physical characteristics are individual traits. This trait construction by its very nature is an abstraction of family life and is potentially too rigid a concept to accommodate its complexities. Thus for example it is unlikely that relatives would be rated high EE in relation to *all* their offspring as the EE ratings are largely based on comments invited about symptoms. The expressed emotion concept therefore needs to be accommodated within a theoretical framework or language of the family interior which is applicable (or possibly unique) to schizophrenia. This then might facilitate the development of the concept of stress in this environment and provide more appropriate measures of family processes to monitor the effects of family interventions.

The next question follows naturally from these considerations: if the characteristics of a high risk stressful family environment remain unclear then what determines the design and goals of a family intervention? As we have seen, clinical intuition and empiricism seem to have been the main guiding lights, because there is no well articulated theory or model to inform their design. The clinically orientated reader might well argue that if we have established successful interventions then what does it matter that they are intuitively designed and their mode of action unknown?

In the first place rationally based interventions will lead to better definitions of the independent variables to be subject to change, and therefore facilitate the essential process of dissemination and replication. Take as an example the intervention of Leff *et al.*, which was, with the exception of the educational component, non-prescriptive and unmonitored in terms of process, and therefore difficult to replicate. The success of their relatives' group may well have depended on the personality of certain low EE families or mix of families and therapists to bring about the 'crucial' changes. Thus even the skilled clinicians in Leff's team may well find difficulty replicating their own work without a clearer understanding and operationalisation of its ingredients.

A further problem is the means by which one might undertake to *improve* family interventions. One reason for this is that family interventions represent 'packages' of interventions with many components which are expensive in terms of time, manpower and resources. There may be redundancy among their components or crucial components may be omitted. The efficacy of the various

components could be examined by comparing them in an experimental design. This might result in the loss of component(s) from
the package. More than likely however some components may be
more effective than others and the 'best' a combination of them all.
The conclusion of such an empirical approach will likely be that
improvements in time, manpower resources etc, can only be
achieved at the *expense* of clinical efficacy. However it may well be
the case that the 'crucial' changes brought about by each component
resides in certain, possibly minor, aspects of their content ('using
a sledge hammer to crack a nut') which could be achieved more
economically. Unless an endless process of empiricism is to be
avoided, the only way in which advances in family interventions are
to be achieved is through greater attention to theory and to the
family processes which these interventions affect (cf. Doane *et al.*
1985).

The same problem emerges if additional or greater emphasis on
certain therapeutic outcomes were required of an intervention (e.g.
reduction in family burden' improvements in social adjustment):
again the most appropriate design would be informed on an *a priori*
basis.

This issue is illustrated by reference to a component common to
all interventions: the provision of education about schizophrenia.
The rationale for this component has never been made explicit, but
clearly its inclusion suggests an assumption that high stress family
environments bear some relationship to their knowledge about
schizophrenia and their often stated need for information. Interventions thus restore this deficit. An empirical approach to its
evaluation might compare this with other components. However it
is becoming clear that the *function* of this component goes beyond
any *specific* consequence of providing information.

Recently Berkowitz *et al.* (1984) analysed the short and longer
term effects of providing information. (The latter was however
confounded with a wider social intervention (cf. Leff *et al.* 1982).)
Their most interesting finding was that they failed to discover any
differences in knowledge between high and low EE families but did
find that high EE's perceive more of the patients' behaviour as
reflecting the presence of schizophrenia. Very little information was
retained by relatives but the high EE's 'knew more about management' and became somewhat less pessimistic about the future. It
would seem that knowledge *per se* is apparently irrelevant. Further
light is shed on this in a study of the specific and non-specific
effects of education by Smith and Birchwood (1987). Their
four session course led to considerable retention of information in
an undifferentiated sample of families. They found that the course
led to actual reductions in stress symptoms, reduced fear of the
patient and an increase in relatives' feelings of being able to exert

some control over the situation. The main result of interest was that they found no correlation between the *amount* of information retained and these non-specific effects, although all participants gained in terms of their knowledge. One important effect of education is therefore to improve 'cognitive mastery' and ability to influence the situation which was an entirely *personal* or *subjective* issue. It is personal for general and specific reasons: *general* because each relative remains unaware of how much they learned and retained overall but the degree of uncertainty which is reduced and their improved mastery is a subject notion; *specific* because in this intervention relatives were prompted by way of homework to *apply* the information to their relative, thus individual families may have learned things which were of significance to their situation.

Education then is important because it reduced disengagement or psychological distance between patient and relative (cf. changes in fear and self efficacy) and the level of stress, born of which might *facilitate* or *enable* their adherence to a more in-depth intervention. Smith and Birchwood (1987) provided families with information about schizophrenia either through the medium of a group discussion, backed up by information booklets, and through the provision of booklets alone which were sent through the post. They found that relatives entering the group condition learned and retained a greater amount of information but the non-specific effects that were observed (stress, burden and fear reduction) were the *same* across both conditions. This underlines, the conclusion that the function of education is in part to improve relatives' *subjective* feeling of greater understanding and control over their situation ('cognitive mastery'). Without knowledge of these wider process factors, we could not undertake a meaningful improvement of this component by empiricism alone.

The lesson to be drawn from this work on education is that in order to be able to improve interventions we need to ask what function they serve and how a particular form achieves this. This presupposes two basic requirements: a model or theory of the family influence incorporating its structural elements and, following from this, appropriate measures of family process.

HOW DO NEUROLEPTIC DRUGS AND PSYCHOSOCIAL INTERVENTIONS INTERACT?

This issue has been dealt with in some detail by Falloon and Liberman (1984) but for present purposes we shall confine ourselves to some major issues. The question is raised as to whether these interventions are independently effective and/or whether they interact in some fashion. This is an important issue because the apparent success of this research invites the question as to whether they might render drugs redundant.

In terms of *negative* symptoms, it is generally accepted that the neuroleptics have relatively little effect, whereas the social environment seems to be much more influential in this respect (Wing and Brown 1970). Thus it may be argued that social interventions exert an independent and unique influence on negative symptoms. However, this has yet to be formally tested in a psychosocial intervention.

As far as social functioning is concerned, evidence suggests that the level of social functioning is constrained by the ambient level of psychotic symptoms. The ability of drugs to suppress symptoms and reduce the likelihood of relapse will therefore have a direct effect on social functioning. However, are drugs sufficient to restore the individual's level of social functioning among those who survive with few symptoms in the community? The study of Hogarty and colleagues has some bearing on this. Across a range of variables relating to social and family functioning, they found that those receiving a combination of drugs and intensive 'sociotherapy' fared much better than those receiving other combinations of treatments. They found that neither drug alone nor the social intervention were sufficient to raise the level of community adjustment. The comparisons with those who received placebo are suspect because those who survive *without* drugs are certainly not representative of 'survivors'. However the 'survivors' on drugs show consistent effects of sociotherapy. The effect is unlikely to have occurred as a result of selective attrition as the combined effect of drugs and socio-therapy occurred after eighteen months and up to two years, a period over which there was little attrition of the sample due to relapse. This result is consistent with that of Doane *et al.* (1985) who, using data from the Falloon study, showed that their family intervention, in combination with drugs, led to an improvement in social func-tioning over nine months.

One might conclude therefore that neither drugs nor psychosocial therapy alone could be relied on to restore social functioning among 'survivors'. On the meagre data available it would seem that psycho-social interventions (of the sort conducted by Falloon and Hogarty) and drugs are both necessary conditions for the significant improve-ment of social functioning among survivors, but neither is sufficient on its own.

Finally, how do drugs and psychosocial interventions interact in respect of relapse? If we refer to the EE research data, Vaughn and Leff (1976) report that the rate of relapse for the low EE group over nine months was 13 per cent *irrespective* of whether patients were taking regular medication. In contrast, among the high EE group, drugs exerted a significant protective effect and under the right conditions the rate of relapse can be 'reduced' to that of the low EE group. Given the success of the experiment to reduce EE (and relapse) one interpretation of these data is that a benign, low stress, low EE environment *alone* can reduce the rate or relapse equivalent, and in some circumstances lower, than that which can be achieved by drugs. This suggests that over a nine month follow-up period, drugs and family interventions may be mutual substitutes. Over two years, however, the rate of readmission steadily rises for low EE patients, possibly as a result of extra familial stress (Leff and Vaughn 1981), to a point where drugs appear to offer some protection against relapse.

The correlational data then imply that family interventions alone may *retard* the rate of relapse, but that drugs alone cannot offer maximum protection against a high stress family environment. The best outcome may be observed by a combination of both. This suggests that drugs and family interventions would be additive in their effects, but that family interventions and drugs on their own would be only of short-term benefit. Do the intervention studies support this? The family interventions have all studied the effect of these interventions in the context of regular medication. As we have seen, the rate of relapse in families receiving these interventions was much lower than would be expected by drugs alone. This is certainly consistent with their being additive, but does not discount the possibility that family interventions are active without drugs.

In the Falloon study, it is reported that family intervention groups were able to be maintained on lower doses of medication compared to the control groups. This suggests that drugs and family intervention are, within limits, mutual substitutes (the higher the 'dose' of family therapy the lower the 'dose' of medication needed). The study of Goldstein and Kopeitan also demonstrated mutual substitution as their high dose/no family therapy and low dose/family therapy group were almost identical in terms of relapse rate (18 per cent vs. 21 per cent). This study also showed that the effect of family therapy on low dose patients was to halve the rate of relapse (48 per cent vs. 21 per cent); in the high dose group the addition of family intervention was not constant across dose levels but *increases* with increasing dose level, which suggests that these interventions are not simply additive but interact in a synergistic fashion. These interventions do not inform us whether family interventions *alone* are effective. The Hogarty study did include a 'placebo/sociotherapy' group which had no influence on relapse, although this was not family-oriented, nor was the success of sociotherapy monitored.

In summary, the evidence to date suggests that family and social interventions represent a considerable advance in addition to the benefit of drugs, and in certain respects they may have unique benefits, but they do not herald the demise of neuroleptic medication.

Chapter twenty

INSTITUTIONAL MANAGEMENT: THE TOKEN ECONOMY

Of the several social learning approaches to the treatment of institutionalised schizophrenics probably the most widely practised and extensively researched is that involving the implementation of ward wide behavioural programmes in the form of token economies (Gripp and Magaro 1974; Hersen 1976; Kazdin 1977).

CHARACTERISTICS OF TOKEN ECONOMY PROGRAMMES

In essence a token economy programme (TEP) represents an attempt to engineer environmental conditions so that multiple adaptive behaviours in several individuals may be developed and maintained by the systematic provision of contingent reinforcement. Such conditions are achieved by the use of generalised conditioned reinforcers (GCR's) in the form of plastic discs, coins, stars, check marks, points or other 'tokens' which are delivered contingent upon the completion of clearly defined and specific target behaviours, and which can be exchanged for a wide range of primary and secondary 'back-up' reinforcers such as consumables, special activities, privileges, consumer goods or money. The use of tokens as the medium through which reinforcement is applied is based on the several theoretical and practical advantages they afford in comparison with other reinforcers such as consumables or activity. Deriving their potency through association with a variety of back-up events, they are for example extremely powerful reinforcers which are capable of maintaining behaviour at a high rate, which are significantly less susceptible to satiation, and which do not involve the deprivation that may be necessary to give other reinforcers their value. They are moreover convenient to administer, they can be given in an immediate and contingent manner, their delivery and receipt does not disrupt the target response, they permit the administration of a single reinforcer to several individuals with different reinforcer preferences, they facilitate the 'parcelling out' of other reinforcers which might otherwise have to be earned in an all- or non-way, and they offer the possibility of working with large numbers of people and many behaviours at the same time. As a further important advantage the use of tokens also helps programme social interaction on the part of the token deliverer, while in addition their tangible nature permits the ready monitoring of their delivery, receipt and expenditure and hence provides immediate quantification of change.

EARLY USES OF TOKEN ECONOMIES WITH SCHIZOPHRENIC POPULATIONS

Following a number of demonstrational studies in which tokens were used with individual patients, the first large scale TEP for chronic schizophrenics was initiated by Ayllon and Azrin at Anna State Hospital, Illinois (Ayllon and Azrin 1968). The rationale for the programme was based squarely on the behavioural analysis of institutionalisation described earlier, Ayllon and Azrin arguing that many of the maladaptive and dependent behaviours they witnessed were fostered by a setting which provided little opportunity for appropriate independent behaviour, which did not require the patient to function appropriately to obtain most of the activities or privileges that were still of interest to them, and which offered little incentive to behave in a adaptive and 'motivated' manner. Through the development of a TEP, Ayllon and Azrin sought therefore to design a 'remotivating' environment in which incentives were readily available for appropriate behaviour and for those skills critical to the re-establishment of independence and initiative. By making the consequences of behaviour clearly discriminable in terms of token loss or gain, it was also hoped that patients would learn that what they did mattered and thus reestablish a sense of individual responsibility. Selection criteria for patient inclusion in the study were broad and simple, involving basically the acceptance of any patient ward staff wished transferred because they were too difficult to manage. Working therefore with forty patients mainly diagnosed as schizophrenic, Ayllon and Azrin devised an elaborate ward wide system in which tokens were awarded for constructive and functional behavioural targets such as self-care, hygiene, kitchen chores, housekeeping tasks and so on, whose absence was considered to prolong hospitalisation and which were easily observed and consequated. Those tokens earned could be exchanged for a variety of back-ups including selection of living quarters, activities on and off the ward, goods from the ward shop, choice of eating group and so on, and since they took the form of metal discs, could be exchanged daily at the commissary, or without staff intervention by operating turnstiles which regulated access to specified areas and activities.

Results of the system were reported to be extremely encouraging, self-care, attendance at activities, general activities on the ward and job-performance on and off the ward all being noted to improve markedly during the operation of the token economy contingency. Moreover suggesting the tokens to be the important treatment variable, the frequencies of target behaviours declined during a reversal phase in which tokens were administered non contingently but again increased when contingent tokens were reinstated. Other early investigations of TEPs were equally encouraging in their results, Atthowe and Krasner for example concluding on the basis of their work with chronic schizophrenics at Palo Alto Veterans Administration Hospital that:

> Thus far, a contingent reinforcement programme represented by a token economy has been successful in combatting institutionalisation, increasing initiative, responsibility and social interaction, and in putting the control of patient behavior in the hands of the patient. The behavioral changes have generalised to other areas of performance. A token economy can be an important adjunct to any rehabilitation programme for chronic or apathetic patients (Atthowe and Krasner 1968: 38).

PROGRAMME OPTIONS

Encouraged by these and other initially positive results, a plethora of further TEPs have been instituted in long-stay hospital settings in both North America and the British Isles. While conforming to the fundamental token-based format, such systems have varied fairly widely in their technical characteristics and specific programme options (Kazdin 1977). The type of contingency utilised has for example ranged from standardised contingencies (where the response requirements are the same for all individuals within a given programme), through group contingencies (where the criterion for token administration is based on the performance of the whole group), to individualised contingencies (where the behavioural targets and criteria for reinforcement are selected for the particular individual). Programmes have also varied in terms of the token deliverer, most relying on members of staff as the principal treatment agents but some involving peer administration of contingencies, or even self-determination of relevant criteria and self-administration of consequences. The range and extent of back-up reinforcers has similarly varied, most programmes employing a wide range of back-ups, but some relying on a single or few reinforcers, or simply on feedback and knowledge or results.

A further programme variation has concerned the extent to which a system incorporates punishment procedures, several making use of such techniques as 'response cost' involving the fining or withdrawal of tokens. Moreover, although many TEPs employ contingencies which are stable and seek to maintain behaviour at a given level of performance, several have introduced 'levelled systems' whereby a client progresses through a number of stages varying in terms of their response requirements and the range of back-up reinforcers available. Typically the first level of such a system would involve fairly rudimentary behavioural requirements and offer a limited range of reinforcers, the next level more complex behaviours and added privileges, and so on to an eventual level whereby the client perhaps has access to many reinforcers without specified token contingencies. Such a system obviously has advantages where the aims are progressive rehabilitation rather than more stable management. Finally programmes have varied in respect of the target behaviours selected for attention. Most of the early systems followed Ayllon and Azrin in selecting targets such as self-care and work activity, for which there is clearly some justification while there are institutions which foster dependent and maladaptive behaviours. More recently however 'output' orientated TEPs have sought to additionally programme targets more clearly related to post-TEP and extra-institutional adjustment, particulrly skills which give the patient the ability to control his environment and have access to a wide range of potential reinforcers. Principal among these targets have been socialisation skills, with an increasing number of TEPs explicitly programming interpersonal interaction either for all patients or as a specific target for individuals. Many systems have also incorporated individualised behavioural programmes aimed at the reduction of specific symptomatic behaviour.

THE EFFICACY OF TOKEN ECONOMY PROGRAMMES

Evaluation of the outcome of most TEPs has consisted of assessments of change in specific targets measured by direct observation frequency counts or time sampling, and in some instances the number of tokens earned. In a few situations, when for example, the target is verbal behaviour as part of an individualised programme, use has also been made of standardised assessment situations (e.g. formal interview), video recordings, and relevant behavioural rating scales. The emphasis on specific target behaviours has also in many cases been complemented by an examination of broad changes in non-targetted responses, use being made variously of rating scales which are well validated and standardised, and local forms less suited to general use.

Despite variation in programme specifications, results of these assessments have continued to be generally positive, Kazdin (1977: 110) in fact suggesting that the success of TEPs in changing a wide variety of behaviours in institutional settings is 'firmly established'. Probably the most consistently and clearly positive results have been reported in respect of behaviours considered adaptive in the hospital, such as getting up, bed making, grooming, personal hygiene, dressing, room cleaning, attending and participating in therapeutic activities, work performance, general activity, compliance with medication, social interaction and so on (e.g. Allen and Magaro 1971; Cohen *et al.* 1972; Glickman *et al.* 1973; Lloyd and Garlington 1968; Maley *et al.* 1973; McReynolds and Coleman 1972; Nelson and Cone 1979; Schaefer and Martin 1966; Steffy *et al.* 1969; Winkler 1970; Woods *et al.* 1984). Although less well established several other studies have suggested that reinforcement of appropriate behaviour may be associated with more general improvements in communication, mood, cooperation, discrimination and neatness, and reductions in shouting, withdrawal, thought disorder, irritability, manifest psychoses and medication (e.g. Di Scipio and Trudeau 1972; Gripp and Magaro 1971; Maley *et al.* 1973; O'Brien and Azrin 1972; Shean and Zeidberg 1971). Similar observations have been made in the present authors' own hospital, when one year after the introduction of a flexible points based token programme improvements in targetted self-care, independence, occupational and interactional behaviours ($p < 0.005$) were associated with significant reductions in non-targetted problem behaviours ($p < 0.005$).

Beneficial effects have also been reported when symptomatic and problem behaviours (e.g. Wincze *et al.* 1972; Winkler 1970), and social skills (e.g. Bennett and Maley 1973; Leitenberg *et al.* 1970; Liberman 1972) are selected as specific targets, while Kazdin (1977) has noted several reports in which tokens have been used to encourage patients to take a more active part in their own treatment by for example making suggestions about ward practices and treatment. Many TEPs have also reported increased rates of discharge and reductions in readmission (e.g. Atthowe and Krasner 1968;

Ellsworth 1969; Heap *et al.* 1970; Lloyd and Abel 1970; McReynolds and Coleman 1972; Shean and Zeidberg 1971) and several have reported greater improvement in subjects receiving token reinforcement than in control groups subject to conventional institutional treatment (e.g. Heap *et al.* 1970; Gripp and Magaro 1971; Maley *et al.* 1973; Schaefer and Martin 1966; Shean and Zeidberg 1971). Maley *et al.* for example concluded their study by noting that:

> . . . results indicate that token economy patients as compared to custodial care patients exhibited more appropriate mood states, were more cooperative, and engaged in more communication with better developed expressive skills. Token economy patients did not show as much 'psychotic behaviour', such as unusual motor activity, confusion, anxiety and bizarreness (Maley *et al.* 1973: 143).

Comparisons of the outcome of TEPs with other non-behavioural social treatments have been rather mixed and less conclusive (e.g. Baker *et al.* 1974; Greenberg *et al.* 1975; Hartlage 1970; Marks *et al.* 1968; Olson and Greenberg 1972). Comparing a TEP with a non-behavioural ward featuring a psychiatric therapy programme emphasising community environment, group discussion of problems, and individual and group psychotherapy, Gershone *et al.* (1977) however concluded that 'the token economy patients, compared with standard therapy patients, were better groomed, attended activities more often, spent less time in bed, and emitted fewer distress comments' (Gershone *et al* 1977: 383). The superiority of a TEP over alternate social therapy was also noted by Stoffelmayr *et al.* (1979), while Paul and Lentz's (1977) massive and rigorous eight year study of state hospital, milieu and social learning treatments clearly favours the programme whose core was a token system modelled on that of Ayllon and Azrin (1968).

Of the numerous studies of TEP effects, that of Paul and Lentz deserves particular attention in view of both its longevity (the psychosocial programmes running for just under four and a half years and being followed by a further one and a half year community placement project), and the sophistication of its methodological design. Thus considerable care was taken in ensuring that staff involved in milieu or social learning settings followed distinctive procedures (conformity to which was carefully assessed throughout the project), and that staff, patient and setting characteristics were equated across conditions. Moreover extremely thorough and objective assessments of change were carried out by independent and trained assessors using a wide battery of measures, including continuous behavioural observations of staff and patient behaviours (e.g. the Staff-Resident Interaction Chronograph, the Time Sample Behavioural Checklist etc). As a result of such design

291

characteristics it was noted that there were no differences between the psychosocial programmes in terms of staff activity, time with or attention to the patients over the duration of the project. Results of the study, while complex, clearly suggest the efficacy of the social learning programme in achieving significant changes in adaptive and maladaptive behaviours (including reducing extremely bizarre and aggressive actions), and in socialising over 90 per cent of the patients into the community, and 10 per cent to independent living. By comparison the milieu programme was significantly less effective in achieving change within the institution and in facilitating successful community adjustment, and it encountered particular difficulties in coping with extremely problematic or aggressive behaviours. The traditional hospital programme made no significant impact on the behaviour of its severely disturbed client group, and Paul and Lentz conclude:

> The overall comparative results on the relative effectiveness of the programs in the current project could not be clearer. The social-learning program was significantly more effective than either the milieu program or the traditional hospital programs. Its greater effectiveness was consistent across all classes of functioning in the intramural setting and in the production of institutional release, based upon the same criteria. Since neither post-release functioning nor rehospitalisation rates differed among those who achieved significant release and received the same aftercare services, the social learning program also maintained greater effectiveness over milieu and hospital programs in community stay. The improvements and release within the social learning program occurred without regard to individual demographic characteristics, previous length or type of treatment, nature of initial level, or severity of deficits or bizarre behaviour and in the relative absence of psychotropic drugs. It was also more efficient and cost-effective, obtaining the superior effects with similar staffing levels to the hospital programs and the same staff, physical plant, activity schedule, and behavioural focus as the milieu program had (Paul and Lentz 1977: 423).

ISSUES IN TOKEN ECONOMY RESEARCH

As suggested by Kazdin (1977), the efficacy of TEPs in effecting beneficial changes in the behaviour of chronic hospitalised schizophrenics would, in the light of the above, appear to be established by a substantial body of supportive evidence. It is however clear that a number of theoretical and practical questions remain concerning the necessary technical specification of an effective TEP, the possibilities of effecting change in the residual group of 'non-responders' reported in most studies, and the extent to which TEPs can promote change which is of clinical and therapeutic significance, which is durable, and which is capable of generalisation beyond the treatment setting. Definite resolution of such issues is of course precluded by the diversity of programme options described earlier, by differences in the characteristics of TEPs operating under the British National Health Service and the American state hospital system (e.g. Mumford *et al.* 1975; Presly *et al.* 1976) and by variability across studies in terms of patient selection criteria, settings and assessment procedures. Indeed Paul and Lentz (1977: 434) have noted that a given TEP 'may be no more related to other token economy procedures than the action of heroin is related to penicillin, even though they are both administered by injection'. A sift of the research literature, with particular emphasis on the results of well designed and controlled studies such as that of Paul and Lentz (1977) does however suggest certain main trends and findings upon which tentative evaluation may be based.

CRITICAL COMPONENTS OF TOKEN ECONOMY PROGRAMMES

The first major area of uncertainty has concerned the identification of components of TEPs critical to their successful function, and particularly the extent to which tokens or similar GCRs are themselves necessary and sufficient therapeutic elements.

The role of instruction, feedback and modelling
TEPs in clinical practice are in fact extremely complex multi-component interventions whose elements include the provision of instructions about the target behaviour required and contingency operative, feedback, modelling, interpersonal interaction and social reinforcement, and the contingent delivery of GCRs backed up by other primary and secondary reinforcers. While each probably makes at least some contribution to the effects of the total package, few direct attempts have however been made to extricate their specific influence or relative importance. A potentially important role for instructions is for example suggested by reports that responsiveness to reinforcement programmes may develop only when contingencies are clearly described (e.g. Ayllon and Azrin 1964), and that significant improvements in the problem behaviour of some chronic schizophrenics may be effected by instructional training alone (e.g. Fraser *et al.* 1981; Suchotliff *et al.* 1970), although others have suggested that mere instruction to behave appropriately may produce little change in performance without the addition of contingent reinforcement (e.g. Liberman 1972; Woods *et al.* 1984). Kazdin

(1977) has argued that clear verbal descriptions of desired behaviour and its consequences are in fact likely to play an important role in TEPs and that they contribute to some of the change more commonly attributed to tokens themselves. In the absence of more direct and extensive controlled investigation the relative importance of instruction and reinforcement however remains uncertain. Similarly few studies have sought to separate the effects of feedback on performance implicit in token delivery from the direct effect of GCRs themselves, and while evidence from other settings (e.g. educational) suggests that token reinforcement is superior to feedback alone, the relative magnitude of change effected by each in psychiatric TEPs is unevaluated. Despite its potential importance, even less attention has been paid to the possible vicarious influence of observing the performance of others and their receipt of reinforcing consequences.

While instruction, feedback and modelling may play an important contributory role, there is at this stage therefore insufficient strong evidence to suggest their influence is primary, or to challenge the view that behaviour change in TEPs does in most instances demand the addition of contingent reinforcement. Since they represent a virtually inevitable aspect of TEP delivery, many clinicians have in fact considered separation of their specific effects to be a matter of theoretical rather than practical interest. That the influence of instruction in particular deserves further attention is however suggested by studies in which significant TEP effects are noted on a group basis, but in which substantial between-subject variability in response is observed. Thus while most studies report group changes on the introduction of tokens, several have noted improvements in some patients in their samples before contingencies are applied (e.g. Ayllon and Azrin 1965; Atthowe and Krasner 1968; Curran *et al.* 1968; Lloyd and Garlington 1968; Lloyd and Abel 1970). In an extreme instance Allen and Magaro (1971) for example reported that of thirty-nine patients required to complete a single target response (attending OT), over 40 per cent performed satisfactorily before the positive token contingency was introduced. Since such reports have rarely sought to investigate the determinants or durability of non-token change, the influence of instructions, staff expectations, non-programmed reinforcers of other types or other factors must remain a matter for conjecture. The possibility that at least some behaviours in some patients may improve without the addition of tokens (if not other reinforcers) is however of potential importance in view of reports that the intrinsic reinforcing properties of a behaviour may be reduced by the addition of an external reinforcer (Levine and Fasnacht 1974). Thus behaviour performed at an adequate level prior to the administration of a token contingency may become 'token bound', being subsequently maintained at a high rate only when tokens are available, and falling below baseline levels when tokens are removed. An instance of this effect has for example been reported by Woods *et al.* (1984) the high baseline levels of some behaviours in one patient being subsequently maintained only during a contingent token condition, and dropping below baseline during non-contingent tokens (in contrast to other behaviours of the patient which were performed at low levels during baseline and for which the TEP had a therapeutic effect). If such problems are to be avoided, the influence of instructions and the identification of individuals in whom behaviour change may occur without tokens, would seem important areas for further investigation.

The role of GCRs versus social reinforcement
Similar issues have been raised in the more hotly contested debate concerning the relative importance in TEPs of GCRs and social reinforcers. In this respect a number of workers have suggested that the introduction of a TEP may involve in addition to GCR administration an increase in staff morale associated with greater interest from other professional groups, an increase in staff efforts to provide better patient care, reorientation in nurse expectancies in the direction of positive results, and the innovation of new activities and routines which provide more structure, promote greater nurse-patient interaction and facilitate the provision of attention for appropriate behaviour. Thus while under normal circumstances nurses may spend less than 25 per cent of their time in patient interaction (Sanson-Fisher *et al.* 1979), there is evidence that both the quantity and quality of staff-patient contact may be changed during token reinforcement (Kazdin 1977). Some studies for example suggest that ward staff participating in a token scheme evaluate their patients more positively (McReynolds and Coleman 1972; Milby *et al.* 1975) and that they reduce their attention to inappropriate behaviour and are less likely to make uses of reprimands and disapproval (Kazdin 1977). Thus Trudel *et al.* (1974) noted that nursing assistants on a TEP ward gave over six times more attention for appropriate behaviour than their colleagues in a non-token setting. It has been suggested therefore that the critical elements of TEPs are not the tokens themselves, but the increase in staff attention and social reinforcement of appropriate behaviour in conjunction with prompting, instruction and feedback (Baker *et al.* 1977; Liberman *et al.* 1974).

Evaluation of the issue is again unfortunately confounded by the relative lack of direct experimental evidence. Some support for the importance of social factors is however provided by Ribes-Inesta *et al.*'s (1973) limited demonstration that responsivity to social reinforcement might be a necessary precondition for the establishment of a functional TEP, and particularly by the work of Baker and associates (Baker *et al*. 1974, 1977; Hall *et al*. 1977) suggesting a critical role for staff orientation towards specific targets and nurse reinforcement and feedback. Thus in a study involving the sequential introduction of staff, increased activity, non-contingent tokens and contingent tokens, Baker *et al*. (1974) noted that the addition of tokens produced no further improvement beyond that achieved during the prior experimental conditions. In a controlled comparison Baker *et al*. (1977) similarly noted that despite an initial positive effect in a contingent token group, a non-contingent token control group provided with equivalent attention did as well in the long run. In contrast however Paul and Lentz's (1977) well controlled comparison of token economy and social-milieu programmes suggested the clear superiority of the former, despite the provision in both conditions of substantial social interaction and attention. While it cannot be certain that social attention was provided on a response contingent basis during milieu therapy, Kazdin (1977) has noted that evidence from TEPs with other types of client group do generally suggest the addition of token contingencies to promote further change over that resulting from prior contingent social reinforcement. Similarly Elliott *et al*. (1979) have noted that a total TEP package produced significant improvements in eighteen chronic schizophrenics, but that the administration of only praise during an experimental phase did not suggest social factors involved in token delivery to be the singularly critical variable (although their data seems to indicate mainly that social reinforcement alone was insufficient to promote additional improvement). Other evidence that GCRs are themselves important is provided by observations that changing the value of tokens relative to back-up reinforcers can lead to changes in the probability of target behaviour (e.g. Ayllon and Azrin 1968; Winkler 1973). Increasing the amount of reward monies available to back up points earning was similarly noted to promote further behavioural improvement in the patients on a token system in the present authors' own hospital (Brookes and Brown 1981; Harvey and Green 1983) and Winkler (1973) has argued that complex economic relationships between GCRs, targets and backups represent in fact important influences on the magnitude of TEP induced change. Thus Winkler (op. cit.) noted for example varying output of target behaviours as a patients' token savings rose and fell, performance improving with low or no savings and deteriorating with high savings which permitted access to back-ups without further target completion.

Improved specification of the relative importance of contingent social and token reinforcement is clearly important in view of the possible disadvantages associated with unnecessary token delivery. As noted earlier the use of tokens to consequate behaviour whose baseline level is already high, or which reaches a high level following instruction and social reinforcement, may result in the development of token bound behaviour which occurs later only if followed by tokens (Levine and Fasnacht 1974). Moreover tokens are in respect of most behaviours 'arbitrary reinforcers' (Ferster 1967), and are not widely used as reinforcing consequences in the 'real world'. Thus while tokens in the form of money represent part of the reinforcement complex maintaining work behaviour, they are not widely employed to encourage self-care, independence or social skills. Their unnecessary use in treatment programmes may therefore present serious obstacles to the generalisation of change, which may be avoided by the use of incentives common to both the treatment and post-training discharge environment.

Clearly the ubiquitous nature of social interaction suggests that for those patients for whom it is effective, social reinforcement offers advantages as a more natural reinforcer which may be available to maintain change after treatment. However even for these patients it may be noted that several studies have suggested that sustained and consistent delivery of contingent social reinforcement may only be possible given the sort of structure provided by a TEP. Ferster (1974) has argued that the structure of a TEP helps staff learn and apply the essentials of functional behavioural analysis, and it is interesting to observe that Baker and Hall (1975) for example reported that staff in their study found it extremely difficult to maintain a control group procedure of contingent attention without the precision afforded by contingent token delivery. Indeed Baker *et al.* (1977) noted that while the TEP in their study was not more effective than an enriched milieu, staff chose to continue the token system since they found it easier to implement. Similar observations have been made by Elliott *et al.* (1979) and in the authors' own hospital. Moreover Rezin *et al.* (1983) have reported that token delivery does indeed facilitate staff-patient interaction even in comparison with attempts to deliver praise in a contingent manner. Thus comparing a group receiving contingent tokens and praise an another given contingent praise but non-contingent tokens, Rezin *et al.* (op. cit.) noted that the length of staff-patient interaction was significantly increased in the contingent token group over a five month period.

Prompts and incentives for behaviour
While no firm conclusions can yet be drawn concerning critical programme elements it does seem reasonable to infer from the above at least two major defining and necessary characteristics from which positive TEP effects are derived. Firstly, TEPs provide a clear and explicit structure within which desirable behaviour is possible, expected and specifically prompted. Such a structure seems to be

important both in facilitating consistent and goal orientated behaviour on the part of staff, and in making behavioural requirements absolutely clear to the patients themselves (perhaps particularly important in view of constraints imposed by cognitive impairment). Secondly, notwithstanding evidence of behaviour change following the provision of structure and instruction alone, there seems little reason to doubt the critical importance of providing, or arranging for the availability of, contingent positive reinforcement (Paul and Lentz 1977). For some patients at least it appears that contingent reinforcement in the form of social attention may be sufficient, although even here the consistent delivery of attention may demand a structure similar to that of a TEP. For many, however, the use of GCRs backed up by an extremely wide range of reinforcers in addition to social attention may be necessary to ensure idiosyncratically relevant contingent reinforcement and to promote initial change. The potential disadvantage of tokens suggests nonetheless that they should be only employed in a flexible, discriminative and selective manner, and that attempts should be made from the outset to programme generalisation and to transfer the responsibility for maintaining change to more natural reinforcers.

Staff support and skill
It may also be noted that the efficacy and indeed very survival of a TEP depends not merely on its technical specification, but also on the skill, motivation and attitudes of its staff, and on the support it enjoys from senior management and hospital administrators. Since it is generally agreed that nurses are crucial to a TEP's success or failure, several authors have emphasised the importance of selecting staff who are pretrained in behavioural techniques, who are favourably disposed to their employment and who will be available on the ward on a consistent basis (e.g. Atthowe 1973; Gripp and Magaro 1974; Hall and Baker 1973; Kazdin and Bootzin 1972). Given the considerable demands involved in running a complex TEP, attention has also been drawn to the importance of maintaining staff morale and motivation by the provision of feedback, recognition and reinforcement for their efforts, the support of hospital administrators being noted to be critical in this respect (Krasner and Atthowe 1971). In the absence of suitably trained and motivated staff there is little doubt that reinforcers will not be applied in a consistent, immediate or contingent manner (Katz *et al.* 1972), and that there is in fact a real danger of inadvertent or deliberate system sabotage (e.g. Atthowe 1973; Hall and Baker 1973; Krasner 1968; Mumford *et al.* 1975). There have indeed been several reports of system breakdown as a consequence of political and organisational difficulties, Woods *et al.* (1984) suggesting the

short life-span of many programmes to be one reason for the relative dearth of long-term follow-up studies. In even Paul and Lentz's (1977) elaborate study political and administrative concerns were throughout intertwined with immediate clinical and research demands, and at several points threatened the project with breakdown. The development and maintenance of a TEP, which may require flexible organisational changes in other parts of the parent institution, clearly therefore demands the engagement of staff, management and administrative support. Its survival may depend not only on the extent to which it can offer reinforcers for patient improvement, but also its ability to offer reinforcers for organisational flexibility and broad based changes in institutional policy.

BETWEEN SUBJECT RESPONSE VARIABILITY

The second issue arousing some debate in the TEP literature is that of between-subject response variability, most studies noting an at least small number of patients who remain unresponsive to the contingencies in operation (Kazdin 1973). The extent and nature of the problem is in fact uncertain since most studies have evaluated programmes by grouping individual data, and have varied in terms of sample size and composition, the number and complexity of behavioural targets, outcome criteria adopted and the length of programme operation. In respect of the latter Woods *et al.* (1984) have for example suggested that the response of some patients may be extremely slow, improvements in some subjects of their five year ongoing TEP being observed only months or even years after continuous contingency administration. Woods *et al.* (op. cit.) speculate therefore that at least some of the reported 'non-responders' may have improved had contingencies been in operation longer than the short time span of many projects. Given evidence for at least some non-responsivity it is however clearly important to determine relevant causes and defining patient characteristics so that TEPs might exercise patient selection or make special arrangements for those 'at risk' for no or slow response.

Non-response and patient characteristics
Unfortunately results of the few studies addressing the issue are neither consistent nor conclusive, and the nature or even existence of characteristics associated with poor response are unclear. Thus while some studies have reported a slight if variable relationship between response and IQ, length of hospitalisation or diagnosis (e.g. Curran *et al.* 1968, Panek 1969; Kowalski 1976), others have found no evidence that variables of a demographic type possess predictive utility (e.g. Allen and Magaro 1971; Ayllon and Azrin

1965; Lloyd and Abel 1970; Woods *et al.* 1984). Behavioural characteristics present before treatment begins have also received some attention, some studies suggesting for example that poor response and treatment difficulties are particularly associated with severely socially withdrawn or hyperactive patients (e.g. Atthowe and Krasner 1968; Ayllon and Azrin 1968; Steffy 1968). In the authors' own hospital some differences in baseline behaviour were similarly observed between patients who showed successful community adjustment on discharge and those who remained on the ward. Thus while all patients showed initial behavioural deficits and problems, and were comparable in terms of baseline self-help and occupational behaviour, those with better outcome tended to have initially higher levels of independence and social skills, and lower levels of problem behaviour. At this stage however there is insufficient evidence to suggest that demographic, diagnostic or general behavioural characteristics are reliably predictive of outcome, and further investigation is clearly required.

Non-response and programme specification

The reasons for non-responsiveness in some patients accordingly remains speculative, and may in fact vary between individuals. Thus it is possible that some patients have particularly unusual response characteristics in relation to conventional reinforcers, or that specific and severe types of cognitive deficit impede the rate of learning and ability to understand relationships between behaviour and its consequences, or that particularly powerful internal stimuli compete with external events for attention, or that very specific types of behavioural excess or deficit interfere with programme operation. It is however precisely because individuals differ in their biological and pre-treatment behavioural characteristics that the most parsimonious explanation of non-responsiveness may in fact be that the contingency system in effect is inappropriate for the given individual. Quite simply an inflexible TEP in which common targets are set for all patients and in which backups are limited, may be insufficiently tailored to meet an individual's idiosyncratic needs and characteristics. Kazdin (1972, 1973) has suggested therefore that non-responsivity may arise because the target response is not in the patient's repertoire, the back-ups are weak or personally irrelevant, the delay between responses and reinforcers is poorly programmed, the patient can earn sufficient reinforcers with a few responses making others unnecessary, poorly designed contingencies conflict with peer group contingencies, the patient has access to reinforcers beyond the systems control, or several other inadequacies of programme design. If this analysis is correct, non-response may in fact at least be alleviated by programme revision involving for example the selection of more appropriate targets, the use of shaping and response priming, the assessment and sampling of reinforcers and provision of better back-ups, the use of individualised contingencies, differential scheduling, altering token values, limiting savings and so on.

Implications for programme design
While the issue of non-response remains uncertain, the above considerations perhaps suggest at least two guidelines for programme design and patient selection. Firstly TEPs should be conceived and designed as convenient but flexible frameworks for the development and delivery of highly individualised behavioural programmes. Thus programme targets for individual patients should be selected and defined on the basis of a full (preferably observational) assessment of their self-care, independence, social, occupational and problem behaviours, a thorough behavioural analysis and the formulation of a tailored goal orientated care plan. Such an analysis may indicate that some target responses can be conveniently addressed through the token system, while others may need the further development of specially configured behavioural programmes employing additional therapeutic techniques. Similarly attempts must be made to identify in the case of each patient idiosyncratically relevant reinforcers which are incorporated into a wide range of other more conventional incentives, and to determine the token value of specific behaviours and back-up exchange rates on an individual basis. Progress on all targets and wide ranging nontargets should then be subject to ongoing review, and the programme changed flexibly as circumstances dictate.

Secondly, in the absence of reliable positive criteria for patient inclusion, TEPs should be designed with particular functions in mind, and should select fairly homogeneous clients with an eye to the targets they are geared to train and the manpower and material resources available. In an attempt to demonstrate the possibilities of behaviour change it was of course reasonable for early TEPs to accept virtually any patient other wards wished to transfer, and their initial promise was perhaps established on these grounds. While however any patient may respond to a contingency programme in principle, there are clearly practical constraints on the possibilities of addressing individual and widely differing needs and problems in a group of heterogeneous composition. It is indeed probable that many early systems adopted limited and common ward wide targets precisely because wide population heterogeneity precluded in practical terms the development of individualised programmes. If TEP effects are to be maximised, it is clearly therefore important that a given system is goal orientated, that it is equipped to promote on an individual basis behaviour necessary for goal achievement, and that it can select patients in need of the training it provides and whose presence will not impede the delivery of individualised programmes to others. If an output orientated TEP is for example geared to promote independence skills, the inclusion of extremely disturbed, overactive or intellectually dull patients demanding excessive staff attention may prove counterproductive, and disrupt ongoing individual work with other clients. Such difficult clients may benefit from a TEP, but one specifically designed to provide the sorts of individual attention they in turn require. Equally if a ward is geared to remediate particular sorts of behavioural deficit, there is little value in including patients already skilled in these areas but having other other sorts of problems. Even given attempts to select patients on an 'exclusion criteria' basis it is likely of course that some will be misidentified as suitable for a given programme. One approach to this problem is to run a one or two week assessment period, during which individual needs, initial response to tokens, the feasibility of particular sorts of individualised programme, the time scale of likely response and so on, can be better assessed. If on the basis of this assessment it seems the system cannot in practice meet the patients' needs without jeopardising its work with others, it may be necessary to exclude them from the programme. Of course if sufficient patients are excluded, it may be necessary to revise the function of the ward so it is better placed to meet the needs of an evidently significant group of potential clients.

THE CLINICAL UTILITY AND GENERALISATION OF TOKEN ECONOMY EFFECTS

The third, and perhaps most contentious issue in the TEP literature has however concerned the clinical relevance, durability and generalisation of programme effects, some critics charging that TEPs may serve as static management systems which provide changes of a merely prosthetic rather than truly therapeutic nature.

Management versus output oriented TEPs

There is in fact little doubt that some TEPs have focused on a limited and common set of self-care and ward work targets whose completion in themselves is of perhaps greater relevance to the smooth running of the institution than the demonstrable needs of individual patients. Of course as Kazdin (1975a) has observed, there may in fact be justification in choosing such targets while there are institutions which foster dependent and maladaptive behaviour. While of a modest nature, their achievement may therefore be crucial if a patient is ever to proceed to a more advanced environment. On their own however such targets are insufficient to promote habilitation, rehabilitation or an improved quality of life and social adjustment, and many TEPs have clearly failed to consider where patients might go on programme completion or to target behaviours required in more advanced environmental settings. In the absence of a progressive rehabilitative framework such systems may well develop into static and permanent management procedures for a stable group of patients.

To a large extent however this problem relates to the inadequacy of system design rather than to any particular theoretical limit on the role of TEPs themselves. Thus as noted earlier many TEPs are now designed as output orientated elements of progressive rehabilitation systems, and seek to select targets of relevance to the individual, to individualise contingencies, and to incorporate specific additional treatment programmes as required. Some have also sought to ensure the relevance of target selection by developing levelled systems (e.g. Lloyd and Abel 1970), Cullen *et al.* (1977) recommending in this respect the initial establishment of a ward for patients with advanced repertoires based on procedures for response maintenance and acquisition similar to those outside the institution, and then working backwards through a series of levelled token programmes. At the bottom of the scale would then be a system requiring the performance of a few behaviours, progressively greater demands being required through stages up to a terminal level rehabilitation ward where behaviours would be closely related to extra-institutional performance demands. Target behaviours at any given level would then be rationally selected in terms of demands at the next level. The point to be emphasised however is that TEPs do not represent a cookbook solution to the problems of chronic institutionalised schizophrenics, but instead a complex tool whose utility will depend upon the use to which it is put and the skill of its design and application. If a TEP is to operate as other than a static management system, it must therefore pay careful attention to selecting as targets those behaviours necessary for survival and successful adjustment in the post-training environment. Even if the realistic goal for some patients is continued hospitalisation, attempts should be made to target skills which give the patient the ability to exercise greater control over their environment, which give access to a wide range of potential reinforcers, and which improve the quality of the patient's life. When the goal is extra institutional survival however the TEP must clearly identify and train those behaviours necessary for adjustment in the local community setting, even if such targets place a premium on institutional flexibility rather than smooth and convenient institutional operation.

The durability and generalisation of change
The durability and generalisation of improvement, the latter

involving both the maintenance of change within a given setting on programme termination and the transfer of learning to other environments, is however a more complex problem. Evaluation of the issue is unfortunately constrained by the surprising scarcity of long-term TEP programmes and follow-up data, reflecting perhaps in part the short-lived nature of many systems and the frequency of collapse because of administrative and political problems. From the few TEPs which have survived on a long-term basis there is at least reasonable evidence for durable behaviour change over long periods of time while contingencies remain in effect (e.g. Paul and Lentz 1977; Woods *et al.* 1984). While of an essentially prosthetic nature, the possibilities of such robust change may be nonetheless of importance for those patients whose realistic prospects involve prolonged hospitalisation. Thus providing targets are set within a positive rather than management framework, improvement maintained by continued token administration may be preferable to an alternative involving regression to apathetic dependence.

The possibilities of maintaining change on programme termination are however more uncertain, on purely theoretical grounds maintenance being in fact not expected unless specifically programmed (Carlson *et al.* 1972; Kazdin 1975a; Liberman *et al.* 1976). Thus Carlson *et al.* (1972) have noted that 'unless specific steps are taken to ensure that post-hospital reinforcement contingencies encountered by the patient are programmed to support changes effected during his hospitalisation, there is no logical or theoretical reason to assume that improvement will be maintained' (Carlson *et al.* 1972: 201). It is perhaps therefore surprising that several studies have reported maintained improvement in some subjects on contingency terminations (see Kazdin 1977), Woods *et al.* (1984) noting for example sustained improvement in several of their subjects on return to baseline conditions which they suggest represents a truly therapeutic effect. Several studies have also of course reported increased rates of discharge and reduced rates of readmission (e.g. Hollingsworth and Foreyt 1975; Shean and Zeidberg 1971), although readmission rates may be poorly correlated with other more direct measures of post-hospital adjustment (e.g. Ellsworth *et al.* 1979). The reasons why responses are maintained after consequences are withdrawn in such studies are unclear, although Kazdin (1977) suggests that behaviour may come under the control of natural reinforcers in the setting, that consequences resulting directly from the performance of the target may be reinforcing or that the behaviour of the agents administering the programme is changed in some permanent way. Thus Woods *et al.* (1984) suggest that the adaptive behaviour of some of their subjects became 'trapped' by natural consequences, the TEP 'priming the pump' by providing opportunities for appropriate behaviour, encouraging their development, and in turn promoting changes in staff expectations and behaviour. Despite this evidence, most studies however report that as expected changes tend not to be maintained once the token contingencies are removed (see Gripp and Magaro 1974; Kazdin 1977; Kazdin and Bootzin 1972).

The enhancement of generalization
In view of the above, several authors (e.g. Peck and Thorpe 1971; Kazdin 1975a, 1977) have argued that specific steps must be taken to promote generalisation, procedures suggested including selecting targets relevant to the discharge environment, increasing the delay and changing the schedule of reinforcement to build resistance to extinction, substituting natural and social reinforcers for the GCRs used in training, varying the stimulus conditions of training, bringing target behaviours under the control of stimuli common to both environments, using gradual approximations to the discharge environment, teaching self control skills as targets (e.g. self re-inforcement, self-cueing, self-instruction) and teaching behavioural methods to staff, relatives and other care givers in the post-training setting. Generalisation is for example more likely if a TEP selects targets for an individual which are idiosyncratically relevant to their personal circumstance and the demands they will face after training, and which will be reinforced by natural consequences in the discharge setting. The adoption of this 'relevance of behaviour rule' (Ayllon and Azrin 1968) demands therefore the selection of targets based not on arbitrary assumption but on direct assessment of the self-care, domestic, independence, social, occupational and other demands the patient will face in the post-TEP environment, the exact skills required to meet these demands, and of course the client's own background, experience and expressed preference.

Similarly since the hospital environment does not in many important respects resemble the 'real world', TEPs training people for community discharge may enhance the chances of generalisation by identifying and utilising training situations which increasingly approximate the discharge environment. While initially all training might be conducted in the 'sheltered' but artificial environment of the hospital, even here attempts should be made to engineer conditions to be as 'realistic' as possible (e.g. setting up social events and situations resembling those outside the hospital). Later as the patient acquires new skills, further training and practice may take place in the real setting (e.g. in a half-way house, local pub, cinema, launderette, etc.) where the demands the patient faces are similar to those he will encounter when fully discharged. A halfway training house may be important in this respect to permit relevant training of domestic skills, skills involved in budgetting etc., and in permit-ting an observable and realistic degree of independence from the hospital while still providing supervision and training. The possibilities of generalisation will also be enhanced by the use wherever possible of 'relevant' incentives which will also be available in the discharge environment. Thus while tokens may be necessary in the first instance to boost motivation and encourage the development of appropriate behaviour, they should be backed up by incentives which are of idiosyncratic interest to the client and their needs, and which are relevant to and readily available in the discharge environment. As noted earlier skills 'pump primed' by the TEP may themselves prove to be intrinsically reinforcing and provide the patient with experience of many naturally available reinforcers to which they had previously little access. While behaviour may become 'caught' by natural consequences, specific programmed attempts should also be made to fade out the use of tokens and to place emphasis on the direct use of natural incentives, and particularly those which normally motivate people to perform the behaviour in question in the post-training environment. Even with such a 'relevant' TEP, it may still be necessary to enhance generalisation by ensuring that staff or family members who live with the patient after discharge continue to prompt and reinforce appropriate behaviour in a systematic manner, particularly if the client's skills remain limited, and insufficient to complete in a harsh real world setting.

The use of such generalisation enhancement procedures has over recent years received increasing attention in the general field of behaviour modification, and Kazdin (1977: 196) has argued that 'the existing literature suggests that there is a technology of establishing the generality of behaviour change'. There are still however very few reported examples of their use in TEPs developed for schizophrenic populations one notable exception being the investigation described by Paul and Lentz (1977). Utilising complex methods to facilitate generalisation, Paul and Lentz did for example choose as targets behaviours necessary for life in the community (changes in which significantly predicted community adjustment), and sought also to develop continuing programmes of involvement with patients discharged into hostels and other partially independent community placements. Results of their work were encouraging, particularly in view of the extremely difficult and aggressive nature of the client group with whom they worked, over 90 per cent of the TEP group remaining in the community one and a half years after programme completion, and 10 per cent living in an independent and self supporting manner. As many as 20 per cent of those living in board and care facilities however displayed low levels of function at follow-up and clearly significant further work is required to establish how generalisation procedures may in practical terms be best employed. Moreover it is clear that while TEPs can help bridge the gap between the institution with its limited demands and incentives to change, and the potentially more rewarding but more challenging and demanding world outside, they cannot function effectively as isolated, independent treatment ventures.

SUMMARY

While their role is not definitely established, there does seem evidence to suggest that TEPs or similar social learning programmes which provide a structure for the prompting and reinforcement of appropriate behaviour, which are capable of generating individualised care plans, which attend to the promotion of generalisation, and which form a component in a progressive and rational rehabilitation framework, may have a significant part to play in the habilitation of chronic schizophrenics. The success of TEPs in producing a more active, sociable and stimulating environment for chronic patients perhaps also suggests the merits of exploring the use of behaviourally organised ward environments for acute patients. Through the systematic provision of prompts and reinforcement for self care, social, work and other positive behaviour, such a regime may help foster independence, social competence and personal well being, and help prevent the slide into chronic apathy and institutionalised dependence. The use of tokens *per se* in such settings may be both unnecessary and undesirable if the environment can be engineered to promote and reinforce adaptive behaviour in more natural ways. The TEP literature however highlights the extent to which ward and hospital practice, policy and organisation may have to change if such engineering is to be feasible.

Chapter twenty-one

THE PROCESS OF REHABILITATION

The last thirty years have witnessed marked changes in the nature of care systems for the mentally ill, advances in treatment technique and mental health philosophy fuelling an increasing emphasis on the provision of community based care and facilitating a steady contraction in the inpatient population of traditional psychiatric hospitals. The optimism for the 1960s and '70s, when the imminent demise of large institutions was widely predicted, has been however necessarily tempered by subsequent evidence concerning both the 'old' and 'new' long stay mentally ill, and the unsatisfactory circumstances of many dischargees living in the community. Despite the upsurge in discharge rates there are still some 69,000 inpatients in psychiatric institutions in England and Wales (Wilkinson 1983) and of those the majority now form a refractory hardcore of ageing, chronically disabled and dependent 'old' long stay residents whose prospects of discharge and community adjustment are increasingly remote. Indeed, it has been estimated that approximately two thirds of mental hospital patients have been resident for more than one year, that nearly half have been hospitalised for over five years, and that long stay patients make up less than 5 per cent of annual hospital discharges (MIND 1980). Significantly, about one-third of patients in hospital for more than two years, and some two-thirds of those whose stay has exceeded a decade, are diagnosed as schizophrenic (Butler and Rosenthal 1978). Epidemiological evidence emerging since the 1960s (e.g. Hailey 1974) has moreover suggested the disturbing accumulation of a younger 'new' long stay population of first and readmissions, who prove unresponsive to treatment and for whom appropriate community provision is unavailable. It is again of note that of the new long stay group almost half are diagnosed as schizophrenic (Mann and Cree 1976). Despite their improved outcome with neuroleptics, the prospects for many schizophrenics therefore remain those of relapse, impairment increasing with each of several episodes, and prolonged hospitalisation. It is also of note that parallel observations have been made in North America, where despite an aggressive policy of discharge from state hospitals some three quarters and one half of their population have been resident for respectively more than one and a half and five years, where an emphasis on community based treatment in short-stay mental health centres has been accompanied by an increase in readmission and multiple admission rates, and where chronically incapacitated psychotic patients continue to 'silt' the care system (Paul and Lentz 1977).

Evidence of a still substantial population of long stay institutional residents has proved of considerable concern to those forecasting the redundancy of psychiatric hospitals and their ready replacement by community based care. Of equal concern however is evidence that for many patients discharged from hospital community maintenance has in itself proved no guarantee of enriched or more independent lifestyles, nor exemption from the restrictive practices which foster dependency in institutional settings. Indeed the disturbing degree of social impoverishment of many schizophrenic and other dischargees has been cogently reflected by use of the phrase 'in-patients living out' to describe those for whom little has changed beyond their address. Surveying 100 dischargees in London, McCowan and Wilder (1976) have for example noted the large percentage who expect to do little during the day, contribute little to their own self maintenance, rarely go out in the evening, have no leisure interests, are unable to obtain or maintain employment, have no friends, feel lonely and have little help from or contact with aftercare services. Other studies have emphasised the similarly severe problems faced by both schizophrenics and their relatives when the discharge environment is home (e.g. Creer 1975). Clearly the transition from inpatient status to effective community functioning involves for many more than the suppression of overt symptomatology, and is easy neither for the dischargee nor those with whom they live and come into contact.

THE IMPORTANCE OF SOCIAL REHABILITATION

Developments in medical technology and mental health philosophy have apparently not in themselves therefore ensured the successful implementation of a policy of deinstitutionalisation and community care. It has accordingly become clear that the social correlates of mental illness must themselves be directly addressed, and specifically that urgent attention must be paid to developing complementary rehabilitation services and systems which can more effectively promote social adjustment and durable community tenure. Indeed social rehabilitation has emerged as matter of critical concern in view not only of the personal and economic costs borne by patients, their families and the community as a whole, but also if the policy of community care is to even continue as one acceptable to the public at large. It is of course fair to say that the importance of rehabilitation is now widely acknowledged, that the provision of adequate services draws the concerned attention of most health authorities, and that significant advances have been made in establishing principles of rehabilitative theory and practice (Royal College of Psychiatrists 1980; Watts and Bennett 1983; Wing and Morris 1981). It is however equally fair to note that in practice the adequacy of rehabilitative provision varies widely across the country as a whole, the form of many services owing relatively little to the adoption of a definite conceptual model or the coordinated implementation of rational strategies based upon experimental research and empirical data. In prefacing the NHS Health Advisory Service Annual Report on services for the mentally ill and elderly, Peter Horrocks has in fact emphasised the:

> . . . great unevenness both in quality and quantity of provision from
> District to District, not significantly related to the overall financial
> status of the particular authorities responsible. The aphorism that 'we
> don't have one National Health Service but two hundred District
> Health Services' is apposite, if not original. Levels of awareness of
> what is possible, let alone desirable, in services for the 'priority'
> groups fluctuate from one locality to the next (Horrocks 1985a: p. 1).

Although the concept of rehabilitation is both familiar and widely employed, a consensus is in practice and application apparently therefore lacking in respect of the procedures and client groups which should form its appropriate area of concern, the system components critical to effective service delivery, and the manner in which rehabilitation services should be structured and organised. What is available in some settings accordingly remains limited in scope, organisationally fragmented, and at best underdeveloped. Indeed in some instances rehabilitation is still seen in traditional terms as referring to activities taking place only after medical treatment is completed, as being appropriate only for long-term patients being prepared for discharge or those failing to respond to chemotherapy, and as involving primarily industrial, occupational or even diversionary activity. If those opportunities afforded by an improved understanding of schizophrenia are to be realised as better client services, continuing priority must clearly be accorded to developing, and implementing on a general basis, more rational, coordinated and effective rehabilitation systems through which even currently available technologies of assessment and behaviour change can be successfully employed. In the absence of such priority a significant gap is likely to remain between what is in principle possible and what is in practice available to alleviate the evidently unsatisfactory lot of many schizophrenics.

The field of psychiatric rehabilitation in general has been covered by Geoff Shepherd (1984), his book recommended to the reader interested in more detailed analysis of many issues of direct relevance to the rehabilitation of schizophrenics in hospital and community settings. In the light of evidence discussed in the present book it is however perhaps important that at least brief consideration be given to the desirable focus, scope and nature of rehabilitation services for schizophrenics, and in particular to the planning, organisational and resource problems which must be addressed if effective provision is in practice to emerge.

GROUPS FOR WHOM REHABILITATION IS APPROPRIATE

In considering the clients who might require rehabilitative support, it may be as suggested in the first instance, that social rehabilitation is in principle an appropriate concern in respect of any individual whose environmental adjustment is impoverished as a correlate of mental illness, or whose psychiatric condition is in part caused, exacerbated or maintained by skill deficits or environmental circumstances. As discussed earlier, psychosocial difficulties in the form of life and social skills deficits, leisure and occupational inactivity, behaviour problems and so on, are in fact fairly pervasive features of schizophrenia which may be observed (if in varying degree), in many community based and young schizophrenics as well as in chronic institutional residents. It may be emphasised therefore that rehabilitation services should desirably develop in such a manner that they are routinely available for most, and probably *all* schizophrenics, and not as is often the case for only a traditional focal group of selected long-term inpatients being prepared for discharge. While the latter group clearly require input to facilitate their resocialisation, the routine attentions of rehabilitation services are equally required by for example acute first episode and admission schizophrenics for whom skill deficits or environmental difficulties are a consequence of, or contribute to, the emergence and continued presence of their disorder. In many instances the initial episode will itself have been precipitated in vulnerable individuals by psychosocial stresses, whose continuing presence in the discharge

311

environment is often further compounded by the personal and social consequences of the breakdown such as loss of employment, rejection by family and friends etc. Even for those discharged in remission such psychosocial factors may well contribute to the later re-emergence of symptomatic problems, relapse and readmission, a course which may to some extent at least be avoided if problems of social adjustment are the direct focus of rehabilitation from the earliest stages. Foci of such efforts might for example include advising on occupational level so that unnecessary life stresses are avoided, teaching clients to cope with stresses via skill training and self control programmes, and training family members to develop patterns of social interaction which promote adaptive functioning. Rehabilitative efforts may similarly be considered appropriate for those schizophrenics who later in the course of their disorder present with a pattern of repeated breakdown and multiple re-admissions, the precipitants of relapse again involving in many cases a failure to cope with the complex demands of daily living which might be countered by active training and support.

The 'new' long stay of course represent a further group for whom rehabilitation is required, interventions of relevance here including not only skill training but also the deliberate engineering of hospital environments such that their structure prevents the development of dependency and inactivity. Another often neglected group of hospitalised schizophrenics requiring rehabilitation, or more strictly, intra-hospital habilitation, are those 'continuing-care' residents for whom there is little realistic prospect of discharge, and who are often therefore excluded from the more active approaches available to those moving to more advanced environments. While having goals of a habilitative rather than movement oriented nature, such patients may be considered equally deserving of active training and support which might combat their further decline into dependent inactivity, encourage their utilisation of, and control over, their environment, and generally promote an enriched quality of life. Moreover, as is clear from evidence discussed in this book, active and ongoing rehabilitation is also needed in respect of many schizophrenics living in the community who present with high degrees of social impoverishment or whose skill deficits put them at risk for later relapse and rehospitalisation. Members of such groups as long-term day patients, the 'low contact' environmentally impoverished, 'revolving-door' clients living in the community, acute patients living at home with their families and so on may all be considered for rehabilitation procedures before hospitalisation with the aim of promoting more effective and durable community functioning. In sum continuing efforts are required to ensure the development of rehabilitation services which are capable of serving preventative as well as remedial functions, and which can address the needs of potentially all schizophrenics whether in primary, secondary or tertiary health care settings.

THE PURPOSE, SCOPE AND NATURE OF REHABILITATION

Evidence concerning the psychosocial problems faced by schizophrenics and their carers suggests as a second issue deserving consideration the desirable purpose, scope and nature of rehabilitative efforts that might be mounted on their behalf. In this respect it may again be noted that a traditional equation of rehabilitation with occupational or industrial therapy, or with simple and often arbitrary activity or stimulation programmes, represents a limited and inadequate perspective which is of perhaps clearer relevance to the established practice of an institution than the requirements of an individual client. In practice such activities are often merely time consuming, lack clear purpose, have little relevance to the idiosyncratic needs of the client, are remote from the economic and social realities of potential discharge environments, and importantly are not rationally determined by reference to an analysis of how the environment and psychosocial factors actually influence behaviour. It is important to emphasise therefore that the needs of schizophrenics demand the provision of far more comprehensive rehabilitation services, which are more active and goal orientated in their approach, which operate across a broader range of residential, social and occupational settings, which employ a wider variety of assessment, (re-)training and environmental management procedures to effect client change, which facilitate the development of a broader range of personally significant 'life' and survival skills, and which thereby more effectively promote the clients' adjustment to and control over their environment, and their enjoyment of an enriched and 'normalised' quality of life. In particular it may be stressed that such services should determine, and help the client achieve, goals and targets which are specifically relevant both to their own individual needs, backgrounds and expectancies and to the demands of the post-training environment. To this end comprehensive rehabilitation services must therefore utilise discriminative and demonstrably effective methodologies of assessment and behaviour change, and employ them in a manner which is reasonably common across settings and complementary to the delivery of other interventions.

In respect of assessment it is in fact fair to say that a reasonable range of fairly objective, reliable, valid and in some instances standardised measurement techniques (including structured interviews, behavioural rating scales, self-completed questionnaires, techniques of direct observation etc), are already available to facilitate the process of planning, decision making and evaluation. Several assessment tools are thus in existence whose employment can for example be of assistance when making decisions about an individual's suitability for a particular environment, when selecting goals, targets, training priorities and appropriate methods of training, when evaluating a client's progress in terms of targetted and non-targetted behaviour, and so on. It is similarly fair to say that a number of specific procedures and methodologies for effecting behaviour change are also now available, and that of these several have potentially wide application in the field of rehabilitation. Of perhaps particular significance in this respect is the broad based and functionally analytic approach of behaviour modification, the utility and efficacy of whose techniques has been demonstrated in a wide range of psychiatric settings. There is thus substantial evidence to suggest that behavioural procedures (e.g. task breakdown, instruction, modelling, prompting, shaping, feedback, rehearsal, reinforcement etc) have an important role to play in teaching or retraining skills whose absence prolongs hospitalisation or limits an individual's control over their environment. As noted earlier there is moreover at least some evidence to suggest a role for social-learning techniques in controlling symptomatic and problem behaviour in schizophrenia. It is however equally fair to note that the availability of such methodologies in principle has in practice proved no guarantee of their widespread use, the extent of their employment in fact varying considerably between and even within rehabilitation services. The provision of relevant and goal orientated rehabilitation for schizophrenics is in some settings therefore still constrained by the inadequate, inconsistent or uncoordinated use of those tools which research and clinical experience has suggested to be objective, demonstrably effective and of potential utility. It is of course clear that the development of even better methods of measurement and behavioural influence remains a priority, the simple suggestion that 'we have the technology' being both premature and complacent. The more effective use of technologies which are already available would however undoubtedly help many more schizophrenics achieve relevant and meaningful goals, and continuing emphasis is still therefore required on ensuring their widespread and routine adoption.

PLANNING, RESOURCE AND ORGANISATIONAL ISSUES

The possibilities of providing goal directed rehabilitation are however critically dependent upon the existence of rehabilitation systems which have available adequate facilities and manpower, and which are organised in a logical and coordinated manner. The final issues deserving consideration therefore concern the interrelated planning, resource and organisational requirements which must be met if effective services for schizophrenics are to be available in practice.

PLANNING ARRANGEMENTS

In respect of the former of these areas it is in fact probably fair to say that the crucial role of coordinated service planning is in many settings the subject of relative neglect. Too frequently developments do not represent the implementation of carefully prepared and coordinated plans, are not based on a thorough consideration of existing services, relevant data or experience gained elsewhere, and are not fully integrated with other aspects of service provision. In some cases therefore fragmented developments emerge which fail to address priority areas of need, which duplicate the efforts of isolated facilities elsewhere in the system, or which through inadequate research prove less useful and effective than anticipated. Clearly therefore attempts must be made to ensure that those systems serving schizophrenics have available clearly defined and effective machineries for planning, and in particular that arrangements exist to facilitate coordinated planning by the several statutory and non-statutory agencies providing services in different settings (including health and social services, other local authority agencies, non-statutory groups such as mental health associations, housing associations etc). Desirably such machinery should incorporate clear and workable channels of communication within and between component service units and agencies, together with specified mechanisms for the assignment of functional responsibilities in terms of decision making, policy formulation and monitoring. It should also include procedures which ensure the availability of information on the efficacy of current services, on local population characteristics and changing patterns of patient need, on national recommendations and guidelines, on the results of epidemiological and experimental research, on the experience of others gained else-

315

where, on sources of funding beyond normal statutory provision, and so on. Machinery for joint planning does of course already exist, and in some areas evidently works in an efficient manner. In other instances however the inadequacy of current provision for schizophrenics suggests that fuller and more effective use of established procedures is still required.

REHABILITATIVE FACILITIES

One major concern of planners is of course the provision of an adequate range of rehabilitation facilities which are backed up by appropriate manpower resources. In considering the needs of schizophrenics in this respect it may be noted that the disorder is characterised by an extensive range of psychosocial difficulties, and by variability between schizophrenics in the degree of their social disability and in the levels of adjustment and independence they might ultimately achieve. It is important to emphasise therefore that comprehensive services for schizophrenics must have available a very wide range of residential, day and evening facilities through which habilitative and rehabilitative procedures can be employed. A psychiatric hospital for example will require not merely a rehabilitative ward, but a variety of facilities of differing size and structure, capable of catering for clients having different needs and goals, and of providing opportunities for and relevant training in a range of domestic, social, leisure and occupational activities. Also required are transitional facilities, whose structures are engineered to resemble discharge environments, and which therefore provide particularly suitable settings for relevant training experience. A wide range of facilities is similarly required in the community, where for example residential provision must be sufficiently varied to meet the needs of clients requiring different levels of training, support and supervision. Depending upon local circumstances and client population characteristics, a particular service may therefore need to consider the provision of medium to long term habilitation hostels, short to medium term training homes, core and cluster schemes, group homes with varying levels of supervision, sheltered housing, warden controlled flats, lodgings, substitute families and 'fostering', and so on, as well as making arrangements to support suitable clients in flats, bedsits and their parental, marital or own home. Given the social isolation and inactivity of many schizophrenics living in the community, a particular concern of rehabilitation systems must also be the provision of a far broader range of day and evening facilities which offer for example further skill training, work, occupation, education, leisure, recreation and social contact.

MANPOWER REQUIREMENTS

While facilities provide an essential service base, the delivery of rehabilitative procedures depends however upon manpower. It is again important to emphasise therefore that services for schizophrenics must be founded upon sufficient numbers of personnel, and upon staff who are drawn from many disciplines, who collectively provide wide ranging skill, expertise and experience, and who operate in an effective multidisciplinary manner. The adequacy of service provision in both hospital and community settings will accordingly depend critically upon the availability of such core professional staff as doctors, nurses, occupational therapists, recreational therapists, industrial therapists, psychologists, social workers, care officers, dieticians, physiotherapists, voluntary service coordinators, and so on. Staffing level guidelines and formulae are of course available in respect of most disciplines, and may be used as yardsticks against which local provision is judged. Importantly however consideration should also be given to determining and meeting manpower requirements in terms of local circumstances, the operational policies of rehabilitative units, and the minimum number of staff required for effective service delivery at any given point in time. Thus guidelines formulated with reference to the provision of more traditional care and supervision may not be appropriate for active rehabilitative work where intensive client assessment and training is required. Similarly attention must be paid to ensuring adequate numbers of staff in not only those traditionally more numerous disciplines such as nursing, but also in paramedical and remedial disciplines whose skills are particularly relevant in rehabilitative settings.

It is unlikely however that the extensive needs of schizophrenics can be met by professional health and social service staff alone. Indeed, if the community is to accept greater responsibility for its disadvantaged members, a response by clinical professionals alone is in fact undesirable. Efforts should be made therefore to incorporate within the overall rehabilitation system the services of many non-clinical and non-professional groups and individuals who can augment, complement and facilitate statutory provision, including mental health concern agencies and the several voluntary and non-statutory groups in the community who provide advice, welfare, counselling, social contact, recreation, transport and so on. The families and friends of schizophrenics should similarly be included as partners in the rehabilitative system, and given support so that they can play an important participatory role as rehabilitative agents.

Arrangements must also exist within the system to ensure that service providers are appropriately trained and motivated. It cannot be assumed for example that general psychiatric experience will in itself equip an individual to work in a rehabilitation setting, and efforts must be made to ensure staff are well trained in the specialist skills of assessment and behaviour change which are employed in programme delivery. In addition to the careful recruitment of appropriately qualified staff, the system must therefore make adequate provision for its own practical staff training. To the extent that volunteers, relatives and so on are involved in rehabilitative work, arrangements must also exist for ensuring that they too are appropriately trained and supervised. Staff motivation, morale and attitudes are further important factors which will influence the efficacy of programme delivery, and attempts must be made not only to select staff specifically interested in the field, but also to ensure their jobs are rewarding, interesting and well supported. It is in this respect significant to note that the impression gained by the Hospital Advisory Service during its visiting programme has been that '. . . too often, extremely committed personnel are struggling to improve and modernise their help to elderly and mentally ill people without comparable commitment or understanding on the part of the managers and authorities for whom they work' (NHS Health Advisory Service Annual Report 1985:1). Clearly the provision of feedback and support by management and administration remains an area for concern.

SERVICE ORGANISATION

The availability of adequate facilities and manpower provides unfortunately no guarantee that services will be delivered to schizophrenics in an efficient or effective manner. Indeed, unless facilities are appropriately structured, unless they have explicit functional roles and definable operational policies, and unless their operation is integrated with that of facilities elsewhere, they may in fact operate as merely static management and prosthetic environments which are incapable of achieving rehabilitative goals. The mere provision of accommodation in the community for example is no guarantee that dischargees will enjoy more independent lifestyles if such facilities are inappropriately structured or lack clear rehabilitative function. Similarly the mere designation of a hospital ward as a rehabilitation unit is insufficient if the ward lacks an effective operational policy through which its supposed function can be achieved. At the level of the component unit within the rehabilitation system therefore attention must be paid to ensuring that goals, objectives and operational policies are clearly specified, documented and widely available. The function of system elements should not of course be inviolate, their role being subservient to and determined by client need, and not vice versa. Changing circumstances and client characteristics may therefore necessitate a change in unit function. At any given point of time however the role and policies of system components should be clearly established and expressed through for example statements concerning objectives, selection criteria, referral policies, procedures in respect of assessment, goal and target setting, programme planning and programme implementation, arrangements for the allocation of key workers, procedures for programme reviews, discharge criteria, methods of pre-discharge preparation, arrangements for follow-up, procedures for service evaluation and so on.

The efficacy of even those facilities which do have clear functions and policies may however be significantly constrained if their operation is not integrated with that of other components of the overall service, or if indeed the service as a whole is essentially fragmented. In the absence of service integration a hospital rehabilitation ward for example is likely to encounter major problems in terms of referral and patient selection, the identification of relevant goals and targets, the movement of clients to other environments and the maintenance of charge therein. Thus, while there may be many clients who would benefit from the wards' training procedures, few or inappropriate referrals may be made because its role is poorly understood elsewhere in the hospital, because its operation is not integrated with that of other wards, or indeed because the hospital as a whole has no generally agreed conception of rehabilitation or policies for progressive and logical movement between its component facilities. Similarly, if the ward does not have available a range of discharge options to which it is rationally linked, it will not be able to determine training priorities which are relevant to the known likely demands the client will face on discharge, and may spend time teaching skills which are arbitrary and irrelevant. Moreover, without the option of moving its patients to other parts of an integrated system, the ward is likely to encounter difficulties when it seeks to make arrangements to ensure the change it achieves will be generalised to and maintained elsewhere.

More generally, if the overall rehabilitation system is fragmented, any rational client movement within and between hospital and community settings will be difficult to arrange, particularly if conditions exist in which staff and agencies in different settings not only fail to coordinate their activities and work in a cooperative manner, but actually view each other's roles with suspicion. It is not uncommon for example for staff in hospitals to perceive community facilities with which they have no clear links as uncooperative and receptive to only 'easy' and uncomplicated discharges, while equally many working in the community view hospitals as all too ready to 'dump' chronic and problem individuals who are unprepared for community maintenance. Clearly such conditions create significant obstacles to rational client movement, and make it more likely that borderline cases will be shuffled between services without receiving adequate assistance from any, and that some facilities will have low turnover and 'silt-up', while others have unacceptably low occupancy, that the potentially useful function of certain facilities cannot be sustained, and so on. Moreover, in the absence of an integrated system crossing hospital and community boundaries, it is likely that the needs of certain client groups will be overserved while those of others are unmet, and that planning will be inefficient and cost-ineffective.

If problems of this type are to be avoided, continuing emphasis must therefore be placed on the development of integrated rehabilitation systems, whose service networks are logically arranged across hospital and community settings, and whose component agencies, facilities and personnel operate in a functionally coordinated manner. The adoption of an integrated, system based organisational arrangement does not of course preclude local initiative or development, nor does it necessitate a rigid interdependence of all service elements. Co-ordination in terms of service planning and delivery can however undoubtedly help ensure that local initiatives are logical and cost effective, that client movement is rational and efficient, and that client programmes are goal orientated, relevant and productive of generalised change.

SUMMARY

By comparison with the often stimulating evidence and provocative speculation generated by experimental and clinical research, the procedural, organisational and related service issues discussed above may seem perhaps rather commonplace and unexciting. Notwithstanding their familiarity, such issues are however of fundamental concern, and must be adequately addressed if schizophrenics are to fully benefit from the opportunities afforded by scientific advance. As noted earlier, the range and quality of rehabilitative provision remains in practice extremely variable, and depends less upon the availability of resources than on awareness of what is desirable and possible in terms of good rehabilitation policy (Horrocks 1985a). Many examples of good practice can in fact be discerned across the country as a whole, and several have been identified and commended by the Hospital Advisory Service in their annual report (HAS 1985). In some settings however deficiencies still remain in terms of the range of schizophrenics whose rehabilitative needs are served, the use made of available technologies of assessment and behaviour change, the provision of an appropriate range of rehabilitation facilities, and the availability of adequate arrangements for integrated service planning and delivery. Unfortunately as noted by Peter Horrocks (1985b:3): 'An excessive amount of self satisfaction exists within some districts that what they are doing is, by definition, the only thing that can be done'! The help that can be offered to schizophrenics clearly depends to a large extent upon the innovation of experimental and clinical scientists, and upon the skill, dedication and commitment of doctors, nurses, paramedical staff and other 'front-line' service providers. It cannot be over-emphasised however that what is offered in practice will depend equally upon the existence of comparable commitment, and genuine and sensitive understanding of need, on the part of managers and authorities ultimately responsible for determining priorities and patterns of service provision.

Part five

AN INTEGRATED MODEL

Chapter twenty-two

AN INTEGRATED MODEL

We have attempted in this book to survey a vast area of research in which the phenomenon of schizophrenia has been subjected to scientific study at numerous levels, from biochemistry to ecology. Our aim in this chapter is to try to bring together these concepts and findings by way of asking two fundamental questions: What is the psychopathology and aetiology of schizophrenia and how can we best meet the needs of those who are affected by this disorder?

With regard to the first question, we believe the research to date suggests a concept which is markedly different from traditional psychiatric or psychological models of psychopathology.

We have argued that schizophrenia should be regarded as a hypothesis or construct and that the various attempts to operationalise the concept are as yet little more than conventions with no intrinsic validity. The research evidence we have reviewed does not yet permit a definitive statement to be made on the definition and nature of schizophrenia. These operational criteria remain conventions. However considerable support for the meaning and utility of the general concept has come from studies of behavioural genetics, neuroleptic drug response, and recent studies of neuropsychology and brain function organisation. The evidence has also allowed us to conclude that schizophrenia is not a unitary disorder but that there are many *schizophrenias*. A broad and largely statistical distinction in terms of phenomenology, demography, familial history, drug responsiveness and neuropathology was consistently suggested between three 'forms' of schizophrenia, which has received support from the more recent studies (Williams *et al.* 1985).

One form is characterised by predominantly negative symptoms at onset, poor premorbid history and tends to occur in males of teenage onset. This group seems to have a lower genetic risk (Flor-Henry 1983), enlarged ventricles on CT scanning and intellectual impairment, show a poor response to neuroleptic medication and have a poorer prognosis.

A second form is characterised by positive symptoms with a strong affective component, good premorbid adjustment, favourable prognosis and is associated with females of later onset ('schizo-affectives'). Many of this group show a familial history of affective disorder, no ventricular enlargement and many seem to respond to lithium carbonate (used in manic-depression). The third group lie in-between so to speak. This large category present with predominantly 'positive' symptoms at onset, have higher but mixed genetic risk for schizophrenia, respond more favourably to neuroleptic medication, is more equally represented in both sexes and the younger age ranges but seem to have a very variable prognosis and premorbid history.

These 'forms' of schizophrenia are delineated not on intuitive clinical grounds (as are the classic subtypes) but on the basis of construct validity arising out of differential phenomenology, treatment response, aetiological factors and to some degree prognosis. We envisage that further clarification of the schizophrenia concept will come from studies addressing construct validity which should eventually lead to a refinement and improvement of therapeutic techniques.

In attempting to bring together the evidence bearing on the aetiology of schizophrenia, we shall concentrate our attention on the above third group. In our view considerable insight into the pathology and phenomenology of this group has been achieved through studies of brain *function* and *organisation* rather than those emphasising structure (e.g. biochemistry). This assumed pathology links in with an aetiological and developmental theory of brain organisation and function. There is also an impressive body of evidence (see Ch. 11) that environmental factors – intrauterine, perinatal, and social – play a significant part in raising the overall liability to schizophrenia *throughout* development. These possibilities are elaborated in a model presented below.

This concept challenges the traditional view that schizophrenia is a functional (i.e. non-organic) disorder. However the evidence reviewed (see Ch. 12) suggests that the pathology of schizophrenia does not inevitably lead to its continued expression in terms of symptoms. Instead the pathology seems to confer a *vulnerability* which depends on other (e.g. exogenous) factors for its continued expression and development. A pure *biological* model would argue that the course of schizophrenia should be viewed as essentially related to endogenous, illness factors. Under this model the episodic nature of the course of schizophrenia might be construed as '. . . temporary respites (of mental health) in the course of a continuing disorder' (Zubin *et al.* 1983:550). An analogy might be drawn between this and Menières disease (a vestibular disorder affecting balance) which can erupt periodically for no clear reason. The vulnerability model on the other hand would construe episodes of schizophrenia as essentially transient punctuations of ill-health in an otherwise normal individual. In this sense schizophrenia might seem closer in this respect to depression or headache than Menières disease.

The vulnerability model is particularly in keeping with the results of cross-cultural studies which have found that some 15 to 20 per cent of patients in developed countries do not relapse following the first episode, irrespective of medication, whereas the corresponding figure in third-world countries lies between 30 and 40 per cent (Waxler 1979). This alone suggests that the social environment might be responsible for the expression of the vulnerability and that drugs function to *protect* against the impact of this environment rather than as a 'cure' for the 'illness' (Leff *et al.* 1983). Evidence for the role of the environment was presented earlier (see Chs. 12, 13) which we shall attempt to synthesise in the following model.

The vulnerability model is presented in Figure 3. The main features of the model are discussed in turn followed by a consideration of its therapeutic implications.

THE PATHOLOGY AND DEVELOPMENT OF VULNERABILITY

In this section a specific model of vulnerability will be forwarded which has two aims. First, to offer a tentative framework, in terms of brain action, which might explain important components of the positive symptoms of schizophrenia referred to earlier as being characteristic of one form of the disorder associated with higher, but mixed, genetic risk. Second, an attempt will be made to highlight possible neurobiological processes which might be important in the development of this form of the disorder. As such the model constitutes a specific type of CNS pathology subsumed under the more general heading of 'vulnerability' referred to in later sections and is not intended to be generally applicable to all forms of schizophrenia.

Before outlining the model it is worthwhile restating certain points briefly which will further clarify the limits of its applicability:

1. The model attempts to draw attention to events and processes which might be of importance in the development of schizophrenia. One critical step in such a developmental sequence which must remain largely unaddressed concerns the nature of the genetic risk factor (see Ch. 4). To paraphrase those

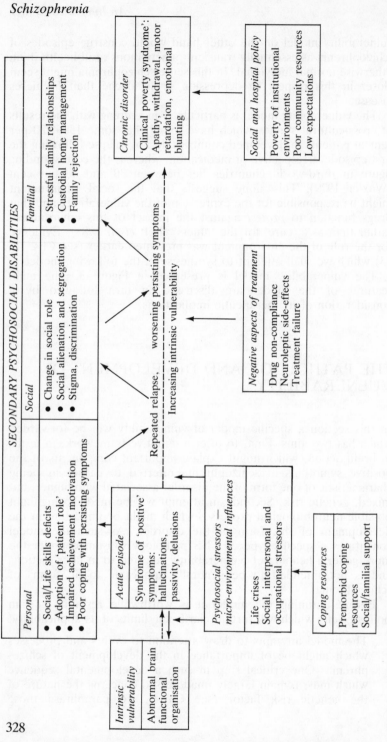

Fig. 3   A vulnerability-interactionist model

SECONDARY PSYCHOSOCIAL DISABILITIES

Personal
- Social/Life skills deficits
- Adoption of 'patient role'
- Impaired achievement motivation
- Poor coping with persisting symptoms

Social
- Change in social role
- Social alienation and segregation
- Stigma, discrimination

Familial
- Stressful family relationships
- Custodial home management
- Family rejection

Chronic disorder
'Clinical poverty syndrome': Apathy, withdrawal, motor retardation, emotional blunting

Social and hospital policy
Poverty of institutional environments
Poor community resources
Low expectations

Repeated relapse, worsening persisting symptoms
Increasing intrinsic vulnerability

Negative aspects of treatment
Drug non-compliance
Neuroleptic side-effects
Treatment failure

Acute episode
Syndrome of 'positive' symptoms: hallucinations, passivity, delusions

Intrinsic vulnerability
Abnormal brain functional organisation

Psychosocial stressors — micro-environmental influences
Life crises
Social, interpersonal and occupational stressors

Coping resources
Premorbid coping resources
Social/familial support

conclusions, we have as yet no firm evidence upon which to differentiate between alternative, and equally plausible, mechanisms of genetic transmission in schizophrenia. Additionally the possibility that a genetic threshold might operate in schizophrenia carries with it the further complication that genetic risk may vary in a weighted fashion across individuals. As such, the possibility of bridging the gap between genes and bio-chemical action seems remote in the absence of a definable genetic marker for the disorder. One factor should be borne in mind, however. There is a general tendency to view genetic mechanisms as blueprints for later behaviour which, once laid down are relatively dormant. It is important to recognise the dynamic role of gene action throughout development which may be 'switched' on and off as a function of multiple triggers.

2. A related area of uncertainty, which would appear to interact with genetic risk, concerns the possible role and influence of the intrauterine environment and the subtle, but as yet unquantified, interactional influences of general obstetric and pregnancy difficulties and viral factors.

3. Whilst the overall model presented here is drawn from a consideration of schizophrenia as being interactional in its course and development the model presented in this section is more explicitly neurological or neuro-behavioural in nature. One reason for this is that early theorists have assumed that, in most important respects, Central Nervous System maturation is completed, or nearly so, at birth, leaving the post-natal period as fair play for the environmentalist. More recent evidence does, however, suggest that significant CNS maturation occurs well into the second decade of life. It must now be considered that the degree to which these biological processes mature is likely to influence, in an ongoing fashion, the extent to which an individual can learn and profit from experience.

POSITIVE SCHIZOPHRENIC SYMPTOMS AND BRAIN FUNCTION

The model attempts to explain certain primary features of the positive symptoms of schizophrenia defined by Schneider (1959) as First Rank (see Ch. 1). These symptoms have a phenomenological commonality in that they appear to reflect the interpretation that thoughts, feelings, actions and sensations are under some degree of independent control or origin and are perceived as being separated from an individual's conscious awareness of his own mental domain.

In constructing a model which might account for the form of

these symptoms in terms of brain activity, it is important to bear in mind that the above symptom cluster does not represent losses of function but rather positive (i.e. novel) qualitatively unusual experiences which are not observed, in a comparable fashion, in any other type of condition of known organic causation. Specifically, there is little evidence that destructive lesions, head trauma or similar pathology results in such phenomena. It is only in relatively rare cases of irritative focal lesions (i.e. temporal lobe epilepsy) or with certain types of callosal tumours that 'schizophrenic-like' symptoms are observed. Even in these instances, where there are similarities in symptomatology, it must also be recognised that there are equally important differences. Any attempt to explain the symptoms of schizophrenia must, therefore, invoke novel mechanisms of cerebral function to account for their presence.

The model put forward here derives from the possibility that schizophrenia might be characterised by a duality of consciousness arising as a function of abnormal interhemispheric integration and communication. The evidence supporting specific difficulties in interhemispheric integration in schizophrenics and children at risk for schizophrenia has already been reviewed in this book.

The majority of the evidence, derived from cognitive assessments, has been gathered by Green and colleagues with adults and by Hallett and colleagues with high-risk children. Additionally, however, independent support for the hypothesis has been obtained from EEG, Evoked Potential, and Neuropsychological investigations (see Chs. 9 and 10).

The simplest explanation of these findings is that schizophrenics are characterised by a primary difficulty in integrating the functions of the two cerebral hemispheres and in transferring complex information from one hemisphere to the other. The most likely structure involved in, or relating to, these abnormalities is the Corpus Callosum. Whilst not active in neural processing, the Callosum consists of an estimated two hundred million axonal fibres and acts as a major channel of communication between the two hemisphere systems, both in terms of transmitting information and in inhibiting the activity of the contralateral hemisphere. To a large extent the Callosal fibres are 'homotopic' (i.e. connecting one specific hemisphere site to its exact counterpart in the opposite hemisphere). It would seem reasonable, then, to argue that an intact Callosum is necessary for complex integrative cerebral functioning which requires coherent flow of information between, and consonant or complementary activity of, interhemispheric sites. The evidence in support of interhemispheric disturbances in schizophrenia does not suggest a total disconnection between the two hemispheres (akin to a functional split-brain condition) but rather a partial disconnection or malconnection. Both partial disconnection and malconnection (whereby *either* Callosal fibres malconnect or stray to an inappropriate processing site, *or* information 'leaks' out into adjacent callosal fibres and ends up at a non-homotopic site) can be invoked to explain a disturbance in transmission across the callosum.

It is, of course, possible that faulty output or reception by a uni-hemispheric site might also result in the phenomenon of poor inter-hemispheric integration (in the same way that a telephone call may be disrupted by electronic or mechanical disturbance at either telephone). The authors however feel that a third possibility, that of a disturbance in the Callosum itself (i.e. the telephone wire), is more consistent with the data and with developmental events during early post-natal life.

Leaving aside these issues for the moment, let us now consider how faulty inter-hemispheric communication might explain the first rank symptoms of schizophrenia. In the diagrams below (see Fig. 4) a simple depiction of inter-hemispheric communication is outlined.

In Figure 4(a), which represents a normal brain, sites A and A' represent exact counterparts in, for example, the left and right temporal speech areas connected clearly in reciprocal fashion by callosal connections. Stimulation of A' (by internal events or afferent input) under normal circumstances gives rise to callosal transmission so that the input or information is coherently available to A. In the Figure 4(b) disrupted callosal transmission is depicted. Here, two distinct processing units are detailed (A and B, with their inter-hemispheric counterparts A' and B'). In this case, however, callosal transmission is degraded from A to A' and from B to B' (and vice versa). Furthermore, if a malconnection is posited, information weakly transmitted from A' may additionally, through neural malconnection or callosal leakage, stimulate a totally different processing site (only one possible malconnection – A' to B – is outlined in the diagram).

In the case of brain 2, information delivered to A' (assuming that the input is a monaural, left ear input of complex verbal information) will become degraded when required to cross the callosum for verbal output. Furthermore, information simultaneously received by A' and A (as in an binaural input) would result in the dominant hemisphere receiving two conflicting units of information – the first being a coherent direct ear to A and the second, a degraded input, indirectly from A'. It is this arrangement which is hypothesised to account for the poor inter-aural performance by schizophrenics reported by Green *et al.* (1983). In a similar fashion, the poor performance of schizophrenics on inter-manual tasks and divided visual field procedures may be explained.

In general, in the normal brain a full integration between the two hemisphere systems would lead to coherent exchange of thoughts, feelings, perceptions, cognitions and intentions resulting in an

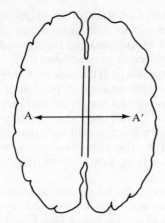

(a) 'Normal' brain

A:A′ = Homotopic temporal lobe processors
B:B′ = Homotopic motor processors

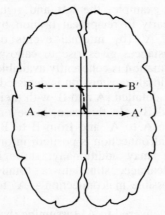

(b) Brain with callosal disruption

Fig. 4 Simplified schematic representation of callosal disruption
(a) 'Normal' brain
(b) Brain with callosal disruption

overall unity of the two spheres of activity and consciousness. In the disintegrated brain this overall unity is degraded raising the possibility that each hemisphere might to some extent regard the other as being 'not-of-the-self'.

If one assumes that A represents the dominant receptive language area, and A′ its non-dominant partner (known to have some language capabilities) it is possible to argue that auditory hallucinations might constitute verbal information from the right hemisphere intruding into the left, verbally dominant, hemisphere which due to partial disconnection interprets the 'thoughts' as arising from an independent source. In a similar fashion, information transferred from A' or B' to A or B might be interpreted as perceptions 'inserted' into the language based conscious awareness of the dominant hemisphere and information from A to A', via callosal transmission, might be interpreted as being withdrawn from conscious experience or broadcast to others.

Passivity feelings might arise through two processes which are not in themselves mutually incompatible. First, commands from A' might be interpreted as arising from an outside source. Second, one might consider the additional possibility of a malconnection from, for example, A' to B. In this case, an auditory percept from A' might also give rise to a stimulation of B, a motor area, such that certain thoughts or auditory input might result in a perceived command (A' − A) and a specific motor action (A' − B). In this situation the individual, finding no correspondence between input, output, and his own thoughts, might interpret the motor movement as being under independent control. Similar problems might arise where motor movements or tactile sensations give rise to auditory percepts.

Primary delusions might constitute an individual's attempt to rationalise, and create order out of, these bizarre occurrences. Alternatively, they may be attempts to identify the 'outside' influences from the right hemisphere (e.g. the devil, computer interference etc), a phenomenon which would inevitably be modified by the person's cultural background and experiences.

In summary, the first-rank symptoms might arise from the right hemisphere's activity being interpreted as being independent from that of the verbally dominant left hemisphere. Intrusions into the left hemisphere or information transferred to the right hemisphere would then be interpreted as coming from or going to an independent source. Primary delusions would then be secondary and consequent on these phenomena and may represent compensatory reactions of the individual to rationalise these perceived experiences.

It is possible to suggest that other symptoms might also reflect a disorder in interhemispheric communication. Thus thought blocking might arise if the left hemispheres ongoing train of thought were interrupted by disparate intrusions from the right which, if frequent, might give rise to a fragmentation of thought and disordered verbalisations.

There is, as yet, no direct evidence which would either support or refute these claims. The above model would predict, however, that first-rank symptoms could not be present in a fully integrated or a totally disconnected interhemispheric system. It is of some interest, then, that both Laitenin (1979) and Wilson *et al.* (1982)

report that partial sectioning of the corpus callosum alleviated schizophrenic symptoms in two patients. The model is further bolstered by the observations that there are no reported accounts of such symptoms in split brain subjects, individuals with callosal agenesis or in cases of right hemispherectomy.

One experimental sequelae of disturbed interhemispheric integration might be a perceived, or indeed actual, dysfunction of unilateral processes. Since many of the tests used to infer such dysfunction are delivered under normal sensory conditions (binaural, binocular, bimanual) both hemispheres would be activated and in the dis-integrated brain might interfere with each other's activity. More specifically, right hemisphere activation might interfere with left hemisphere processing and in some instances be perceived or interpreted as indicative of left hemisphere dysfunction. If the conclusions of Green and colleagues are valid, we would expect significant differences in performance on complex auditory tests if they were delivered under monaural/binaural listening conditions. These possibilities need to be explored to determine whether, in some studies, hypothesised unilateral dysfunction might more parsimoniously be accounted for in terms of interhemispheric dysfunction (indeed the study of Buchsbaum *et al.* (1979) tends to support this contention). These arguments do not, of course, apply to all studies which have inferred left hemisphere dysfunction in schizophrenics. Nevertheless, Nasrallah (1985), having reviewed the literature suggests that the results are equally consistent with a weakening of left hemisphere dominance or a shift in laterality.

Objectively it is difficult to determine whether callosal and unilateral dysfunction co-exist in schizophrenia, whether unilateral dysfunction may arise as a consequence of callosal disturbance, or whether unilateral dysfunction in some way disrupts interhemispheric processes because of its nature or location. In the present model it is argued that the primary dysfunction may be callosal in origin and that the precursors of this disturbance can be traced within the developmental years of post-natal life.

In summary the model presented so far outlines a few of the potential difficulties in interhemispheric integration which might account for the form of first-rank symptoms (a more detailed account being described by Hallett and Quinn (1987).

One assumption which has been addressed only superficially, but which is fairly central to this model concerns the extent to which the non-dominant hemisphere in a dis-integrated brain can process and transmit complex linguistic information. Nasrallah's (1985) analysis does indicate that schizophrenics may exhibit abnormalities of language lateralisation rather than a 'pure' unilateral dysfunction. In the next section we will direct attention to the second aspect of our model and will suggest that abnormal language lateralisation may be a logical sequela of developmental disturbances in inter-hemispheric integration.

DEVELOPMENTAL PERSPECTIVE

The observations of Hallett and Green (1983) and Hallett *et al.* (1986) suggest that significant deficits of inter-hemispheric integration are present in at-risk children well before the onset of psychosis, and raise the question as to whether such abnormalities might be of aetiological significance. The results of the latter study also suggested that the high-risk group exhibited performance decrements consistent with abnormal or anomalous language specialisation. Like the abnormalities or neurological integration documented by Fish (1984) the present authors propose that the disturbances of inter-hemispheric integration might reflect developmental neurological deviation which might be of genetic origin. Whilst there is, as yet, no direct evidence to support such a contention it is useful at this stage to describe some of the implications of this statement.

Of the structures of the CNS it is noteworthy that the Corpus Callosum and certain intra-hemispheric fibres are actively maturing after birth. The study by Salamy (1978), which measured inter-hemispheric transmission time in young children, suggests that callosal maturation, in terms of its myelination of specific fibres, continues at least until five years of age. Furthermore, Yakovlev and Lecours (1967) suggest that the myelogenetic cycle of inter-hemispheric fibres continues well after this age, and Randall (1983) has argued for its continuation to roughly the fifteenth year of life. Whilst, therefore, most of the callosal connections are likely to be established early in life, the process of myelination (whereby certain fibres are surrounded by a fatty myelin sheath), which speeds up and increases efficiency of neural conduction, may well proceed for many years and possibly to adolescence. Correlating Salamy's measures of inter-hemispheric conduction time with behavioural procedures of intermanual performance indicates a close temporal association between callosal maturation and efficiency in inter- and bi-manual performance and, by inference, interhemispheric integration (Galin *et al.* 1977; O'Leary 1980). It could, therefore, be proposed that delays in, or abnormalities of, this maturational process might severely disturb inter-hemispheric integration and communication which becomes more apparent as greater cognitive demands are made upon the two hemisphere systems.

One important developmental process which may be strongly related to callosal functioning concerns the lateralisation of specific functions to one hemisphere. This process of lateral specialisation is most clearly observed in language functions. Whilst for the majority of people the left temporal lobe appears to be anatomically predisposed to develop language function there is evidence that callosal integrity may be a critical feature in this normal process of lateralisation. The evidence to support this derives from two lines of research.

First, the emergence of a stable right ear (left brain) advantage on a verbal dichotic listening task appears to correlate temporally with increasing efficiency of callosal transmission. Thus Geffan (1976) reports no significant ear advantage in children below the age of five years but documents the emergence of a relatively stable REA beyond that time. This correlates well with the decrease in interhemispheric conduction time (Salamy 1978) and improved performance on intermanual tasks (O'Leary 1980).

The second line of evidence derives from studies of children with callosal agenesis in whom the callosum is completely absent at birth and fails to develop thereafter. Whilst there are many difficulties in interpreting the results from these studies (in view of the other CNS difficulties apparent in acallosal children) there is some evidence of bilaterally symmetrical language representation in this group (Cook 1984). The data is, as yet, not well established since the type of procedure which would directly address the issue of bilateral representation in this group have not been utilised (although Jeeves (1976) clearly demonstrated bilateral language in a small group of acallosals using a verbal dichotic listening task). Nevertheless, the role of callosal transmission in the emergence of lateralised function is implicit in Selnes' (1974) and Gazzanaga's (1974) models of the establishment of cerebral dominance.

It is proposed here that normal development of lateral specialisation of language occurs when the verbally predisposed hemisphere callosally 'inhibits' the non-dominant partner, preventing it from developing all but the most rudimentary of language abilities and, more importantly, from duplicating the functions of the dominant hemisphere. In the absence of a callosum (as in callosal agenesis) no interhemispheric inhibition would occur and hence the non-dominant hemisphere would be 'freed' to develop and specialise the same functions. As such, a disturbance of inter-hemispheric communication during the critical developmental years might result in a more bilateral representation of language due to partial or incomplete inhibition. The non-dominant hemisphere would not develop total equivalence of function but rather be able to process more complex verbal information than would normally be the case. It is the dual operation of callosal disruption and anomalous language specialisation which is hypothesised to characterise some adult schizophrenics and 'at-risk' children. While the data to address these issues has yet to be fully analysed, an initial report by Hallett *et al.* (1986) is suggestive of abnormal language lateralisation in high-risk children.

The exact mechanisms which might give rise to the inferred primary abnormality in callosal maturation are not known. It is useful, however, to speculate on the nature of these mechanisms and two possibilities are forwarded. First, an abnormality in the migration of callosal axons during the latter part of intrauterine development, leading to inappropriate straying of the axons to the wrong target site (a 'neuroanatomical malconnection'). Ultimately this might point to a specific abnormality in the production or transfer of Nerve Growth Factor which chemically 'guides' the axons to their target sites. This process is itself fundamentally influenced by the growth and subsequent function of astrocytic (glial) processes in the developing brain.

A second candidate might be an abnormality in the post-natal production, and laying down, of the oligodendroglia which make up the myelin sheath surrounding the axons. Such an abnormality would ultimately reduce callosal transmission by temporary blockade and might additionally result in a leakage of signal across to adjacent callosal fibres (an 'electrochemical malconnection'). For both these processes to proceed normally they rely on adequate functioning of glial cells. Since both astrocytic processes and the oligodendroglia ultimately derive from the same prototypic structure it might be reasonable to speculate that the process of axonal migration and myelination might be affected by a common defect which could be genetically determined. There is, as yet, no evidence to support such claims but it is of interest that Nasrallah *et al.* (1983) have observed abnormal gliosis in the corpus callosums of schizophrenics at autopsy. A third possibility, put forward by Randall (1983) suggests that malconnection may occur because of an abnormal increase in the number of callosal axons which results in extra 'non-homotopic' connections.

Finally, in constructing a developmental profile or sequence it is necessary to account for the 'time-lag' between the onset of the inferred disturbance of callosal maturation and schizophrenic breakdown (the risk period for which begins at approximately fifteen years of life). Several possibilities, each plausible and not mutually exclusive, may be forwarded. First, the symptoms might not manifest until the termination of the callosal myelogenetic cycle (possibly at the fifteenth year) particularly in view of the plasticity of the brain during early life, *or* they may only become apparent as more complex demands are made upon an individual's system. On this issue Randall (1983) argues that the emergence of more complex and advanced cognitive processes might indeed depend on the maturation of systems, such as the corpus callosum, which are likely to facilitate integrative cerebral function, and that there is a

337

close association between progressive stages of cognitive development (as forwarded by Piaget), increments in brain size, and the known interhemispheric myelination cycle. He also argues that there is temporal relationship of these factors to the onset of schizophrenia.

A third possibility is that the breakdown to schizophrenia arises at a time when other important CNS changes occur during the adolescent period. Feinberg (1972) documents several important processes in normal individuals which occur roughly between the ages of ten and sixteen. These include: a reduction of cerebral oxygen metabolism; a surge in adrenal function; EEG changes (specifically a reduction in delta amplitude); a significant reduction in cerebral synaptic density; a reduction in the latency of the endogenous P300 evoked potential response, and a reduction in neuroanatomical plasticity. Whilst the significance of some of these events is not, as yet, fully understood they do represent important changes in brain structure and activity and it is of interest that delta amplitude and P300 abnormalities have been reported in adult schizophrenics and high-risk children (see Chs. 8 and 10). Whether these changes may in some way be thought of as general cerebral stressors, or whether they reflect the operation of more specific factors in the breakdown of schizophrenia, cannot as yet be ascertained. What is of importance here is the close association of many cerebral and cognitive changes within a very limited time period which relates temporally to the onset of the schizophrenic risk period.

Finally, it may be put forward that in those individuals who are predisposed, due to faulty interhemispheric maturation, specific stressors (either environmental or biochemical) might play an important role in precipitating the onset of observable symptomatology. Thus only those individuals who are exposed to highly specific stress eventually break down. Under this general heading, for example, we might include those individuals in whom abnormal connection is present and who subsequently develop focal epilepsy. It may be this group of individuals who might constitute the relatively rare cases of dominant temporal lobe epilepsy with first-rank symptoms reported by Flor-Henry (1969).

In conclusion the protracted time course of fibre myelination within the callosum relates closely to the time at which adult schizophrenic symptoms are reported to emerge, although other influences may need to be invoked to account fully for this phenomenon. Whilst florid schizophrenic symptoms are proposed to emerge only at the end of the myelogenetic cycle of the callosum it is possible that certain vague and subclinical signs might be present earlier in life, although, as Randall (1983) points out, these may to some extent be masked because of the brain's plasticity and ability to compensate in the early years of life. One specific difficulty which might be present in young 'at-risk' children is more rudimentary difficulties of integration as, for example, observed by Fish (1984) and also difficulties in the acquisition of language or problems in communication and subsequent interaction with others.

Figure 5 summarises the major characteristics and processes outlined above as being important in the developmental phase of this specific vulnerability model.

In this model an attempt has been made to outline one possible, but complex, process which might account for the first-rank symptoms of schizophrenia and for its development. In view of the proposed possible types of factors which might influence the onset of schizophrenia it has only been possible to draw attention to what might be major and significant epochs and events in an individual's developmental history. It does seem possible that environmental influences play a role during the early years of life of the developing individual but that these influences themselves may not be crucial until significant phases of CNS maturation have occurred. Whilst children of schizophrenic parents are, therefore, indeed likely to be influenced by their parents' behaviour this in itself cannot account for subsequent breakdown. It would seem more parsimonious to assume that the major environmental influences occur later in life, or that they may contribute to the course and onset of the disorder in a more insidious manner (see Ch. 17).

COURSE AND OUTCOME

The vulnerability model speculates that episodes of schizophrenia are prompted by 'ordinary' stressing environmental events in vulnerable individuals. The threshold at which an episode occurs is modelled as an inverse relationship between intrinsic vulnerability and the level of stress i.e. the higher the vulnerability, the lower the level of stress required and vice versa.

Three kinds of psychosocial influences are posited. The first kind are independent environmental events (i.e. independent of the presence of schizophrenia) which, for a short period, tax the individual's ability to adjust in emotional and behavioural terms, and thereby lead to acute 'stress'. Such 'ordinary' life experiences (interpersonal, social, work-related) are known antecedents of episodes and for most people tend to accumulate in the late teens and twenties when major life changes are occurring. The ability of the individual to cope effectively may vary as a function of the level of

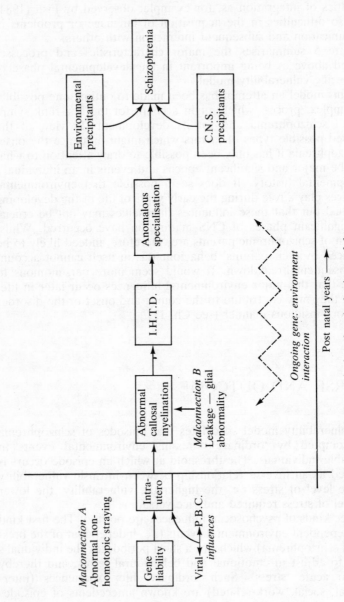

Fig. 5 Major developmental phases in interhemispheric model
(a) Major process in development of constitutional vulnerability to schizophrenia

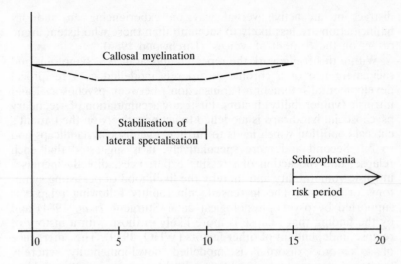

(b) Maturation of callosum in relation to language specialisation

support and contact there is with other individuals and the quality of his premorbid coping resources.

The second source of psychosocial influence are those which may occur as a secondary response to the emergence of schizophrenia. The stress-prone lifestyles of many schizophrenics in developed, urbanised countries (unemployment, geographical mobility, alienation/segregation) and the stressful circumstances which many patients seem to create for themselves, may directly influence the appearance of symptoms. The accumulation of secondary handicap in the form of social isolation and impairments of social and life skills might increase the impact of stressing experiences as they reflect, in part, the individual's resources to cope with the vicissitudes of life. It was precisely these characteristics which Hogarty and colleagues (1974) attempted to improve and which developing countries seem so adept at maintaining.

The seemingly stressful and relapse-inducing nature of some family environments we also model as a secondary handicap as the evidence pointed towards the conclusion that the chronic stressful qualities of these environments are emergent ones resulting from families' difficulty in adjusting to the behavioural changes associated with schizophrenia. Finally we would argue that schizophrenics' manner of responding to their hallucinations and delusions, particularly during periods of insight, might well determine whether a full-blown relapse occurs. Thus for example patients who ignore or distract in an active verbal way on experiencing an auditory hallucination are less likely to succumb than those who listen, argue or act on the content of 'voices' (Birchwood 1986).

Within this framework the repeated appearance of symptoms and the emergence of a chronic disorder is modelled as a reciprocal developmental interaction ('transaction') between psychosocial and intrinsic (vulnerability) factors. First, any accumulation of secondary psychosocial handicaps is modelled to act negatively on the patient's clinical condition which leads to further psychosocial handicaps and so on. Second and more speculatively, it is suggested that each relapse, and the action of stressing experiences, directly increases intrinsic vulnerability and thereby the likelihood of persisting symptoms or relapse. The increased vulnerability following relapse is supported by psychophysiological data (Sturgeon *et al.* 1984) and by the finding that relapse is more likely in those with a history of relapse, independent of other factors (WHO, 1979). The emergence of a chronic disorder is modelled developmentally whereby increased intrinsic vulnerability is raised to a degree that symptoms persist between episodes, fading imperceptibly with time into a chronic unremitting disorder. Entry into institutions further exacerbates negativity and social decline as the individual learns and accepts the role of patienthood. The negative effect of unstimulating, custodial environments (which can include family and other community settings) was vividly demonstrated by the study of Wing and Brown (1970) and by the dramatic changes achieved by Paul and Lentz (1977) in their intensive rehabilitation programmes with chronic severely disturbed patients.

We are suggesting then that a synergistic relationship exists between psychosocial factors, intrinsic vulnerability and symptomatic status which can represent a potent force 'driving' an individual toward chronicity and social disablement. The prevention or early amelioration of any psychosocial handicaps and the use of regular medication will clearly serve to retard the process.

Finally we would speculate that the three kinds of schizophrenia referred to at the beginning of this chapter, respond differently to these environmental factors. The first group, which tend to be characterised by negative symptoms at onset, poor premorbid personality, ventricular enlargement, male and of early onset, are known to have a poorer prognosis. It is suggested that this group possess an initially high level of intrinsic vulnerability and require little in the way of a psychosocial process to initiate a chronic deterioration. The schizo-affectives on the other hand are known to have a better prognosis (Ch 12) which we would speculate as being due to a low intrinsic vulnerability requiring exceptionally adverse environmental circumstances to initiate a chronic decline. The action of the transactional process will occur maximally with the third ('nuclear') group of intermediate vulnerability whose variable outcome we would model as a function of (variable) environmental influences.

TREATMENT IMPLICATIONS

PREVENTATIVE MEASURES

The ideal treatment for any problem is, of course, some form of prevention. For this to become a practical possibility for schizophrenia, important contributors to the disorder would need to be defined with clarity. As yet our understanding of the determinants of the disorder and the precise factors important in its development are clearly inadequate for the task of primary prevention. We have no comprehensive map of the role of genetic mechanisms contributing to the liability of schizophrenia and we are presently unable to document a clear natural history of the pre-schizophrenic period in terms of defining the complex interaction between biological and psychosocial variables. Whilst prevention is therefore likely to be a future goal it is likely that, at least, three important issues would contribute to this goal.

Genetic/post-natal counselling
The prospect of some form of genetic counselling raises several important ethical and social questions but it is important to bear in mind that this does not constitute an attempt at clearing the 'schizophrenic genes' from the overall gene pool. Rather, it should be viewed as a humane attempt at alleviating the suffering of individuals by aiming to reduce or minimize the actualisation of risk.

This might take the form of informing parents of the nature of that risk and the possible biological and environmental interactions that may be significant. Rather than just advising parents of the potential risk or likelihood of future children developing schizophrenia, and hence placing the parents in the intolerable position of deciding whether or not to have further children, we should envisage this practice as being one of post-natal advice, counselling, and education.

This, of course, may be fine in principle, but might raise additional difficulties by alerting parents such that they change their behaviour towards the child in a manner as to cause iatrogenic effects on the child's psychosocial development. This can be avoided but, ultimately, the validity of the approach relies on the ability to identify an at-risk child from essentially statistical data derived from population genetics. Attempts to address this problem have been considered (eg. Reveley 1984) and used in practise, and involve extensive evaluation of each individual within the immediate and extended family to produce a 'pedigree' of affected and non-affected individuals. Clearly, however, this approach is limited at present, in part by diagnostic uncertainties, and also because of our ignorance of the precise number and interaction of genes which are presumed to contribute towards liability.

A necessary adjunct to identifying risk on the basis of genetic liability would be the identification of early biological signs of the disorder.

Early screening
The ability to identify a biological marker, observable in early life by non-obtrusive methods, might pave the way for prevention. Thus, for example, in the model presented earlier abnormal inter-hemispheric integration, delayed language acquisition and abnormal lateral specialisation would in principle be observable in the early years of life and thus might be useful as screening measures, should future research support our present findings. The extent to which it might be possible to identify reliable markers depends on fulfilling two fundamental criteria. First, that the evidence clearly confirms a relationship between early indices and future breakdown. For this to occur extensive and independent longitudinal investigation with high-risk groups would be essential. Thus the study of Fish (1984) suggests that significant indices of future breakdown may be identified as early as four to nine months of life.

Obviously to establish these findings as being of general significance would require international agreement and co-operation among existing and future high-risk projects. Second, it would be vital to demonstrate that the abnormalities or pathology observed early in life are exclusively pathognomic of schizophrenia. This requires a complex and exhaustive examination of the processes in question.

Primary prevention
Should it be feasible to identify early predictors of schizophrenic breakdown it might be possible to consider preventative methods. The authors, however, do not wish to convey the idea that since the constitutional vulnerability may be biological in nature that this necessarily points us only in the direction of pharmacological or surgical procedures. Rather, since the vulnerability is more likely to reflect abnormalities of cerebral function and organisation, (rather than gross anatomical disruption) a variety of psychological, educational, and perhaps prosthetic techniques, in conjunction with

psychosocial intervention might minimise the influence, or full behavioural expression, of the constitutional vulnerability. Particularly in view of the brain's functional plasticity in early life, discrete and specific techniques might arrest the progress of adverse 'soft' neurological processes. It is therefore of interest that Green (1985) reports some success in alleviating the difficulties of some Learning Disabled children by psychological procedures developed from research of brain function.

Of necessity this section has been somewhat general and vague and has served merely to highlight the need for a combined approach, implicit in a transactional model, which would need to consider the exact nature of the genetic liability and the putative biological and psychosocial precursors. Until this occurs prevention remains more of an ideal than a practical option. Having said this, the continued reporting from the wide variety of studies considered throughout this book does offer the promise of prevention and we should be optimistic that the results of these studies will have implications for prevention in the not-too-distant future.

AMELIORATION

We have argued in this book that, in itself, a diagnosis of schizophrenia embodies relatively weak therapeutic implications compared to diagnoses in conventional medicine. This is partly a statement of fact in that the limitations of drugs are now well appreciated; the high probability of relapse, their lack of effectiveness with negative symptoms and the continuing problems of chronic deterioration and social disablement. The model also suggests that in terms of amelioration, there are, *a priori*, reasons to question the view that classifying a person as a member of the category 'schizophrenia' will ultimately be a sufficient decision to help the individual with the problems he is faced with. If the model is correct, then the nature and degree of the *individual* secondary psychosocial response is equal if not more crucial to the outlook for an individual than his/her category membership. It is our strong view that if both the 'individual' and 'categorical' implications of this model are met then it should be possible to ameliorate the clinical and social consequences of schizophrenia to a highly significant degree.

The model we have offered and our review of psychosocial and drug intervention suggests the utility of an integrated psychosocial-medical intervention programme, emphasising a number of components, some of which are already well-developed, some requiring further research and development. The following programme of intervention is based on two assumptions. First, the notion of a developmental progression carries with it the need to consider interventions at different stages and in response to different problems. Strategies that may be appropriate for an older, socially withdrawn, institutionalised patient will be more concerned with amelioration both of the individual's problems and the constraints imposed by hospital rehabilitation policy. For the younger schizophrenic there will be a greater accent on prevention. Second, we believe there must be an effective marriage between psychosocial and medical interventions given the nature of schizophrenia that we have outlined. This will require some professional adaptation but also considerable change in the philosophy and structure of mental health care, away from notions of 'disease' and 'treatment' (as embodied in the psychiatric hospital) in favour of a view which sees schizophrenia in the total context of the individual, i.e. as a life problem.

The elements of an integrated programme through which this might be achieved are described below.

The amelioration of intrinsic vulnerability

It would be misguided to assume that the intrinsic vulnerability to schizophrenia is a static phenomenon which is presumed to lay down the biologial template for schizophrenia and not subject to amelioration after breakdown. It has, for example, already been discussed in earlier chapters of this book that the use of prosthetic agents, such as the occlusion of monaural stimulation (Birchwood 1986) and certain psychological techniques (generally subsumed under the heading of 'voice control') may achieve considerable success in reducing the frequency and intensity of psychotic symptoms in some schizophrenics. It is therefore important to reiterate that these techniques were developed from hypotheses which seek to understand the phenomenology of positive symptoms in terms of abnormal cerebral function – specifically in terms of defective inter-hemispheric integration.

As our knowledge of the precise nature of this phenomenon increases it is hoped that other 'bio-behavioural' techniques may be developed and tested.

Similarly, as growing knowledge of the action of drugs increases, it seems likely that more specific forms of medication may be developed. In the reverse manner, the elucidation of alternative models of the aetiology and phenomenology of schizophrenia may result in a revision of our current explanations of the mechanisms of drug action. It is, therefore, of importance here to determine how the vulnerability model presented earlier might explain the anti-psychotic effects of certain neuroleptic drugs. Chlorpromazine, the archetypal neuroleptic, is generally considered to achieve its therapeutic effects via antidopaminergic action. In terms of the presented model two possibilities may be forwarded.

First, that the major cause of symptom relief is indeed through antidopaminergic mechanisms, but that specifically it achieves its effect via the cortico-cortical (i.e. interhemispheric) dopaminergic networks. A second possibility derives from the observation of a considerable time delay between drug administration and its 'anti psychotic' effects. Randall (1983) argues, and has subsequently demonstrated (pers. comm.) that this time delay is inconsistent with selective drug uptake at the neural body but more compatible with uptake into the fatty myelin sheath. Indeed chlorpromazine appears to be selectively absorbed by fatty myelin (the rate of absorption being much slower than that observed through neural body intake) and displaces cholesterol from the internal lipid layer. Having said this, the exact mechanisms by which chlorpromazine subsequently achieves its therapeutic effect is not known. Randall (1980) suggests that the effect is due to a local anaesthetic action which leads to blockade of axonal conduction ameliorates schizophrenic symptoms by virtue of a chemical 'callosectomy' or split brain.

Experiments with chlorpromazine on infra-humans, however, indicates that the drug has the effect of speeding up transcallosal (or interhemispheric) transmission (Guirgea and Moyersoons 1977). If this is the case, it is possible to speculate that the primary therapeutic action of this drug is achieved by enhancing callosal transmission (possibly by 're-insulating' the myelin sheath and hence reducing electrochemical leakage) and thus reduce symptoms which are argued to be due to disrupted callosal transmission. Whilst this provides only a partial and incomplete explanation, further research in this area might prove fruitful.

The self-control of schizophrenic symptoms

It has been pointed out that in spite of drugs, persisting symptoms, often with insight, are major problems in acute schizophrenia. Such symptoms also frequently emerge as 'early warning signs' of relapse. We have reviewed a number of encouraging single-case reports in which symptoms such as auditory hallucinations and delusions have been brought under control using self-directed management strategies. In the case of hallucinations, those strategies involving concurrent verbalisations, and others, derived from hemispheric integration theory seem to be particularly useful. We feel that further research in this area will be fruitful with younger, acute, episodic schizophrenics with persisting symptoms. This is partly because such strategies are dependent upon the individual's recognition of the maladaptive nature of his experiences and on his motivation and ability to implement a treatment programme. These prerequisites may be absent in chronic schizophrenia. Also, in acute schizophrenia, it is known that the symptom profile is largely repeated at each relapse (WHO 1979). Thus, it may be feasible to train patients and their relatives to recognise the early signs of schizophrenic relapse, while the patient retains insight, and to utilise the self-control strategies in order to avert a relapse.

Improving the outlook of schizophrenia through social intervention

Managing life crises and changes As indicated in a previous chapter, there have been no attempts to explore the therapeutic implications of the well established finding that episodes of schizophrenia can be triggered by stressful life episodes. It was suggested that this might be explored in two forms: reducing exposure to these events or improving patients' ability to respond effectively to them. One might for example advise against lifestyles which are constantly changing such as in the case of patients who drift from job to job or who are geographically mobile. However improving patients' ability to respond to life changes seems more realistic. As we argued in the previous chapter much research is awaiting to be done on the nature of these coping responses in normal and pathological populations but we would suggest that an intervention designed to improve social, interpersonal and vocational functioning is likely to have a beneficial spin-off in terms of improved resources to meet stressful life circumstances.

Psychosocial rehabilitation The concept of rehabilitation has traditionally been associated with chronic institutionalised populations. We would strongly advocate the application of rigorous psychosocial rehabilitation techniques to the younger acutely disturbed person. This would improve the individual's ability to meet life demands and avert the possibility of repeated relapse and the slide into chronicity. The model suggests that the social disabilities associated with (and we would suggest instrumental in creating) chronicity, have their origins at or sometimes before the onset. If the synergy between social and clinical functioning is to be broken more than temporarily, then maximum effort should be applied as early as possible to restore and improve social and community functioning. This may include a number of components.

First, the environment in which the person is treated should be structured in such a way as to reduce the likelihood of dependency and passivity. Hospital ward environments do not seem to promote independence (Goffmann 1961; Wing and Brown 1970) The emphasis of the treatment environment should be positive, fostering patients' independence, social competence and personal well-being through a systematic structure which expects, trains and encourages these characteristics. The experience of successful social learning programmes (e.g. Paul and Lentz 1977) could be applied to these environments to facilitate change. It is recognised that such a change is limited by the philosophy and organisation of psychiatric hospitals which foster 'patient-role' expectations among staff and residents alike. Clearly changes in the organisation, structure and activities of acute treatment units towards greater autonomy and privacy for its residents will be essential. The situation of such units attached to their local community rather than in amorphous hospital environments will enable these changes.

We would suggest that a routine function of these acute units should include that of needs-oriented discharge planning. Each individual should be assessed and life goals discussed and agreed e.g. in occupational, social and recreational spheres. Appropriate training in relevant interpersonal self-help and independence skills should be routinely provided based on goal-oriented decision making and resolution of problems. Perhaps most important of all, the involvement of the psychiatric service should be criterion oriented (i.e. goal achievement) rather than time oriented. This would help to avoid the problem whereby discharge generally sees the end of the hospital's responsibility and commitment of resources, and facilitate true continuity of help. Clearly, this would require a closer integration of 'hospital' and 'community' resources which in Britain is hindered by the hiatus between the Health and Social Services. An integrated, centrally funded 'Mental Health Service' is needed which can organise itself and set its own priorities unfettered by the demands of expensive general medical health services.

Family interventions A crucial 'community' resource of the acute schizophrenic is his family. We have advocated the close involvement of the family in maintaining the well-being of the acute schizophrenic. However, the continuing emphasis on relapse and the general medical orientation in family interventions, casts families in the role of a potential 'pathology', to be removed by social intervention, which hinder the benefits of medication. Families should on the contrary be regarded as a potential asset and partner in psychiatric treatment. For example the role which families might play in acute psychosocial rehabilitation has been a neglected aspect of family interventions. The authors have worked with numerous families providing them with the structure and necessary training to encourage and maintain basic community survival skills in their relative. Thus we see no reason why families cannot form a valued part of an integrated psychiatric service.

One model of this 'partnership' has been explored by the authors in the West Birmingham Health District at All Saints Hospital in the UK. The 'Family Centre For Advice Resources and Education' has been set up as a form of training and liaison service on a research basis to facilitate a constructive therapeutic alliance between professionals and the family. The Centre functions to: (a) provide education courses about schizophrenia to families, designed to be applied to their own situation, (b) training families to recognise and report early signs of relapse so as to abort the relapse through a prompt increase in medication, (c) assist families to overcome negative emotional reactions, and other consequences of schizophrenia including stigma, worry, stress and disturbed family relationships, (d) help families to manage disturbed behaviour and to improve social functioning in their relative, and (e) act as a support through the provision of a drop-in advice facility.

Drug treatment

Changes brought about in the outlook for schizophrenia through the introduction of neuroleptics has reached a plateau; drug companies continue to market slight variants of the established compounds but with little additional tangible benefit. Disquiet is now also expressed about the side-effects of medication; as to whether they do outweigh their benefits and, in the third decade of their use, what their long-term effects are likely to be. In the light of this concern, we would advocate the following clinical and research strategies:

1. Our review of psychosocial interventions concluded that there was evidence that these interventions could act in whole or partial substitution for drug therapy. Future investigations should therefore routinely manipulate the dose of maintenance medication; for example no drugs, low dose and conventional dose. This kind of research is expensive and a case justifiably might be made for their funding in part by the drug companies.
2. High doses are frequently used with little empirical reason to do so (Hogarty *et al.* 1976) and are associated with greater side-effects (Kane and Smith 1982). Low dose drug strategies should therefore be explored, possibly in combination with an effective 'early warning system' to identify impending relapse such as that outlined with families in the previous section.
3. Two kinds of non-responders to medication are often observed by research studies, those who remain well without drugs and those who remain unwell in spite of drugs (Carpenter and Heinrichs 1981). Although this is a statistical rather than an individual fact, these results ought to be applied more rigorously both clinically and on an experimental basis (cf. Ch. 21).
4. Among drug 'responders', continued medication is crucial but drug non-compliance is a continual problem. Drug non-compliance can be predicted by questionnaire (Hogan *et al.* 1983; Mantonakis *et al.* 1985) and these 'at risk' individuals and their families should receive education about its advantages and costs. However as Hogan *et al.* (1980) point out, non-

compliance is frequently associated with side-effects; this then is another reason for the investigation of low-dose maintenance regimes.

Prevention and rehabilitation in chronic schizophrenia

The model suggests that one route by which a chronic disorder arises is a developmental one: the effects of repeated relapse, the accumulation of secondary psychosocial handicap, negative aspects of treatment and adverse social/hospital policies. We would argue therefore that the implementation of the steps outlined above should considerably reduce the prevalence of the social disability associated with chronicity if not the chronicity itself.

In respect of those chronic schizophrenics who are already long-term residents of psychiatric hospitals, the impressive results of Paul and Lentz's (1977) social learning approach to rehabilitation suggest that many problems characteristic of 'institutionalisation' may be ameliorated by a process of prudent environmental and behavioural management. While Paul and Lentz commend their approach as a model for further practice, it may however be emphasised that token economies provide a means for engineering an environment to encourage behaviour which the institutional environment does not. The token economy may therefore help remediate the deficiencies of an institution whose physical and social structure inadvertently promotes passivity, withdrawal and dependence. If however ill-conceived or carelessly applied, the token economy may encourage the view that only 'specialised techniques' can promote and motivate behaviour. Token systems which provide a structure for systematically cuing and reinforcing relevant behaviour, which are capable of individualised programme development, and which operate within the context of a progressive rehabilitative framework, may indeed have a useful role to play in promoting independence and social adjustment. They should not however be seen simply as prostheses for deficient institutional environments. Improving the quality of these environments in general, and establishing a coherent system of rehabilitation, should therefore remain as primary objectives. Indeed the efforts of those concerned with the management and rehabilitation of chronic schizophrenia might be best directed to examining alternative systems of rehabilitation other than those which focus exclusively on the psychiatric hospital.

CONCLUSION

The introduction of neuroleptic medication in the 1950s heralded a new era in the treatment of schizophrenia, and significantly improved the outlook for those suffering the most debilitating of the psychiatric disorders. Chemotherapy has not in itself however provided a sufficient solution to the problems of schizophrenics, and continuing efforts are clearly required if we are to develop more effective and rational ameliorative, remedial and preventative intervention strategies. We firmly believe that further significant advances in the field will depend not upon the initiative of a single discipline operating within a unitary and confined theoretical framework, but upon the genuine integration of medical, social and psychological approaches and the adoption of a broad interactional model as a guide for research and clinical practice.

REFERENCES

Achte K A 1967, *On Prognosis and Rehabilitation in Schizophrenia and Paranoid Psychoses*. Copenhagen: Munksgaard

Adams J 1983, Interhemispheric language dysfunction in schizophrenia. Unpublished MSc. dissertation, University of Birmingham

Adelstein A M, Downham D Y, Stein Z and Susser M W 1968, *Social Psychiatry* 3: 47–63

Albrecht P, Torrey E F, Boone E, Hicks J T and Daniel N 1980, Raised cytomegalovirus-antibody level in cerebrospinal fluid of schizophrenic patients, *Lancet*, ii: 767–72

Alford G S, Fleece L and Rothblum E 1982, Hallucinatory-delusional verbalizations: modification in a chronic schizophrenic by self-control and cognitive restructuring *Behavior Modification*, 6: 421–35

Alford G S and Turner S M 1976, Stimulus interference and conditioned inhibition of auditory hallucinations, *Journal of Behavior Therapy and Experimental Psychiatry* 7: 155–60

Al-Issa I 1978, Sociocultural factors in hallucinations, *International Journal of Social Psychiatry*, **23–24**: 167–75

Allen D J and Magaro P A 1971, Measures of change in token-economy programs, *Behaviour Research and Therapy*, 9: 311–18

Alpert M, Rubenstein, H and Kesselman M 1976, Asymmetry of information processing in hallucinators and nonhallucinators, *Journal of Nervous and Mental Disease*, **162**: 258–65

Alumbaugh R V 1971, Use of behavior modification techniques towards reduction of hallucinatory behavior: A case study, *Psychological Record* **21**: 415–417

Anderson L T and Alpert M 1974, Operant analysis of hallucination frequency in a hospitalized schizophrenic, *Journal of Behavior Therapy and Experimental Psychiatry* 5: 13–18

Anderson W H, Kuehnle J C and Catanzand D M, 1976, Rapid treatment of acute psychosis, *American Journal of Psychiatry* **133**: 1076–8

Andreasen N C 1982, The relationship between schizophrenic language and the aphasias. In F A Henn and H A Nasrallah (eds) *Schizophrenia as a Brain Disease*. New York: Oxford University Press, pp 99–111

Andreasen N C 1985, Positive vs. negative schizophrenia: a critical evaluation. *Schizophrenia Bulletin* **11**: 380–9

353

Andreasen N C , Dennert J W, Olsen S A and Damasio A L 1982a, Hemisphere asymmetries and schizophrenia, *American Journal of Psychology* **139**: 427–30

Andreasen N C, Olsen S A, Dennert J W and Smith M R 1982b, Ventricular enlargement in schizophrenia: relationship to positive and negative symptoms, *American Journal of Psychiatry* **193** 297–302

Andreasen N C, Smith M R, Jacoby C G, Dennert, J W and Olsen S A 1982c, Ventricular enlargement in schizophrenia: definition and prevalence, *American Journal of Psychiatry* **139**: 292–6

Andrews G, Hell N, Goldstein G, Lapsley H, Bartels R and Silove D 1985, The economic costs of schizophrenia, *Archives of General Psychiatry* **42**: 537–43

Angrist B, Gershon S, Sathananthan G, Walker R W, Lopez-Ramos B, Mandel L R and Vandenheuvel T 1976, Dimethyltryptamine levels in blood of schizophrenic patients and control subjects, *Psychopharmacology* **47**: 29–32

Angrist B, Sathananthan G, Wilk S and Gershon S 1974, Amphetamine psychosis: Behavioural and biochemical aspects, *Journal of Psychiatric Research* **11**: 13–23

Ariel R N, Golden C J, Berg R A, Quaife M A, Dirksen I W, Forsen T, Wilson J and Graber B 1983, Regional blood flow in schizophrenics: Tests using the Xenon XE-133 inhalation method, *Archives of General Psychiatry* **40**: 258–63

Arieti S 1967, *The Intrapsychic Self*, New York: Basic Books

Asano N 1967, Pneumoencephalographic study of schizophrenia. In H Mitsuda (ed), *Clinical Genetics in Psychiatry. Problems of Nonsociological Classification*, Tokyo: Igaku Shoin Ltd, 209–19

Ashkenazi A, Krasilowsky D, Levin S, Idar D, Kalian M, Or A, Ginat Y and Halperin B 1979, Immunologic reaction of psychotic patients to fractions of gluten, *American Journal of Psychiatry* **136**: 1306–9

Astrup C 1962, *Schizophrenia: Conditional reflex studies*, Springfield III: Charles C Thomas

Atthowe J M 1973, Token economies come of age, *Behavior Therapy* **4**: 646–54

Atthowe J M and Krasner L 1968, Preliminary report on the application of contingent reinforcement procedures (token economy) on a 'chronic' psychiatric ward, *Journal or Abnormal Psychology* **73**: 37–43

Ayllon T 1963, Intensive treatment of psychotic behavior by stimulus satiation and food reinforcement, *Behaviour Research and Therapy* **1**: 53–61

Ayllon T 1965, Some behavioral problems associated with eating in chronic schizophrenic patients. In L P Ullmann and L Krasner (eds), *Case Studies in Behavior Modification* New York: Holt, Rinehart and Winston: 73–7

Ayllon T and Azrin N H 1964, Reinforcement and instructions with mental patients, *Journal of the Experimental Analysis of Behavior* **7**: 327–31

Ayllon T and Azrin N H 1965, The measurement and reinforcement of behavior of psychotics, *Journal of the Experimental Analysis of Behavior* **8**: 357–83

Ayllon T and Azrin N H 1968, *The Token Economy: A motivational system for therapy and rehabilitation*. New York: Appleton-Century-Crofts

References

Ayllon T and Haughton E 1962, Control of the behavior of schizophrenic patients by food, *Journal of the Experimental Analysis of Behavior* **5**: 342–52

Ayllon T and Haughton E 1964, Modification of symptomatic verbal behaviour of mental patients, *Behaviour Research and Therapy* **2**: 87–97

Ayllon T and Kandel H 1976, 'I hear voices but there's no one there' (A functional analysis of auditory hallucinations). In H J Eysenck (ed), *Case Studies in Behaviour Therapy* London: Routledge and Kegan-Paul

Ayllon T and Michael J 1959, The psychiatric nurse as a behavioral engineer, *Journal of the Experimental Analysis of Behavior* **3**: 324–34

Babigian H M 1975, in A M Freedman H, Kaplan and B J Sadock (eds), *Comprehensive Textbook of Psychiatry II*, Vol 1, Baltimore: Williams and Wilkins

Bakan P 1971, The eyes have it, *Psychology Today* **4**: 64–7

Baker R 1971, The use of operant conditioning to reinstate speech in mute schizophrenics, *Behaviour Research and Therapy* **9**: 329–36

Baker R and Hall J N 1975, A controlled study of a token economy. Paper presented at the annual conference of the British Association for Behavioural Psychotherapy, York, England

Baker R, Hall J N and Hutchinson K 1974, A token economy project with chronic schizophrenic patients, *British Journal of Psychiatry* **124**: 367–84

Baker R, Hall J N, Hutchinson K and Bridge G 1977, Symptom changes in chronic schizophrenic patients on a token economy: A controlled experiment, *British Journal of Psychiatry* **131**: 381–93

Baldessarini R J, Stramentinoli G and Lipinski J F 1979, Methylation hypothesis, *Archives of General Psychiatry* **36**: 303–7

Ban T 1964, *Conditioning and Psychiatry* Chicago: Aldine

Bannister D and Fransella F 1966, A grid test of schizophrenic thought disorder, *British Journal of Social and Clinical Psychology* **5**: 95–102

Barry H and Barry H 1961, Season of birth, *Archives of General Psychiatry* **5**: 292–300

Barton R 1959, *Institutional Neurosis* Bristol, England: J Wright & Sons Ltd

Bateson G, Jackson D D, Haley J, Weakland J H 1956, Toward a theory of schizophrenia, *Behavioural Sciences* **1**: 251–64

Bauman E 1979, Schizophrenic short-term memory: A deficit in subjective organisation, *Canadian Journal of Behavioural Science* **3**: 55–65

Bazhin E F, Wasserman L I and Tonkonogii I M 1975, Auditory hallucinations and left temporal lobe pathology *Neuropsychologia* **13**: 481–7

Beaumont J G 1983, *Introduction to Neuropsychology* Oxford: Blackwell Scientific Publications

Beaumont J G and Dimond S J 1973, Brain disconnection and schizophrenia, *British Journal of Psychology* **123**: 661–2

Beck A T, Ward C H, Mendelson M, Mock J E and Erbaugh J K 1962, Reliability of psychiatric diagnosis: II A study of clinical judgements and ratings, *American Journal of Psychiatry* **119**: 351–7

Beck A T, Rush A J, Shaw B F and Emery G 1979, *Cognitive Theory of Depression*, Wiley

Beck J C and Worthen K 1972, Precipitating stress, crisis theory and hospitalisation in schizophrenia and depression, *Psychiatry* **26**: 123–9

Beckman M and Haas S 1980, High dose diazepam in schizophrenia,

Psychopharmacology **71**: 79–82

Bellack A S, Hersen M and Turner S M 1976, Generalization effects of social skills training in chronic schizophrenics: an experimental analysis, *Behaviour Research and Therapy* **14**: 391–8

Bellack A S, Hersen M and Lamparski D 1979, Role-playing tests for assessing social skills: are they valid? Are they useful?, *Journal of Consulting and Clinical Psychology* **47**: 335–42

Benes F, Sunderland P, Jones B D, LeMay M, Cotten B M and Lipinski J F 1982, Normal ventricles in young schizophrenics, *British Journal of Psychiatry* **141**: 90–3

Bennett P S and Maley R F 1973, Modification of interactive behaviors in chronic mental patients. *Journal of Applied Behavior Analysis* **6**: 609–20

Berger P A 1981, Biochemistry and the schizophrenias: Old concepts and new hypotheses, *The Journal of Nervous and Mental Disease* **169**: 90–9

Berger P A, Faull K F, Kilkowski J, Anderson P J, Kraemer H, Davis K L and Barchas J D 1980, CSF monoamine metabolites in depression and schizophrenia, *American Journal of Psychiatry* **137**: 174–80

Berger P A, Watson S J, Akil H, Elliott G R, Rubin R T, Pfefferbaum A, Davis K L, Barchas J D and Li C H 1980, B-Endorphin and schizophrenia, *Archives of General Psychiatry* **37**: 635–40

Bergsma D and Goldstein A L (eds) 1978, *Neurochemical and Immunologic Components in Schizophrenia*, New York: A R Liss

Berkowitz R, Eberlein-Vries R, Kuipers L and Leff J 1984, Educating relatives about schizophrenia, *Schizophrenia Bulletin* **10**: 418–29

Bigelow L B, Nasrallah H A and Rauscher F P 1983, Corpus callosum thickness in chronic schizophrenia, *British Journal of Psychiatry* **142**: 284–7

Birchwood M J 1983, Family coping behaviour and the course of schizophrenia: A two year follow-up study, Unpublished PhD, University of Birmingham

Birchwood M J 1986, The control of auditory hallucinations through the occlusion of monaural auditory input, *British Journal of Psychiatry* **149**: 104–7

Bird E D, Spokes E G and Iversen L L 1979, Brain Norepinephrine and Dopamine in schizophrenia, *Science* **204**: 93–4

Birley J L T and Brown G 1970, Crises and life changes preceding the onset or relapse of schizophrenia, *British Journal of Psychiatry* **116**: 327–33

Blackman D 1974, *Operant Conditioning: An experimental analysis of behaviour* London: Methuen and Co Ltd

Bleuler E 1950, *Dementia Praecox or the Group of Schizophrenias*, 1911 English Translation J Zinkin, New York: International Universities Press

Bleuler M 1978, Die schizophrenen geistesstoerungen im lichte langjaehriger kranken und familiengeschichten thieme, Stuttgart. *The Schizophrenic Disorders: Long Term Patient and Family Studies* translated by S M Clemens, Newhaven & London, Yale University Press

Blumenthal R, Kreisman D and O'Connor P A 1982, Return to the family and its consequences for rehospitalisation among recently discharged mental patients, *Psychological Medicine* **12**: 141–7

Bocca E, Calaero C, Cassinari V and Magliavacca F 1955, Testing 'cortical' hearing in temporal lobe tumours, *Acta-Oto-Laryngology* **45**: 289–304

Boehme D H, Cottrel J C, Dohan F C and Hillegass L M 1973, Fluorescent antibody studies of immunoglobulin binding by brain tissues, *Archives of General Psychiatry* **28**: 202–7

Boklage C E 1977, Schizophrenia, brain asymmetry development and twinning: Cellular relationship with etiological and possibly prognostic implications, *Biological Psychiatry* **12**: 19–35

Bolin B J 1953, Left-handedness and stuttering as signs diagnostic of epileptics, *Journal of Mental Science* **99**: 483–8

Book J A 1953, A genetic and neuropsychiatric investigation of a North-Swedish population with special regard to schizophrenia and mental deficiency, *Acta Genetica et Statistics Medica (Basel)* **4**: 1–100

Bowers M B 1973, 5-Hydroxyindoleacetic acid (5-HIAA) & Homovanillic acid (HVA) following Probenecid in acute psychotic patients treated with Phenothiazines, *Psychopharmacologia* **28**: 309–18

Brandon S, Gonley P, McDonald C, Neville P, Palmer R and Wellstood-Eason S 1985, Leicester ECT trial: Results in schizophrenia, *British Journal of Psychiatry* **146**: 177–83

Brecher M and Begleiter H 1983, Event-related brain potentials to high-incentive stimuli in unmedicated schizophrenic patients, *Biological Psychiatry* **18**: 661–74

Brenner M H 1963, *Mental Illness and the Economy*, Cambridge: Harvard University Press

Brenner R and Shopsin B 1980, The use of Monoamine Oxidase inhibitors in schizophrenia *Biological Psychiatry*, **15**: 633–47

Brockington I F, Kendell R E and Leff J P 1978, Definitions of schizophrenia: Concordance and prediction of outcome, *Psychological Medicine* **8**: 387–98

Brockington I F and Meltzer H Y 1982, Documenting an episode of psychiatric illness, *Schizophrenia Bulletin* **8(3)**: 485–92

Broen W E and Storms L H 1967, A theory of response interference in schizophrenia. In B A Maher (ed), *Progress in Experimental Personality Research*, Vol. 4, New York: Academic Press: 269–312

Brookes D J and Brown C A 1981, A behavioural approach to psychiatric rehabilitation, *Nursing Times* 367–70

Brown G W and Birley J 1968, Crises and life changes and the onset of schizophrenia, *Journal of Health and Social Behaviour* **9**: 203–14

Brown G W and Birley J L T 1970, Social precipitants of severe psychiatric disorders. In E H Hare & J K Wing (eds) *Psychiatric Epidemiology* London: London University Press

Brown G W, Birley J L T and Wing J K 1972, The influence of family life on the course of schizophrenic disorders: A replication, *British Journal of Psychiatry* **121**: 241–58

Brown G W, Bone S, Dalison L and Wing J K 1966, *Schizophrenia and social care*, London: Oxford University Press

Brown G W, Carstairs G M and Topping G 1958, Post-hospital adjustment of chronic mental patients, *Lancet* **2**: 685–9

Brown G W and Harris T 1979, *Social Origins of Depression: A study of psychiatric disorder in women*, London: Tavistock

Brown G W, Harris T and Peto J 1973, Life events and psychiatric disorders II: Nature of a causal link, *Psychological Medicine* **3**: 159–76

Brown G W, Monck E M, Carstairs G M and Wing J K 1962, Influence of family life on the course of schizophrenic illness, *British Journal of Preventive and Social Medicine* **16**: 55–68

Brown G W and Rutter M L 1966, The measurement of family activities and relationships, *Human Relations* **19**: 241–63

Bruder G E 1983a, Cerebral laterality and psychopathology: A review of dichotic listening studies, *Schizophrenia Bulletin* **9**: 134–50

Bruder G E 1983b, Dichotic listening laterality in schizophrenia and affective disorders: The role of diagnostic subtype and clinical state. In P Flor-Henry and J Gruzelier (eds), *Laterality and Psychopathology*, Amsterdam: Elsevier Science Publishers: 411–26

Bucher B and Fabricatore J 1970, Use of patient-administered shock to suppress hallucinations, *Behavior Therapy* **1**: 382–5

Buchsbaum M S 1977, The middle evoked response components in schizophrenia, *Schizophrenia Bulletin* **3**: 93–104

Buchsbaum M 1981, Lateralised asymmetries in glucose uptake assessed by PET in patients with schizophrenia and in normal controls, *Paper Presented at the Second International Conference on Laterality and Psychopathology* Banff, Alberta, Canada

Buchsbaum M S, Carpenter W T, Fedio P, Goodwin F K, Murphy D L and Post R M 1979, Hemisphere differences in evoked potential enhancement by selective attention to hemiretinally presented stimuli in schizophrenic, affective and post-temporal lobectomy patients. In J Gruzelier and P Flor-Henry (eds), *Hemisphere Asymmetries of Function in Psychopathology* Elsevier/North Holland Biomedical Press: 317–28

Buchsbaum M and Ingvar D H 1982, New visions of the schizophrenic brain: Regional differences in electrophysiology, blood flow and cerebral glucose use. In F A Henn and H A Nasrallah (eds), *Schizophrenia as a Brain Disease*, New York: Oxford University Press: 235–52

Budzinski J 1977, Turning on in the twilight zone, *Psychology Today* **11**: 38–44

Burns G W 1980, *The Science of Genetics* New York: MacMillan Publishing Co, Inc

Butler S R and Glass A 1974, Asymmetries in the electroencephalogram associated with cerebral dominance, *Electroencephelography and Clinical Neurophysiology* **36**: 481–91

Butler R J and Rosenthall G 1978, *Behaviour and Rehabilitation* Bristol, England: John Wright and Sons

Callaway E 1975, *Brain Electrical Potentials and Individual Psychological Differences*, New York: Grune and Stratton

Carlson C G, Hersen M and Eisler R M 1972, Token economy programs in the treatment of hospitalized adult psychiatric patients, *Journal of Nervous and Mental Disease* **155**: 192–204

Carlsson A and Lindqvist M 1963, Effect of Chlorpromazine and Haloperidol on formation of 3-Methoxytyramine and Normetanephrine in mouse brain, *Acta Pharmacologica et Toxicologica* **20**: 140–4

Carpenter W T and Heinrichs D N 1981, Treatment of relevant subtypes of schizophrenia, *Journal of Nervous and Mental Disease* **169**: 113–9

References

Carpenter W T and Heinrichs D N 1983, Early intervention, time-limited targetted pharmacotherapy of schizophrenia, *Schizophrenia Bulletin* **9(4)**: 533–42

Carr S A 1980, Interhemispheric transfer of stereognostic information in chronic schizophrenics, *British Journal of Psychiatry* **136**: 53–8

Carter R L, Holenegger N and Satz P 1980, Handedness and aphasia: An inferential method for determining the mode of cerebral speech specialisation, *Neuropsychologica* **18**: 569–74

Castellani S, Ziegler M G, Van Kammen D P, Alexander P E, Siris S G and Lake C R 1982, Plasma Norepinephrine and Dopamine-beta-Hydroxylase activity in schizophrenia, *Archives of General Psychiatry* **39**: 1145–9

Cerletti V and Bini L 1938, L'elettroshock, *Archivo Generale di Neurologia, Psichiatria e Psicoanalisi* **19**: 266

Cheek F 1965, The father of the schizophrenic, *Archives of General Psychiatry* **13**: 336–45

Cheek F E 1967, Parental social control mechanisms in the family of the schizophrenic – A new look at the family environment of schizophrenia, *Journal of Schizophrenia* **1(i)**: 19

Ciompi L 1980, Three lectures on schizophrenia: The natural history of schizophrenia in the long term, *British Journal of Psychiatry* **136**: 413–20

Clarke A M and Clarke A D B 1974, Genetic-environmental interactions in cognitive development. In Clarke A M and Clarke A D B, *Mental Deficiency: The Changing Outlook* London: Methuen

Clausen J A and Kohn M L 1966, In D Jackson (ed), *The Etiology of Schizophrenia*, New York: Basic Books

Cochrane R 1984, *The Social Creation of Mental Illness* England: Longman

Coffey V P and Jessop W J E 1959, Maternal influenza and congenital deformities: A prospective study, *Lancet* **11**: 935–8

Coger R W, Dymond A M and Serafetinides E A 1979, Electroencephalographic similarities between chronic alcoholics and chronic, non-paranoid schizophrenics, *Archives of General Psychiatry* **36**: 91–4

Cohen C and Sokolovsky J 1978, Schizophrenia and social networks: Expatients in the inner city, *Schizophrenia Bulletin* **4**: 546–60

Cohen R, Florin I, Grusche A, Meyer-Osterkamp S and Sell H 1972, The introduction of a token economy in a psychiatric ward with extremely withdrawn chronic schizophrenics, *Behaviour Research and Therapy* **10**: 69–74

Cohen S M, Nichols A, Wyatt R J and Pollin W 1974, The administration of Methionine to chronic schizophrenic patients: A review of ten studies, *Biological Psychiatry* **8**: 209–25

Colbourn C J and Lishman W A 1979, Lateralisation of function and psychotic illness: A left hemisphere deficit? In J Gruzelier and P Flor-Henry (eds), *Hemisphere Asymmetries of Function in Psychopathology*, Amsterdam: Elsevier/North Holland Biomedical Press: 539–59

Connolly J F 1982 Correspondence, *British Journal of Psychiatry* **140**: 429–36

Connolly J F, Gruzelier J H, Manchanda R and Hirsch S R 1983, Visual evoked potentials in schizophrenia. Intensity effects and hemisphere asymetry, *British Journal of Psychiatry* **142**: 152–5

Cook N D 1984, Callosal inhibition: The key to the brain code, *Behavioural Science* **29**: 98–110

Cooklin R, Sturgeon D and Leff J 1983, The relationship between auditory hallucinations and spontaneous fluctuations of skin conductance in schizophrenia, *British Journal of Psychiatry* **142**: 47–52

Cooper B 1978, Epidemiology. In J K Wing (ed), *Schizophrenia: Towards a New Synthesis*, London: Academic Press

Cooper B and Sylph J 1973, Life events and the onset of neurotic illness. An investigation in general practice, *Psychological Medicine* **3**: 421–35

Cooper J E, Kendell R E, Gurland B J 1972, *Psychiatric Diagnosis in New York and London* New York: Oxford University Press

Corey G 1977, *Theory and Practice of Counseling and Psychotherapy*, Belmont, California: Wadsworth

Cottrell A C, McCleod M F and McCleod W R 1977, A Bufotenin-like substance in the urine of schizophrenics, *American Journal of Psychiatry* **134**: 322–3

Coursey R D, Buchsbaum M S and Murphy D L 1979, Platelet MAO activity and evoked potentials in the identification of subjects biologically at risk for psychiatric disorders, *British Journal of Psychiatry* **134**: 372–81

Cowden R C and Ford L I 1962, Systematic desensitization with phobic schizophrenics, *American Journal of Psychiatry* **119**: 241–5

Craighead W E, Kazdin A E and Mahoney M J 1976, *Behavior Modification: Principles, Issues and Applications*, Boston: Houghton Mifflin Co.

Creer C 1975, Living with schizophrenia, *Social Work Today* **6**: 2–7

Creer C and Wing J K 1973, *Schizophrenia in the home*, Surbiton, Surrey: National Schizophrenia Fellowship

Creese I, Burt D R and Snyder S H 1976, Dopamine receptor binding predicts clinical and pharmacological potencies of antischizophrenic drugs, *Science* **192**: 481–3

Cross A J, Crow T J and Owen F 1981, ^{3}H-Flupenthixol binding in post-mortem brains of schizophrenics: Evidence for a selective increase in Dopamine D2 Receptors, *Psychopharmacology* **74**: 122–4

Crow T J 1980, Molecular pathology of schizophrenia: More than one disease process?, *British Medical Journal* **280**: 66–8

Crow T J 1981a, Biochemical determinants of schizophrenic and toxic psychoses. In H M Van Praag, M H Lader, O J Rafaelsen and E J Sachar (eds), *Handbook of Biological Psychiatry. Part IV. Brain Mechanisms and Abnormal Behaviour, Chemistry*: 3–80

Crow T J 1981b, Positive and negative schizophrenic symptoms and the role of Dopamine, *British Journal of Psychiatry* **139**: 251–4

Crow T J, Baker H F, Cross A J, Joseph M H, Lofthouse R, Longden A, Owen F, Riley G J, Glover V and Killpack W S 1979a, Monoamine mechanisms in chronic schizophrenia: Post mortem neurochemical findings, *British Journal of Psychiatry* **134**: 249–56

Crow T J, Cross A J, Johnstone E C and Owen T 1982a, Two syndromes in schizophrenia and their pathogenesis. In F A Henn and H A Nasrallah (eds), *Schizophrenia as a Brain Disease*, New York: Oxford University Press: 196–234

Crow T J, Cross A J, Johnstone E C, Owen F, Owens D G C, Bloxham C, Ferrier I N, Macreadie R M and Poulter M 1982b, Changes in D2 Dopamine receptor numbers in post-mortem brain in schizophrenia in relation to the presence of the Type 1 syndrome and movement disorder. In R Collu *et al.* (eds) *Brain Peptides and Hormones* New York: Raven Press

Crow T J, Ferrier I N, Johnstone E C, MacMillan J F, Owens D G C, Parry R P and Tyrrell D A J 1979b, Characteristics of patients with schizophrenia or neurological disease and virus-like agent in cerebrospinal fluid, *Lancet* **1**: 842–44

Cullen C N, Hattersley J and Tennant L 1977, Behaviour modification: Some implications of a radical behaviourist view, *Bulletin of the British Psychological Society* **30**: 65–9

Curran J P, Jourd S and Whitman H 1968, Behaviour change techniques on a closed psychiatric unit, Unpublished manuscript, Anoka State Hospital, Anoka, Minnesota

Dalen P 1974, *Season of Birth: A Study of Schizophrenia and other Disorders*, Amsterdam: North Holland Publishing Co.

Damasio A R and Maurer R G 1978, A neurological model for childhood autism, *Archives of Neurology* **35**

Davidson G S and Neale J M 1974, The effects of signal-noise similarity on visual information processing of schizophrenics, *Journal of Abnormal Psychology* **83**: 683–6

Davis G C, Bunney W E, Buchsbaum M S *et al.* 1979, Use of narcotic antagonists to study the role of endorphins in normal and psychiatric patients. In E Usdin, W E Bunney, jnr and N S Kline (eds), *Endorphins in Mental Health Research*, London: MacMillan Press: 393–406

Davis K L, Hollister L E and Tepper J 1978, Cholinergic inhibition of Methylephenidate induced stereotypy with Oxotremorine, *Psychopharmacology* **56**: 1–4

Davis K L, Livesey J, Hollister L E and Berger P A 1979, Cerebrospinal fluid Acetylcholinesterase in psychosis and movement disorders. In K Davis and P A Berger (eds), *Brain Acetylcholine and Neuropsychiatric Disease*, New York: Plenum Publishing Corporation: 53–62

Davis K L, Hollister L E and Berger P A 1980, Choline chloride in schizophrenia, *American Journal of Psychiatry* **136**: 1581–3

Davis J M 1965, Efficacy of tranquillising and antidepressant drugs, *Archives of General Psychiatry* **13**: 552–72

Davis J M and Janowsky D 1975, Cholinergic and adrenergic balance in mania and schizophrenia. In E F Domino and J M Davis (eds), *Neurotransmitter Balances Regulating Behavior*, Ann Arbor: NPP Books: 135–48

Davis J R, Wallace C J, Liberman R P and Finch B F 1976, The use of brief isolation to suppress delusional and hallucinatory speech, *Journal of Behavior Therapy and Experimental Psychiatry* **7**: 269–75

Dawson M E and Neuchterlein K H 1984, Psychophysiological dysfunctions in the developmental course of schizophrenic disorders, *Schizophrenia Bulletin* **10**: 2, 204–32

Delay J and Deniker P 1952, Le traitment des psychoses par une methode neurolytique derivee d'hibernotherapie; Le 4560 RP utilise seul en cure prolongee et continuee, *Congres des Medicins Alienstes et Neurologistes de France et des Pays du Langue Francaise* **50**: 503–13

DeLisi L E, Neckers L M, Weinberger D R and Wyatt R J 1981, Increased whole blood serotonin concentrations in chronic schizophrenic patients, *Archives of General Psychiatry* **38**: 647–50

Dimond S J 1976, Depletion of attentional capacity after total commissurotomy in man, *Brain* **99**: 347–56

Dimond S J, Scammell R E, Pryce I G, Huws D and Gray C 1979, Callosal transfer and left-hand anomia in schizophrenia, *Biological Psychiatry* **14**: 735–9

Dimond S J, Scammell R E, Pryce I G, Huws D and Gray C 1980, Some failures on intermanual and cross-lateral transfer in chronic schizophrenics, *Journal of Abnormal Psychology* **89**: 505–9

Discipio W J, Glickman H and Hollander M A 1973, Social learning and operant techniques with hospitalized psychotics, *Proceedings of 81st Annual Convention of the American Psychological Association*: 453–4

Discipio W J and Trudeau P F 1972, Symptom changes and self-esteem as correlates of positive conditioning of grooming in hospitalized psychotics, *Journal of Abnormal Psychology* **80**: 244–8

Dohan F C 1966, Cereals and schizophrenia: Data and hypothesis, *Acta Psychiatrica Scandinavica* **42**: 125–52

Dohan F C 1976, The possible pathogenic effect of cereal grains in schizophrenia – Celiac disease as a model, *Acta Neurologica* **31**: 195–205

Dohrenwend B P and Egri G 1981, Recent stressful life events and episodes of schizophrenia, *Schizophrenia Bulletin* **1**: 12–24

Domschke W, Dickschas A and Mitznegg P 1979, CSF Beta-Endorphin in schizophrenia, *Lancet* **1**: 1024

Domino E F, Krause R R and Bowers J 1973, Various enzymes involved with putative neurotransmitters. Regional distribution in the brain of deceased mentally normal, chronic schizophrenic or organic brain syndrome patients, *Archives of General Psychatry* **29**: 195–201

Dunham W 1965, Community and schizophrenia: An epidemiological analysis, Detroit: Wayne State University Press

Durell J and Archer E G 1976, Plasma proteins in schizophrenia: A review, *Schizophrenia Bulletin* **2**: 147–159

Dvirskii A E 1976, Functional asymmetry of the cerebral hemispheres in clinical types of schizophrenia, *Neurosciences and Behavioural Physiology* **7**: 236–9

Eaton E M, Busk J, Maloney M P, Sloane R B, Whipple K and White K 1979, Hemisphere dysfunction in schizophrenia: Assessment by visual perception tasks, *Psychiatry Research* **1**: 325–32

Edelstein B and Eisler R M 1976, Effects of modeling and modeling with instructions and feedback on the behavioral components of social skills of a schizophrenic, *Behavior Therapy* **7**: 382–9

Edwards S and Kumar V 1984, A survey of psychotropic drugs in a Birmingham psychiatric hospital, *British Journal of Psychiatry* **145**: 502–7

Eisler R M, Blanchard E B, Fitts H L and Williams J G 1978, Social skills training with and without modelling for schizophrenic and nonpsychotic hospitalized psychiatric patients, *Behaviour Modification* **2**: 147–72

Eisler R M, Hersen M and Miller P M 1973, Effects of modeling on components of assertive behaviour, *Journal of Behavior Therapy and Experimental Psychiatry* **4**: 1–6

El-Islam M F 1979, A better outlook for schizophrenics living in extended families, *British Journal of Psychiatry* **135**: 343–7

El-Islam M F, Ahmed S A and Erfan M E 1970, The effect of unilateral ECT on schizophrenic delusions and hallucinations, *British Journal of Psychiatry* **117**: 447–8

Elliott F A 1969, The corpus callosum, cingulate gyrus, septum pellucidum, septal area and fornix. In P J Vinkent and G S Bruyn (eds), *Handbook of Clinical Neurology* **2**, New York: Elsevier/North Holland Biomedical Press: 758–65

Elliott P A, Barlow F, Hooper A and Kingerlee P E 1979, Maintaining patients improvements in a token economy, *Behaviour Research and Therapy* **17**: 355–67

Ellsworth J R 1969, Reinforcement therapy with chronic patients, *Hospital and Community Psychiatry* **20**: 36–8

Ellsworth R B, Collins J F, Casey N A, Schoonover R H, Hickey R H, Hyer L, Twemlow S W and Nesselroade J R 1979, Some characteristics of effective treatment programs, *Journal of Consulting and Clinical Psychology* **47**: 799–817

Emrich H M, Hollt V, Kissling W, Fischer M, Laspe H, Heinemann H, von Zerssen D and Herz A 1979, Beta-endorphin-like immunoreactivity in cerebrospinal-fluid and plasma of patients with schizophrenia and other neuropsychiatric disorders, *Pharmakopsychiatry Neuropsychopharmakology* **12**: 269–76

Erdelyi E, Elliot G R, Wyatt R J and Barchas J D 1978, S-Adenosylmethionine-dependent N-Methyltransferase activity in autopsied brain parts of chronic schizophrenics and controls, *American Journal of Psychiatry* **135**: 725–8

Erickson G and Gustafson G 1968, Controlling auditory hallucinations, *Hospital and Community Psychiatry* **19**: 327–9

Erlenmeyer-Kimling L 1968, Studies on the offspring of two schizophrenic parents. In D Rosenthal and S S Kety (eds), *The Transmission of Schizophrenia* New York: Pergamon Press

Erlenmeyer-Kimling L 1977, Issues pertaining to prevention and interaction in genetic disorders affecting human behaviour. In G W Albee and J M Joffe (eds), *Primary Prevention in Psychopathology*, New Hampshire: University Press of New England

Erlenmeyer-Kimling L, Cornblatt B, Friedman D, Marcuse Y, Rutschmann J, Simmens S and Devi S 1982, Neurological, electrophysiological and attentional deviations in children at risk for schizophrenia. In F A Henn and H A Nasrallah (eds), *Schizophrenia as a Brain Disease* New York: Oxford University Press: 61–98

Errickson E, Darnell M H and Labeck L 1978, Brief treatment of hallucinatory behavior with behavioral techniques, *Behavior Therapy* **9**: 663–5

Esser A H 1967, Behavioral changes in working chronic schizophrenic patients, *Diseases of the Nervous System* **28**: 433–40

Etevenon P, Pidoux B, Peron-Magnon P, Verdeaux G and Deniker P 1982,

Computerized EEG in schizophrenia and pharmacopsychiatry, *Electroencephelography and Clinical Neurophysiology* (supp. 1) **36**: 516–23

Etevenon P, Pidoux B, Rioux P, Peron-Magnon P, Verdeaux G and Deniker P 1979, Intra- and interhemispheric EEG differences quantified by spectral analysis, *Acta Psychiatrica Scandinavica* **60**: 57–80

Eysenck H J 1966, *The Effects of Psychotherapy* New York: International Science Press

Falloon I R, Boyd J L, McGill C W, Razani J, Moss H B and Gilderman A M 1982, Family management in the prevention or exacerbation of schizophrenia: A controlled study, *New England Journal of Medicine* **306**: 1437–40

Falloon I R and Liberman R 1983, Interactions between drug and psychosocial therapy in schizophrenia, *Schizophrenia Bulletin* **9(4)**: 543–54

Falloon I R and Talbot R E 1981, Persistent auditory hallucinations: Coping mechanisms and implications for management, *Psychological Medicine* **11**: 329–39

Falloon I R, Watt D C and Sheperd M 1978, A comparative controlled trial of Pimozide and Fluphenazine Decanoate in the continuation therapy of schizophrenia, *Psychological Medicine* **8**: 59–70

Famuyiwa O O, Eccleston D, Donaldson A A and Garside R F 1979, Tardive Dyskinesia and Dementia, *British Journal of Psychiatry* **135**: 500–4

Faris R E L and Dunham H N 1939, *Mental Disorders in Urban Areas* Chicago: University of Chicago Press

Farkas T 1980, Biochemical imaging of the brain, *A Presentation at the 35th Annual Convention of the Society of Biological Psychiatry* Boston Mass.

Feinberg I, Schizophrenia and late maturational changes in man, *Psychopharmacology Bulletin* **18**: 29–31

Feinsilver D B and Gunderson J G 1972, Psychotherapy for schizophrenics – Is it indicated?, *Schizophrenia Bulletin* **1**: 11–23

Feldberg W 1976, Possible association of schizophrenia with a disturbance in prostaglandin metabolism: A physiological hypothesis, *Psychological Medicine* **6**: 359–69

Ferreira A J and Winter W D 1965, Family interaction and decision making, *Archives of General Psychiatry* **13**: 214–23

Ferster C B 1967, Arbitrary and natural reinforcement, *Psychological Record* **17**: 341–7

Ferster C B 1974, The difference between behavioral and conventional psychology, *Journal of Nervous and Mental Diseases* **159**: 153–7

Field W and Ruelke W 1973, Hallucinations and how to deal with them, *American Journal of Nursing* **4**: 638–40

Finch B E and Wallace C J 1977, Successful interpersonal skills training with schizophrenic inpatients, *Journal of Consulting and Clinical Psychology* **45**: 885–90

Fischer E, Spatz H, Saavedra J M, Reggiani H, Miro A H and Heller B 1972, Urinary elimination of Phenethylamine, *Biological Psychiatry* **5**: 139–47

Fischer M, Harvald B and Hange M 1969, A Danish twin study of schizophrenia, *British Journal of Psychiatry* **115**: 981–90

Fish B 1975, Biological antecedents of psychosis in children. In D X

Freedman (ed), *Biology of the Major Psychoses* New York, Raven Press: 49–80

Fish B 1977, Neurobiologic antecedents of schizophrenia in children, *Archives of General Psychiatry* **34**: 1297–313

Fish B 1984, Offspring of schizophrenics from birth to adulthood. In N Watt, E J Anthony, L Wynne and J Rolf (eds), *Children at Risk for Schizophrenia: A Longitudinal Perspective* New York: Cambridge University Press

Fitts W H 1972, The self concept and psychopathology, Wallace Center Monograph IV. Nashville, Tennessee: Counsellor Recordings and Tests

Fleminger J J, Dalton R and Standage K F 1977, Handedness in psychiatric patients, *British Journal of Psychiatry* **131**: 448–52

Flor-Henry P 1969, Psychosis and temporal-lobe epilepsy: A controlled investigation, *Epilepsia* **10**: 365–95

Flor-Henry P 1976, Lateralised temporal limbic dysfunction and psychopathology, *Annals of the New York Academy of Science* **280**: 777–97

Flor-Henry P 1979, Laterality, shifts of cerebral dominance, sinistrality and psychosis. In J Gruzelier and P Flor-Henry (eds), *Hemisphere Asymmetries of Function in Psychopathology* Amsterdam: Elsevier/North Holland Biomedical Press: 3–19

Flor-Henry P 1981, The influence of gender on psychopathology, *Unpublished Manuscript*

Flor-Henry P 1983, Commentary and synthesis. In P Flor-Henry and J Gruzelier (eds), *Laterality and Psychopathology*, Amsterdam: Elsevier Science publishers: 1–18

Flor-Henry P, Fromm-Auch D and Schopflocher D 1983, Neuropsychological dimensions in psychopathology. In P Flor-Henry and J Gruzelier (eds), *Laterality and Psychopathology* Amsterdam: Elsevier Science Publishers: 59–82

Flor-Henry P and Gruzelier J (eds) 1983, *Laterality and Psychopathology* Amsterdam, Elsevier Science Publishers

Flor-Henry P, Koles Z J, Bo-Lassen P and Yeudell L T 1975, Studies of the functional psychoses: Power spectral EEG analyses (Abstract), *ICRS Medical Science* **3**: 87

Flor-Henry P, Koles Z J, Howarth B G and Burton L 1979, Neurophysiology studies of schizophrenia, mania and depression. In J Gruzelier and P Flor-Henry (eds), *Hemisphere Asymmetries of Function in Psychopathology* Amsterdam: North Holland Biomedical Press: 189–222

Fonagy P and Slade P 1982, Punishment vs. negative reinforcement in the aversive conditioning of auditory hallucinations, *Behaviour Research and Therapy* **20**: 483–92

Fraser D, Black D and Corckram L 1981, An examination of the effectiveness of instructional training and response cost procedures in controlling the inappropriate behaviour of male schizophrenic patients, *Behavioural Psychotherapy* **9**: 256–67

Frederiksen L W, Jenkins J O, Foy D W and Eisler R M 1976, Social skills training to modify abusive verbal outbursts in adults, *Journal of Applied Behavior Analysis* **9**: 117–25

Freedman D X, Belendiuk K, Belenduik G W and Crayton J W 1981,

Blood Tryptophan metabolism in chronic schizophrenics, *Archives of General Psychiatry* **38**: 655–9

Freeman H 1978, Pharmacological treatment and management. In J K Wing (ed), *Schizophrenia: Towards a New Synthesis* London: Academic Press

Freeman W and Williams J 1952, Human sonar: The amydaloid nucleus in relation to auditory hallucinations, *Journal of Nervous and Mental Disease* **116**: 456–62

Fremming K H 1951, The expectation of mental infirmity in a sample of the Danish population, *Occasional Papers on Eugenics* **7**: London: Cassell

Friedhoff A J and Van Winkle E 1962, Isolation and characterization of a compound from the urine of schizophrenics, *Nature* **194**: 897–8

Friedman D, Frosch A and Erlenmeyer-Kimling L 1979, Auditory evoked potentials in children at high-risk for schizophrenia. In H Begleiter (ed), *Evoked Brain Potentials and Behaviour* New York: Plenum Press

Friedman D, Vaughan Jr H G and Erlenmeyer-Kimling L (1980) The late positive complex to unpredictable auditory events in children at high risk for schizophrenia, *Psychophysiology* **17**: 310–11

Fromm-Reichmann F 1952, Some aspects of psychoanalytic therapy with schizophrenics. In E Brady and F C Bedlich (eds), *Psychotherapy with Schizophrenics* New York: International Universities Press

Furman W, Geller M, Simon S J and Kelly J A 1979, The use of a behavior rehearsal procedure for teaching job interviewing skills to psychiatric patients, *Behavior Therapy* **10**: 157–67

Galin D, Dimond R and Herron J 1977, Development of crossed and uncrossed tactile localisation of the fingers, *Brain and Language* **4**: 558–90

Garbutt J C and Van Kammen D P 1983, The interaction between GABA and Dopamine: Implications for schizophrenia, *Schizophrenia Bulletin* **9**: 336–53

Garmezy N 1966, The prediction of performance in schizophrenia. In P Hoch and J Zubin (eds), *Psychopathology of Schizophrenia* New York: Grune and Stratton: 129–81

Garmezy N 1978, Observations on high-risk research and premorbid development in schizophrenia. In L C Wynne, R L Cromwell and S Mattysse (eds), *The Nature of Schizophrenia* New York: John Wiley and Sons: 460–72

Gattaz W F, Waldmeler P and Beckmann H 1982, CSF Monoamine Metabolites in schizophrenic patients, *Acta Psychiatrica Scandinavica* **66**: 350–60

Gazzaniga M S 1974, Cerebral dominance viewed as a decision system. In S Dimond and J G Beaumont (eds), *Hemisphere Function in the Human Brain* London: Paul Elik

Geffan G 1976, Development of hemisphere specialisation for speech perception, *Cortex* **12**: 337–46

Gerner R H, Catlin D H, Gorelick D A, Hui K K and Li C H 1980, Beta-Endorphin: Intravenous infusion causes behavioural change in psychiatric inpatients, *Archives of General Psychiatry* **37**: 642–7

Gershone J R, Errickson E A, Mitchell J E and Paulson D A 1977, Behavioral comparison of a token economy and standard psychiatric treatment ward, *Journal of Behavior Therapy and Experimental*

Psychiatry **8**: 381–5

Gibbons J S, Horn S H, Powell J M and Gibbons J L 1984, Schizophrenic patients and their families: A survey in a psychiatric service based on a DGH Unit, *British Journal of Psychiatry* **144**: 70–7

Gillin J C, Kaplan J A and Wyatt R J 1976, Clinical effects of Tryptophan in chronic schizophrenic patients, *Biological Psychiatry* **11**: 635–9

Gillin J C, Stoff D M, Wyatt R J 1978, Transmethylation hypothesis: A review of progress. In M A Lipton, A Dimascio and K F Killam (eds), *Psychopharmacology: A Generation of Progress* New York: Raven Press: 1097–112

Giurgea C E and Moyersoons F 1979, The pharmacology of callosal transmission: A general survey. In I S Russell, M W Van Hoff and G Berlucchi (eds), *Structure and Function of Cerebral Commissures* London: The MacMillan Press Ltd: 283–98

Gjerde P F 1983, Attentional capacity dysfunction and arousal in schizophrenia, *Psychological Bulletin* **93**: 57–72

Glaister B 1985, A case of auditory hallucination treated by satiation, *Behaviour Research and Therapy* **23**: 231–5

Glick S D 1983, Cerebral lateralisation in the rat and tentative extrapolations to man. In M S Myslobodsky (ed), *Hemisyndromes: Psychobiology, Neurology, Psychiatry* New York: Academic Press: pp 7–26

Glickman H, Plutchik R and Laudau H 1973, Social and biological reinforcement in an open psychiatric ward, *Journal of Behavior Therapy and Experimental Psychiatry* **4**: 121–4

Goffman E 1961, *Asylums*, New York: Anchor Press, Doubleday

Goldberg E M and Morrison S L 1963, Schizophrenia and social class, *British Journal of Psychiatry* **109**: 785–802

Goldberg S C, Schooler N R, Hogarty G E and Roper M 1977, Prediction of relapse in schizophrenic outpatients treated by drug and social therapy, *Archives of General Psychiatry* **34**: 171–84

Golden C J, Graber B, Coffman J, Berg R A, Bloch S and Brogan D 1980a, Brain density defects in chronic schizophrenia, *Psychiatry Research* **3**: 179–84

Golden C J, Graber B, Coffman J, Berg R A, Newlin D B and Bloch S 1981, Structural brain defects in schizophrenia, *Archives of General Psychiatry* **38**: 1014–17

Golden C J, Moses J A, Zelazowski M A, Graber B, Zataz L M, Horvath T B and Berger P A 1980b, Cerebral ventricular size and neuropsychological impairment in young chronic schizophrenics, *Archives of General Psychiatry* **37**: 619–23

Goldsmith J B and McFall R M 1975, Development and evaluation of an interpersonal skill training program for psychiatric inpatients, *Journal of Abnormal Psychology* **84**: 51–8

Gomés-Schwartz B 1979, The modification of schizophrenic behavior, *Behavior Modification* **3**: 439–68

Gottesman I I and Shields J 1972, *Schizophrenia and Genetics: A Twin Study Vantage Point* New York: Academic Press

Gottesman I I and Shields J 1977, Obstetric complications and twin studies of schizophrenia: Clarifications and affirmations, *Schizophrenia Bulletin* **3**: 351–4

Gottesman I I and Shields J 1982, *Schizophrenia: The Epigenetic Puzzle*

Cambridge: Cambridge University Press

Gould L N 1948, Verbal hallucinations and activity of vocal musculature: An electromyographic study, *American Journal of Psychiatry* **105**: 367–72

Gould L N 1949, Auditory hallucinations and subvocal speech: Objective study in a case of schizophrenia, *Journal of Nervous and Mental Disease* **109**: 418–27

Gould L N 1950, Verbal hallucinations as automatic speech. Reactivation of dormant speech habit, *American Journal of Psychiatry* **107**: 110–19

Green P 1978, Defective interhemispheric transfer and schizophrenia, *Journal of Abnormal Psychology* **87**: 427–80

Green P 1985, Abnormal asymmetries of speech comprehension in psychotic and cerebral-lesioned patients. Unpublished Doctoral Thesis, England: University of Birmingham

Green P, Glass A and O'Callaghan M 1979, Some implications of abnormal hemisphere interaction in schizophrenia. In J Gruzelier and P Flor-Henry (eds), *Hemisphere Asymmetries of Function in Psychopathology* Amsterdam: Elsevier/North Holland Biomedical Press: 431–48

Green P and Preston M 1981, Reinforcement of vocal correlates of auditory hallucinations by auditory feedback: A case study, *British Journal of Psychiatry* **139**: 204–8

Green P, Hallett S and Hunter M 1983, Abnormal interhemispheric integration and hemispheric specialisation in schizophrenia and high-risk children. In P Flor-Henry and J Gruzelier (eds), *Laterality and Psychopathology* Amsterdam: Elsevier Science Publishers: 443–70

Green P and Kotenko V 1980, Superior speech comprehension in schizophrenics under monaural versus binaural listening conditions, *Journal of Abnormal Psychology* **89**: 339–408

Green W P and O'Callaghan M J 1980, Incompatible vocalisation as a means of reducing auditory hallucinations. Unpublished Manuscript, Department of Psychology, All Saints Hospital, Birmingham, England

Greenberg D J, Scott S B, Pisa A and Friesen D D 1975, Beyond the token economy: A comparison of two contingency programs, *Journal of Consulting and Clinical Psychology* **43**: 498–503

Gripp R F and Magaro P A 1974, The token economy programme in the psychiatric hospital: A review and analysis, *Behaviour Research and Therapy* **12**: 205–28

Gripp R F and Magaro P A 1971, A token economy programme evaluation with untreated control ward comparisons, *Behaviour Research and Therapy* **9**: 137–49

Gross G, Huber G and Schuttler R 1982, Computerised tomography studies on schizophrenic diseases, *Arch Psychiatr Nervenkr* **231**: 519–26

Gruzelier J H 1980, Cerebral laterality and psychopathology: Fact and fiction, *Psychological Medicine* **11**: 93–108

Gruzelier J H 1983, Conundrums in methods and theory in Laterality research. In P Flor-Henry and J Gruzelier (eds), *Laterality and Psychopathology* Amsterdam: Elsevier Science Publications: 19–28

Gruzelier J H and Flor-Henry P 1979, *Hemisphere Asymmetries of Function in Psychopathology* Amsterdam: Elsevier/North Holland Biomedical Press

Gruzelier J H and Hammond N V 1976, Schizophrenia: A dominant hemisphere temporal-limbic disorder?, *Research Communications in Psychology, Psychiatry and Behaviour* **1**: 33–72

Gruzelier J H and Hammond N V 1980, Lateralised deficits and drug influences on the dichotic listening of schizophrenic patients, *Biological Psychiatry* **15**: 759–79

Gruzelier J H, Mednick S and Schulsinger F 1979, Lateralised impairments in the WISC profiles of children at genetic risk for psychopathology. In J Gruzelier and P Flor-Henry (eds), *Hemisphere Asymmetries of Function in Psychopathology* Amsterdam: Elsevier/North Holland Biomedical Press: 105–10

Gulmann N C, Wildschiodtz G and Orbaek K 1982, Alteration of interhemispheric conduction through corpus callosum in chronic schizophrenia, *Biological Psychiatry* **17**: 585–94

Gunderson J G and Mosher L R 1975, The cost of schizophrenia, *American Journal of Psychiatry* **132**: 1437–40

Gur R E 1975, Conjugate lateral eye movements as an index of hemispheric activation, *Journal of Personality and Social Psychology* **31**: 751–7

Gur R E 1977, Motoric laterality imbalance in schizophrenia, *Archives of General Psychiatry* **34**: 33–7

Gur R E 1978, Left hemisphere dysfunction and left hemisphere overactivation in schizophrenia, *Journal of Abnormal Psychology* **87**: 226–30

Gutride M E, Goldstein A P and Hunter G F 1973, The use of modelling and role-playing to increase social interaction among asocial psychiatric patients, *Journal of Consulting and Clinical Psychology* **40**: 408–15

Hailey A M 1974, The new chronic psychiatric population, *British Journal of Preventative and Social Medicine* **28**: 180–6

Haley J 1968, Testing Parental instructions of schizophrenic and normal children, *Journal of Abnormal Psychology* **73**: 559–65

Halgren E, Squires N K, Wilson C L 1980, Endogenous potentials generated in the human hippocampal formation and amygdala by infrequent events, *Science* **210**: 803–5

Halgren E, Walter R D, Cherlow D G and Crandall P H 1978, Mental phenomena evoked by electrical stimulation of the human hippocampal formation and amygdala, *Brain* **101**: 83–117

Hall J N and Baker R D 1973, Token economy systems: Breakdown and control, *Behaviour Research and Therapy* **11**: 253–63

Hall J N, Baker R D and Hutchinson K 1977, A controlled evaluation of token economy procedures with chronic schizophrenic patients, *Behaviour Research and Therapy* **15**: 261–83

Hallett S E and Green P 1983, Possible defects of interhemispheric integration in children of schizophrenics, *The Journal of Nervous and Mental Disease* **171**: 421–5

Hallett S E and Quinn D A, Schizophrenia: The dis-integrated brain (In Submission)

Hallett S E, Quinn D and Hewitt J 1986, Defective interhemispheric integration and anomalous language lateralisation in children at risk for schizophrenia, *The Journal of Nervous and Mental Disease* **174**: 418–27

Hanson D R, Gottesman I I and Heston L L 1976, Some possible childhood indications of adult schizophrenia inferred from children of schizophrenics, *British Journal of Psychiatry* **129**: 142–54

369

Schizophrenia

Hanssen T, Heyden T, Sundberg I, Alfredsson G, Nyback H and Watterberg L 1980, Propranolol in schizophrenia: Clinical, metabolic and pharmacologic findings, *Archives of General Psychiatry* **37**: 685–90

Haracz J L 1982, The Dopamine hypothesis: An overview of studies with schizophrenic patients, *Schizophrenia Bulletin* **8**: 438–69

Harder D N, Strauss J S, Kokes R F, Ritzler B A and Gift T E 1980, Life events and psychopathology severity among first psychiatric admissions, *Journal of Abnormal Psychology* **89**: 162–80

Hare E H 1956, Mental illness and social conditions in Bristol, *Journal of Mental Science* **102**: 349–57

Hare E H, Price J and Slater E 1974, Mental disorder and season of birth: A national sample compared with the general population, *British Journal of Psychiatry* **124**: 81–6

Hare E and Price J S 1968, Mental disorder and season of birth: Comparison of psychosis with neurosis, *British Journal of Psychiatry* **115**: 533–40

Harrow M and Grossman L S 1984, Outcome in schizo-affective disorders: A critical review, *Schizophrenia Bulletin* **10**: 1, 87–108

Hartlage L C 1970, Subprofessional therapists' use of reinforcement versus traditional psychotherapeutic techniques with schizophrenics, *Journal of Consulting and Clinical Psychology* **34**: 181–3

Hartman L M and Cashman F E 1983, Cognitive-behavioural and psychopharmacological treatment of delusional symptoms: A preliminary report, *Behavioural Psychotherapy* **11**: 50–61

Harvey T K and Green P 1983, Effects of increased reward money, *Nursing Times* **79**: 58–60

Hatta T, Yamamoto M, Kawabata Y 1984, Functional differences in schizophrenia: Interhemispheric transfer deficit or selective hemisphere dysfunction, *Biological Psychiatry* **19**: 1027–36

Haug J O 1962, Pneumoencephalographic studies in mental disease, *Acta Psychiatrica Scandinavica* (suppl 165) **38**: 1–114

Hawk A B, Carpenter W T, Strauss J S 1975, Diagnostic criteria and 5-year outcome in schizophrenia: A report from the International Pilot Study of Schizophrenia, *Archives of General Psychiatry* **32**: 343–56

Haynes S T and Geddy P 1973, Suppression of psychotic hallucinations through time-out, *Behavior Therapy* **4**: 123–7

Heap R F, Boblitt W E, Moore C H and Hord J E 1970, Behavior-milieu therapy with chronic neuropsychiatric patients, *Journal of Abnormal Psychology* **76**: 349–54

Heath R G and Krupp I M 1967, Schizophrenia as an immunologic disorder: 1. demonstration of antibrain globulins by fluorescent antibody techniques, *Archives of General Psychiatry* **16**: 1–9

Helgosan T 1964, *Acta Psychiatrica Scandinavica* **40**: (supp 1, 73)

Helzer J E, Brockington I F, Kendell R E 1981, Predictive validity of DSM III and Feighner definitions of schizophrenia, *Archives of General Psychiatry* **38**: 791–7

Hemsley D R 1977, What have cognitive deficits to do with schizophrenic symptoms? *British Journal of Psychiatry* **130**: 167–73

Hemsley D R 1978, Limitations of operant procedures in the modification of schizophrenic functioning: The possible relevance of studies of

370

cognitive disturbance, *Behavioural Analysis and Modification* **2**: 165–73

Hermon J A F, Mirsky N F, Ricks N L and Gallant D 1977, Behaviour and electrographic measures of attention in children at risk for schizophrenia, *Journal of Abnormal Psychology* **86**: 27–33

Herrnstein R J 1966, Superstition: A corollary of the principles of operant conditioning. In W K Honig (ed), *Operant Behaviour: Areas of Research and Application* New York: Appleton-Century-Crofts

Hersen M 1976, Token economies in institutional settings: Historical, political, deprivation, ethical and generalization issues, *Journal of Nervous and Mental Disease* **162**: 206–11

Hersen M and Bellack A S 1976, A multiple baseline analysis of social skills training in chronic schizophrenics, *Journal of Applied Behavior Analysis* **9**: 239–45

Hersen M, Eisler R M and Miller P M 1974, An experimental analysis of generalization in assertiveness training, *Behaviour Research and Therapy* **12**: 295–310

Hersen M, Kazdin A E, Bellack A S and Turner S M 1979, Effects of live modelling, covert modelling and rehearsal on assertiveness in psychiatric patients, *Behaviour Research and Therapy* **17**: 369–77

Hersen M, Turner S M, Edelstein B A and Pinkston S G 1975, Effects of Phenothiazines and social skills training in a withdrawn schizophrenic, *Journal of Clinical Psychology* **31**: 588–94

Herz M I and Melville C 1980, Relapse in schizophrenia, *American Journal of Psychiatry* **137**: 801–5

Herz M I, Szymouski H V and Simon J C 1982 Intermittent medication for stable schizophrenic outpatients: An alternative to maintenance medication, *American Journal of Psychiatry* **139**: 918–22

Heston L L 1966, Psychiatric disorders in foster home reared children of schizophrenic mothers, *British Journal of Psychiatry* **112**: 819–25

Heston L L and Denny D 1968, Interactions between early life experience and biological factors in schizophrenia. In D Rosenthal and S S Kety (eds), *The Transmission of Schizophrenia*, Oxford: Pergammon Press: 363–76

Higgins J 1966, Effect of child rearing by schizophrenic mothers, *Journal of Psychiatric Research* **4**: 153–67

Hirsch S R and Leff J P 1975, *Abnormalities in Parents of Schizophrenics*, Maudsley Monograph No. 22, London: Oxford University Press

Hoffer A and Osmond H 1964, Treatment of schizophrenia with nicotinic acid: A ten year follow-up, *Acta Psychiatrica Scandinavica* **40**: 171–89

Hofner H and Reiman H 1970, In E H Hare and J K Wing (eds), *Psychiatric Epidemiology* London: Oxford University Press

Hogan T P, Awad A G, Eastwood R 1983, A self report scale predictive of drug compliance in schizophrenics: Reliability and discriminative validity, *Psychological Medicine* **13**: 177–83

Hogarty G E 1984, Depot neuroleptics, *Journal of Clinical Psychiatry* **45**: 36–42

Hogarty G E, Goldberg S C and Schooler N R 1974, Drug and sociotherapy in the aftercare of schizophrenic patients: II two year relapse rates, *Archives of General Psychiatry* **31**: 603–8

Hogarty G E and Katz M M 1971, Norms of adjustment and social behaviour, *Archives of General Psychiatry* **25**: 470–80

Hogarty G E, Schooler N, Ulrich R F, Mussare F, Ferro P and Herron E 1979, Fluphenazine and social therapy in the aftercare of schizophrenic patients: Relapse analyses of a two year controlled study of Fluphenazine Decanoate and Fluphenazine Hydrochloride, *Archives of General Psychiatry* **36**: 1283–94

Hogarty G E, Ulrich R F, Mussare F and Aristigetz N 1976, Drug discontinuation among long term, successfully maintained schizophrenic outpatients, *Diseases of the Nervous System* **37**: 494–500

Holden J M C, Itil T, Keskiner A and Gannon P 1971, A clinical trial of an antiserotonin compound, Cinanserin, in chronic schizophrenia, *Journal of Clinical Pharmacology* **11**: 220–6

Hollander M and Horner V 1975, Using environmental assessment and operant procedures to build integrated behaviors in schizophrenics, *Journal of Behavior Therapy and Experimental Psychiatry* **6**: 289–94

Hollingshead A B and Redlich F C 1958, *Social class and mental illness*, New York: John Wiley and Sons

Hollingsworth R and Foreyt J P 1975, Community adjustment of released token economy patients, *Journal of Behavior Therapy and Experimental Psychiatry* **6**: 271–4

Holmes T H and Rahe R H 1967, The social readjustment rating scale, *Journal of Psychosomatic Research* **11**: 213–18

Holzman P S and Levy D L 1977, Smooth pursuit eye movements in functional psychoses: A review, *Schizophrenia Bulletin* **3**: 15–27

Horn J M, Green M and Erickson M T 1975, Bias against genetic hypotheses in adoption studies, *Archives of General Psychiatry*, **32**: 1365–7

Horrobin D F 1977, Schizophrenia as a prostaglandin deficiency disease, *Lancet* **1**: 936–7

Horrocks P 1985a, Introduction In *National Health Service Health Advisory Service, Annual Report (June 1984–June 1985)* NHS Health Advisory Service, 29–37 Brighton Road, Sutton, Surrey, England

Horrocks P 1985b, Managers are failing to back up the professions (Interview), *Speech Therapy and Practice*, December 3

Ihezue U H and Kumaraswamy N 1984, A psychological study of Igbo schizophrenic patients treated at a Nigerian psychiatric hospital, *Acta Psychiatrica Scandinavica* **70**: 310–15

Inanaga K, Nakazawa Y, Inoue K, Tachibana H, Ochima M, Kotorii T, Tanaka M and Ogawa N 1975, Double-blind controlled study of L-Dopa therapy in schizophrenia, *Folia Psychiatrica et Neurologica Japonica* **29**: 123–43

Inglis J 1966, *The Scientific Study of Abnormal Behaviour*, New York: Aldine

Ingvar D H and Franzen G 1974, Abnormalities in cerebral blood flow distributions in patients with chronic schizophrenia, *Acta Psychiatrica Scandinavica* **54**: 425–62

Ingvar D H and Schwartz M S 1974, Blood flow patterns induced in the dominant hemisphere by speech and reading, *Brain* **97**: 273–88

Itil I M, Hsu W, Saletu B and Mednick S 1974, Computer EEG and auditory evoked potential investigations in children at high risk for schizophrenia, *American Journal of Psychiatry* **131**: 892–900

Iversen L L 1978, Biochemical and pharmacological studies: The dopamine hypothesis. In J K Wing (ed), *Schizophrenia: Towards a New Synthesis*, London: Academic Press: 89–116

Iversen L L 1982, Neurotransmitters and CNS disease: Introduction, *Lancet* **2**: 914–18

Jablensky A and Sartorius N 1975, Culture and schizophrenia, *Psychological Medicine* **5**: 113–24

Jackson D D 1960, A critique of the literature on the genetics of schizophrenia. In D D Jackson (ed), *The Etiology of Schizophrenia* New York: Basic Books

Jacob T 1975, Family interaction in disturbed and normal families: A methodological and substantive review, *Psychological Bulletin* **82**: 33–65

Jacobs S and Myers J 1976, Recent life-events and acute schizophrenic psychosis: A controlled study, *Journal of Nervous and Mental Disease* **162**: 75–87

Jacobs S, Prusoff B A and Paykel E S 1974, Recent life events in schizophrenia and depression, *Psychological Medicine* **4**: 444–53

Jaffe P G and Carlson P M 1976, Relative efficacy of modeling and instructions in eliciting social behavior from chronic psychiatric patients, *Journal of Consulting and Clinical Psychology* **44**: 200–7

James D A E 1983, The experimental treatment of two cases of auditory hallucinations, *British Journal of Psychiatry* **143**: 515–16

Janowsky D S, Segal D S and Bloom F 1977, Lack of effect of Naloxone on schizophrenic symptoms, *American Journal of Psychiatry* **134**: 926–7

Jeeves M A 1969, A comparison of interhemispheric transmission times in acallosals and normals, *Psychonomic Science* **16**: 245–7

Jernigan T L, Zatz L M, Moses Jr J A and Berger P A 1982, Computed tomography in schizophrenic and normal volunteers. 1: Fluid volume, *Archives of General Psychiatry* **39**: 765–70

Jeste D V, Doongaji D R, Panjwani D, Datta M, Potkin S G, Karoum F, Thatte S, Sheth A S, Apte J S and Wyatt R J 1981, Cross-cultural study of a biochemical abnormality in paranoid schizophrenia, *Psychiatry Research* **3**: 341–52

Johnson D A W 1976, The expectation of outcome from maintenance therapy in chronic schizophrenic patients, *British Journal of Psychiatry* **128**: 246–50

Johnson D A W 1977, Practical considerations in the use of depot neuroleptics for the treatment of schizophrenia, *British Journal of Hospital Medicine* **17**: 546–68

Johnson D A W 1985, Anti-psychotic medication: Clinical guidelines for maintenance therapy, *Journal of Clinical Psychiatry* **46**: 6–15

Johnson O and Crockett D 1982, Changes in perceptual asymmetries with clinical improvement of depression and schizophrenia, *Journal of Abnormal Psychology* **91**: 45–54

Johnstone E C, Crow T J, Frith C D, Husband J and Kreel I 1976, Cerebral ventricular size and cognitive impairment in chronic schizophrenia, *Lancet* **2**: 924–6

Johnstone E C, Crow T J and Mashiter K 1977, Anterior pituitary hormone secretion in chronic schizophrenia: An approach to neurohumoural mechanisms, *Psychological Medicine* **7**: 223–8

Johnstone E C, Cunningham D G, Owens A G, Crow T J and MacMillan J F 1981, Institutionalisation and the defects of schizophrenia, *British Journal of Psychiatry* **139**: 195–203

Johnstone E C, Owens D G C, Gold A, Crow T and Macmillan J F 1984, Schizophrenic patients discharged from hospital – A follow-up study, *British Journal of Psychiatry* **145**: 586–90

Jones G H and Miller J J 1981, Functional tests of the corpus callosum in schizophrenia, *British Journal of Psychiatry* **139**: 553–57

Jones I H and Frei D 1979, Seasonal births in schizophrenia: a southern hemisphere study using matched pairs, *Acta Psychiatrica Scandinavica* **59**: 164–72

Joseph M H, Baker H F, Johnstone E C and Crow T J 1976, Determination of 3-Methoxy-4-Hydroxy-Phenyl-Glycol conjugates in urine. Application to the study of central noradrenaline metabolism in unmedicated chronic schizophrenic patients, *Psychopharmacology* **51**: 47–51

Joseph M H, Owen F, Baker H F and Bourne R C 1977, Platelet Serotonin concentration and Monoamine Oxidase activity in unmedicated schizophrenic and in schizoaffective patients, *Psychological Medicine* **7**: 159–62

Kale R J, Kaye J H, Whelan P A and Hopkins B L 1968, The effects of reinforcement on the modification, maintenance and generalization of social responses of mental patients, *Journal of Applied Behavior Analysis* **1**: 307–14

Kalinowsky L B and Hoch P H 1952, *Shock Treatments, Psychosurgery and other Somatic Treatments in Psychiatry* (*2nd edition*) New York: Grune and Stratton

Kallman H J 1977, Asymmetry and monaurally-presented sounds, *Neuropsychologia* **15**: 833–6

Kane J M, Rifkin A, Woerner M 1983, Low dose neuroleptic treatment of outpatient schizophrenics, *Archives of General Psychiatry* **40**: 893–6

Kane J M and Smith J 1982, Tardive Dyskinesia: prevalence and risk factors 1959–1979, *Archives of General Psychiatry* **39**: 473–82

Karlsson J L 1966, *The Biological Aspect of Schizophrenia*, Springfield Ill: C. C. Thomas

Katz J (ed) 1978, *Handbook of Clinical Audiology* Baltimore: Williams and Wilkins

Katz M M 1963, Methods of measuring adjustment and social behaviour in the community I. Rationale, description, discriminative validity and scale development, *Psychological Reports* **13**: 503–35

Katz R C, Johnson C A and Gelfand S 1972, Modifying the dispensing of reinforcers: Some implications for behavior modification with hospitalized patients, *Behavior Therapy* **3**: 579–88

Kaur J 1984, Interhemispheric memory dysfunction in schizophrenia, Unpublished BSc Dissertation, University of Aston

Kazdin A E 1972, Non-responsiveness of patients to token economies, *Behavior Research and Therapy* **10**: 417–18

Kazdin A E 1973, The failure of some patients to respond to token programs, *Journal of Behavior Therapy and Experimental Psychiatry* **4**: 7–14

References

Kazdin A E 1975a, Recent advances in token economy research. In M
Hersen, R M Eisler and P Mitler (eds), *Progress in Behavior Modification* Vol. 1, New York: Academic Press

Kazdin A E 1975b, *Behavior Modification in Applied Settings* Homewood, Illinois, Dorsey Press

Kazdin A E 1977, *The Token Economy: A Review and Evaluation* New York: Plenum Press

Kazdin A E and Bootzin R R 1972, The token economy: An evaluative review, *Journal of Applied Behavior Analysis* 5: 343–72

Keith S J, Gunderson J G, Reifman A, Buchsbaum S and Mosher L R 1976, Special report: Schizophrenia, *Schizophrenia Bulletin* 2: 509–65

Kendler K S 1983, Overview: A current perspective on twin studies of schizophrenia, *American Journal of Psychiatry* 140: 1413–25

Kendler K, Gruenberg A, Strauss J 1981, An independent analysis of the Danish adopted study of schizophrenia, *Archives of General Psychiatry* 38: 982–4

Kendell R E 1975, *The Role of Diagnosis in Psychiatry* London: Blackwell

Kennedy T 1964, Treatment of chronic schizophrenia by behavior therapy: Case reports, *Behaviour Research and Therapy* 2: 1–6

Kessler S 1980, The genetics of schizophrenia: A review, *Schizophrenia Bulletin* 6: 14–26

Kessler P and Neale J M 1974, Hippocampal damage and schizophrenia: A critique of Mednick's theory, *Journal of Abnormal Psychology* 83: 91–7

Kety S S 1983, Mental illness in the biological and adoptive relatives of schizophrenia adoptees: Findings relevant to genetic and environmental factors in aetiology, *American Journal of Psychiatry* 140: 720–7

Kety S S, Rosenthal D, Wender P H and Schulsinger F 1971, Mental illness in the biological and adoptive families of adopted schizophrenics, *American Journal of Psychiatry* 128: 302–6

Kety S S, Rosenthal D, Wender P H, Schulsinger F and Jacobsen B 1975, Mental illness in the biological and adoptive families of adopted individuals who have become schizophrenic: A preliminary report based on psychiatric interviews. In R R Fieve, D Rosenthal and H Brill (eds), *Genetic Research in Psychiatry* Baltimore: John Hopkins University Press; pp 147–65

Kety S S, Rosenthal D, Wender P H, Schulsinger F and Jacobsen B 1978, The biological and adoptive families of adopted individuals who became schizophrenic: Prevalence of mental illness and other characteristics. In L C Wynne, R L Cromwell and S Matthysse (eds), *The Nature of Schizophrenia: New Approaches to Research and Treatment* New York: Wiley: 25–37

Kety S S, Woodford R B, Hormel M H, Freyhan F A, Appel K E and Schmidt C F 1948, Cerebral blood flow and metabolism in schizophrenia, *American Journal of Psychiatry* 104: 765–70

King D J, Cooper S J, Earle J A P, Martin S J, McFerran N V and Wisdom G B 1985, Serum and CSF antibody titres to seven common viruses in schizophrenic patients, *British Journal of Psychiatry* 147: 145–9

King G F, Armitage S G and Tilton J R 1960, A therapeutic approach to schizophrenics of extreme pathology: An operant-interpersonal method, *Journal of Abnormal and Social psychology* **61**: 276–86

King L W, Liberman R P, Roberts J and Bryan E 1977, Personal effectiveness: A structured therapy for improving social and emotional skills behaviour, *Behaviour Analysis and Modification*, **2**: 82–91

Kinney D K and Jacobsen B 1978, Environmental factors in schizophrenia: New adoption study evidence. In L C Wynne, R L Cromwell and S Matthyse (eds), *The Nature of Schizophrenia: New Approaches to Research and Treatment*, New York: Wiley: 38–51

Kinsbourne M 1972, Eye and head turning indicates cerebral lateralisation, *Science* **176**: 539–41

Kinsbourne M and Smith W L (eds) 1974, *Hemispheric Disconnection and Cerebral Dysfunction*, Illinois: Thomas

Klee W A, Ziodrou C and Streaty R A 1978, Exorphins-Peptides with opioid activity isolated from wheat gluten and their possible role in the etiology of schizophrenia. In E Usdin (ed), *Endorphins in Mental Health Research* New York: MacMillan Publishing Co

Klein D F and Davis J M 1969, *Diagnosis and Drug Treatment of Psychiatric Disorders* Baltimore: Williams and Wilkins

Kleinman J E, Weinberger D R, Rogol A D, Bigelow L B, Klein S T, Gillin J C and Wyatt R J 1982, Plasma prolactin concentrations and psychopathology in chronic schizophrenia, *Archives of General Psychiatry* **39**: 655–7

Knight J G 1982, Dopamine-receptor-stimulating autoantibodies: A possible cause of schizophrenia, *Lancet* **II**: 1073–6

Koh S D, Kayton L and Berry R 1973, Mnemonic organisation in young non-psychotic schizophrenics, *Journal of Abnormal Psychology* **81**: 299–310

Koh S D, Kayton L and Schwartz C 1972, Remembering of connected discourse by young non-psychotic schizophrenics, *Abstract Guide, Twentieth International Congress of Psychology* **407**

Kohn M L 1973, Social class and schizophrenia: A critical review and reformulation, *Schizophrenia Bulletin* **7**: 60–76

Kolb B and Wishaw I Q 1983, Performance of schizophrenic patients on tests sensitive to left or right frontal, temporal and parietal function in neurological patients, *The Journal of Nervous and Mental Disease* **171**: 435–43

Kowalski P A, Daley G D and Gripe R F, Token economy: Who responds how?, *Behaviour Research and Therapy* **14**: 372–4

Krasner L 1968, Assessment of token economy programmes in psychiatric hospitals. In R Porter (ed), *CIBA Foundation Symposium: The Role of Learning in Psychotherapy* London: Churchill Livingstone

Krasner L and Atthowe J M 1971, The token economy as a rehabilitative procedure in a mental hospital setting. In H C Richard (ed), *Behavioral Intervention in Human Problems* New York: Pergamon Press: 311–33

Kringlen E 1967, *Heredity and Environment in the Functional Psychoses* London: Heinemann

Kruse W 1959, Effect of Trifluoperazine on auditory hallucinations in schizophrenics, *American Journal of Psychiatry* **116**: 318–21

Kugler B T and Caudrey D J 1983, Phoneme discrimination in schizophrenia, *British Journal of Psychiatry* **142**: 53–9

Kugler B T, Caudrey D J and Gruzelier J H 1982, Bilateral auditory acuity of schizophrenic patients: Effects of repeated testing, time of day and medication, *Psychological Medicine* 12: 775–81

Kuipers L 1979, Expressed emotion: A review, *British Journal of Social and Clinical Psychology* 18: 237–53

Kuipers L, Sturgeon D, Berkowitz R and Leff J 1983, Characteristics of expressed emotion: Its relationship to speech and looking, *British Journal of Psychiatry* 22: 257–64

Kulhara P and Wig N N 1978, The chronicity of schizophrenia in North-west India: Results of a follow-up study, *British Journal of Psychiatry* 132: 186–90

Kurachi M, Kobayashi K, Matsubara R, Hiramatsu H, Yamagnchi N, Matsuda H, Maeda T, Hisardy K 1985, Regional cerebral blood flow in schizophrenic disorders, *European Neurology* 24: 176–81

Kuriansky J B, Deming W E and Gurland B J 1974, On trends in the diagnosis of schizophrenia, *American Journal of Psychiatry* 131: 402–8

Lagache D 1935, Les hallucinations verbal et le parole, *Psychological Abstracts* 9: 529

Laitinen L V 1972, Stereotactic lesions in the knee of the corpus calosum in the treatment of emotional disorders, *The Lancet* Feb. 26: 472–5

Lamb R and Goertzel V 1971, Discharged mental patients – Are they really in the community?, *Archives of General Psychiatry* 24: 29–34

Lambley D 1973, Behavior modification techniques and the treatment of psychosis: A critique of Alumbaugh, *Psychological Record* 23: 93–7

Lamontagne Y, Audet N and Elie R 1983, Thought-stopping for delusions and hallucinations: A pilot study, *Behavioural Psychotherapy* 11: 177–84

Langer G, Sachar E J, Gruen P H and Halpern F S 1977, Human prolactin responses to neuroleptic drugs correlate with antischizophrenic potency, *Nature* 266: 639–40

Lazarus R S 1966, *Psychological Stress and the Coping Process* New York: McGraw Hill

Lazarus R S, Averill J R and Opton E M 1970, Toward a cognitive theory of emotions. In M Arnold (ed), *Feelings and Emotions* New York: Academic Press

Leckman J F, Bowers M B and Sturges J S 1981, Relationship between estimated premorbid adjustment and CSF homovanillic acid and 5-hydroxyindoleacetic acid levels, *American Journal of Psychiatry* 138: 472–7

Lee J H, Lee Y J and Oh S W 1985, Schizophrenia and cerebral laterality, *Ann Acad Med (Singapore)* 14: 91–4

Leff J P 1982, *Psychiatry Around The Globe: A Transcultural View* Marcel Dekker Inc

Leff J P and Brown G W 1977, Family and social factors in the course of schizophrenia (letter), *British Journal of Psychiatry* 130: 417–20

Leff J P, Hirsch S R, Gaind R, Rohde P D and Stevens B C 1973, Life events and maintenance therapy in schizophrenia relapse, *British Journal of Psychiatry* 123: 659–60

Leff J P, Kuipers L, Berkowitz R, Eberlein-Vries R and Sturgeon D 1982, A controlled trial of social intervention of schizophrenic patients, *British Journal of Psychiatry* 141: 121–34

Leff J P, Kuipers L, Berkowitz R, Vaughn C and Sturgeon D A 1983, Life events, relatives 'expressed emotion' and maintenance neuroleptics in schizophrenic relapse, *Psychological Medicine* **13**: 799–806

Leff J P and Vaughn C 1980, The interaction of life events and relatives' expressed emotion in schizophrenia and depressive neurosis, *British Journal of Psychiatry* **136**: 146–53

Leff J P and Vaughn C 1981, The role of maintenance therapy and relatives' expressed emotion in relapse of schizophrenia: A two year follow-up, *British Journal of Psychiatry* **139**: 102–4

Leff J P and Wing 1971, Trial of maintenance therapy in schizophrenia *British Medical Journal* **III**: 559–604

Lehmann H, Vasavan Nair N P and Kline N S 1979, Beta-endorphin and naloxone in psychiatric patients: Clinical and biological effects, *American Journal of Psychiatry* **136**: 762–6

Leitenberg H, Wincze J, Butz R, Callahan E and Agras W 1970, Comparison of the effect of instructions and reinforcement in the treatment of a neurotic avoidance response: A single case experiment, *Journal of Behavior Therapy and Experimental Psychiatry* **1**: 53–8

LeMay M 1967, Changes in ventricular size during and after pneumoencephalography, *Radiology* **88**: 57–63

LeMay M 1976, Morphological cerebral asymmetries of modern man, fossil man, and non-human primates, *Annals of the New York Academy of Science* **280**: 349–66

LeMay M and Kido D K 1978, Asymmetries of cerebral hemispheres on computed tomograms, *Journal of Computer Assisted Tomography* **2**: 470–6

Lerner J, Nachson I and Carmon A 1977, Responses of paranoid and non-paranoid schizophrenics in a dichotic listening task, *Journal of Nervous and Mental Disease* **164**: 247–52

Lerner P, Goodwin F K, Van Kammen D P, Post R M, Major L F, Ballenger J C and Lovenberg W 1978, Dopamine-beta-hydroxylase in the cerebrospinal fluid of psychiatric patients, *Biological Psychiatry* **13**: 685–94

Levine F M and Fasnacht G 1974, Token rewards may lead to token learning, *American Psychologist* **29**: 816–20

Levit R A, Sutton S and Zubin J 1973, Event potential correlates of information processing in psychiatric patients, *Psychological Medicine* **3**: 487–94

Lewinsohn P M 1967, Characteristics of patients with hallucinations, *Journal of Clinical Psychology* **23**: 423

Lewis M S and Griffin P A 1981, An explanation for the season of birth effect in schizophrenia and certain other diseases, *Psychological Bulletin* **89**: 589–96

Liberman R P 1972, Reinforcement of social interaction in a group of chronic mental patients. In R D Rubin, H Fensterheim, J D Henderson and L P Ullmann (eds), *Advances in Behavior Therapy* New York: Academic Press

Liberman R P, Lillie F, Falloon I R H, Harpin R E, Hutchinson W and Stoute B 1984, Social skills training with relapsing schizophrenics: An experimental analysis, *Behaviour Modification* **8**: 155–79

Liberman R P, McCann M J and Wallace C J 1976, Generalization of behaviour therapy with psychotics, *British Journal of Psychiatry* **129**: 490–6

Liberman R P, Teigen J, Patterson R and Baker V 1973, Reducing delusional speech in chronic paranoid schizophrenics, *Journal of Applied Behavior Analysis* **6**: 57–64

Liberman R P, Wallace C J, Falloon I R H and Vaughn C E 1981, Interpersonal problem solving therapy for schizophrenics and their families, *Comprehensive Psychiatry* **22**: 627–30

Liberman R P, Wallace C J, Teigen J and Davis J 1974, Intervention with psychotic behaviors. In K S Calhoun, H E Adams and K M Mitchell (eds), *Innovative Treatment Methods in Psychopathology* New York: Wiley

Lidz T, Blatt S and Cook B 1981, Critique of the Danish-American studies of the adopted-away offspring of schizophrenic parents, *American Journal of Psychiatry* **138**: 1063–8

Lidz T, Hotchkiss G and Greenblatt M 1957, Patient-family hospital interrelationships: Some general considerations. In M Greenblatt, D Levinson and R Williams (eds), *The Patient and the Mental Hospital*, Glencoe. Ill.: The Free Press.

Lindsley O R 1960, Characteristics of the behavior of chronic psychotics as revealed by free-operant conditioning methods, *Diseases of the Nervous System Monograph Supplement* **21**: 66–78

Lindsley O R 1963 Direct measurement and functional definition of vocal hallucinatory symptoms, *Journal of Nervous and Mental Disease* **136**: 293–7

Lipinski J, Meyer R, Kornetsky C and Cohen B M 1979 Naloxone in schizophrenia: Negative result, *Lancet* **1**: 1292–3

Lipton R B, Levy D L, Holzman P S and Levin S 1983, Eye movement dysfunctions in psychiatric patients, *Schizophrenia Bulletin* **9**: 13–32

Lishman W A and McMeekan E R L 1976, Hand preference in psychiatric patients, *British Journal of Psychiatry* **129**: 158–66

Lishman W A, Toone B K, Colbourn C J, McMeekan E R L and Mance R M 1978, Dichotic listening in psychotic patients, *British Journal of Psychiatry* **132**: 333–41

Little L K 1966, Effects of the interpersonal interaction on abstract thinking performance in schizophrenics, *Journal of Consulting Psychology* **30**: 158–64

Lloyd K E and Abel L 1970, Performance on a token economy psychiatric ward: A two year summary, *Behaviour Research and Therapy* **8**: 1–9

Lloyd K E and Garlington W K 1968, Weekly variations in performance on a token economy psychiatric ward, *Behaviour Research and Therapy* **6**: 407–10

Logan D G and Deodhar S D 1970, Schizophrenia, an immunological disorder?, *Journal of the American Medical Association* **212**: 1703–4

Lowing P A, Mirsky A F and Pereira R 1983, The inheritance of schizophrenic spectrum disorders: A reanalysis of the Danish adoptive study data, *American Journal of Psychiatry* **140**: 1167–71

Luchins D J 1982, Computed tomography in schizophrenia: Disparities in the prevalence of abnormalities, *Archives of General Psychiatry* **39**: 859–60

Luchins D J, Weinberger D R and Wyatt R W 1979, Anomalous lateralisation associated with a milder form of schizophrenia, *American Journal of Psychiatry* **136**: 1598–9

Luchins D J, Weinberger D R and Wyatt R W 1982, Schizophrenia and cerebral asymmetry detected by computed tomography, *American Journal of Psychiatry* **139**: 753–7

Lukoff D, Snyder K, Ventura J and Neuchterlein K H 1984, Life events, familial stress and coping in the developmental course of schizophrenia, *Schizophrenia Bulletin* **10(2)**: 258–92

Lytton H 1977, Do parents create, or respond to, differences in twins?, *Developmental Psychology* **13**: 456–9

McCowan P and Wilder J 1976, *Lifestyle of 100 Psychiatric Patients*, Psychiatric Rehabilitation Association, 21a Kingsland High Street, London, England

McGuffin P 1979, Schizophrenics who wear ear-plugs, *British Journal of Psychiatry* **134**: 651

McGuigan F J 1966, Covert oral behaviour and auditory hallucinations, *Psychophysiology* **3**: 73–80

McKinney W T and Moran E C 1981, Animal models of schizophrenia, *American Journal of Psychiatry* **138**: 478–83

McNeil T F and Kaij L 1973, Obstetric complications and physical size of offspring of schizophrenic, schizophrenic-like and control mothers, *British Journal of Psychiatry* **123**: 341–8

McNeil T F and Kaij L 1978, Obstetric factors in the development of schizophrenia: Complications in the births of preschizophrenics and in reproduction by schizophrenic parents. In L C Wynne, R L Cromwell and S Matthysse (eds), *The Nature of Schizophrenia: New Approaches to Research and Treatment* New York: Wiley: 401–29

McReynolds W T and Coleman J 1972, Token economy: Patient and staff changes, *Behaviour Research and Therapy* **10**: 29–34

Machon R A, Mednick S A and Schulsinger F 1983, The interaction of seasonality, place of birth, genetic risk and subsequent schizophrenia in a high risk sample, *British Journal of Psychiatry* **143**: 383–8

Mackay A V P, Bird E D, Spokes E G, Rossor M, Iversen L L, Creese I and Snyder S H 1980, Dopamine receptors and schizophrenia: Drug effect or illness? *Lancet* **2**: 915–16

Maley R F, Feldman G L and Ruskin R S 1973, Evaluation of patient improvement in a token economy treatment program, *Journal of Abnormal Psychology* **82**: 141–4

Mann S A and Cree W 1976, 'New' long stay patients: A national sample of fifteen mental hospitals in England and Wales 1972–3, *Psychological Medicine* **6**: 603–16

Mantonakis J, Markidis M, Kontaxakis V and Liakos A 1985, A scale for detection of negative attitudes towards medication among relatives of schizophrenic patients, *Acta Psychiatrica Scandinavica* **71**: 186–9

Marcus J 1974, Cerebral functioning in offspring of schizophrenics. A possible genetic factor, *International Journal of Mental Health* **3**: 57–73

Marcus J, Auerbach J, Wilkinson L and Busack C M 1984, Infants at risk for schizophrenia: the Jerusalem infant development study. In N Watt, E J Anthony, L Wynne and J Rolf (eds), *Children at Risk for Schizophrenia: A Longitudinal Perspective* New York: Cambridge University Press

Margo A, Hemsley D R and Slade P D 1981, The effects of varying auditory input on schizophrenic hallucinations. *British Journal of Psychiatry* **139**: 122–7

Marin R S and Tucker G J 1981, Psychopathology and hemispheric dysfunction: A review, *The Journal of Nervous and Mental Disease* **169**: 546–57

Marks J, Sonoda B and Schalock R 1968, Reinforcement vs. relationship therapy for schizophrenics, *Journal of Abnormal Psychology* **73**: 397–402

Marzillier J S and Birchwood M J 1981, Behavioural treatment of cognitive disorders. In L Michelson, M Hersen and S M Turner (eds), *Future Perspectives in Behaviour Therapy*, New York: Plenum Press

Mathews R J, Duncan G C, Weinman M L and Barr D L 1982, Regional cerebral blood flow in schizophrenia, *Archives of General Psychiatry* **39**: 1121–4

Mathews R J, Meyer J S, Francis D J, Schooler J C, Weinman M and Mortel K F 1981, Regional cerebral blood flow in schizophrenia: A preliminary report, *American Journal of Psychiatry* **138**: 112–13

Matson J L and Zeiss R A 1978, Group training of social skills in chronically explosive, severely disturbed psychiatric patients, *Behavioural Engineering* **5**: 41–50

Matussek N, Ackenheil M, Hippus H, Muller F, Schroder H T, Schultes H and Wasilewski B 1980, Effect of clonidine on growth hormone release in psychiatric patients and controls, *Psychiatry Research* **2**: 25–36

May P R A 1974, Psychotherapy research in schizophrenia – Another view of present reality, *Schizophrenia Bulletin* **1**: 126–32

May P R A, Tuma A H, Yale C, Potepan P and Dixon W J 1976, Schizophrenia – A follow-up study of results of treatment: II Hospital stay over two to five years, *Archives of General Psychiatry* **33**: 481–6

Mednick B R 1973, Breakdown in high-risk subjects: Familial and environmental factors, *Journal of Abnormal Psychology* **82**: 469–75

Mednick S A 1970, Breakdown in individuals at high risk for schizophrenia: Possible predispositional perinatal factors, *Mental Hygiene* **54**: 50–63

Mednick S A and Schulsinger F 1965, A longitudinal study of children with a high risk for schizophrenia: A preliminary report. In S Vandenberg (ed), *Methods and Goals in Human Behaviour Genetics* New York: Academic Press: 255–96

Mednick A and Schulsinger F 1968, Some premorbid characteristics related to the breakdown of children with schizophrenic mothers. In D Rosenthal and S S Kety (eds), *The Transmission of Schizophrenia* New York: Pergamon Press: 267–92

Mednick S A and Schulsinger F 1973, A learning theory of schizophrenia: 13 years later. In M Hammer, K Salzinger and S Sutton (Eds), *Psychopathology: Contributions from Social, Behavioural and Biological Sciences* New York: John Wiley and Sons

Meichenbaum D H 1966, Effects of Social Reinforcement on the Level of Abstraction in Schizophrenics, *Journal of Abnormal and Social Psychology* **71**: 354–62

Meichenbaum D H 1969, The effects of instructions and reinforcement on thinking and language behavior of schizophrenics, *Behaviour Research and Therapy* **7**: 101–14

Meichenbaum D H and Cameron R 1973, Training schizophrenics to talk to themselves: A means of developing attentional control, *Behavior Therapy* **4**: 515–34

Meltzer H Y 1982, What is schizophrenia? *Schizophrenia Bulletin* **8**: 3, 433–4

Meltzer H Y, Busch D, So R, Holcomb H and Fang V S 1980a, Neuroleptic induced elevations in serum prolactin levels: Etiology and significance. In C Baxter and T Melnechuk (eds), *Perspectives in Schizophrenia Research* New York: Raven Press: 149–76

Meltzer H Y, Duncavage M B, Jackman H, Arora R C, Tricou B J & Young M 1982, Effect of neuroleptic drugs on platelet monoamine oxidase in psychiatric patients, *American Journal of Psychiatry* **139**: 1242–8

Meltzer H Y, Jackman H & Arora R C 1980b, Brain and skeletal muscle monoamine oxidase activity in schizophrenia, *Schizophrenia Bulletin* **6**: 208–12

Mertens G C and Fuller G B 1963, Conditioning of motor behaviour in 'regressed' psychotics. I: An objective measure of personal habit training with 'regressed' psychotics, *Journal of Clinical Psychology* **19**: 333–7

Meyers A, Mercatoris M and Sirota A 1976, Use of covert self-instruction for the elimination of psychotic speech, *Journal of Consulting and Clinical Psychology* **44**: 480–3

Miklowitz D J, Goldstein M J, Falloon I R H and Doane J A 1984, Interactional correlates of expressed emotion in families of schizophrenics, *British Journal of Psychiatry* **144**: 482–7

Mikulic M A 1971, Reinforcement of independent and dependent patient behaviors by nursing personnel: An exploratory study, *Nursing Research* **20**: 162–5

Milby J B, Pendergrass P E and Clarke C J 1975, Token economy versus control ward: A comparison of staff and patient attitudes toward ward environment, *Behavior Therapy* **6**: 22–9

Miller E 1983, A note on the interpretation of data derived from neuropsychological tests, *Cortex* **19**: 131–2

Milner P M 1971, *Physiological Psychology*, London: Holt, Rinehart and Winston

Milton F, Patwa V K and Hafner R J 1978, Confrontation vs belief modification in persistently deluded patients, *British Journal of Medical Psychology* **51**: 127–30

MIND 1980, *Mental Health Statistics* MIND, London

Mintz S and Alpert M 1972, Imagery vividness, reality testing and schizophrenic hallucinations, *Journal of Abnormal Psychology* **79**: 310–16

Mirdal G K M, Mednick S A, Scholsinger H and Teasdale T W 1974, Perinatal complications children of schizophrenic mothers, *Acta Psychiatric Scandinavica* **50**: 553–68

Mischel W 1968, *Personality and Assessment* New York: Wiley

Mischel W 1973, Towards a cognitive social learning reconceptualisation of personality, *Psychological Review* **80**: 252–83

Mitchell W S and Stoffelmayr B E 1973, Application of the Premack principle to the behavioral control of extremely inactive schizophrenics, *Journal of Applied Behavior Analysis* **6**: 419–23

Monakhov K 1981, A reflection of physiological mechanism or a programme of brain activity, *Advances in Biological Psychiatry* **6**: 5–11

Moniz E 1936, *Tentatives Opératories dans le Traitement de Certaines Psychoses* Paris: Masson

Morais J and Bertleson P 1973, Laterality effects in dichotic listening, *Perception* **2**: 107–11

Morais J and Darwin C J 1974, Ear differences for same-different reaction times to monaurally presented speech, *Brain and Language* **1**: 388–90

Morihisa J M, Duffy F H and Wyatt R J 1983, Brain electrical activity mapping (BEAM) in schizophrenic patients, *Archives of General Psychiatry* **40**: 719–28

Morley S 1987, Modification of Auditory Hallucinations: Distraction *vs* Attentuation, *Behavioural Psychotherapy* (in press)

Morstyn R, Duffy F H and McCarley R W 1983, Altered topography in schizophrenia, *Archives of General Psychiatry* **40**: 729–34

Moser A J 1974, Covert punishment of hallucinatory behavior in a psychotic male *Journal of Behavior Therapy and Experimental Psychiatry* **5**: 297–9

Moses J A, Cardellino J P and Thompson L L 1983, Discrimination of brain damage from chronic psychosis by the Luria-Nebraska neuropsychological battery: A closer look, *Journal of Consulting and Clinical Psychology* **15**: 441–9

Mosher L R, Pollin N and Stabenav J R 1971a, Families with identical twins discordant for schizophrenia, *British Journal of Psychiatry* **118**: 29–42

Mosher L R, Pollin N and Stabenav J R 1971b, Identical twins discordant for schizophrenia: Neurologic findings, *Archives of General Psychiatry* **24**: 422–30

Mumford S J, Lodge Patch I C, Andrews N and Wynder L 1975, A token economy ward programme with chronic schizophrenic patients, *British Journal of Psychiatry* **126**: 60–72

Murphy D L and Wyatt R J 1972, Reduced platelet monoamine oxidase activity in chronic schizophrenia, *Nature* **238**: 225–6

Murphy H B M 1978, Cultural influences on incidence, course and treatment response. In L C Wynne, R L Cromwell and S Matthysse (eds), *The Nature of Schizophrenia* New York: Wiley

Murphy H B M and Rahman A C 1971, The chronicity of schizophrenia in indigenous tropical peoples, *British Journal of Psychiatry* **118**: 489

Naber D, Pickar D, Post R M, Van Kammen D P, Waters R N, Ballenger J C, Goodwin F K and Bunney W E 1981, Endogenous opioid activity and beta-endorphin immunoreactivity in CSF of psychiatric patients and normal volunteers, *American Journal of Psychiatry* **138**: 1457–62

Nachmani G and Cohen B D 1969, Recall and recognition free learning in schizophrenics, *Journal of Abnormal Psychology* **74**: 511–16

Narasimhachari N, Baumann P, Pak H S, Carpenter W T, Zoochi A F, Hokanson L, Fujimori M and Himwich H E 1974, Gas chromatographic-mass spectrometric identification of urinary bufotenin and dimethyltryptamine in drug-free chronic schizophrenic patients, *Biological Psychiatry* **8**: 293–305

Nasrallah H A 1982, Laterality and hemisphere dysfunction in schizophrenia. In F A Henn and H A Nasrallah (eds), *Schizophrenia as a Brain Disease* New York: Oxford University Press: 273–94

Nasrallah H A 1985, The unintegrated right cerebral hemispheric consciousness as alien intruder: A possible mechanism for Schneiderian delusions in schizophrenia, *Comprehensive Psychiatry* 26: 273–82

Nasrallah H A, Bigelow L B, Rauscher F P and Wyatt R J 1979, Corpus callosum thickness in schizophrenia, *New Research Abstracts*, American Psychiatric Association, 132nd Annual Convention: 15

Nasrallah H A, Jacoby C G, McCalley-Whitters M and Kuperman S 1982a, Cerebral ventricular enlargement in subtypes of chronic schizophrenia, *Archives of General Psychiatry* 39: 774–7

Nasrallah H A, McCalley-Whitters M and Jacoby C G 1981b, Cerebral ventricular enlargement in young manic males, *Journal of Affective Disorders* 4: 15–19

Nasrallah H A, McCalley-Whitters M and Kuperman S 1982d, Neurological differences between paranoid and non-paranoid schizophrenia: Part I Sensory-motor lateralisation, *Journal of Clinical Psychiatry* 43: 305–6

Nasrallah H A, McCalley-Whitters M, Rauscher F P and Bigelow L B 1982c, Histopathology of the corpus callosum in early and late onset schizophrenia, *Proceedings of the Annual Meeting of the American Association for the Advancement of Science*, Washington D.C.

Nasrallah H A, Schroeder C, Keelor K and McCalley-Whitters M 1981a, Motoric lateralisation in schizophrenic males, *American Journal of Psychiatry* 138: 1114–15

Nasrallah H A, Tippin J, McCalley-Whitters M and Kuperman S 1982b, Neurological differences between paranoid and non-paranoid schizophrenia: Part 3, Neurological soft signs, *Journal of Clinical Psychiatry* 43: 310–12

National Health Service Health Advisory Service 1985, *Annual Report (June 1984–June 1985)* NHS Health Advisory Service, 29–37 Brighton Road, Sutton, Surrey, England

Neale J M 1971, Perceptual span in schizophrenia, *Journal of Abnormal Psychology* 77: 196–204

Neale J M and Oltmanns T F 1980, *Schizophrenia* New York: Wiley

Nelson G L and Cone J D 1979, Multiple-baseline analysis of a token economy for psychiatric patients, *Journal of Applied Behavior Analysis* 12: 255–71

Neuchterlein K H 1983, Signal detection in vigilance tasks and behavioural attributes among offspring of schizophrenic mothers and among hyperactive children, *Journal of Abnormal Psychology* 92: 4–28

Neuchterlein K H and Dawson M E 1984, Information processing and attentional functioning in the developmental course of schizophrenic disorders, *Schizophrenia Bulletin* 10(2): 160–203

Newlin D B, Carpenter B and Golden C J 1981, Hemisphere asymmetries in schizophrenia, *Biological Psychiatry* 16: 561–82

Niwa S-I, Hiramatsu K-I, Kameyama T, Saitoh O, Itoh K and Utena H 1983, Left hemisphere's inability to sustain attention over extended time periods in schizophrenia, *British Journal of Psychiatry* 142: 477–81

Nodder 1980, *Organisation and Management of Mental Illness Hospitals* DHSS, HMSO

Nydegger R V 1972, The elimination of hallucinatory and delusional behavior by verbal conditioning and assertive training: A case study, *Journal of Behavior Therapy and Experimental Psychiatry* 3: 225–7

O'Brien F and Azrin H H 1972, Symptom reduction by functional displacement in a token economy: A case study, *Journal of Behavior Therapy and Experimental Psychiatry* 3: 205–7

Oddy H C and Lobstein T J 1972, Hand and eye dominance in schizophrenia, *British Journal of Psychiatry* 120: 231–2

Odegard O 1974, Season of birth in the general population and in patients with mental disorder in Norway, *British Journal of Psychiatry* 125: 397–405

Offord D R 1974, School performance of adult schizophrenics, their siblings and age mates, *British Journal of Psychiatry* 125: 12–19

O'Leary D S 1980, A developmental study of interhemispheric transfer in children aged 5 to 10, *Child Development* 51: 743–50

Olson R P and Greenberg D J 1972, Effects of contingency-contracting and decision-making groups with chronic mental patients, *Journal of Consulting and Clinical Psychology* 38: 376–83

Osmond H and Smythies J 1952, Schizophrenia: A new approach, *The Journal of Mental Science* 98: 309–15

Owen F, Cross A J, Crow T J, Longden A, Poulter M and Riley G J 1978, Increased dopamine receptor sensitivity in schizophrenia, *Lancet* 11: 223–6

Palmour R, Ervin F, Wagemaker H and Cade R 1979, Characterisation of a peptide from the serum of psychotic patients. In E Usdin, W E Bunney Jr and N S Kline (eds), *Endorphins in Mental Health Research* London: Macmillan Press: 581–93

Pandey G N, Garver D L, Tamminga C, Ericksen S, Ali S R and Davis J M 1977, Postsynaptic supersensitivity in schizophrenia, *American Journal of Psychiatry* 134: 518–22

Panek M 1969, *Token Economies on a Shoestring: Successes and Failures*, Unpublished Research Report, Northern State Hospital, Sedro-Wooley, Washington

Panse 1936, Quoted in D Rosenthal 1970 *Genetic Theory and Abnormal Behaviour* New York: McGraw Hill

Parker G and Neilson M 1976, Mental disorder and season of birth. A Southern hemisphere study, *British Journal of Psychiatry* 129: 355–61

Parnes J, Schulsinger F, Teasdale T W, Schulsinger H, Feldman P M and Mednick S A 1982, Perinatal complications and clinical outcome within the schizophrenic, *British Journal of Psychiatry* 140: 416–20

Parrish E 1897, Hallucinations and illusions: A study of fallacious perception (quoted in Gould 1949)

Patterson R and Teigen J 1973, Conditioning and Post-Hospitalization Generalization of Non-delusional responses in a Chronic Psychotic Patient, *Journal of Applied Behavior Analysis* 6: 65–70

Pattison E M, DeFrancisco D, Wood P, Frazier H and Crowder J 1975, A psychosocial kinship model for family therapy, *American Journal of Psychiatry* 132: 1246–51

Paul G L 1969, Chronic mental patient: Current status – Future directions, *Psychological Bulletin* 71: 81–94

Paul G L and Lentz R J 1977, *Psychological Treatment of Chronic Mental Patients: Milieu vs Social Learning Programs* Cambridge Mass: Harvard Univeristy Press

Paykel E S 1978, Contribution of life events to causation of psychiatric illness, *Psychological Medicine* **8**: 245–53

Pearlson G D and Veroff A E 1981, Computerised tomographic scan changes in manic-depressive illness, *Lancet* **2**: 470

Peck D F and Thorpe G L 1971, Experimental foundations of token economies: A critique. Paper presented at 3rd Behaviour Modification Conference, Wexford, Ireland

Penfield W and Perot P 1963, The brain's record of auditory and visual experience, *Brain* **86**: 595–696

Phillips L 1953, Case history data and prognosis in schizophrenia, *Journal of Nervous and Mental Disease* **117**: 515–25

Pic'l A K, Magara P A and Wade E A 1979, Hemisphere functioning in paranoid and non-paranoid schizophrenia, *Biological Psychiatry* **14**: 891–903

Platt J J and Spivack G 1972, Problem-solving thinking of psychiatric patients, *Journal of Consulting and Clinical Psychology* **39**: 148–51

Pollack M, Levenstein S and Klein D F 1968, A three-year post-hospital follow-up of adolescent and adult schizophrenics, *American Journal of Orthopsychiatry* **38**: 94–109

Pollin W, Allen M G, Hoffer A, Stabenau J R and Hrubec Z 1969, Psychopathology in 15,909 pairs of veteran twins, *American Journal of Psychiatry* **7**: 597–609

Pollin W, Cardon P V, Kety S S 1961, Effects of amino acid feedings in schizophrenic patients treated with iproniazid, *Science* **133**: 104–5

Pollin N and Stabenav J R 1968, Biological psychological and historical differences in a series of monozygotic twins discordant for schizophrenia. In D Rosenthal and S S Kety (eds), *The Transmission of Schizophrenia* Oxford: Pergamon Press

Portnoff L A 1982, Schizophrenia and semantic aphasia: A clinical comparison, *International Journal of Neuroscience* **16**: 189–97

Post R M, Fink E, Carpenter W T & Goodwin F K 1975, Cerebrospinal fluid amine metabolities in acute schizophrenia, *Archives of General Psychiatry* **32**: 1063–9

Presly A S, Black D, Gray A, Hartie A and Seymour E 1976, The Token Economy in the National Health Service: Possibilities and Limitations, *Acta Psychiatrica Scandinavica* **53**: 258–70

Price J and Hopkinson G 1968, Monoamine oxidase inhibitors and schizophrenia, *Psychiatria Clinica* **1**: 65–84

Puente A E, Heidelberg-Sanders C and Lund N L 1982, Discrimination of schizophrenics with and without nervous system damage using the Luria-Nebraska neuropsychological battery, *International Journal of Neuroscience* **16**: 59–62

Pulkkinen E 1977, Immunoglobulins, psychopathology and prognosis in schizophrenia, *Acta Psychiatrica Scandinavica* **56**: 173–82

Pulver A E, Sawyer J W and Childs B 1981, The association between season of birth and the risk for schizoprenia, *American Journal of Epidemiology* **114**: 735–49

Pulver A E, Stewart W, Carpenter W T and Childs B 1983, Risk factors in schizophrenia: Seasons of birth in Maryland, USA, *British Journal of Psychiatry* **143**: 389–96

Purves M J 1972, *The Physiology of Cerebral Circulation* London: Cambridge University Press

Rabkin J G 1980, Stressful life events and schizophrenia: A review of the research literature, *Psychological Bulletin* **87 (2)**:408–25

Randall P L 1980, A neuroanatomical theory on the aetiology of schizophrenia, *Medical Hypotheses* **6**: 645–58

Randall P L 1983, Schizophrenia, abnormal connection and brain evolution, *Medical Hypotheses* **10**: 247–80

Rasmussen T and Milner B 1975, Clinical and surgical studies of the cerebral speech areas in man. In K J Zulch, O Creutzfeldt and G C Galbraith (eds), *Cerebral Localisation* Berlin: Springer-Verlag

Ravensborg M R 1972, An operant conditioning approach to increasing interpersonal awareness among chronic schizophrenics, *Journal of Clinical Psychology* **28**: 411–13

Reisine T D, Rossor M, Spokes E, Iversen L L & Yamamura H I 1980, Opiate and neuroleptic receptor alterations in human schizophrenic brain tissue, *Advances in Biochemical Psychopharmacology* **21**: 443–50

Reveley A M, Reveley M A and Murray R M 1984, Cerebral ventricular enlargement in non-genetic schizophrenia: A controlled fourth study, *British Journal of Psychiatry* **144**: 89–93

Reveley A M, Reveley M A, Clifford C A and Murray R M 1982, Cerebral ventricular size in twins discordant for schizophrenia, *Lancet* **i**: 540–1

Reveley M A, Glover V, Sandler M and Spokes E G 1981, Brian monoamine oxidase activity in schizophrenics and controls, *Archives of General Psychiatry* **38**: 663–5

Reynolds G P, Ruthven C R J, Goodwin B L and Sandler M 1979, Phenylethylamine, a putative dopaminergic agonist: its possible role in the pathogenesis of schizophrenia. In E Usdin, I J Kopin and J D Barchas (eds), *Catecholamines: Basic and Clinical Frontiers Vol. 2* New York: Pergamon Press: 1854–6

Reynolds G P, Riederer P, Jellinger K and Gabriel E 1981, Dopamine receptors and schizophrenia: The neuroleptic drug problem, *Neuropharmacology* **20**: 1319–20

Rezin V A, Elliott P A and Paschalis P 1983, Nurse-patient interaction in a token economy, *Behavioural Psychotherapy* **11**: 225–34

Ribes-Inesta E, Duran L, Evans B, Felix G, Rivera G and Sanchez S 1973, An experimental evaluation of tokens as conditioned reinforcers in retarded children, *Behaviour Research and Therapy* **11**: 125–8

Richardson R, Karkalas Y, Lal H 1972, Application of operant procedures in treatment of hallucinations in chronic psychotics. In R D Rubin, H Fensterheim, J D Henderson and L P Ullmann (eds), *Advances in Behaviour Therapy* New York: Academic Press: 147–50

Rickard H C, Dignam P J and Horner R F 1960, Verbal manipulation in a psychotherapeutic relationship, *Journal of Clinical Psychology* **16**: 364–7

Rieder R O, Rosenthal D, Wender P and Blumenthal H 1975, The offspring of schizophrenics, *Archives of General Psychiatry* **32**: 200–11

Rinquette E L and Kennedy T 1966, An experimental study of the double-bind hypothesis, *Journal of Abnormal Psychology* **71**: 136–41

Risberg J, Halsey J H, Wills E L and Wilson E M 1975, Hemisphere specialisation in normal man studied by bilateral measurements of the regional cerebral blood flow. A study with the 133-Xe inhalation technique, *Brain* **98**: 511–24

Ritzler B and Rosenbaum G 1974, Bilateral transfer of inhibition in the motor learning of schizophrenics and normals, *Journal of Motor Behaviour* **6**: 205–15

Roberts E 1972, An hypothesis suggesting that there is a defect in the GABA system in schizophrenia, *Neurosciences Research Program Bulletin* **10**: 468–81

Roberts E 1976, Disinhibition as an organising principle in the nervous system – The role of the GABA system. Application to neurologic and psychiatric disorder. In E Roberts, T Chase and D Tower (eds), *GABA in Nervous System Function* New York: Raven Press: 515–39

Rodnight R, Murray R M, Oon M C H, Brockington I F, Nicholls P and Birley J L T 1976, Urinary dimethyltryptamine and psychiatric symptomatology and classification, *Psychological Medicine* **6**: 649–57

Rogers C R, Gendlin G T, Kiesler D V and Truax C B 1967, *The Therapeutic Relationship and its Impact: A Study of Psychotherapy with Schizophrenics* Madison: University of Wisconsin Press

Rosen A J, Tureff S E, Davona J H, Johnson P B, Lyons J S and Davis J M 1980, Pharmacotherapy of schizophrenia and affective disorders, *Journal of Abnormal Psychology* **89**: 373–89

Rosen J N 1946, A method of resolving acute catatonic excitement, *Psychiatric Quarterly* **20**: 183–98

Rosenthal D 1970, *Genetic Theory and Abnormal Behaviour* New York: McGraw-Hill

Rosenthal D 1975, Discussion: The concept of schizophrenic disorders. In R R Fieve, D Rosenthal and H Brill (eds), *Genetic Research in Psychiatry*, Baltimore: John Hopkins University Press: 199–208

Rosenthal D, Wender P H, Kety S S, Schulsinger F, Welner J and Ostergaard L 1968, Schizophrenics' offspring reared in adoptive homes. In D Rosenthal and S S Kety (eds), *The Transmission of Schizophrenia* Oxford: Pergamon Press: 377–91

Rosenthal D, Wender P H, Kety S S, Schulsinger F, Welner J and Reider R 1975, Parent-child relationships and psychopathological disorder in the child, *Archives of General Psychiatry*, **32**: 466–76

Rosenthal R and Bigelow L B 1972, Quantitative measurements in chronic schizophrenia, *British Journal of Psychiatry* **121**: 259–64

Rosenthal R and Bigelow L G 1973, The effects of Physostigmine in Phenothiazine resistant chronic schizophrenic patients: Preliminary observations, *Comprehensive Psychiatry* **14**: 489–95

Rosensweig M R 1951, Representation of the two ears at the auditory cortex, *American Journal of Physiology* **167**: 147–58

Ross E D and Mesuram M M 1979, Dominant language functions of the right hemisphere? Prosody and emotional gesturing, *Archives of Neurology* **36**: 144–8

Roth W T and Cannon E H 1972, Some features of the auditory evoked response in schizophrenia, *Archives of General Psychiatry* **27**: 466–71

Rotrosen J, Angrist B, Gershon S, Paquin J, Branchey L, Oleshansky M, Halpern F & Sachar E J 1979, Neuroendocrine effects of apomorphine: Characterization of response patterns and application to schizophrenia research, *British Journal of Psychiatry* **135**: 444–56

Rotrosen J, Miller A D, Mandio D, Traficante L J and Gershon S 1980, Prostaglandins, platelets and schizophrenia, *Archives of General Psychiatry* **37**: 1047–54

Royal College of Psychiatrists 1980, *Psychiatric Rehabilitation in the 1980s. Report of Working Party*, Royal College of Psychiatrists: London

Rutner I T and Bugle C 1969, An experimental procedure for the modification of psychotic behavior, *Journal of Consulting and Clinical Psychology* **33**: 651–3

Rutter M and Brown G W 1966, The reliability and validity of measures of family life and relationships in families containing a psychiatric patient, *Social Psychiatry* **1**: 38–53

Saitoh O, Hiramatsu K-I, Niwa S-I, Kameyama T and Itoh K 1983, Abnormal ERP findings in schizophrenia with special regards to dichotic detection tasks. In P Flor-Henry and J Gruzelier (eds), *Laterality and Psychopathology*, Amsterdam: Elsevier Science Publishers: 379–94

Sakel M 1938, The pharmacological shock treatment of schizophrenia, *Nervous and Mental Disease Monograph* **62**

Salamy A 1978, Commissural transmission: Maturational changes in humans, *Science* **200**: 1409–11

Saletu B, Saletu M, Itil T and Jones J 1976a, Somatosensory evoked potential changes during thioxthixene treatment in schizophrenic patients, *Psychopharmacologia* **20**: 242–52

Saletu B, Saletu M, Itil T and Jones J 1976b, Somatosensory evoked potential changes during haloperidol treatment of chronic schizophrenics, *Biological Psychiatry* **3**: 299–307

Salokanges R K R 1983, Prognostic implications of the sex of schizophrenic patients, *British Journal of Psychiatry* **142**: 145–51

Salzinger K 1968, Behavior theory models of abnormal behaviour. Paper Read at the Biometrics Research Workshop on Objective Indicators of Psychopathology, Sterling Forest Conference Centre, Tuxedo, New York

Salzinger K 1973, *Schizophrenia: Behavioural Aspects* New York: Wiley

Salzman L F and Kelin R H 1978, Habituation and conditioning of electrodermal responses in high risk children, *Schizophrenia Bulletin* **4**: 210–22

Samaan N 1975, Thought-stopping and flooding in a case of hallucinations, obsessions and homicidal-suicidal behaviour, *Journal of Behavior Therapy and Experimental Psychiatry* **6**: 65–7

Sameroff A J and Chandler M J 1975, Reproductive risk and the continuum of caretaker casualty. In F D Horowitz, M Hetherington, S Scarr-Salapatek and G Siegel (eds), *Review of Child Development Research* **4**: Chicago: University Press

Sandler M and Reynolds G P 1976, Does phenylethylamine cause schizophrenia?, *Lancet* **1**: 70–1

Sanson-Fisher R W, Poole A D and Thomson V 1979, Behaviour patterns within a general hospital psychiatric unit: An observational study, *Behaviour Research and Therapy* **17**: 317–32

Satz P 1979, A test of some models of hemispheric speech organisation in the left and right handed, *Science* **203**: 1131–3

Scarone S, Gambini O and Pieri E 1983, Dominant hemisphere dysfunction in chronic schizophrenia: Schwartz test and short aphasia screening test. In P Flor-Henry and J Gruzelier (eds), *Laterality and Psychopathology* Amsterdam: Elsevier Science Publishers: 129–42

Scarr S, Carter and Saltzman L 1979, Twin method: Defence of a critical assumption, *Behaviour Genetics* **9**: 527–42

Schaeffer H H and Martin P L 1966, Behavioural therapy for 'apathy' of hospitalised schizophrenics, *Psychological Reports* **19**: 1147–58

Scheibel A, and Kovelman J 1981, Disorientation of the hippocampal pyramidal cell and its processes in the schizophrenic patient, *Biological Psychiatry* **16**: 101–2

Schneider K 1959, *Clinical Psychopathology* New York: Grune and Stratton,

Schneider S J 1976, Selective attention in schizophrenia, *Journal of Abnormal Psychology* **85**: 167–73

Schulsinger H 1976, A ten-year follow-up of children of schizophrenic mothers: clinical assessment, *Acta Psychiatrica Scandinavica* **53**: 371–90

Schultz S C, Van Kammen D P, Barlow J E, Flye M W and Bunney W E Jr 1981, Dialysis in schizophrenia: a double blind study, *Science* **211**: 1066–8

Schwartz C C and Myers J K 1977, Life events and schizophrenia: I. Comparison of schizophrenics with a community sample, *Archives of General Psychiatry* **34**: 1238–41

Schwartz S 1978, *Language and Cognition in Schizophrenia* Lawrence Erlbaum Associates

Schweitzer L 1979, Differences of cerebral lateralisation among schizophrenic and depressed patients, *Biological Psychiatry* **14**: 721–33

Schweitzer L 1982, Evidence of right cerebral hemisphere dysfunction in schizophrenic patients with left hemisphere dysfunction, *Biological Psychiatry* **17**: 655–73

Schweitzer L, Becker E and Welsh H 1978, Abnormalities of cerebral lateralisation in schizophrenic patients, *Archives of General Psychiatry* **35**: 982

Sedvall G C and Wode-Helgodt B 1980, Aberrant monoamine metabolite levels in CSF and family history of schizophrenia: Their relationships in schizophrenic patients, *Archives of General Psychiatry* **37**: 1113–16

Seeman P and Lee T 1975, Antipsychotic drugs: Direct correlation between clinical potency of presynaptic action on dopamine neurons, *Science* **188**: 1217–9

Seidman L J 1983, Schizophrenia and brain dysfunction; An integration of recent neurodiagnostic findings, *Psychological Bulletin* **94**: 195–238

Selnes D A 1974, The corpus callosum: Some anatomical and functional considerations with special reference to language, *Brain and Language* **1**: 111–39

Serban G S 1975, Stress in normals and schizophrenics, *British Journal of Psychiatry* **126**: 397–407

Serber M and Nelson P 1971, The ineffectiveness of systematic desensitization and assertive training in hospitalised schizophrenics, *Journal of Behavior Therapy and Experimental Psychiatry* 2: 107–9

Shagass C 1977, Twisted thoughts – Twisted brainwaves? In L C Shagass, S Gershon and A J Friedhoff (eds), *Psychopathology and Brian Dysfunction* New York: Raven Press: 353–78

Shagass C, Roemer R A and Straumanis J J 1983, Evoked potential studies of topographic correlates of psychopathology. In P Flor-Henry and J Gruzelier (eds), *Laterality and Psychopathology* Amsterdam, Elsevier Science Publishers: 395–408

Shagass C, Roemer R A, Straumanis J J and Amadeo M 1979, Evoked potential evidence of lateralised hemispheric dysfunction in the psychoses. In J Gruzelier and P Flor-Henry (eds), *Hemisphere Asymmetries of Function in Psychopathology*. Amsterdam: Elsevier/North Holland Biomedical Press: 293–316

Shapiro A K 1971, Placebo effects in medicine, psychotherapy and psychoanalysis. In A E Bergin and S L Garfield (eds), *Handbook of Psychotherapy and Behavior Change: An Empirical Analysis* New York: J. Wiley and Sons: 439–73

Sharan S N 1966, *Journal of Abnormal Psychology* 71: 345–53

Shaw J C, Brookes S, Colter N and O'Connor K P 1979, A comparison of schizophrenic and neurotic patients using EEG power and coherence spectra. In J Gruzelier and P Flor-Henry (eds), *Hemisphere Asymmetries of Function in Psychopathology* Amsterdam: Elsevier/North Holland Biomedical Press: 257–84

Shean G D and Zeidberg Z 1971, Token reinforcement therapy: A comparison of matched groups, *Journal of Behavior Therapy and Experimental Psychiatry* 2: 95–105

Sheppard G J 1981, O[15] positron emission tomography in schizophrenia, *Paper Presented at the Second International Conference on Laterality and Psychopathology* Banff, Alberta, Canada

Shepherd G W 1977, Social skills training: The generalization problem, *Behavior Therapy* 8: 1008–9

Shepherd G W 1978, Social skills training. The generalization problem – some further data, *Behaviour Research and Therapy* 16: 287–8

Shepherd G W 1984, *Institutional Care and Rehabilitation* London: Longman

Sherman J A 1965, Use of reinforcement and imitation to reinstate verbal behavior in mute psychotics, *Journal of Abnormal Psychology* 70 155–64

Shields J 1978, Genetics. In J K Wing (ed), *Schizophrenia: Towards a New Synthesis* London: Academic Press: 53–88

Shields J, Heston L L and Gottesman I I 1975, Schizophrenia and the schizoid: The problem for genetic analysis. In R R Fieve, D Rosenthal and H Brill (eds), *Genetic Research in Psychiatry*, Baltimore: John Hopkins University Press: 167–97

Shimura M, Nakamwa I and Mivra T 1977, Season of birth of schizophrenics in Tokyo, Japan, *Acta Psychiatrica Scandinavica* 55: 275–82

Shur E 1982, Season of birth and high and low genetic risk schizophrenics, *British Journal of Psychiatry* 140: 410–15

Shur E and Hare E 1983, Age prevalence and the season of birth effect in schizophrenia: a response to Lewis and Griffin, *Psychological Bulletin* **93**: 373–7

Siegal J M 1975, Successful systematic desensitization of a chronic schizophrenic patient, *Journal of Behavior Therapy and Experimental Psychiatry* **6**: 345–6

Silverstein M L and Meltzer H Y 1983, Neuropsychological dysfunction in the major psychoses: Relation to premorbid adjustment and social class. In P Flor-Henry and J Gruzelier (eds), *Laterality and Psychopathology* Amsterdam: Elsevier Science Publishers: 143–52

Simons R F 1982, Physical anhedonia and future psychopathology: an electrocortical continuity?, *Psychophysiology* **19**: 433–41

Singer M T and Wynne L C 1963, Differentiating characteristics of parents of childhood schizophrenics, childhood neurotics and young adult schizophrenics, *American Journal of Psychiatry* **120**: 234–43

Slade P D 1972, The effects of systematic desensitization on auditory hallucinations, *Behaviour Research and Therapy* **10**: 85–91

Slade P D 1973, The psychological investigation and treatment of auditory hallucinations: A second case report, *British Journal of Medical Psychology* **46**: 293–6

Slade P D 1974, The external control of auditory hallucinations: An information theory analysis, *British Journal of Social and Clinical Psychology* **13**: 73–9

Slade P D 1975, Unpublished Case Study Cited in Slade 1976(b) op. cit.

Slade P D 1976a, Editorial: hallucinations, *Psychological Medicine* **6**: 7–13

Slade P D 1976b, Towards a theory of auditory hallucinations: Outline of an hypothetical four-factor model, *British Journal of Social and Clinical Psychology* **15**: 415–23

Slade P D 1976c, An investigation of psychological factors involved in the predisposition to auditory hallucinations, *Psychological Medicine* **6**: 123–32

Slater E and Beard A W 1963, The schizophrenia-like psychoses of epilepsy I. Psychiatric aspects, *British Journal of Psychiatry* **109**: 95–150

Slater E and Cowie V 1971, *The Genetics of Mental Disorders* London: Oxford University Press

Smith C 1970, Heritability of liability and concordance in monozygous twins, *Annals of Human Genetics* **34**: 578–88

Smith C 1971, Discriminating between different modes of inheritance in genetic disease, *Clinical Genetics* **2**: 303–14

Snyder S H 1982, Neurotransmitters and CNS disease: Schizophrenia, *Lancet* **2**: 970–4

Sokoloff L 1977, Relation between physiological function and energy metabolism in the central nervous system, *Journal of Neurochemistry* **29**: 13–26

Sokolovsky J, Cohen C, Berger D and Geiger J 1978, Personal networks of ex-mental patients in a Manhatten SRO hotel, *Human Organisation* **37**: 5–15

Sparks R and Geschwind N 1968, Dichotic listening in man after section of the neocortical commissures, *Cortex* **4**: 3–16

Spitzer R L and Fleiss J L 1979, A re-analysis of the reliability of psychiatric diagnosis, *British Journal of Psychiatry* **125**: 341–7

Spivack G, Platt J J and Shure M B 1976, *The Problem-Solving Approach to Adjustment* San Francisco: Jossey-Bass

Sophn H E and Larson J 1983, Is eye tracking dysfunction specific to schizophrenia?, *Schizophrenia Bulletin* **9**: 50–4

Spohn H E and Patterson T 1980, Recent studies of psychophysiology in schizophrenia, *Schizophrenia Bulletin (Special Report)* 38–68

Springer S P and Deutsch G 1981, *Left Brain, Right Brain*, San Francisco: W H Freeman and Company

Stahl J R, Thomson L E, Leitenberg H and Hasazi J E 1974, Establishment of praise as a conditioned reinforcer in socially unresponsive psychiatric patients, *Journal of Abnormal Psychology* **83**: 488–96

Steffy R A 1968, Service applications: Psychotic adolescents and adults. Treatment of aggression, Paper presented to American Psychological Association, San Fransisco

Steffy R A, Hart J, Craw M, Torney D and Marlett N 1969, Operant behavior modification techniques applied to severely regressed and aggressive patients, *Canadian Psychiatric Association Journal* **14**: 59–67

Stein L and Wise C D 1971, Possible etiology of schizophrenia: Progressive damage to the noradrenergic reward system by 6-hydroxydopamine, *Science* **171**: 1032–6

Sternberg D E, Charney D S, Heninger G R, Leckman J F, Hafstad K M and Landis D H 1982, Impaired presynaptic regulation of norepinephrine in schizophrenia: Effects of clonidine in schizophrenic patients and normal controls, *Archives of General Psychiatry* **39**: 285–9

Sternberg D E, Van Kammen D P, Lake C R, Ballenger J C, Marder S R and Bunney W E 1981, The effect of pimozide on CSF norepinephrine in schizophrenia, *American Journal of Psychiatry* **138**: 1045–51

Stevens J R 1982a, Editorial: The neuropathology of schizophrenia, *Psychological Medicine* **12**: 695–700.

Stevens J R 1982b, Neuropathology of schizophrenia. *Archives of General Psychiatry* **39**: 1131–9.

Stevens J R, Bigelow L, Penneym D, Lipkin J, Livermore A H, Rauscher F and Wyatt R J 1979, Telemetered EEG-AEOG during psychotic behaviours of schizophrenia, *Archives of General Psychiatry* **36**: 251–62

Stoffelmayr B E, Faulkner G E and Mitchell W S 1979, The comparison of token economy and social therapy in the treatment of hard core schizophrenic patients, *Behavioural Analysis and Modification* **3**: 3–17

Stone A H and Eldred S H 1959, Delusional formation during the activation of chronic schizophrenic patients, *Archives of General Psychiatry* **1**: 177–9

Storms L H, Clopton J M and Wright L 1982, Effects of gluten on schizophrenics, *Archives of General Psychiatry* **39**: 323–7

Strahilevitz M, Narasimhachari N, Fischer G W, Meltzer H Y and Himwich H E 1975, Indolethylamine-N-Methyltransferase activity in psychiatric patients and controls, *Biological Psychiatry* **10**: 287–302

Strauss J and Carpenter W 1973, Characteristic symptoms and outcome in schizophrenia, *Archives of General Psychiatry* **30**: 429–34

Strauss J and Carpenter W T 1974, The prediction of outcome in schizophrenia II: Relationships between predictor and outcome variables, *Archives of General Psychiatry* **31**: 37–42

Strauss J and Carpenter W T 1977, The prediction of outcome in schizophrenia III: Five year outcome and its predictors, *Archives of General Psychiatry* **34**: 159–63

Sturgeon D, Turpin G, Kuipers L, Berkowitz R and Leff J 1984, Psychophysiological responses of schizophrenic patients to high & low expressed emotional relatives: a follow-up study, *British Journal of Psychiatry* **145**: 62–9

Suchotliff L, Greaves S, Stecker H and Berke R 1970, Critical variables in a token economy, *Proceedings of the 78th Annual Convention of the American Psychological Association* **5**: 517–18

Szasz T D 1979, *Schizophrenia: The Sacred Symbol of Psychiatry* London: Oxford University Press

Tamminga C A, Tighe P J, Chase T N, Defraites G and Schaffer M H 1981, Des-Tyrosine-Gamma-Endorphin administration in chronic schizophrenics: a preliminary report, *Archives of General Psychiatry* **38**: 167–8

Tarrier N, Vaughn C E, Lader M H and Leff J P 1979, Bodily reactions to people and events in schizophrenia, *Archives of General Psychiatry* **36**: 311–15

Taylor M and Abrams R 1983, Cerebral hemisphere dysfunction in the major psychoses. In P Flor-Henry and J Gruzelier (eds), *Laterality and Psychopathology* Amsterdam: Elsevier Science Publishers: 143–52

Taylor P J, Dalton R and Fleminger J J 1980, Handedness in schizophrenia. *British Journal of Psychiatry* **136**: 375–83

Teng E L 1981, Dichotic ear difference is a poor index for the functional asymmetry between the cerebral hemispheres, *Neuropsychologia* **19**: 235–40

Thomson N, Fraser D and McDougall A 1974, The reinstatement of speech in near-mute chronic schizophrenics by instructions, imitative prompts and reinforcements, *Journal of Behavior Therapy and Experimental Psychiatry* **5**: 83–9

Thudichum H 1884, *A Treatise on the Chemical Constitution of the Brain* London: Bailliere, Tindall and Cox

Tienari P 1963, Psychiatric illness in identical twins, *Acta Psychiatrica Scandinavica* Supp 171

Tienari P 1971, Schizophrenia and monozygotic twins, *Psychiatrica Fennica* 97–104

Tolsdorf C C 1976, Social networks, support and coping: An exploratory study, *Family Process* **4**: 407–18

Toone B K, Cooke E and Lader M H 1981, Electrodermal activity in the affective disorders and schizophrenia, *Psychological Medicine* **11**: 497–508

Torrey E F 1980, Neurological abnormalities in schizophrenic patients, *Biological Psychiatry* **15**: 381–8

Torrey E F, Torrey B B and Burton-Bradley B G 1974, The epidemiology of schizophrenia in Papua New Guinea, *American Journal of Psychiatry* **131**: 567–73

Torrey E F, Torrey B B and Peterson M R 1977, Seasonality of schizophrenic births in the United States, *Archives of General Psychiatry* **34**: 1065–9

Trudel G, Boisvert J, Maruca F and Leroux P 1974, Unprogrammed reinforcement of patients' behaviors in wards with and without token economy, *Journal of Behavior Therapy and Experimental Psychiatry* **5**: 147–9

True J E 1966, Learning of abstract responses by process and reactive schizophrenic patients, *Psychological Reports* **18**: 51–5

Turner R J and Wagonfield M O 1967, Occupational mobility and schizophrenia. An assessment of the social causation and social selection hypothesis, *American Sociological Review* **32**: 104–13

Turner S M, Hersen M and Bellack A S 1977, Effects of social disruption, stimulus interference and aversive conditioning on auditory hallucinations, *Behaviour Modification* **1**: 249–58

Turner W J and Merlis S 1959, Effect of some Indolealkylamines on man, *AMA Archives of Neurology and Psychiatry* **81**: 121–9

Tyrrell D A J, Crow T J, Parry R P, Johnstone E and Ferrier I N 1979, Possible virus in schizophrenia and some neurological disorders, *Lancet* **1**: 839–41

Ullmann L P, Forsman R G, Kenny J W, McInnes T C, Unikel I P and Zeisset R M 1965, Selective reinforcement of schizophrenics' interview responses, *Behaviour Research and Therapy* **2**: 205–12

Ullmann L P and Krasner L 1975, *A Psychological Approach to Abnormal Behaviour*, (2nd edition) New Jersey: Prentice-Hall

Ullmann L P, Krasner L and Edinger R L 1964, Verbal conditioning of common associations in long-term schizophrenic patients *Behaviour Research and Therapy* **2**: 15–18

Van Dyke J L, Rosenthal D and Rasmussen P V 1974, Electrodermal functioning in adopted-away offspring of schizophrenics, *Journal of Psychiatry Research* **10**: 199–215

Van Kammen D P 1977, Gamma-Aminobutyric Acid (GABA) and the dopamine hypothesis of schizophrenia. *American Journal of Psychiatry* **134**: 138–43

Van Kammen D P, Bunney W E, Docherty J P, Marder S R, Ebert M H, Rosenblatt J E and Rayner J N 1982a, Alpha-Amphetamine-Induced heterogeneous changes in psychotic behavior in schizophrenia, *American Journal of Psychiatry* **139**: 991–7

Van Kammen D P, Sternberg D E, Hare T A, Waters R N, Bunney W E 1982b, CSF levels of Gamma-Aminobutyric Acid in schizophrenia. Low values in recently ill patients, *Archives of General Psychiatry* **39**: 91–7

Vaughn C and Leff J 1976, The influence of family and social factors on the course of psychiatric patients, *British Journal of Psychiatry* **129**: 125–37

Venables P H 1982, Cerebral mechanisms, autonomic responsivity and attention in schizophrenia, *Paper Presented at the Nebraska Symposium on Motivation*, University of Nebraska

Verhoeven W M A, Van Ree J M, Heezius-Van Bentum A, De Wied D and Van Praag H M 1982, Antipsychotic properties of Des-Enkephlin-Gamma-Endorphin in treatment of schizophrenic patients, *Archives of General Psychiatry* **39**: 648–54

Volavka J, Abrams R, Taylor M A and Reker D 1981, Hemispheric lateralisation of fast EEG activity in schizophrenia and endogenous depression, *Advances in Biological Psychiatry* **6**: 72–5

Wagemaker H and Cade R 1977, The use of hemodialysis in chronic schizophrenia, *American Journal of Psychiatry* **134**: 684–5

Wahl O F 1976, Handedness and schizophrenia, *Perceptual Motor Skills* **42**: 944–6

Walker E and Green M 1982, Soft signs of neurological dysfunction in schizophrenia: an investigation of lateral performance, *Biological Psychiatry* **17**: 381–6

Walker E, Hoppes E and Emory E 1981, A reinterpretation of findings on hemispheric dysfunction in schizophrenia, *The Journal of Nervous and Mental Disease* **169**: 378–80

Walker E and McGuire M 1982, Intra- and interhemispheric processing in schizophrenia, *Psychological Bulletin* **92**: 701–25

Walker E, Marwit S J and Emory E A 1980, A cross-sectional study of emotion recognition in schizophrenics, *Journal of Abnormal Psychology* **84**: 428–36

Wallace C J 1984, Community and interpersonal functioning in the course of schizophrenic disorders, *Schizophrenia Bulletin* **10**: 233–57

Wallace C J, Nelson C, Liberman R P, Lukoff D, Aitchison R A and Ferris C 1980, A review and critique of social skills training with chronic schizophrenics, *Schizophrenic Bulletin* **6**: 42–64

Walsh K W 1978, *Neuropsychology* London: Churchill-Livingstone

Waring M and Ricks D F 1965, Family patterns of children who become adult schizophrenics, *Journal of Nervous and Mental Disease* **140**: 351–64

Warner R 1983, Recovery from schizophrenia in the Third World, *Psychiatry* **46**: 197–212

Watson C G, Kucala T, Angulski G and Bronn C 1982, Season of birth and schizophrenia: a response to the Lewis and Griffin critique, *Journal of Abnormal Psychology* **91**: 120–5

Watson C G, Thomas R W, Anderson D and Felling J 1968, Differentiation of organics from schizophrenics at two chronicity levels by use of the Reitan-Halstead organic test battery, *Journal of Consulting and Clinical Psychology* **32**: 679–84

Watson S J, Akil H, Berger P A and Barchas J D 1979, Some observations on the opiate peptides and schizophrenia, *Archives of General Psychiatry* **36**: 220–3

Watson S J, Berger P A, Akil H, Mills M J and Barchas J D 1978, Effects of Naloxone on schizophrenia: Reduction in hallucinations in a subpopulation of subjects, *Science* **201**: 73–6

Watt D C, Katz K and Shepherd M 1983, The natural history of schizophrenia: A 5 year prospective follow-up of a representative sample of schizophrenics by means of a standardised clinical and social assessment, *Psychological Medicine* **13**: 603–70

Watt N F 1978, Patterns of childhood social development in adult schizophrenics, *Archives of General Psychiatry* **35**: 160–70

Watts F N and Bennett D H 1983, (eds), *Theory and Practice in Psychiatric Rehabilitation* Chichester: Wiley

Watts F N, Powell G E and Austin S V 1973, The modification of abnormal beliefs, *British Journal of Medical Psychology* **46**: 359–63

Waxler N E 1979, Is outcome for schizophrenia better in nonindustrial societies? The case of Sri Lanka, *Journal of Nervous and Mental Diseases* **167**: 144–58

Weidner F 1970, In vivo desensitization of a paranoid schizophrenic, *Journal of Behavior Therapy and Experimental Psychiatry* **1**: 79–81

Weinberger D R, DeLisi L E, Penman G P, Torgum S and Wyatt R J 1982, Computed tomography in schizophreniform disorder and other acute psychiatric disorders, *Archives of General Psychiatry* **39**: 778–83.

Weinberger D R and Wyatt R J 1982, Cerebral morphology in schizophrenia: In vivo studies. In F A Henn and H A Nasrallah (eds), *Schizophrenia as a Brain Disease* New York: Oxford University Press

Weingaertner A H 1971, Self-administered aversive stimulation with hallucinating hospitalized schizophrenics, *Journal of Consulting and Clinical Psychology* **36**: 422–9

Weinman B, Gelbart P, Wallace M and Post M 1972, Inducing assertive behavior in chronic schizophrenics: a comparison of socio-environmental, desensitization and relaxation therapies, *Journal of Consulting and Clinical Psychology* **39**: 246–52

Weintraub S, Prinz R and Neale J M 1978, Peer evaluations of the competence of children vulnerable to psychopathology, *Journal of Abnormal Child Psychology* **6**: 461–73

Weller M and Montagu J D 1979, Electroencephalographic coherence in schizophrenia: A preliminary study. In J Gruzelier and P Flor-Henry (eds), *Hemisphere Asymmetries of Function in Psychopathology* Amsterdam: Elsevier/North Holland Biomedical Press: 285–92

Wender P H, Rosenthal D, Kety S S, Schulsinger F and Weiner J 1974, Cross-fostering: A research strategy for clarifying the role of genetic and experimental factors in the etiology of schizophrenia, *Archives of General Psychiatry* **30**: 121–8

Wexler B E and Heninger G R 1979, Alteration in cerebral laterality during acute psychotic illness, *Archives of General Psychiatry* **36**: 278–84

Whitaker P M, Crow T J and Ferrier I N 1981, Titrated LSD binding in frontal cortex in schizophrenia, *Archives of General Psychiatry* **38**: 278–80

Wiersma D, Giel R, DeJong A and Sloof C J 1983, Social class and schizophrenia, *Psychological Medicine*, **13**: 141–50

Wigan A L 1844, *The Duality of the Mind. A New View of Insanity* London: Longman, Brown, Green and Longman

Wilkinson G 1985, Community care: Planning mental health services, *British Medical Journal* **290**: 1371–3

Williams A O, Reveley T, Kolakowska T, Arden M and Mandelbrote B M 1985, Schizophrenia with good and poor diagnosis II: Cerebral ventricular size and clinical significance, *British Journal of Psychiatry* **146**: 237–44

Williams M T, Turner S M, Watts J G, Bellack A S and Hersen M 1977, Group social skills training for chronic psychiatric patients, *European Journal of Behavioural Analysis and Modification* **1**: 223–9

Wilson F S and Walters R H 1966, Modification of speech output of near mute-schizophrenics through social learning procedures, *Behaviour Research and Therapy* **4**: 59–67

Wilson S F, Reeves A G and Gazzaniga M S 1982, Central commissurotomy for intractible epilepsy: Series two, *Neurology* **32**: 687–97

Wincze J P, Leitenberg H and Agras W S 1972, The effects of token reinforcement and feedback on the delusional verbal behavior of chronic paranoid schizophrenics, *Journal of Applied Behavior Analysis* **5**: 247–62

Wing J K 1978, The management of schizophrenia. In J K Wing (ed) *Schizophrenia: Towards a New Synthesis* London: Academic Press

Wing J K, Birley J L, Cooper J E, Graham P and Isaacs A 1967, Reliability of a procedure of measuring and classifying 'present psychiatric state', *British Journal of Psychiatry* **113**: 499–515

Wing J K and Brown G W 1970, *Institutionalism and Schizophrenia* London: Cambridge University Press

Wing J K, Cooper J E, Sartorius N 1974, *The Measurement and Classification of Psychiatric Symptoms* London: Cambridge University Press

Wing J K and Morris B (eds) 1981, *Handbook of Psychiatric Rehabilitation Practice* Oxford: Oxford University Press

Winkler R C 1970, Management of chronic psychiatric patients by a token economy reinforcement system, *Journal of Applied Behavior Analysis* **3**: 47–55

Winkler R C 1973, An experimental analysis of economic balance, savings and wages in a token economy, *Behavior Therapy* **4**: 22–40

Wise C D, Baden M M and Stein L 1974, Post-mortem measurement of enzymes in human brain: Evidence of a central noradrenergic deficit in schizophrenia, *Journal of Psychiatric Research* **11**: 185–98

Wise C D and Stein L 1969, Facilitation of brain self-stimulation by central administration of norepinephrine, *Science* **163**: 299–301

Wood C C, Allison T, Goff W R, Williamson P D and Spencer P S 1980, On the neural origin of P300 in man. In H H Kornhuber and L Decke (eds), *Progress in Brain Research* Amsterdam: Elsevier Science Publishers **54**: 322–30

Woods P A, Higson P J and Tannahill M M 1984, Token economy programmes with chronic psychotic patients: The importance of direct measurement and objective evaluation for long-term maintenance, *Behaviour Research and Therapy* **22**: 41–51

World Health Organisation 1973, *The International Pilot Study of Schizophrenia (Vol. I)* Geneva: World Health Organisation

World Health Organisation 1979, *Schizophrenia: An International Follow-Up Study* New York, John Wiley & Sons

Wyatt R J, Bigelow L B and Gillin J C 1979c, Catecholamine related substances and schizophrenia: A review. In E Usdin, I J Kopin and J D Barches (eds), *Cathecholamines: Basic and Clinical Frontiers* Vol. 2 New York: Pergamon Press: 1820–5

Wyatt R J, Gillin J C, Stoff D M, Mojo E A and Tinklenberg J R 1977, Beta-Phenylethylamine and the neuropsychiatric disturbances. In E Usdin, D Hamburg and J D Barchas (eds), *Neuroregulators and Psychiatric Disorders* New York: Oxford University Press: 31–45

Wyatt R J, Murphy D L, Belmaker R, Cohen S, Donnelly C H and Pollin N 1973, Reduced monoamine oxidase activity in platelets: A possible genetic marker for vulnerability to schizophrenia, *Science* **179**: 916–18

Wyatt R J, Potkin S G, Bridge T P, Phelps B H and Wise C D 1980, Monoamine oxidase in schizophrenia: An overview, *Schizophrenia Bulletin* **6**: 199–207

Wyatt R J, Potkin S G, Cannon H E *et al* 1979b, Phenylethylamine (PEA) and chronic schizophrenia. In E Usdin, I J Kopin and J D Barchas (eds),

Catecholamines: Basic and Clinical Frontiers, Vol. 2 New York: Pergamon Press: 1833–5

Wyatt R J, Potkin M D and Murphy D L 1979a, Platelet monoamine oxidase activity in schizophrenia: a review of the data, *American Journal of Psychiatry* **136**: 377–85

Wyatt R J, Saavedra J M and Axelrod J 1973, A dimethyltryptamine forming enzyme in human blood, *American Journal of Psychiatry* **130**: 754–60

Wyatt R J, Termini B A and Davis J M 1971, Biochemical and sleep studies of schizophrenia: A review of the literature 1960–1970: I: Biochemical studies, *Schizophrenia Bulletin* **4**: 10–44

Wynne L C, Cromwell R L and Mattysse S (eds) 1978, *The Nature of Schizophrenia* New York: John Wiley and Sons

Wynne L C, Singer M T and Toohey M L 1976, Communication of the adoptive parents of schizophrenics. In J Horsted and E Ugelsad (eds), *Schizophrenia 75: Psychotherapy, Family Studies, Research* Oslo: Universitetsforlaget

Yakovlev P and Lecours A 1967, The myelogenetic cycles of regional maturation of the brain. In A Minkowski (ed), *Regional Development of the Brain in Early Life* Oxford: Blackwell Scientific Publications

Yolles S F and Kramer M 1969. In L Bellack and L Loeb (eds), *The Schizophrenia Syndrome* New York: Grune and Stratton

Yorkston N J, Zaki S A, Malik M K, Morrison R C and Havard C W H 1974, Propranolol in the control of schizophrenic symptoms, *British Medical Journal* **4**: 633–5

Yosawitz A, Bruder G, Sutton T, Sharpe L, Gurland B, Fleiss J and Costa L 1979, Dichotic perception: Evidence for right hemisphere dysfunction in affective psychosis, *British Journal of Psychiatry* **135**: 224–37

Young D and Scoville W B 1938, Paranoid psychosis in narcolepsy and the possible danger of benzedrine treatment, *Medical Clinics of North America* **22**: 637–46

Zeisset R M 1968, Desensitization and relaxation in the modification of psychiatric patients' interview behaviour, *Journal of Abnormal Psychology* **73**: 18–24

Zubeck J P 1969, *Sensory deprivation: Fifteen years of research*, New York: Appleton Century Crofts

Zubin J, McGaziner J and Steinhaver S R 1983, The metamorphosis of schizophrenia: from chronicity to vulnerability, *Psychological Medicine* **13**: 551–71

Zubin J, Salsinger S, Burdock E 1961, A biometric approach to prognosis in schizophrenia. In P Hoch, J Zubin (eds), *Comparative Epidemiology of the Mental Disorders* New York, Grune and Stratton Inc

Zusman J 1967, Some explanations of the changing appearance of psychotic patients: Antecedents of the social breakdown syndrome concept, *International Journal of Psychiatry* **3**: 216–37

INDEX

acetylcholine, 46
and schizophrenia, 62–3
acute dystonic reaction, 235
adoption studies, 33–7, 162–5
adrenaline, 46
akathisia, 235
amphetamine psychosis, 56
amygdala and P300, 104
anhedonia and P300, 104
anticholinergic drugs, 236
aphasia and schizophrenic language,
124–6
asphyxia, 157
audible thoughts, 21
auditory hallucinations, 237–51
and anxiety, 239–40
and systematic desensitisation,
239–40
and subvocalisations, 244–55

balanced polymorphism, 33
BEAM, 104–5
birth complications, 151
birth-season effect, 153–5
birthweight, 33
of discordant twins, 150
brain damage, 153
butyrophenones, 253

callosal agenesis, 336
cerebral
asymmetry, 83
function and high-risk children,
138–9
lateralisation, 33 108
laterality, 83
organisation, 96
chlorpromazine, 233

cognitive
appraisal, 269
deficits, 167
handicaps, 169
commissurotomy, 115
communication disturbance, 776
compliance with medication, 270–3
computed tomography, 43, 77, 79–86
concordance,
definitions, 19, 20
of twins, 148
Copenhagen risk project, 133
coping skills, 269
core phenomenology, 20
corpus callosum, 78, 97, 99, 140, 128,
330–1, 335–9
and EEG, 105
CT scans, 151

delusional beliefs, 251–5
and cognitive restructuring, 252–3
delusions, 4, 5, 251, 341, 348
of influence, 21
of persecution, 10
and cognitive restructuring, 252–3
and operant conditioning, 252
and self-management, 253
and subcultural beliefs, 25
Dementia praecox, 15
Depixol, 233
diagnosis, 20, 278
and outcome, 175
dichotic listening in schizophrenia,
112–16
disagreements in diagnosis, 16
disjunctive definitions, 17
dizygotic twins, 31
dopamine, 46
dopamine hypothesis, 47–56